Board-Level Employee Representation in Europe

Board-Level Employee Representation in Europe analyses the role, activities and networking of board-level employee representatives in sixteen European countries and their counterparts operating in companies that have adopted European status. Board-level employee representation is viewed as a key element of worker participation in Europe, but there has been only limited international comparative research that establishes what board-level employee representatives do and how their activities vary between countries.

Based on a large-scale survey distributed to board-level employee representatives (more than 4,000 respondents), this study identifies the personal characteristics and industrial location of board-level employee representatives, what they do and how they interact with other parties within and outside of the company. This study fills in a knowledge gap at a time when policy debates are considering stakeholder models of corporate governance as a means on the way out of the crisis and the achievement of sustainable economies.

Board-Level Employee Representation in Europe allows direct comparisons between clusters of countries for the first time, as the same survey instrument has been employed in all the participating countries. The research findings demonstrate a large variation in what constitutes board-level employee representation; in practice, including the relations between board-level employee representatives and parties within and external to the company, and the pattern of influence of board-level employee representatives on strategic company decision-making.

Aimed at practitioners, researchers and policymakers alike, this book makes a vital contribution to the field and will be the definitive work on board-level employee representation for the foreseeable future.

Jeremy Waddington is professor of Industrial Relations at the University of Manchester and the Project Coordinator for the European Trade Union Institute, Brussels.

Aline Conchon is a senior researcher at the European Trade Union Institute, Brussels.

Routledge Research in Employment Relations

Series editors: Rick Delbridge and Edmund Heery *Cardiff Business School, UK.*

Aspects of the employment relationship are central to numerous courses at both undergraduate and postgraduate level.

Drawing from insights from industrial relations, human resource management and industrial sociology, this series provides an alternative source of research-based materials and texts, reviewing key developments in employment research.

Books published in this series are works of high academic merit, drawn from a wide range of academic studies in the social sciences.

11 European Works Councils
Pessimism of the intellect optimism of the will?
Edited by Ian Fitzgerald and John Stirling

12 Employment Relations in Non-Union Firms
Tony Dundon and Derek Rollinson

13 Management, Labour Process and Software Development
Reality bytes
Edited by Rowena Barrett

14 A Comparison of the Trade Union Merger Process in Britain and Germany
Joining forces?
Jeremy Waddington, Marcus Kahmann and Jürgen Hoffmann

15 French Industrial Relations in the New World Economy
Nick Parsons

16 Union Recognition
Organising and bargaining outcomes
Edited by Gregor Gall

17 Towards a European Labour Identity
The case of the European Work Council
Edited by Michael Whittall, Herman Knudsen and Fred Huijgen

18 Power at Work
How employees reproduce the corporate machine
Darren McCabe

19 Management in the Airline Industry
Geraint Harvey

20 Trade Unions in a Neoliberal World
British trade unions under New Labour
Gary Daniels and John McIlroy

21 Diversity Management in the UK
Organizational and stakeholder experiences
Anne-marie Greene and Gill Kirton

22 Ethical Socialism and the Trade Unions
Allan Flanders and British industrial relation reform
John Kelly

23 European Works Councils
A transnational industrial relations institution in the making
Jeremy Waddington

24 The Politics of Industrial Relations
Labor unions in Spain
Kerstin Hamann

25 Social Failures of EU Enlargement
A case of workers voting with their feet
Guglielmo Meardi

26 Trade Unions and Workplace Training
Issues and international perspectives
Edited by Richard Cooney and Mark Stuart

27 Men, Wage Work and Family
Edited by Paula McDonald and Emma Jeanes

28 Gendering and Diversifying Trade Union Leadership
Edited by Sue Ledwith and Lise Lotte Hansen

29 Gender and Leadership in Trade Unions
Gill Kirton and Geraldine Healy

30 Minimum Wages, Pay Equity, and Comparative Industrial Relations
Edited by Damian Grimshaw

31 The Transformation of Employment Relations in Europe
Institutions and outcomes in the age of globalization
Edited by James Arrowsmith and Valeria Pulignano

32 Financial Services Partnerships
Labor-management dynamics
Peter J. Samuel

33 Voice and Involvement at Work
Experience with non-union representation
Edited by Paul J. Gollan, Bruce E. Kaufman, Daphne Taras and Adrian Wilkinson

34 Corporate Social Responsibility and Trade Unions
Perspectives from Europe
Edited by Lutz Preuss, Michael Gold and Chris Rees

35 Gender Equality and Work-Life Balance: Glass Handcuffs and Working Men in the U.S.
Sarah Blithe

36 Board-Level Employee Representation in Europe
Priorities, Power and Articulation
Jeremy Waddington and Aline Conchon

Board-Level Employee Representation in Europe

Priorities, Power and Articulation

Jeremy Waddington and Aline Conchon

Routledge
Taylor & Francis Group
LONDON AND NEW YORK

First published 2016 by Routledge

2 Park Square, Milton Park, Abingdon, Oxfordshire OX14 4RN
711 Third Avenue, New York, NY 10017

Routledge is an imprint of the Taylor & Francis Group, an informa business

First issued in paperback 2018

Library of Congress Cataloging-in-Publication Data
Waddington, Jeremy.
Board-level employee representation in Europe : priorities, power and articulation / by Jeremy Waddington & Aline Conchon. — 1 Edition.
pages cm. — (Routledge research in employment relations ; 36)
Includes bibliographical references and index.
1. Industrial management—Employee participation—Europe.
2. Management—Employee participation—Law and legislation—Europe. 3. Industrial relations—Europe. I. Conchon, Aline. II. Title.
HD5660.E9W32993 2015
331.01'12094—dc23 2015017433

ISBN: 978-1-138-79202-9 (hbk)
ISBN: 978-1-138-61687-5 (pbk)

Typeset in Sabon
by Apex CoVantage, LLC

Contents

Tables

Abbreviations

ABVV/FGTB	Algemeen Belgisch Vakverbond/ Fédération Générale du Travail de Belgique
AGM	Annual General Meeting
BDA	Bundesverband der Deutschen Arbeitgeberverbände
BDI	Bundesverband der Deutschen Industrie
BLER	Board-Level Employee Representative
CEE	Central and Eastern Europe
CEO	Chief Executive Officer
CFDT	Confédération française démocratique du travail
CFE-CGC	Confédération générale des cadres- Confédération française de l'encadrement
CFTC	Confédération française des travailleurs chrétiens
CG	Corporate Governance
CGIL	Confederazione generale italiana del lavoro
CGT	Confédération générale du travail
CISL	Confederazione italiana sindicati lavoratori
CME	Coordinated Market Economy
CSR	Corporate Social Responsibility
DG	Directorate General
DGB	Deutscher Gewerkschaftsbund
EC	European Commission
EEA	European Economic Area
EME	Emerging Market Economy
EMF	European Metalworkers' Federation
EWC	European Works Council
EU	European Union
FAFO	Forskningsstiftelsen
FO	Force ouvrière
GIIPS	Greece, Ireland, Italy, Portugal and Spain
ICTU	Irish Congress of Trade Unions
IDA	Ingeniørforeningen i Danmark
IGS	Ireland, Greece and Spain
LME	Liberal Market Economy

LO	Landsorganisationen i Sverige
MME	Mixed Market Economy
NAMA	National Asset Management Agency
NMS	New Member States
OECD	Organisation for Economic Cooperation and Development
ÖGB	Österreichischer Gewerkschaftsbund
SE	Societas Europaea (as defined by the European Company Statute, Council Regulation (EC) No. 2157/2001)
SME	Small and Medium-sized Enterprises
SNB	Special Negotiation Body
TUC	Trades Union Congress
UK	United Kingdom
US	United States

Preface

The representation of workers on the board of companies with similar rights as other board members is a distinctive feature of European social models. Board-level employee representation was introduced throughout much of Western continental Europe during the 1970s and 1980s. Subsequent developments in Central and Eastern Europe during the 1990s resulted in board-level employee representation throughout much of continental Europe. Furthermore, after many failed initiatives the European Union adopted the European Company Statute (2157/2001) in October 2001 and the accompanying measure on the involvement of employees in companies that adopt this European status (2001/86/EC) as a means to develop the social dimension. The eventual success of this initiative paved the way for the adoption of two further measures of European company law that embraced board-level employee representation: the Statute for a European Cooperative Society in July 2003 and the Cross-border Merger directive in October 2005. By 2009, when this study commenced, board-level employee representation was thus present in some form in eighteen European countries and at European level. This book examines the views of more than 4,000 board-level employee representatives operating in no fewer than sixteen countries and in European Companies on their role, the interventions they make at the board, the power they exert, and the manner in which they articulate with other board members, managers and other labour representatives.

Board-level employee representation is contested among both policy-makers and academics. Some employers tend to oppose board-level employee representation on the grounds that it infringes on managerial prerogative, may slow decision-making and does not necessarily lead to improved decision-making. Many, but by no means all, trade unionists support the principle of board-level employee representation, but argue that the terms of its implementation need to be improved if representatives are to exert a meaningful influence on board-level decision-making. Similarly, among academics there are those that argue against board-level employee representation as it fails to address the fundamental principal–agency issue of corporate governance or that it may lead to the incorporation of representatives into managerial decision-making processes. Taking a different tack, other academics view board-level employee representation as a means to unify the economic and social spheres of the operation of firms and to integrate the insider knowledge held by employees to the benefit of the firm. The nature of this contestation and the debates that arise therefrom are examined here in the context of questionnaire-based survey data generated from more than 4,000 board-level employee representatives. In addition, it is acknowledged by all parties to these debates that economic, social and political circumstances have changed markedly since board-level employee representation was initially implemented in Western Europe. The ascendency of neo-liberal ideologies and economic policies, financialisation and the weakening of trade unionism have all served to bring into question the viability of board-level employee representation as conceived at the point of its implementation. This book assesses how these changes have promoted a gap between initial *de jure* intention and current *de facto* practice.

Two interrelated points of departure inform the analysis and resonate throughout the book. The corporate governance point of departure places the firm at centre stage and assesses the implications of board-level employee representation for the operation, performance and coordination of the firm. In addition, such analyses attempt to identify the features of national political economies that promote or inhibit the development of particular forms of corporate governance, including board-level employee representation. The industrial relations point of departure, in contrast, situates board-level employee representation as an element of industrial democracy and, in consequence, focuses on the differences in interests and power between capital and labour, whether these differences can be reconciled and, if so, the institutional form of the reconciliation. Two features are common to the corporate governance and industrial relations points of departure and figure large in this book. First, the focus in both points of departure is on the absence or presence of board-level employee representation and, if present, the institutional form taken by board-level employee representation. Theoreticians from neither corporate governance nor industrial relations focus on the influence and power exerted by board-level employee representatives within the different institutional forms, the assumption being that institutional presence results in influence and power. This study examines the extent of influence and power exerted by board-level employee representatives. Second, neither corporate governance nor industrial relations literature explicitly examine the character and the implications of articulation between board-level employee representation and other institutions of labour representation within and outside the firm. Such articulation may contribute to the influence and power exercised by board-level employee representatives, will certainly enhance coordination among labour representatives with interests in the firm and is integral to the achievement of industrial democracy. This study assesses the character and intensity of articulation involving board-level employee representatives.

The book argues that there are marked differences in the national character of board-level employee representation that extend beyond the constitutional variation that underpins its operation. In particular, the extent and the manner in which board-level employee representatives exercise power cannot be treated as a uniform category. Similarly, the character and the intensity of articulation involving board-level employee representatives are shown to vary widely between national clusters with the intensity of articulation involving Germanic board-level employee representatives, trade unions and other institutions of labour representation within the firm being unsurpassed. More uniform, however, are the views of board-level employee representatives towards the agenda of board meetings, confidentiality and the timeliness and quality of the available information. The book also demonstrates that a substantial minority of European board-level employee representatives participate at the board in terms of either information or consultation with the result that they can exert no power over and can, at best, only influence company strategic decision-making, thus confirming that *de jure* intention is not matched by *de facto* practice in a substantial minority of cases.

This book is the result of several years of research and engagement with academics and practitioners. We would like to take this opportunity to thank all those who have contributed to the research on which the book is based. The Hans-Böckler-Stiftung generously funded the research and was thus integral to its completion. Guidance from the Beirat (Advisory Board), established by the Hans-Böckler-Stiftung to oversee the research, was also invaluable. Members of the Beirat included Inger-Marie Hagen, Reiner Hoffmann, Tanja Jacquemin, Norbert Kluge, Roland Köstler, Inge Lippert, Stefan Lücking, Ruth Naderer, Werner Nienhüser, Alice Niklas, Thomas Otto, Udo Rehfeldt, Marie Seyboth, Karsten Schneider, Michael Stollt, Rainer Trinczek and Sepp Zuckerstätter. We are grateful for all the critical and helpful comments from the members of the Beirat on drafts of each of the book chapters, which contributed significantly and positively to the final manuscript. Study leave granted by the University of Manchester facilitated the completion of the project and allowed time to be put aside for writing. The European Trade Union Institute acted as the hub of the research and through its various networks of researchers, particularly the SEEurope Network, ensured a continual critical review of progress and outputs.

The complexity of the mechanics of the project necessitated assistance from a wide range of people from within the different participating countries at successive stages of the research: questionnaire design, questionnaire translation, identification of board-level employee representatives and questionnaire distribution. We would like to express our heartfelt thanks to all those throughout Europe who spared their hard-pressed time to assist in this process without whom the project would never have been completed. At the time of their involvement in the research, the affiliation of those who assisted was as follows: Amsterdam Instituut voor ArbeidsStudies

(AIAS) researchers (Robbert van het Kaar, Elwin Wolters); Arbeiterkammer (AK) Wien officers (Ruth Naderer, Heinz Leitsmüller, Sepp Zuckerstätter); Centralorganisationen af industriansatte i Danmark (CO-Industri) officers (Erling Jensen, Peter Rimfort, Rune Siglev); Českomoravská Konfederace Odborovych Svazu (ČMKOS) legal advisor (Jaroslav Stránský) and coordinator of European affairs (Hana Málková); Deutscher Gewerkschaftsbund representatives (Thomas Otto, Marie Seyboth); Energeticko-Chemický Odborový Zväz (ECHOZ) international secretary (Erika Bršelová); European Trade Union Confederation deputy general secretary (Reiner Hoffmann, now President of the Deutsche Gewerkschaftsbund); European Trade Union Institute colleagues (Birgit Buggel-Asmus, Romuald Jagodziński, Carmen Lorenzo, Michael Stollt); Finnish Industrial Union Cooperation working group secretary (Sari Vaittinen); Forskningsstiftelsen (FAFO) researcher (Inger Marie Hagen); Friedrich-Ebert-Stiftung research officer (Vladimir Špánik); Hans-Böckler-Stiftung officers (Irene Ehrenstein, Roland Köstler); Ingeniørforeningen i Danmark (IDA) officer (Lisbeth Michala Keldsen); Institut de Recherches Economiques et Sociales (IRES) senior researcher (Udo Rehfeldt); Institute for Political Science of the Hungarian Academy of Sciences, senior research fellow (László Neumann); Konfederacija sindikatov Slovenije PERGAM (KSS PERGAM) international cooperation adviser (Nina Mežan); Οργανισμός Μεσολάβησης και Διαιτησίας (Organisation for Mediation and Arbitration) researcher (Christos Ioannou); Privattjänstemannakartellen (PTK) officer (Eva Karnehed); research unit 'Relations professionnelles et emploi' (REPREM) researcher (Franz Clément); Technische Universität München (TUM) senior researcher (Rainer Trinczek); Wissenschaftscentrum Berlin für Socialforschung (WZB) senior researcher (Inge Lippert); Worker Director Group chairman (Pat Compton); Združenje nadzornikov Slovenije (ZNS) legal secretary (Valerija Božič); Zveze svobodnih sindikatov Slovenije (ZSSS) executive secretary (Marjan Urbanč); and three independent researchers (Marie-Nöelle Auberger, Kevin O'Kelly, Klas Levinson). In addition, Denise Kasperkiewicz, with good humour, ensured that the survey data were efficiently coded and analysed. Administrative assistance from Lut Coremans and help with documentation and literature from Giovanna Corda throughout the duration of the project has also been invaluable. Of course, none of the above bears any responsibility for the final manuscript.

Jeremy Waddington
University of Manchester and European Trade Union Institute

Aline Conchon
European Trade Union Institute

1 Setting the Scene

The representation of employees at the board level within enterprises is a defining characteristic of the political economy of a nation. Such representation and the character of coordination within and between firms that it generates is integral to the distinction drawn between the competitive managerial capitalism of the US and the personal capitalism of the UK, on one hand, and the cooperative managerial capitalism of Germany, on the other (Chandler 1977, 1990), to the categorisation of business systems (Whitley 1992, 1999) and, most recently, to the differentiation between liberal market economies and coordinated market economies in the latter of which board-level employee representation facilitates intra-firm coordination (Hall and Soskice 2001a). Furthermore, debates on the economic performance of nation states in the context of globalisation, the internationalisation of capital markets and more intense regime competition highlight board-level employee representation as influential on company decision-making and competitiveness (Vitols 2010). During the 1990s, for example, the short-term time horizons of company boards in the UK and the US from which board-level employee representatives are excluded were linked to industrial decline. Among the remedies proposed was the broadening of stakeholder representation to act as a constraint on the influence of the chief executive officer (CEO) and to limit shareholder-value-oriented business decision-making (Hutton 1995; Porter 1990). In contrast, some post-2000 analyses focus on the limitations of board systems that allow stakeholder representation and detect movement towards Anglo-American systems in hybrid forms that combine elements of the shareholder and stakeholder models, as companies adjust to liberalisation and financialisation (Barker 2010; Höpner 2003; Lazonick 2010; Vitols 2004). Irrespective of the detail of these debates, the protagonists assume that board-level employee representatives influence decision-making within the firm. The principal purpose of this study is to identify the role of board-level employee representatives, the character of the power they exert and the extent of articulation of their relations with other parties inside and outside of the firm. To achieve these objectives a questionnaire survey was conducted to which more than 4,000 board-level employee representatives from sixteen countries responded, together with their counterparts who serve on the boards of companies that have adopted European status.

The recent rapid rise in the number of transnational company mergers and acquisitions (*Acquisitions Monthly* various; Buiges 1993), the development and implementation of corporate social responsibility programmes (EMF 2004; Schömann et al. 2008) and scandals involving the failure of company boards to oversee the financial practices of companies *inter alia* at Enron, Worldcom and Parmalat (Blackburn 2002; Coffee 2005) are indicative of the changing roles and challenges faced by company boards. Similarly, changes to work organisation and decentralisation reflect the complexity of decision-making within companies. In combination, these developments heightened the intensity of the public debate on the role, composition and performance of company boards in changing economic and political circumstances. Committees were established in many countries to review corporate governance and, in particular, the practices of company boards on financial management and reporting.[1] These reviews were supplemented by recommendations from public bodies to promote engagement with stakeholders (OECD 1999, 2004) and, at European level, by the adoption of the European Company Statute (2157/2001) together with a directive on the establishment of institutions of employee involvement within companies that adopt such a status (2001/86/EC).

The point here is twofold. First, the role of company boards and the board-level employee representatives that sit on them has changed markedly since much of the legislation was enacted on which the presence of board-level employee representatives is based (Lazonick and O'Sullivan 2000; Williams 2000). This study assesses how these changes have impinged on board-level employee representatives by identifying their actions at the board and their views towards their representative functions. Second, there is no *a priori* reason to expect board-level employee representatives to respond in a similar manner to change in different institutional circumstances. This study identifies the range of actions taken by board-level employee representatives in different national circumstances.

Analyses of board-level employee representation rely on one of two points of departure: corporate governance or industrial relations. While analyses based on these two points of departure are by no means mutually exclusive, there are marked differences in emphasis. The literature on corporate governance takes the relationship between owners and managers as the basic problematic from which assessments are undertaken regarding issues of ownership and control within the firm, the objectives to which control within the firm may be put, variation in the pattern of corporate governance, and the efficacy of different regulatory regimes. The focus of corporate governance analyses is thus the firm. Analyses of corporate governance highlight the terms of company law whereas those of industrial relations are more reliant on legislation originating in collective labour law.

In contrast to the corporate governance literature, industrial relations situates employee representation at board level within a framework of employee participation and industrial democracy (Blumberg 1968; Clegg 1960). Alongside collective bargaining and systems of workplace participation, board-level employee representation is viewed as a means to democratise work and the employment relationship (Dachler and Wilpert 1978; King and van de Vall 1978) and to reduce the powerlessness and alienation of workers (Poole 1975, 1982). Implicit in such analyses is that shareholders and managers cede some power in decision-making to employees or their representatives. The manner of this concession may be voluntary or compulsory, the latter typified by legislation introduced by the state. As with the analyses that take corporate governance as the point of departure, analyses founded on participation and democracy assume that board-level employee representatives can exert power over decision-making within enterprises. This study examines whether board-level employee representatives have a 'democratising' effect.

The nature of the power of board-level employee representation and its linkage to reductions in the powerlessness and alienation of workers is rarely elaborated. What is clear is that the power exercised through board-level employee representation is not necessarily reflected in the immediate work situation, the terms and conditions of employment or the nature of the work undertaken by individual employees (Bernstein 1976; Lippert et al. 2014). With the objective of furthering employee participation, no fewer than eighteen of the twenty-eight Member States of the European Union (EU) and Norway have introduced rights of board-level representation. Regulations underpinning these rights on board-level representation vary by reference to the structure of the board: in particular whether the board is single tier or dual tier; the coverage: the sector, size and legal status of the companies covered; the board composition: the proportion of all board members that comprise employee or other stakeholder representatives; and the subject matter on which board-level employee representatives may intervene (Kluge and Stollt 2009). The impact of this institutional variation on the activities and influence of board-level employee representatives are examined.

The issue of articulation between board-level employee representatives and other institutions of labour representation within the firm and beyond is explicit in neither corporate governance nor industrial relations analyses. Articulation is essential to both analytical strands, because the recognition of board-level employee representatives by those on whose behalf they act as representatives underpins any influence the representatives may have on the workforce and other representatives of labour within the firm. Board-level employee representatives acting as isolated individuals separate from the workforce are unlikely to have a pronounced influence over, or to adequately represent the interests of, the workforce. Similarly, if board-level employee representatives are to have a strategic effect, as envisaged by the legislation that underpins their position, their views should be articulated with other institutions of labour representation in order that decision-making on the labour side incorporates information from the board level and is articulated between board and workplace.

This study assesses whether board-level employee representatives are articulated with institutions of labour representation within the firm and, if so, identifies the character and impact of such articulation. Beyond the firm, articulation primarily involves trade unions. In this context, information gleaned by board-level employee representatives may assist in the strategic decision-making of trade unionists and vice versa. Trade unions may also make available training and other support services to assist the employee representative to undertake his/her duties on the board. This study investigates whether two-way exchanges of information between trade unions and board-level employee representatives are in place and, if so, their impact on decision-making. The study also identifies the views of board-level employee representatives towards the support they receive from trade unions and how this support may be improved.

The purpose of this chapter is to introduce the issues of concern to a study of the activities of board-level employee representatives in Europe. To this end, this chapter is composed of three further sections. The first and second sections review the literature on corporate governance and industrial relations with the objective of isolating some of the variables that may affect the activities of board-level employee representatives and the objectives to which these activities may be directed. The third section identifies some further research questions and briefly outlines the structure of the book.

CORPORATE GOVERNANCE AS THE POINT OF DEPARTURE

A wide range of literature on corporate governance explores the linkages between finance and management. This literature focuses on ownership and control within the firm, the objectives sought through the achievement of control, and the manner in which control is exercised. Comparative analyses of corporate governance tend to contrast outsider with insider, shareholder with stakeholder and market with relational systems (Mayer and Alexander 1990; Prowse 1994; Becht and Röell 1999). Company finance is generated via public equities and market-based debt in market/shareholder systems in which equity markets are wide ranging. Within this framework, firms operate outsider forms of corporate governance based on strong legal rights for investors, and are characterised by dispersed shareholdings and high rates of mergers and acquisitions, including hostile takeovers, which exert financial discipline on company board members (Manne 1965). In contrast, corporate finance is more likely to be drawn from banks and other financial institutions in relational/stakeholder systems and investments are viewed as long term. Insider systems of corporate governance are employed in such circumstances, characterised by direct relationships between managers and owners, lower rates of corporate restructuring and, thus, less external financial discipline, and concentrated shareholdings. Archetypically, the UK and the US are viewed as market/shareholder systems and Germany as a prominent relational/stakeholder system.

Although the distinctions between these two forms of corporate governance have narrowed over recent years in function if not in form (Deeg 1999, 2009; Goergen et al. 2008; Höpner 2003; Vitols 2004), the differentiation of insider and outsider systems informs much of the analysis of corporate governance and relies on a dichotomy drawn between the economic and social spheres within a firm (Conchon 2011a). Advocates of the superiority of outsider systems of corporate governance view the economic and the social as essentially separate spheres within the firm (Fama 1980; Jensen and Meckling 1976). Members of the company board and senior managers are exclusively responsible for strategic financial decision-making within the economic sphere of the firm. In contrast, the separate social sphere includes collective bargaining between managers and workers' representatives on terms and conditions of employment. Proponents of insider systems argue that the analytical dichotomy between the economic and social spheres in corporate governance is not sustainable in practice, because decisions made in either sphere have ramifications elsewhere (Harrison and Freeman 1999; Piore 2003). Within the terms of this argument a central policy objective is to articulate the economic and the social; hence, the composition of company boards should embrace a range of stakeholders.

To highlight the principal features of these competing positions, the analysis proceeds in two stages. The first stage identifies the features of economic and legal perspectives within which the economic and social spheres tend to be treated as separate. The second stage addresses sociopolitical perspectives, a focus of which is to analytically integrate the economic and social spheres. An objective of this assessment is to identify the role assigned to labour representation within these competing analytical positions.

Economic and Legal Perspectives

In writing *Wealth of Nations* (originally published in 1776), Adam Smith noted a problematic tendency for the separation of ownership from control in companies in that the interests of managers differed from those of owners. More than 150 years later, the separation of ownership and control was systematically assessed by reference to the impact of industrialisation and the development of markets (Berle and Means 1932). The focus of analysis was how disparate shareholders can reduce the costs of delegating control over financial capital to managers. In particular, where legislation protected minority shareholders and, thus, encouraged diversified shareholdings, as in the UK and the US, the separation of ownership and control was viewed as problematic.

Finance or principal–agency models of corporate governance build on the initial observation that ownership and control may be separated within companies. The finance model regards owners or shareholders as the 'principal' who delegate responsibility for decision-making to managers, the 'agents' (Fama 1980; Fama and Jensen 1983, 1985; Jensen and Meckling

1976). Within the terms of the finance model it is argued that managers may not necessarily act in the best interests of shareholders, because the former may seek monetary, career enhancing or other benefits, adopt different time horizons, and have a different view of risk (Butler and Ribstein 1995). Furthermore, managers are likely to have access to a broader portfolio of information on which to base decision-making than are shareholders. The finance model established that managerial agency costs faced by corporate owners are a significant form of transaction cost, necessitating the identification of systems of corporate governance that minimise these agency costs and the means whereby managers can be monitored to maximise the benefits for shareholders (Jensen and Meckling 1976). Advocates of the finance model argue that markets, particularly those for capital, corporate control and managerial labour, limit managerial discretion and that the voting rights of shareholders act to ensure that the resources of firms will be deployed by managers to maximise the value of the firm (Easterbrook and Fischel 1983). The voting rights of shareholders are complemented by the presence of a board that is accountable to shareholders, comprising non-executive directors and independent auditors, which, in combination, ensure that managers are monitored and made accountable (Hart 1995). Advocates of the finance model acknowledge that failings in corporate governance can occur. The remedy, however, is not to broaden the composition of company boards but to remove restrictions on the market for corporate control, thereby imposing greater financial discipline on managers (Jensen 1986), or to reward managers through share option schemes, thereby aligning the interests of managers and shareholders more closely (Lazonick and O'Sullivan 2000). The inclusion of employees on the board is rejected within the finance model as employee representatives would be expected to act only to protect jobs and wages, thereby acting in a manner inconsistent with the maximisation of shareholder value (Lippert et al. 2014; Williams 2000).

Four principal critiques of the finance model have been tabled. First, the description of the system of control within the modern firm is unrealistic as such firms are dominated by boards, which function as self-perpetuating oligarchies, and adequate monitoring of managers is not feasible though the means proposed within the terms of the finance model (Kay and Silberston 1995). Second, the finance model assumes that executive remuneration will be related to, if not commensurate with, corporate performance. The rapid rises in executive remuneration compared to average earnings since the 1980s have occurred in the absence of a consistent relationship between executive pay and corporate performance, indicating that market mechanisms are of insufficient regulatory effect (Conyon et al. 1995; Gregg et al. 1993). Third, the finance model assumes that the knowledge of shareholder representatives and non-executive directors is sufficient to ensure the competitiveness of the company. This assumption has been questioned by those who argue that to gain a sustainable competitive advantage, company boards should rely more on insiders elected by employees who can transfer firm-specific knowledge to the board (Osterloh and Frey 2006). Fourth, the dispersed shareholdings, which are at the source of the problematic of monitoring managers, are characteristic of Anglo-Saxon economies. Elsewhere, the separation of ownership and control is not as pronounced, with the consequence that dominant shareholders often have both the means and the incentive to discipline managers (Morck et al. 1988), that is, the problematic of the finance model is of restricted geographical coverage.

A legal perspective was developed to move away from the focus on Anglo-Saxon economies characteristic of the finance model and inject a more encompassing comparative dimension to the analysis of corporate governance (La Porta et al. 1997; Shleifer and Wolfenzon 2002). The legal perspective is directed toward explaining the more diversified shareholdings in Anglo-Saxon economies compared to their continental European counterparts. The legal perspective accepts many of the tenets of the principal–agent distinction, particularly the dominant economic rationale and the need to discipline managers, and assumes that legislation may modify markets to maximise shareholder value. The analytical focus is the distinction between common law and civil law systems. The common law systems of Anglo-Saxon countries assign to judges a key role in the development of law through the setting of precedents, whereas judges interpret detailed legal codes in the civil law systems of continental Europe (La Porta et al. 1997). The legal perspective argues that institutions found in common law systems offer superior protection to minority shareholders from adverse decisions made by either majority shareholders or managers than institutions within civil law systems (Johnson et al. 2000). In particular, regulations and institutions in the fields of accounting standards and financial transparency, corporate law, stock exchange controls and corporate restructuring through mergers and acquisitions encourage diversified shareholdings in common law systems (Coffee 2006; La Porta et al. 2000).

Three points arise from these initial observations. First, drawing on the finance model, advocates of the legal perspective argue that the form and the extent of agency costs vary between national systems of corporate governance (La Porta et al. 2000). Second, variations in the content of civil law provide different degrees of protection to shareholders: French civil law is viewed as offering less protection than does German civil law, which, in turn, is weaker than Nordic civil law (Enriques and Volpin 2007; La Porta et al. 1997). Third, the initial analysis of corporate governance has been extended to embrace a wider range of institutions and markets. In particular, civil law systems rely on more detailed legislation governing the employment relationship and the conduct of industrial relations that is directly implemented by governments compared to common law regimes (Botero et al. 2004). These points are of concern to the analysis of the activity of board-level employee representatives insofar as they imply that institutional variation in corporate governance will be associated with different strategic choices for employee representatives and that the relationship between board-level employee representatives and labour management will vary according to institutional arrangements.

The legal perspective is open to question on three principal counts.[2] First, the distinction between common law and civil law systems assumes a consistency within each system that is not present (Armour et al. 2009; Gourevitch and Shinn 2005:83–87). Institutional variation in corporate governance regimes within both common law and civil law systems is wide ranging, indicating an analytical limitation of the distinction drawn between the two systems. Similarly, political decisions have eroded some of the distinctions between common law and civil law systems (Gourevitch 2003; Roe 1994, 2003). Political approaches to corporate governance also highlight the impact of political views towards shareholder value, which may be more influential on the development of corporate governance than the impact of legal systems (Roe 2003). Second, the argument that the control of agency costs underpins the institutional variation in corporate governance regimes is to downplay the impact of other features of a national political economy, which also impinge on the decision to legislate and the character of any legislation. A decision to incorporate employee participation into the regulatory regime, for example, clearly moves beyond the concern of controlling agency costs. Third, the impact of legislation or institutional change is contingent on the context of its introduction (Aguilera et al. 2008). Although proponents of the legal perspective acknowledge that a wide range of factors may influence the development of legal systems, the impact of these factors is not viewed as influencing the operation of these legal systems (Mahoney 2001). In other words, the legal perspective lacks analytical consistency.

Within the finance and legal perspectives, employees and employee representation are rarely discussed. The arguments deployed within these perspectives to favour shareholders, however, are also applicable to workers (Blair 1995; Greenfield 1998; Kaufman and Englander 2005; O'Connor 1993). Whereas shareholders yield control of money to managers, employees yield control of skill, time and effort. In both instances the party yielding control does so to achieve benefits: shareholders may benefit in terms of money while employees may benefit in terms of wages, job security and training. Similarly, the economic and legal perspectives assign to shareholders a residual claim; that is, shareholders are viewed as entitled to the residual when all other claims against the firm have been met. The extent of the residual is dependent on the performance of the firm. 'Insider labour' also has claims against the firm that are dependent on the performance of the firm (Rueda 2006, 2007). Pensions and other retirement benefits or understandings on job security, for example, may become worthless if the firm fails. Promotion, training and the safety standards of employees are also influenced by the performance of the firm. In short, in assigning primacy to the interests of shareholders, the finance and legal perspectives downplay the similarities between the positions of shareholders and employees. Furthermore, both finance and legal perspectives exclude analysis of how profits or a surplus over costs are generated within firms in presenting profits as a residual (Lazonick 2010, 2013). Employee representation at board level is viewed within the finance model as unnecessary: only shareholders need monitor the activities of managers because their sunk investment must be safeguarded. Furthermore, the expertise and experience of employee representatives are not regarded as likely to make a positive contribution to decision-making at board level. To the contrary, the presence of employee representatives is viewed as likely to increase agency costs and thus restrict shareholder value.

Sociopolitical Perspectives

Those arguing that the economic and social spheres are necessarily interrelated, criticise finance and legal perspectives on four principal counts: first, finance and legal perspectives exclude labour as an actor within the firm; second, the shareholder–manager relationship is analysed in the abstract, removed from its institutional setting; third, there is no recognition of the range of divergent interests within and between the categories shareholders, managers and labour; and fourth, actors within a firm are not passive, bound by markets, legislation or the behaviour of shareholders, as implied by finance and legal perspectives, but are in a position to develop and implement strategic choices (Aguilera and Jackson 2003; Blair 1995; Gospel and Pendleton 2005). In developing these criticisms, a body of sociopolitical literature on corporate governance has developed which emphasises the networks of relationships within firms and between stakeholders in firms and individuals, organisations and institutions beyond the firm (Aoki 2001; Gourevitch and Shinn 2005; Hall and Soskice 2001b; Whitley 1992, 1999). From within sociopolitical perspectives the effective management of firms is dependent on aspects of the polity (Roe 2003) or on engagement of those within the firm with different 'spheres' of the political economy (Hall and Soskice 2001a:6–7), which, in turn, influence the range of actions that are available to stakeholders. In short, stakeholders are embedded in political and social networks of institutions. The different emphases within sociopolitical perspectives are examined below to illustrate the nature of the networks that influence corporate governance and the role assigned to employee representatives at board level.

Political perspectives. Proponents of political perspectives argue that finance and legal approaches are too narrow insofar as variations in the pattern of corporate governance cannot be reduced to the pursuit of economic efficiency and shareholder value. To the contrary, political perspectives view variation in the pattern of corporate governance to result from economic and, particularly, political conflict. Within political perspectives are two competing emphases. The first argues that differences in corporate governance and ownership arise from variation in the intensity at which market-oriented policies are supported within the polity (Roe 1994, 2003).

The second focuses on the alliances that may be formed by stakeholders in corporate governance and the impact of political power and conflict on the practices and institutions of corporate governance (Gourevitch 2003; Gourevitch and Shinn 2005).

Legal perspectives argue that the more diversified shareholdings characteristic of Anglo-Saxon economies result from differences in common and civil law systems (La Porta et al. 1997). In developing a political perspective, Roe (2003) took the same problematic of explaining diversified or concentrated shareholdings and argued that small investors are less likely to invest in Western continental European and Japanese companies because of the prevailing political environment that imposes restrictions on the activities of senior managers. In consequence of these restrictions, managers implement policies that are not consistent with the short-term maximisation of shareholder value, thereby deterring small investors. Politics are thus viewed as the key influence. Prominent among the features of the political environment that act as restrictions on the activities of senior managers are the protections offered to employees against the adverse effects that may result from the unrestricted pursuit of shareholder value. Institutional variation in corporate governance within Western continental Europe and Japan should not disguise the impact of the polity in promoting concentrated share ownership (Roe 2003:63–98). The political complexion of the national polity is associated with patterns of corporate governance. In particular, 'left-wing governments' promote concentrated shareholdings in order to counteract the tendency among managers to engage in 'empire building', whereas right-of-centre governments favour shareholders at the expense of managers and employees in the form of protective legislation (Roe 2003:51–56).

The political perspective advanced by Roe has been questioned on three counts. First, in assigning politics primacy over institutions Roe emphasises the impact of class in the form of the political right and left. Other constellations of interest groups that are not explicable by reference to such a polarisation are not addressed. The impact of industrial sectors, religion and geographical regions, for example, may impinge on the implementation and subsequent development of institutions of corporate governance. Furthermore, the type of electoral system has been shown to be associated with the character of political alliances and, in turn, the relative levels of protection available to employees and shareholders: proportional systems are linked with strong employee rights compared to those of shareholders, whereas the opposite is the case in majoritarian electoral systems (Pagano and Volpin 2005).[3] Second, in several Western continental European countries alliances that embraced sections of the political right and left were responsible for labour market and welfare regulation that promoted alternatives to a shareholder value orientation (Esping-Andersen 1990; Schmitter 1995; Swenson 2002). In other words, alliances may cross the right–left political divide. Third, a growing body of evidence suggests that in the context of corporate governance 'left' political parties are concerned primarily with the interests of those with secure employment, labour insiders, rather than labour *per se* (Rueda 2005); that is, Roe fails to differentiate between different segments of labour.

To accommodate these points a second strand within the political perspective emphasises the impact of political power and conflict on corporate governance by means of an identification of the range of alliances that stakeholders might enter (Gourevitch 2003; Gourevitch and Shinn 2005). The issue of alliances, considered a limitation of the perspective developed by Roe, is thus placed centre stage. Whereas Roe focuses exclusively on class expressed in terms of the political right and left, Gourevitch and Shinn argue that stakeholders can enter into different alliances as tactical or strategic choices (2005:149–186). Based on a model comprising stakeholders, shareholders, managers and employees, a range of alliances is shown to be feasible. Furthermore, the preferences of each group of stakeholders are not monolithic, suggesting that the range of possible alliances is wide and that alliances may differ in composition from issue to issue (Gourevitch and Shinn 2005:205–241). Changes to institutional context may also result in alterations to the composition of alliances. The injection of more shareholder-value-oriented practices into firms within coordinated market economies, for example, may promote alliances between employees and shareholders with the objective of improving managerial transparency to the benefit of both parties to the alliance (Gourevitch and Shinn 2005:160–166; Jackson 2005).

Institutional variation is incorporated into the analysis. First, the impact of an alliance is dependent on the institutional framework within which the alliance is embedded. Institutions thus influence the composition of alliances as stakeholders assess the likely impact of any alliance in its institutional context. Second, differentiation between majoritarian and proportional electoral systems is introduced on the understanding that proportional systems are not subject to marked shifts in public policy with small changes in the distribution of votes, whereas significant public policy changes may result from small changes in the distribution of votes in majoritarian systems (Pagano and Volpin 2005). The formation of alliances in the context of variants of political institutions encourages the development of varied arrangements in corporate governance, industrial relations, skill formation and inter-firm relations, which, in turn, produce different ownership structures within firms (Gourevitch and Shinn 2005:205–241). This causal chain results in two forms of corporate governance comprising proportional political systems, coordinated market institutions and concentrated corporate ownership on the one hand, as well as majoritarian political systems, liberal market institutions and diverse corporate ownership on the other hand. These categories are not dissimilar to those employed in sociological perspectives, a point to which the argument returns later.

The implications of political perspectives for an investigation of the activities of board-level employee representatives are wide ranging. Both variants of the political perspective acknowledge that labour is an active stakeholder within the firm and, by inference, that board-level employee representatives have specific interests that they are concerned to further. The implication of Roe's (2003) position is that the interests of labour diverge from those of capital along class lines, suggesting marked differences in objectives between board-level employee representatives and those of shareholder representatives. While Gourevitch and Shinn would not regard the position of Roe as impossible, they would regard it as one of several possibilities rather than a universal situation. Other possibilities are dependent on the particular configuration of the alliances in place on the issue(s) under consideration. The inference here is that alliances entered into by board-level employee representatives are likely to vary on an issue-by-issue basis. Relationships between board-level employee representatives and potential allies on the board are assessed in Chapter 6.

Sociological perspectives. Although the legal perspective introduces some sociological factors, it is concerned to explain the range of legislative and institutional forms of corporate governance by reference to the maximisation of shareholder value. In contrast, sociological perspectives treat the firm as embedded within networks comprising *inter alia* cultural and social norms, systems of market regulation, and wide-ranging and varied relationships within firms and between firms and other organisations and institutions (Hollingsworth 1997). Whereas the political perspective treats the direction of causality of corporate governance arrangements and, in particular, the structure of ownership as dependent on the interaction between the preferences of stakeholders and political institutions mediated by the manner in which firms coordinate their activities (Gourevitch and Shinn 2005), sociological perspectives treat the networks within which firms are embedded as conditioning, but not determining, the strategy of firms towards corporate governance. Sociological perspectives thus question the direction of causality of political perspectives (Hall 2005, 2007). What may be permissible within one network may not be permissible elsewhere. Similarly, combinations of corporate governance practices deemed effective within one network may not be effective elsewhere. New institutions or actions, however, are more likely to be adopted and implemented if they are consistent with extant networks and the social norms that they generate. Sociological perspectives thus acknowledge a degree of path dependency and institutional complementarity.

With reference to our focus on board-level employee representation, several implications arise from the assumptions that underpin sociological perspectives. First, the object of analysis is the firm and the various stakeholders therein. The shareholder–manager relationship that forms the core of financial and legal perspectives is one of many relationships that require analysis. Employees and employee representatives thus merit detailed examination as stakeholders within the firm. Second, to assess the functioning of board-level employee representatives, it is necessary to analyse the networks they develop and within which they operate. Although sociological perspectives tend to take the nation state as the basis of analysis, it is accepted that networks may vary by region and/or by sector within nation states (Aguilera et al. 2008; Herrigel 1996).[4] A third, and associated, issue is that a similar relationship within two national or sectoral networks may function very differently because of the character of the network within which the relationship operates. A unionised board-level employee representative in Sweden, for example, may function with superior training, advice and support from his or her relatively well-resourced trade union, compared to a counterpart in Hungary, where the resources available to trade unions are more limited and experience of supporting board-level employee representation is more short-lived.

Based on the founding assumptions mentioned earlier, sociological perspectives have developed to accommodate a variety of criticisms.[5] The much-cited varieties of capitalism approach and issues concerned with conflict are examined here to highlight the dichotomy between sociological perspectives and finance and legal perspectives, and to identify further elements of the analytical framework that informs this study. The distinction between liberal market economies (LMEs) and coordinated market economies (CMEs) underpins the varieties of capitalism approach (Hall and Soskice 2001b; Hancké et al. 2007). Market mechanisms regulate relations within firms, between companies and their suppliers and customers, and between providers and users of capital in LMEs. Sophisticated financial markets facilitate the establishment of new firms and the transfer of resources from contracting to expanding sectors of an economy. Labour is mobile, thereby encouraging employers and employees to invest in general rather than specific skills (Culpepper 1999; Herrigel 1996). In contrast, in CMEs long-term relationships between companies and providers of capital and detailed collaboration between firms within industries in setting standards, vocational training and research, coupled with commitments to provide firm- and industry-specific skills, are supplemented by labour market regulation, which are often implemented through tripartite organisations, to encourage labour retention during economic downturns.

The UK and the US (LMEs) were initially contrasted with Germany (CME) to illustrate the distinction between LMEs and CMEs (Hall and Soskice 2001a).[6] In terms of the European focus of this study, three categories introduced in recognition of variation beyond the LME–CME distinction add to the analytical complexity: mixed market economies (MMEs), which comprise market and coordinated regulation and are exemplified by France (Hall and Gingerich 2009; Molina and Rhodes 2007); and emerging market economies (EMEs) where coordinated regulation, if present at all, is by no means stable, illustrated by the new Member States (NMS) of the EU from Central and Eastern Europe (CEE) (King 2007; Mykhnenko 2007)[7] and the 'GIIPS' group, comprised here of Greece, Ireland and Spain, where structural weakness in the capitalisation of financial sectors have been addressed by stronger externally driven regulation during the recent crises (Schweiger 2014).[8] Acknowledging that there are degrees of coordinated regulation within Europe implies variation in the density of the networks within which firms are embedded and that the networks established by board-level employee representatives are likely to vary in intensity and form dependent on the type of capitalism within which they operate. To accommodate this variation the sixteen European countries covered by this study are assessed as CMEs, MMEs or EMEs or as belonging to the GIIPS group.

Critics argue that the impact of political and social conflict in the promotion of institutional diversity and on different types of capitalism cannot be incorporated into the varieties of capitalism approach, as the analysis of the power relations that underpin coordination is inadequately developed (Crouch 2005; Howell 2003; Regini 2003). Political and social conflict in this context may take different forms. Changes in US legislation were shown to present opportunities to finance managers to promote corporate diversification and enhance their strategic advantage within firms (Fligstein 1990). Similarly, the varieties of capitalism approach has been criticised as emphasising stability and failing to incorporate analysis of the dynamics of institutional change (Deeg and Jackson 2007; Mahoney and Thelen 2010). As economies become more open to foreign capital, for example, extant networks may be disturbed: long-standing coalitions among shareholders, managers and employees in Germany have been disturbed during debates over shareholder value (Höpner 2001; Streeck 2009:77–89) and the reform of the financial system (Deeg 2005).

The implications of introducing political and social conflict into the analysis of corporate governance are wide ranging for an examination of the activities of board-level employee representatives. First, there is no *a priori* reason to anticipate a congruence of interests between employee representatives and other board members. How employee representatives act to secure their chosen objectives in such a contested environment is thus an objective of this study. Second, arguments about the impact of political and social conflict acknowledge the generation of pressures to adapt or to change in response to altered environmental circumstances, particularly in CMEs. Such processes of adaptation or change are contested. A further purpose of this study is thus to identify the roles undertaken by board-level employee representatives in processes of adaptation or change. Moreover, in contested situations board-level employee representatives may find it necessary to seek alliances with other board members or groups thereof. This study investigates the nature of these alliances.

INDUSTRIAL RELATIONS AS THE POINT OF DEPARTURE

Industrial relations situates board-level employee representation in debates on industrial democracy and employee participation. Industrial democracy and employee participation are 'intricate' and 'enigmatic' terms

(Müller-Jentsch 2008) and are contested by reference to definition, institutional means of achievement and effect. For example, industrial democracy has been viewed as a means to transfer the democratic principles that permeate civil society to the workplace (Dachler and Wilpert 1978; King and van de Vall 1978), to addresses the unequal distribution of power at the workplace (Blumberg 1968; Poole 1975, 1982), and to improve the quality of corporate decision-making, thereby, facilitating the implementation of change and reducing the likelihood of industrial conflict (Bullock 1977). In contrast, managerial critics argue that measures intended to promote industrial democracy raise the operating costs of firms, result in unqualified and inexperienced people serving as board members, complicate or jeopardise decision-making processes on the boards of firms (Brannen 1983), and, more recently, introduce unnecessary regulation when deregulation is required to improve economic competitiveness (Speth 2004). Marxists argue that measures implemented to achieve industrial democracy result in the incorporation of employees to the goals of the firm and the containment of conflict within institutions of joint regulation, thus mystifying the inherent differences of interest between capital and labour (Clarke 1977; Hyman 1975:141–149).

Similarly, employee participation has been deployed as a means to examine alienation and worker satisfaction (Blumberg 1968), work design and organisation (Berggren 1993; Sandberg 1995), political democracy (Pateman 1970) and the economic performance of firms (Ichniowski et al. 1997; MacDuffie 1995). As a consequence of this wide disciplinary involvement, definitions of employee participation also differ markedly. Narrow definitions of employee participation view it as a process whereby two or more parties with divergent interests influence each other (French et al. 1960), while others see employee participation as leading to the progressive control of the production process by employees together with the education and development required to undertake incrementally more demanding tasks (Vranicki 1965). Within these parameters, the focus of industrial relations approaches to board-level employee representation is on differences in interests and power between capital and labour, whether these differences can be reconciled and, if so, the institutional form of reconciliation. Contrary to some perspectives within corporate governance, economic efficiency and company performance tend to be downplayed within industrial relations.

To disentangle these competing positions for the purposes of a study of board-level employee representatives it should be acknowledged that participation may be direct or indirect. Direct participation schemes are usually management inspired and centre on the involvement of individual or small groups of employees at workplace level, with the objective of generating higher levels of employee motivation or commitment to managerial objectives. Management-led direct communication, upward problem solving and employee involvement schemes are forms of direct participation (Kessler et al. 2004; Marchington and Wilkinson 2005). Indirect participation usually results from a collective agreement or legislation and requires the selection of representatives to act on behalf of a group of employees at various levels within an organisation. Board-level employee representation is a form of indirect participation. Industrial democracy and employee participation are thus fundamentally different from direct participation, although the use of indirect and direct participation schemes may be associated with power shifts between capital and labour (Ackers et al. 1992; Martinez Lucio 2010).

To situate board-level employee representation within these debates, this section includes two parts. The first part traces the development of the notion of industrial democracy within industrial relations and identifies some of the institutional forms envisaged in its achievement. The second part critically assesses how shifts in power between capital and labour have been used to explain the introduction of different forms of employee participation. This assessment constitutes an introduction to the legislation of board-level employee representation in Europe examined in Chapter 2.

Industrial Democracy as an Industrial Relations Construct

The Anglo-Saxon and German industrial relations traditions underpin different approaches to industrial democracy (Frege 2007; Kaufman 2004; Müller-Jentsch 1986, 2003). Within the Anglo-Saxon tradition, industrial democracy initially embraced issues concerned with the constitutions and internal practices of trade unions, and trade union engagement with employers and the state (Webb and Webb 1913). Trade union constitutional arrangements and practices were viewed as addressing the fundamental challenge inherent in democracy: the reconciliation of administrative efficiency and popular control (Webb and Webb 1913:38). The engagement of trade unions with employers at the workplace and through collective bargaining ensures 'voice' within the firm and influence over the employment contract, while relations with the state allow participation in national political processes (Webb and Webb 1913:807–850). Within the same tradition, industrial democracy was later defined in terms of providing 'mechanisms for protecting the rights and safeguarding the interests of industrial workers' (Clegg 1960:83) and collective bargaining regarded as the means whereby these rights and interests could be safeguarded (Clegg 1976). Underpinning this position was the observation that 'three main elements' characterise industrial democracy: the independence of trade unions from both the state and management, a recognition that only trade unions can represent the interests of workers, and that for the purposes of industrial democracy it is irrelevant whether an enterprise is in the public or private sector (Clegg 1960:21–25). Trade unionism is thus at the core of the Anglo-Saxon approach to industrial democracy.

In contrast to Anglo-Saxon approaches to industrial democracy, the German tradition focuses on works councils and co-determination (Müller-Jentsch 2003, 2008). Originating as a political response to the production necessities of World War I and the German revolution of 1918, works councils were introduced through the *Gesetz über den Väterlandischen*

Hilfsdienst in 1916, which covered companies essential to the war effort that employed fifty or more people; and, more generally, at all workplaces where twenty or more were employed through the *Betriebsrätegesetz* of February 1920.[9] Works councils allowed employee participation and voice at establishment and enterprise levels but were not viewed as 'pioneers of a new socio-economic order' (Naphtali 1928, quoted by Müller-Jentsch 2008:261). Instead, they were seen as standing 'for the democratisation of the industrial system and the attainment, in the economic sphere, of the same rights of self-government and self-determination' as was thought had been achieved politically by the revolution of 1918 (Guillebaud 1928:212). More central to the practice of *Wirtschaftsdemokratie*, however, was co-determination at industry and national levels, which allowed employee representatives an influence on macroeconomic policy formulation (Müller-Jentsch 1986:40–47, 2008), and was enacted through works councils at industry and national levels that were underpinned by Article 165 of the Weimar constitution (Mommsen 1989:51–88).[10] While trade unionists subsequently sought to secure positions on works councils, the German approach to industrial democracy initially did not, and currently does not, centre exclusively on trade union activity. Furthermore, statutory provisions enacted in 1920 and 1922 allowed one or two works council members to sit on the supervisory boards of joint stock companies, thereby introducing board-level employee representation. Three interrelated points pertinent to this study arise from the German approach to industrial democracy.

First, the idea of legislation underpinning institutions and practices of industrial democracy contrasts markedly with the 'voluntarist' tradition that underpinned the Anglo-Saxon approach. In Norway and in seventeen of the eighteen EU Member States where board-level employee representation is in place, legislation supports the practice. While in some Nordic countries legislation originated from collective agreements and Spanish board-level representation relies on collective agreements, the point remains that the juridified approach characteristic of Germany was adopted in most other Western European countries because of differences in state traditions toward trade union organisation between continental European and Anglo-Saxon countries (Bendix 1964; Rokkan 1970; Sorge 1976). Only where this juridified approach assumed precedence during the first half of the twentieth century has board-level employee representation been established, albeit along very different timelines and with varied coverage, as Chapter 2 demonstrates.[11] Furthermore, attempts to introduce board-level employee representation at EU level rely on a similar juridified approach. This is not to argue that the content and impact of legislation is the same across countries but to move towards an explanation of why trade union movements that traditionally advocated voluntarism (Britain and Ireland) or were wary of statutory intervention (Belgium and Italy) tended to treat the achievement of board-level employee representation as a low political priority (Sorge 1976).

Second, in introducing co-determination, the German tradition raises issues concerning the strength of rights of employee participation. Variation in the strength of rights of employee participation is usually expressed in terms of information, consultation and joint decision-making. Continental European systems of employee participation tend to link rights of information, consultation and joint decision-making to different issues, with the strongest rights for employees on joint decision-making available on welfare and some operational issues, whereas the weaker information rights apply to long-term and strategic issues pertinent to the firm (Rogers and Streeck 1995). This situation has significant consequences for what has been referred to as the 'intensity of participation' or the extent of employee influence (Gold and Hall 1990:4; Knudsen 1995:8–10). In practice, the intensity of participation is dependent, *inter alia*, on the range of rights assigned to employee representatives and the breadth and strategic importance of the issues to which the rights are allocated. A purpose of this study is to establish whether the rights assigned to employee representatives at the board, coupled with the issues to which these rights apply, are sufficient to generate the intensity of participation required to enable employee representatives to exert power over strategic decision-making within the firm.

A third point linked to the German tradition concerns the shift away from collective bargaining and trade unions that characterise Anglo-Saxon approaches. The Anglo-Saxon emphasis on the independence of trade unions from employers and the state in the conduct of adversarial collective bargaining 'distances' employee representatives from issues concerned with the management and performance of the firm. In contrast, the German focus on co-determination and works councils ensures the engagement of employee representatives with such issues. Furthermore, collective bargaining is primarily conducted outside of the firm in Germany. Two implications arise at this juncture. First, the engagement of employee representatives through co-determination ensures that managers are made more accountable within the firm because managers have to justify and negotiate strategic decisions with employee representatives (Streeck 1992). Bringing managers to account assumes that board-level representatives receive information in sufficient time to enable them to formulate considered positions on its content, have the capacity and training to interpret documents, and are networked with other institutions of labour representation within and outside the firm. Second, if board-level employee representatives negotiate strategic decisions with managers, issues of alliances with other stakeholders represented on the board arise, as suggested in the corporate governance literature (Gourevitch and Shinn 2005).

Ebbs and Flows: The Views of the Social Partners

At the height of union density and strike activity in Europe during the late 1960s and 1970s employee participation was located in industrial relations literature by reference to cycles of worker resistance and managerial responses (Huiban 1984; Ramsay 1977, 1980). Managers were attracted to participation when they perceived their control over labour to be under pressure. Participation was thus a zero-sum game driven by the struggle between capital and labour at the point of production. Appendix B charts the legislation on board-level employee representation.[12] As is apparent from Appendix B much Western European legislation on board-level representation was enacted during the 1970s suggesting an association between the power of labour and the introduction or extension of board-level representation. Furthermore, in both Germany and Sweden the legislation enacted in 1976 and from 1973 through 1976 was bitterly contested (Hamskär 2012; Kjellberg 1992:124–131; Markovits 1986:53–60). A specific association between the introduction of board-level representation in several countries and high level of labour power does not, however, corroborate a general cycles of participation explanation. Three points are problematic.

First, the only variable force in the cycles of participation explanation is labour power: when labour is strong management yields participation in order to regain control. This focus is 'narrow and partisan' (Ackers et al. 1992), fails to take into account the interests and objectives of management and the state, and treats labour as uniform thereby failing to address why some trade union movements, or trade unions/confederations within such movements, opt for board-level representation and others reject board-level representation. Indeed, the narrow focus on labour influenced the academic shift to situate the firm rather than labour at the analytical centre of sociological perspectives on corporate governance (Höpner 2005).

Second, the cycles of participation explanation focuses on systems based on indirect participation. A founding assumption of the explanation is that management has no interest in encouraging participation other than on the occasions when it is necessary to regain control. The burgeoning of management-inspired direct-participation initiatives (Kessler et al. 2004) and financial-participation schemes (Poutsma 2001; Würz 2003) during the 1980s and 1990s in Europe when labour was relatively weak, suggest that management interests may also be furthered through the introduction of participation schemes. Managerial objectives sought by the introduction of such schemes include higher levels of employee commitment (Watanabe 1991) and productivity (Jones and Kato 1995), shifts to high-performance work systems (Appelbaum et al. 2000) and weakening workplace unionism (Blasi and Kruse 1991). In short, it is not only labour that may strive for forms of employee participation. Furthermore, different forms of participation may be advocated by different groups of managers (Marchington et al. 1993), suggesting that relations within management, as well as between management and employees, may influence the institutions and practice of participation.

Third, neither the cycles of participation argument nor arguments based on the pursuit of different forms of participation by management are sufficient to explain the legislation on board-level representation introduced in West Germany in 1951 and 1952 and in the NMS of the EU after 1988 (see

Appendix B). In West Germany the initiative for the legislation enacted in 1951 came from an agreement concluded in the British sector in 1947 between the Trust Administration and trade unions concerning the governance of coal and steel companies. As the British military government intended to 'decartelise' the steel industry, German trade unionists became strategic allies in the implementation of the British plan. In the absence of opposition from German managers and from former owners, who were concerned to avoid the dismantling of the coal and steel industries, the agreement stipulated parity representation of employee and shareholder representatives on the supervisory boards of the 30 or so independent and publicly-owned companies (Beal 1955; Köstler et al. 2013). Although the Christian Democratic government led by Adenauer opposed the initiative, it introduced the *Montanmitbestimmungsgesetz* when confronted by overwhelming support for strike action within *Industriegewerkschaft Metall* (Metalworkers' Union) and *Industriegewerkschaft Bergbau* (Mineworkers' Union) (Müller 1987, 1991). By 1952, however, the political position of the Adenauer administration was more secure, with the consequence that it was able to resist union efforts to extend parity co-determination throughout the economy and force through the *Betriebsverfassungsgesetz*, which introduced employee representation comprising one-third of the supervisory boards of companies that employ between 500 and 2,000 employees. The legislation of 1951 and 1952 was thus consistent with the principle of co-determination established in 1920 and 1922, extended the scale of employee participation on supervisory boards compared to the Weimar period and was influenced by trade union interventions. Post-war politics, however, particularly regarding the break-up of the steel conglomerates, constituted the specific circumstances within which the legislation was adopted.

The introduction of board-level employee representation in the NMS of 2004 and 2007 took place between 1988 (Hungary) and 1993 (Slovenia). Although this period was marked by wide-ranging unrest and the political transformation of Soviet-style command economies, there is no evidence of significant pressure from labour for the introduction of board-level representation (in Hungary e.g. see Hughes 1992; Neumann 1997). Furthermore, the *acquis communautaire*, under which accession to the EU was negotiated, did not require the NMS to introduce board-level employee representation. Neither political pressure from labour nor preparations for membership of the EU thus appear to have prompted the introduction of board-level employee representation. More influential appear to be long-standing state traditions regarding labour representation that originated during industrialisation. Analyses of these traditions locate several of the NMS in the same category as much of Western continental Europe insofar as both the freedom of association and the right for workers to combine were initially withheld by the state (Crouch 1993; Rokkan 1970; Sorge 1976). In addition, a number of the NMS of 2004 were subsumed within the Austro-Hungarian Empire during industrialisation within which the impact of the German approach to industrial democracy was apparent (Czech Republic, Kořalka 1990; Hungary, Hitchens 1990).[13] The influence of Germanic systems were still present at the time of the economic transition illustrated by the design of company law systems that followed the Germanic pattern in the then Czechoslovakia, Hungary and Slovenia (Bedrač 2005; Havel 2005; Vliegenhart 2009).

The cycles of participation explanation is thus problematic as an analytical framework and does not offer leverage as a means to assess the introduction of board-level employee representation in Germany during the early-1950s and in the NMS of the EU after 1988. Two points, however, emerge from the assessment of the cycles of participation explanation that are relevant to an analysis of board-level representation in Europe. First, board-level employee representation is a recent phenomenon that is not necessarily stable in the NMS.[14] The survey of board-level employee representatives thus presents the opportunity to compare and contrast the activities of board-level employee representatives in 'mature' institutions elsewhere in Europe with those of their counterparts in 'emerging' institutions. Second, board-level employee representation was introduced in some NMS without marked trade union political pressure with the consequence that unionists had to adjust to change, which they did not necessarily promote. The survey enables an examination of the networks established by board-level employee representatives that involve trade unions and institutions of workplace representation, the quality of support offered by trade unions to employee representatives at the board level and the manner in which employee representatives acquire the expertise necessary to participate at the board.

Putting aside the peculiarities of the NMS, it is apparent that a substantial number of Western European trade union movements have tended to support board-level representation underpinned by legislation. Throughout Austria, Germany, Luxembourg and most of the Nordic countries, for example, trade union support for board-level representation has been constant since the 1960s, albeit pursued at different intensities over time (Crouch 1993; Sorge 1976). In general terms, two forms of rejection of board-level employee representation were in evidence: the UK and Ireland, where a tradition of voluntarism remained in place throughout much of the twentieth century, and among key sections of the union movements in Belgium, France, Greece and Italy.

Although the Trades Union Congress (TUC) in 1978 formally supported the $2X + Y$ formula proposed by the Bullock Commission in 1977, opposition within several large TUC-affiliated unions and employers effectively led to the proposal being sidelined (Gold 2005).[15] Unions that rejected the proposal objected to industrial democracy by legal means and argued that the task of trade unions through collective bargaining is 'to consider, contest and oppose, if necessary, the exercise of managerial prerogatives. It is not the responsibility of work people to manage the enterprise; indeed, it is essential that trade unions retain their independence' (Electrical, Electronic, Telecommunications and Plumbing Union evidence to Bullock 1977: cited at page 124). Instead of industrial democracy by legal means, the objective was a 'self-managed society of producer associations' achieved through the extension of collective bargaining to result in workers' control (Coates and Topham 1977). The election of the Conservative government led by Margaret Thatcher effectively removed industrial democracy in the form of board-level employee representation from political debate. Concurrent with the political debate on the Bullock Commission in the UK, the Irish trade union movement accepted proposals tabled in the Worker Participation (State Enterprises) Act 1977 to allow board-level employee representation in seven state-owned enterprises. Although acceptance of the proposal was not consistent with the voluntarism then advocated by the Irish Congress of Trade Unions (ICTU), the limited public-sector coverage of the measure resulted in its acceptance.

Within the second group of largely southern European countries, where trade unions had opposed board-level employee representation, ideology rather than a tradition of voluntarism underpinned rejection of board employee representation. In particular, legal mechanisms to introduce board-level employee representation were viewed as leading to the incorporation of employee representatives and thus distancing the stated objective of *contrôle ouvrier*. Rejection of employee representation at the board introduced by legal means was most strongly expressed from within the union confederations with links to the Communist Party such as the Confederazione generale italiana del lavoro (CGIL, Italy) and Confédération générale du travail (CGT, France). The CGT opposed board-level employee representation in the private sector well into the twentieth century while having supported its introduction in state-owned companies since 1919 (Guglielmi 2005).[16] Confederations linked to the Socialist Party including the Confederazione italiana sindicati lavoratori (CISL, Italy), Confédération française démocratique du travail (CFDT, France) and the Algemeen Belgisch Vakverbond/ Fédération Générale du Travail de Belgique (ABVV/ FGTB, Belgium) were prepared to sanction information and consultation rights at the workplace, but excluded employee representation at the board as a means to improve such rights. There are no legal arrangements for board-level employee representation in Belgium and Italy. In France and Greece, Socialist Party–led governments introduced schemes restricted to the public sector during the 1980s.[17] Although there was no union opposition to the measures, in Greece there was little union pressure for the legislation. In short, where union organisations have not promoted board-level employee representation in the private sector there is either no legislation to support such representation or the systems that are in place tend to be restricted to the public sector. The research questions arising from this analysis are: have employee representatives at board level in France, Greece and Ireland taken measures to avoid their incorporation as was anticipated within some union confederations and, if so, what has been the impact of the measures that they implemented?

Critics of the cycles of participation explanation argue that employers do not oppose participation *per se* but favour voluntary and direct rather than statutory and indirect systems. There is certainly no evidence of employers' organisations lobbying for the introduction of statutory board-level employee representation or for increases in the proportion of employee representatives that sit on boards within existing systems. Individual employers and managers, however, express some support for board-level employee representation (Paster 2012). In contrast, the evidence on the growth of voluntary and direct systems of participation from around the mid-1980s is wide ranging (Gill and Krieger 1999; Kessler et al. 2004). The growth of voluntary and direct participation systems has led some to question whether such systems are alternatives rather than complements to statutory and indirect systems (Jacobi and Hassel 1995). In a similar vein, sociological perspectives on corporate governance acknowledge that firms within CMEs are coming under increasing competitive pressure to adopt more features characteristic of their counterparts operating in LMEs (Goyer 2006; Iversen 2007). Indeed, hybrid board arrangements are appearing as a means to increase international competitiveness (Barker 2010; Höpner 2003; Vitols 2004).

The variation in the character of employer strategies to reform or circumvent extant institutions within CMEs is of concern here. The case of Germany, the archetypical CME, illustrates the variation and impact of employer strategies. The strategy of German employers operates at the national political level and within the firm (Kinderman 2005). At the national political level, employers organised into the *Bundesverband der Deutschen Arbeitgeberverbände* (BDA) and the *Bundesverband der Deutschen Industrie* (BDI) have lobbied for greater deregulation, established the New Social Market Initiative to accelerate economic liberalisation and institutional reform, and have eroded the coverage of industry-wide collective agreements through the negotiation of *Öffnungsklauseln* (opening clauses) (Massa-Wirth and Seifert 2005; Schmidt 2002). In November 2004 the president of the BDI referred to board-level co-determination as an 'error of history' (quoted in Paster 2012:485). The flight of German capital, particularly in the form of investments in CEE, provides the backdrop to these political campaigns. In addition, some German companies are adopting a foreign legal status in greater numbers as a means, *inter alia*, to circumvent German regulations on board-level employee representation (Sick 2015). Within the firm the strategy of employers is not necessarily to seek the reform or the removal of institutions but to shape their content and function in a manner consistent with deregulation (Paster 2012; Pongratz and Voß 2003), thereby altering the purpose rather than the form of board-level representation. Boyer (2005), for example, argues that German employee participation has changed from being a mechanism to pursue the interests of employees to an institution that is concerned to promote corporate competitiveness.

While the extent and the impact of employer strategies are subject to intense debate (Hassel 1999; Thelen 2000; Thelen and van Wijnbergen

2003), they raise two key arguments in the context of a study of board-level employee representation. First, if employer strategies are directed to altering the content and function of employee representation at board level, the nature of change will be recorded in the survey evidence in the form of the perceptions of the board-level employee representatives. In other words, the survey data will contribute to the debate on the extent and impact of the strategies of employers, particularly German employers. Second, the strategies of employers raise *de jure* and *de facto* comparisons. Board-level employee representation is *de jure* a contribution to industrial democracy and a defining feature of the stakeholder category of corporate governance. If the strategies of employers have altered the practice of board-level representation to serve purposes associated with deregulation and economic liberalisation, however, the *de facto* function will differ from the original *de jure* intention.

WHERE DO WE GO FROM HERE?

Analyses of board-level employee representation within the corporate governance and industrial relations perspectives argue that board-level employee representatives exert power over strategic board decisions. The complication within both analytical perspectives is that several of the key variables are endogenous and indirect. To illustrate, the economic performance of a firm is likely to have been influenced by past directors and may influence the selection of subsequent directors. From within corporate governance literature, economic perspectives focus on the impact on corporate economic performance of the presence of board-level employee representatives (Jirjahn 2011). Similarly, the industrial relations literature focuses on the relation between board-level employee representation and the management of labour (Gospel and Pendleton 2005; Jackson 2005). In both cases, economic performance and the management of labour are not a direct outcome of employee representation on the board, may be influenced by a range of factors additional to employee representation on the board, and may affect the approach of board-level employee representatives as well as being influenced by them. In short, establishing connections between the presence and activities of board level representatives and the outcomes anticipated from within the corporate governance and industrial relations perspectives is methodologically fraught.

Two further points regarding the approach adopted here are apposite at this juncture. First, no attempt is made to review in detail extant empirical evidence on the impact of board-level employee representatives. Instead, such evidence is assessed in conjunction with the findings presented in Chapters 3 through 6. This approach is adopted because the vast majority of extant evidence has been generated by means of studies based in single countries, whereas the approach here is comparative. Second, no attempt is made to demonstrate associations between board-level employee representation and the economic performance of companies. Underpinning this approach is the recognition that evidence of the economic effects of board-level employee representation is far from conclusive. Recent reviews, for example, demonstrate that about one-third of the findings show a positive effect on company economic performance, one-third show a negative effect, and a final third fail to demonstrate any correlation (Conchon 2011b; Kommission zur Moderniserung der deutschen Unternehmensmitbestimmung 2006). Furthermore, 'macro-economic policies, competition, industry structure and the education and motivation of managers and employees affect competitiveness and productivity much more than governance alone' (Roe 1994:233). In view of this ambiguity the emphasis here is placed on issues associated with the power and articulation of board-level employee representatives.

To identify the means to assess the impact of the presence and the activities of employee representatives at that board level, this section is composed of two parts. In the first part, some further research questions and some additional variables that may influence the activities of board members are identified. In the second part the structure and the broad argument of the book are briefly outlined.

Further Research Questions

At the core of any framework for analysing the activities of board-level employee representatives is the question, what do board-level employee representatives do? Legislation may stipulate what board-level employee representatives *should* do, but this may differ from day-to-day practice. In addition to the functions undertaken by employee representatives are issues arising from variations in the structure of the board and the manner in which the board operates (Adams et al. 2010).

In general terms, two issues underpin what board-level employee representatives do: the setting and monitoring of corporate strategy, and the appointment, assessment and dismissal of senior managers. At a minimum, board members endorse corporate strategies proposed by managers, if they do not propose strategies. Surveys indicate, however, that the majority of directors view themselves as originators of corporate strategy rather than as monitors or overseers of the activities of senior managers (Demb and Neubauer 1992). Three issues arise in this context regarding a study of board-level employee representatives. First, to exert a meaningful influence on or power over corporate strategy, employee representatives require access to the same information within the same time frame as other board members. This issue is assessed by reference to the wide range of agenda items considered by company boards to establish whether information flows are consistent and equitable across the range of the agenda and are sufficiently timely to enable employee representatives at the board the opportunity to prepare a position for presentation at a board meeting. Second, corporate strategy covers a wide range of issues, including investments, performance and restructuring, that are traditionally linked with shareholder preferences; and 'social' issues, such as collective bargaining, health and safety, and environmental matters that are often viewed as the priorities of stakeholders other than shareholder representatives. In this context the research establishes the attitude of board-level employee representatives to these different aspects of corporate strategy and investigates whether their interest and influence varies according to the topic. Third, within the board, strategic preferences may be contested and the role of the CEO in influencing strategy has come under increasing scrutiny, particularly in the light of the financialisation of corporations and the associated growth in personal rewards available to some CEOs. In this context, information transmission from the CEO to board members and vice versa, and the independence of board members from the CEO are central to transparent and effective governance (Boone et al. 2007; Ryan and Wiggins 2004). The research questions examined in this study are the extent employee representatives exert control over the agenda of the board and the independence of board-level employee representatives from the CEO.

The appointment, assessment and dismissal of senior managers are also viewed as a key component of what board members do. In two-tier boards an explicit function of the supervisory board involves the supervision of senior managers. It is difficult to imagine board-level employee representatives being able to monitor effectively the activities of senior managers directly, thus the study also examines the extent to which board-level employee representatives view themselves as supervisors of senior managers.

A second range of research questions relates to the structure of company boards. Board members are typically divided into two groups: insiders, who are usually full-time employees of the company, and outsiders, whose primary employment is not with the company. Outsiders are often referred to as independent board members, but the degree of this independence has been recently questioned (Blackburn 2002; Coffee 2005). Within this framework board-level employee representatives may be either insiders (employees) or outsiders (trade union officers), albeit operating with the expectation that they retain a degree of independence to pursue issues of concern to labour. This study examines the nature and extent of the influence or power exercised by board-level employee representatives, and identifies the agenda items introduced and pursued at the board by employee representatives.

Further structural variables that may influence the performance of a company board include single-tier or dual-tier structure and, in particular, whether the roles of CEO and chair of the board are undertaken by the same or different individuals (Adams et al. 2005; Brickley et al. 1997); the size of the board (Yermack 1996); and the proportion of employee representatives that sit on the board and their capacity to act collectively. Specifically, are employee representatives able to caucus to establish a uniform position to present at the board? The scope to examine each of these variables is available within the terms of this study. In addition, there is a vast array of evidence to indicate that women employee representatives pursue different agendas to their male counterparts (Farrell and Hersch 2005; Fonow and Franzway 2009; McBride 2001), a point examined here in the context of the power exercised by board-level employee representatives and their nature of their articulation with other institutions of labour representation.

Structure of the Book

In the context of studies of board-level employee representation, this book is innovative in four respects. First, the priorities, influences and the mode of action of board-level employee representatives constitute a thread that runs throughout the text. Variation between board-level employee representatives from different country clusters in each of these fields demonstrates that board-level employee representation is not monolithic but is subject to wide-ranging internal variation. Second, this study identifies the nature and the extent of the power exerted by board-level employee representatives and thus examines whether they are able to co-determine strategic corporate decision-making. Third, the articulation of board-level employee representatives with other institutions within and outside of the company is a recurring theme of the book. Such articulation underpins the efficacy of many of the activities of board-level employee representatives and is integral to the generation of a coordinated position by labour within the company and, if appropriate, between companies. Fourth, these issues are evaluated by reference to large-scale survey evidence comprising data from board-level employee representatives based in sixteen countries together with their counterparts operating in European Companies. Apart from differences to accommodate institutional variation, the questionnaires were identical across the sample, thereby allowing the first large-scale, direct comparisons of the activities of board-level employee representatives.

The first phase of the analysis establishes the key features of board-level employee representation and representatives in Europe. Chapter 2 introduces the situation *de jure* regarding the expectations of board-level employee representation. As Appendix B shows, much of the relevant legislation, particularly in Western Europe, was enacted when different economic and political circumstances prevailed compared to the current situation. Chapter 2 thus 'sets up' the analysis of what board-level employee representatives do now by identifying the initial expectations regarding their role as established in law. Chapter 3 identifies the characteristics of board-level employee representatives; locates them by reference to company status, sector/industry and size and establishes the features of the company boards on which they sit.

The second phase of the analysis presents the data disaggregated into country clusters, together with a separate category for the European Companies. Chapter 4 focuses on the board meeting and identifies the priorities of board-level employee representatives, the manner in which the agenda is compiled, the timeliness and quality of information provided for the board meeting, confidentiality and how board-level employee representatives intervene at the board. Chapter 5 retains a focus on the board meeting but shifts emphasis to the influence of board-level employee representatives on company restructuring decisions, the nature and extent of the power exercised by board-level employee representatives and the participation of board-level employee representatives in subcommittees of the board and in pre-meetings. Chapter 6 assesses the articulation of board-level employee representatives with institutions of labour representation within the company, with trade unions outside of the company and with other board members, thereby extending the analysis of the power of board-level employee representatives.

Chapter 7 concludes the book by reviewing the features of board-level employee representation in the different country clusters and by examining the views of corporate governance and industrial relations theorists in the light of the presented evidence. Appendix A details the procedures used to compile the database on which these analyses are founded while Appendix B outlines the legislation that underpins board-level employee representation in Europe.

NOTES

1. Among such reviews were the Cadbury Report for the UK in 1992, the first Vienot Report for France in 1995, the Nørby Report for Denmark in 2001, the Cromme Code for Germany in 2002 and the US Commission on Public Trust and Private Enterprise in 2003.
2. For more detailed criticisms of the legal perspective, see Goyer (2010).
3. In this instance, electoral victory in a proportional electoral system is defined as requiring a majority of votes cast, whereas in a majoritarian system electoral victory results from achieving victory in a majority of districts or constituencies.
4. Differences between small and medium-sized enterprises and large companies are also noted as influencing the character of networks and the objectives sought by stakeholders therein (Berndt 2000; Kinderman 2005). This issue is pursued here for countries in which the minimum size threshold for board-level employee representation includes smaller companies.
5. Among the criticisms of the sociological perspectives are that they are static and fail to accommodate change (Hancké and Goyer 2005); they do not elaborate with an analysis of the service sector but focus on manufacturing (Blyth 2003); they do not recognise linkages between nation states, particularly in the context of the EU (Crouch 2005; Pontusson 2005); and they downplay the role of the state (Regini 2003; Schmidt 2002). These issues are explored in detail in Hancké et al. (2007).
6. Whereas Germany was viewed as the exemplary CME, Austria, Belgium, the Netherlands, Japan, the Nordic countries and Switzerland were also categorised as CMEs.
7. Other non-European EMEs include Brazil, India and Russia.

8. Italy and Portugal are also assigned to this group but are excluded here because there is no board-level employee representation in Italy and in Portugal the legislation that is in place is not implemented in practice (see Appendix A).
9. More restricted legislation had been enacted earlier to introduce works councils in particular sectors. The legislation of 1916 and 1920 introduced works councils as an institution of national coverage.
10. Article 165 of the Weimar Constitution stated that 'workers and staff are appointed to participate with equal rights together with the company in the regulation of wages and working conditions, as well as in the complete economic development of the producing powers'.
11. Although the theoretical underpinning of the distinction between state traditions differs from that drawn between common law and civil law systems in the legal perspective (La Porta et al. 1997, 2000), the categorisation of countries based on the two approaches is very similar.
12. The timings of the survey and the reasons for excluding Croatia, the Netherlands and Portugal from the analysis are provided in Appendix A.
13. This argument would also apply to Croatia, which was subsumed within the Austro-Hungarian Empire.
14. Chapter 7 discusses some of the recent developments in this regard.
15. The $2X + Y$ formula included equal representation for shareholder and employee representatives ($2X$) plus a number of independent directors acceptable to both shareholder and employee representatives (Y).
16. The CGT campaigned during the 1960s and 1970s for the nationalisation of large segments of the French economy with a tripartite administration introduced to nationalised companies included in which was board-level employee representation.
17. Although the first law generalising board-level employee representation in French state-owned companies was enacted in 1983, board-level employee representation was already in place in some state owned companies as the nationalisation plan adopted during the 'liberation period' (1944–1945) included employee representation on the boards of strategic companies, including Air France, Électricité de France, Gaz de France and Renault.

2 The Situation *De Jure*
The Regulation of Board-Level Employee Representation

Chapter 1 established that board-level employee representation is underpinned by varied regulatory mechanisms. In Spain bipartite agreements support board-level employee representation that is specific to particular enterprises. Elsewhere legislation buttresses board-level employee representation. The origins of this legislation lie in either corporate governance or industrial relations. Regulation in the case of corporate governance comprises company law supplemented recently, in many countries, by codes of conduct of varying legal status. Although the distinction is far from robust, industrial relations legislation tends to emphasise issues associated with industrial democracy whereas the corporate governance regulations focus, *inter alia*, on the duties and responsibilities of board members. The purpose of Chapter 2 is to establish the extent of variation in the regulations that underpin board-level employee representation. Chapter 2 thus identifies the *de jure* position on board-level employee representation that serves as the basis of the comparison with the *de facto* analyses of subsequent chapters.

Both the corporate governance and industrial relations literatures presented in Chapter 1 allow the identification of several points of departure for an examination of the regulation of board-level employee representation. The legal perspective within the corporate governance literature, for example, anticipates consistent differences in the form of regulation between civil law and common law systems. Sociological perspectives and, in particular, the varieties of capitalism approach suggest a different point of departure. By definition, board-level employee representation is not widespread in LMEs, where reliance is placed on market mechanisms to regulate relations within firms. Within CMEs, MMEs, and EMEs, however, there are different expectations regarding board-level employee representation. In essence, stronger regulations on board-level employee representation are anticipated in CMEs than in either MMEs or EMEs, and the regulations in EMEs are expected to be less stable than the regulations in CMEs and MMEs (Grabbe 2003; Hall and Soskice 2001a; King 2007). In this context, what constitutes the 'strength' of regulations remains a moot point. This chapter investigates the strength of the regulations by reference to coverage, the proportion of the board comprising employee representatives, and the rights and obligations of board-level employee representatives. Further attention is paid to the formal support in the context of selection procedures and the types of actors involved, both of which facilitate articulation between board-level employee representatives and other employee representation bodies at company level. As established in Chapter 1, perspectives developed within the industrial relations literature emphasise the importance of connections between employee representatives and their constituents in order to anchor industrial democracy and to reinforce the capacity of labour institutions to exert influence and power.

With the intention of testing the assumptions stemming from each of these different points of departure, Chapter 2 comprises three sections. The first section examines the scope and coverage of board-level employee representation in Europe. The second section assesses the means of selection of board-level employee representatives and how these might influence articulation between board-level employee representatives and other institutions of labour representation. The third section identifies features of the constitution of the board and how these impinge on the practices of board-level employee representatives. Throughout, the term *board* refers to the institution on which the employee representatives sit unless otherwise stated.

In Belgium, Bulgaria, Cyprus, Estonia, Italy, Latvia, Lithuania, Malta, Romania and the UK there is no legislation to support board-level employee representation. In companies in which board-level employee representation exists in these countries, it results from specific voluntary arrangements that have been agreed at company level. These countries are thus excluded from the analysis. With the exception of the UK, these countries operate with civil law systems in a manner similar to much of continental Europe. The distinction between civil law and common law systems and their uniform effects on approaches to corporate governance (La Porta et al. 1997) would thus appear to be overstated (Ahlering and Deakin 2007).

In addition to national-level regulations, board-level employee representation stands as a European-level feature insofar as it is anchored in primary and secondary European law. In European primary law, it has been recognised as a fundamental right as it is enshrined in both the 1989 Community Charter of Fundamental Social Rights for Workers,[1] to which Member States are committed following the Fifth Recital of the European Treaty, and in the treaty field devoted to the European social policy.[2] Employee representation at board level became an element of European secondary law in 2001 when a European company legal status was initially adopted in the form of the European Company, known as the 'SE' after its Latin name *Societas Europæa*.[3] This enactment paved the way for the adoption of two further components of European company law, the Statute for a European Cooperative Society (2003) and the Cross-Border Mergers Directive (2005), which include provisions on board-level employee representation, based to a large extent on the European Company Statute (SE). These cases led to the emergence of Europeanised boards on which sit employee representatives from the 'home country' of the company and from the 'participating countries' in the establishment of an SE, a European Cooperative Society or a merged company. Because of the low number of established European Cooperative Societies (25 throughout Europe as of July 2012) and the lack of data regarding the use of the Cross-Border Mergers Directive compared to more than 2,000 SEs registered as of 1 January 2015,[4] this research exclusively focuses on SEs. Data and information on the regulation of board-level employee representation in SEs are thus added to that on national legislation as the focus of this *de jure* study.

THE SCOPE OF BOARD-LEVEL EMPLOYEE REPRESENTATION IN EUROPE

For current purposes, the scope of board-level employee representation in Europe includes issues associated with the sectoral coverage of the regulations and, in particular, with indicators found within the regulations of the sixteen countries of the capacity of board-level employee representatives to exert power and influence. The coverage of regulations, for example, may be all-inclusive or restricted to specific sectors or companies. Similarly, the influence and power of employee representation on the board is likely to vary, dependent, *inter alia*, on the proportion of the membership of the board comprised by employee representatives. In addition, national differences in the structure of company boards are identified and assessed by reference to the scope of the regulations. Examination of the variation in the scope of board-level employee representation thus moves the analysis towards the identification of country categories on a *de jure* basis, which subsequent chapters assess by reference to *de facto* practices. The data are presented in Table 2.1 on a country-by-country basis.

The analysis is based on regulations in force at the time the survey was conducted (2009–2013) rather than those introduced by the initial regulations. Reference to Table 2.1 reveals four categories of countries, with SEs being specific and relying so much on national rules that they comprise a stand-alone category. The categories of countries are presented in ascending order of coverage.

The most restricted coverage of the regulations is in Ireland, Greece and Spain. In these countries the regulations cover only state-owned companies. In Ireland coverage initially included sixteen semi-state or state-sponsored bodies.[5] Privatisation has restricted the coverage of the regulation in Ireland and has diluted representation in a number of organisations (TASC 2012). Furthermore, the public sector agencies established in recent years, notably the National Asset Management Agency (NAMA), do not have employee representation arrangements at the board level (Ribarova et al. 2010:104). Estimates suggest that there were about 50 board-level employee representatives throughout Ireland (O'Kelly 2004). The impact of the financial

Table 2.1 The Scope of Board-Level Employee Representation in Europe

Country	Date of Regulation[1]	Coverage of Board-level Employee Representation		Company Board Structure	Number/Proportion of Employee Representatives
		Sector	Company Size		
Austria	1947 (1974, Arbeitsverfassungsgesetz)	Limited liability companies	300 or more employees	Dual board	33% of the supervisory board
		Joint stock companies	All	Dual board	33% of the supervisory board
Czech Republic	1990 (1997, Zákon č. 77/1997 Sb., o státním podniku)	State enterprises[2]	All	Dual board	33% of the supervisory board
	1991, Zákon č. 513/1991 Sb., obchodní zákoník[3]	Joint stock companies	50 or more employees, but lower thresholds may be agreed through articles of association	Dual board	33% of the supervisory board, but articles of association may allow up to 50%
Denmark	1973 (2009, selskabsloven)	Joint stock and limited liability companies	35 or more employees	Choice[4]	33% with a minimum of 2 (minimum of 3 on the board of a parent company)

(Continued)

Table 2.1 (Continued)

Country	Date of Regulation[1]	Coverage of Board-level Employee Representation		Company Board Structure	Number/Proportion of Employee Representatives
		Sector	Company Size		
Finland	1990, Laki henkilöstön edustuksesta yritysten hallinnossa	Joint stock and limited liability companies	150 or more employees	Choice	Based on agreement. If no agreement, minimum standards apply: 20% of the board with a maximum of 4
	1987 (2010, Laki valtion liikelaitoksista)	State enterprises	All	Unitary board	At least one
France[5]	1983, Loi de démocratisation du secteur public	State enterprises	All (single or parent companies)	Choice	Single or parent companies: 2% to 33% in companies with fewer than 200 employees.
			200 or more employees (in case of subsidiaries)		Subsidiaries: 3 in companies with between 200 and 1,000 employees. 33% of the board in all other cases
	1994, Loi relative à l'amélioration de la participation des salariés dans l'entreprise 2006, Loi pour le développement de la participation	Privatised companies	All		Minimum of 1 up to 3 depending on the applicable privatisation Act and size of the board

Germany	1951, Montan-Mitbestimmungsgesetz	Joint stock and limited liability companies in the mining, iron and steel industry	1,000 or more employees	Dual board	50% of the supervisory board (on which also sits an additional 'neutral external person' agreed by both the shareholders' and employees' sides)
	1952 (2004, Drittelbeteiligungsgesetz)	Joint stock and limited liability companies (inter alia)	From 500 to 2,000 employees	Dual board	33% of the supervisory board
	1976, Mitbestimmungsgesetz	Joint stock and limited liability companies (inter alia)	2,000 or more employees	Dual board	50% of the supervisory board, with the chair (appointed by shareholders) having a casting vote in the event of a tie
Greece	1983 (2005, Νόμος 3429/2005 Δημόσιες Επιχειρήσεις και Οργανισμοί)	State enterprises	All	Unitary board	Either 1 or 2 (depending on the size of the board and of the company)
Hungary	1988 (2013, évi V. törvény a Polgári Törvénykönyvrõl)	Joint stock and limited liability companies	200 or more employees	Choice	33% of the supervisory board Extent of representation agreed between works council and board if unitary board in place

(Continued)

Table 2.1 (Continued)

Country	Date of Regulation[1]	Coverage of Board-level Employee Representation		Company Board Structure	Number/Proportion of Employee Representatives
		Sector	Company Size		
Ireland	1977 (1988, Worker Participation (State Enterprises) Act)	State enterprises and agencies	All	Unitary board	33% of the board of directors
Luxembourg	1974, Loi instituant des comités mixtes dans les entreprises du secteur privé et organisant la représentation des salariés dans les sociétés anonymes	Joint stock companies	1,000 or more employees	Choice	33% of the board
		State enterprises in which the state has a minimum 25% holding	All	Choice	Minimum 3 board members, maximum 33% of the board
Norway	1972 (1997, Lov om aksjeselskaper, Lov om allmennaksjeselskaper)	Joint stock and limited liability companies	30 or more employees	Unitary board	30–50 employees: 1 board member 50 or more employees: minimum of 2 board members up to 33% of the board More than 200 employees and no corporate assembly: 33% of the board of directors and an additional board member
	1991, Lov om statsforetak	State enterprises			

Poland	1981, Ustawa r. o przedsiębiorstwach państwowych	State enterprises	All	Dual board	All of the 'workers council' which is the main governing body
	1990 (1996, Ustawa r. o komercjalizaji i prywatyzacji przedsiębiorstwach państwowych)	'Commercialised' companies (limited liability or joint stock companies with the state as sole shareholder) and privatised companies (in which the state is no longer the sole shareholder)	All	Dual board	40% of the supervisory board of 'commercialised' companies Between 2 and 4 members on the supervisory board of privatised companies (depending on the size of the board)
Slovakia	1991, Zákon č. 513/1991 Sb., obchodný zákoník	Joint stock companies	50 or more employees, but lower thresholds may be agreed through articles of association	Dual board	33% of supervisory board, but articles of association may allow up to 50%
	1990, Zákon č. 111/1990 o štátnom podniku	State enterprises	All	Dual board	50% of supervisory board, except the position of chairman (who has a casting vote in the event of a tie)

(Continued)

Table 2.1 (Continued)

Country	Date of Regulation[1]	Coverage of Board-level Employee Representation		Company Board Structure	Number/Proportion of Employee Representatives
		Sector	Company Size		
Slovenia	1993, Zakon o sodelovanju delavcev pri upravljanju	Joint stock and limited liability companies that are not regarded as being 'small'	50 or more employees	Choice	Minimum 1 member up to 25% in unitary boards. Between 33% up to 50% of supervisory board
Spain	1986, Acuerdo sobre participación sindical en la empresa pública 1993, Acuerdo colectivo para las empresas del sector del Metal del Grupo INI-TENEO	State enterprises	1,000 or more employees. A lower threshold (500 or more employees) applies in the metal sector	Unitary board	2 or 3 members of the board of directors (1 member per trade union entitled to participate in nomination)
Sweden	1973 (1987, Lag om styrelserepresentation för de privatanställda)	Joint stock and limited liability companies	25 or more employees	Unitary board	In companies between 25 and 1,000 employees: 2 board members In larger companies which operate in several industries: 3 board members, maximum of 50% of the board

Sources: Büggel (2010); Calvo et al. (2008); Fulton (2013a); HBS and ETUI (2004); Kluge and Stollt (2006, 2009 updated by Conchon in 2015); SDA and ETUI (2005), authors' own research with the support of the members of the SEEurope network (http://www.worker-participation.eu/European-Company-SE/SEEurope-network/Network-members).

Notes:

1. The date of the regulation is that of the initial measure in the country concerned after 1945 or the initial measure for a major sector of the economy in countries where the regulations are sector specific. The coverage, company board structure and the number/proportion of board-level employee representatives are those specified in the most recent legislation, which is mentioned in parentheses.
2. The case of state enterprises is mentioned only with regard to countries that regulate them by a specific legislation. When not specified, board-level employee representation in state enterprises is regulated as in private companies insofar as state enterprises have adopted the legal statute of a private limited liability or a joint-stock company.
3. Since the beginning of this research project, provisions relating to compulsory board-level employee representation in Czech joint-stock companies were repealed, with effect from 1 January 2014. Legal provisions reported in this table refer to the situation in force at the time the survey was conducted.
4. The term *choice* in the 'company board structure' column refers to national arrangements that allow for either unitary or dual board arrangements.
5. Since the beginning of this research, provisions relating to compulsory board-level employee representation were extended to large private-sector (joint-stock) companies in France, with effect from 2014. The situation of privatised companies was also modified by an Edict of 2014 that repealed the provisions related to board-level employee representation found in the Acts of 1994 and 2006. These legal developments are not reported in Table 2.1, which refers to the situation in force at the time the survey was conducted.

crisis since 2007 and privatisation have significantly reduced the coverage of board-level employee representation in the Spanish and Greek public sectors (Conchon 2012). Unitary boards operate in Ireland, Greece and Spain. Employee representation on the board in Ireland cannot exceed 33 per cent of board membership and is usually between one and five members. In Spain employee representation is limited to two or three members, while the extent of board-level employee representation in Greece is even more confined with only one or two board members representing employees.

A second country category comprises France and Poland. Legislation in these countries limits board-level employee representation to the public sector, although arrangements are in place for privatised companies to retain board-level employee representation. Both unitary and dual-board arrangements are available in France, while in Poland only dual-board arrangements are allowed. In each of these countries the legislation allows for minority representation up to a maximum of 33 per cent in France and 40 per cent in Poland of board members. As in Ireland, Greece and Spain, privatisation has effectively curtailed the coverage of the legislation in Poland. At December 2003, for example, about 700 single-shareholder companies of the Polish State Treasury operated with board-level employee representation plus an unknown number of companies in which the State Treasury retains stocks or shares (Stelina 2005),[6] resulting in more than 1,000 board-level employee representatives. Following drastic privatisation plans, only 400 of those representatives remained by 2011 (Conchon 2012). Privatisation has also muddied the explicit distinction between the public and private sectors. In France, for example, two pieces of legislation, the Act of 1994 regarding the improvement of employee participation in the company and the Act of 2006 regarding the development of employee participation, require privatised companies to retain a minimum of one board-level employee representative. This obligation is not indefinite. A decision of the Annual General Meeting (AGM) of shareholders may remove employee representatives' reserved seats from the board. Board-level employee representation, however, has been retained in the majority of the companies privatised since the enactment of the legislation (Conchon 2009). This practice paved the way for a recent extension of the coverage of board-level employee representation in France, with legislation enacted in 2013, making it compulsory for large private-sector companies to assign one or two board seats to employee representatives (Fulton 2013a). The Polish situation could have changed dramatically had a government bill submitted in 2010 on the reform of corporate governance within privatised companies not been stalled. The Polish Treasury Ministry proposed legislation intended, amongst other things, to eliminate employee representation at board level, to ensure a level playing field with private-sector companies (Skupień 2010). Although the government proposal was eventually removed from the political agenda because of other pressing matters, particularly pension reform, the longevity of arrangements for board-level employee representation in Poland is open to question.

Common to the two country categories with the most restricted systems of board-level employee representation are traditions of adversarial industrial relations and trade union movements with ambivalent attitudes towards the practice. A consequence of trade union ambivalence is that there are no encompassing trade union campaigns to extend the coverage of board-level employee representation, although there are rhetorical demands. Furthermore, when proposals to privatise public-sector companies with board-level employee representation have been implemented in these countries trade unionists have neither tended to mount significant campaigns in defence of board-level employee representation nor been unified in their defence, with some trade unions remaining indifferent.

A third country category includes the Czech Republic, Finland, Luxembourg and Slovakia. Countries in this category operate board-level employee representation throughout the economy but have a threshold based on employment numbers for the private sector, whereas the public sector is covered irrespective of employment numbers. The employment threshold is set at 50 employees in the Czech Republic and Slovakia, at 150 employees in Finland, and at 1,000 employees in Luxembourg. In Luxembourg and Finland unitary and dual-board arrangements are in place, while in the Czech Republic and Slovakia dual-board structures operate with employee representatives sat on the supervisory board. Independent of the board structure, employee representatives comprise a minimum of 20 per cent of the board in these four countries. In addition, voluntary arrangements in the Czech Republic and Slovakia may raise the proportion of board members that represent the workforce to 50 per cent.

Implementation of the legislation does not correspond to its scope in the two CEE countries. In 2003 in the Czech Republic, for example, survey evidence showed that only about 14,000 companies, or 4.1 per cent of the total number, operated with board-level employee representation (Heppnerová 2005). Similarly, in Slovakia is evidence of reductions in the number of employee representatives serving on the boards of companies in which voluntary company-level arrangements set the parameters of employee participation (Krajcir 2005). In the Czech Republic and Slovakia the scale of post-transition privatisation has had a marked effect on the coverage and practice of board-level employee representation (Grabbe 2003; Meardi 2002). A combination of weak or non-existent workplace trade union organisation, a lack of interest amongst the workforce and managerial opposition ensured that board-level employee representation was not necessarily retained on privatisation or was diluted in effect. Dilution equates to the disappearance of compulsory provisions in the Czech case. On 1 January 2014, a new act (No. 90/2012) on commercial corporations came into force. As none of the previous provisions related to board-level employee representation were repeated in this act, the obligation for Czech private-sector companies to have employee representatives on their board was effectively withdrawn.

A fourth country category comprises seven countries: Austria, Denmark, Germany, Hungary, Norway, Slovenia and Sweden. Legislation on board-level employee representation in these countries covers the entire economy and, with the exception of Austria, there is no distinction between the private and public sectors in terms of employment thresholds or other coverage criteria. In Austria there is an employment threshold of 300 employees but only for limited liability companies. There is national variation in the employment size thresholds for inclusion in the regulations ranging from 25 employees in Sweden to 500 in Germany. The possibility of a dual board is available in five of the seven countries, with only Sweden and Norway committed to a unitary board structure. Since 2010 in Denmark and since 2006 in Hungary and Slovenia, however, a choice of board arrangements has been available, with the consequence that there is no obligation to establish dual board structures. The presence of employee representatives on a board varies from one individual in Norwegian and Slovenian unitary boards, to 50 per cent in German and Slovenian supervisory boards.

Insofar as the other five countries are generally classified as CMEs, Hungary and Slovenia are the outliers within this category. The relatively recent regulations on board-level employee representation in Hungary and Slovenia are more encompassing in law than in practice and, as in the Czech Republic, Poland and Slovakia, the interest expressed by trade unionists in, and their capacity to defend, board-level employee representation at company level is very much open to question (Neumann 2006; Vliegenthart 2007). Reports from Slovenia show that the implementation of the legislation is irregular and that employees are often unaware of their rights and the available enforcement mechanisms (Bedrač 2005). Recent change in Hungarian legislation aimed at allowing a choice between governance structures has deregulated aspects of board-level representation. There is now a greater reliance on company agreements rather than hard law to specify the terms of employee representation on unitary boards (Neumann 2006). The practice of board-level employee representation in Hungary and Slovenia is thus unlikely to reproduce that found in the CMEs. In contrast, in the five CMEs the trade union movements have consistently advocated board-level representation and in Germany and Norway campaigned vigorously for improvements in the terms of its introduction in the face of opposition from employers (Conchon 2011b:26–28; Dukes 2005; Müller 1987). Despite unequivocal trade union support for board-level representation in the CMEs, in practice the coverage is mixed. In Germany in 2004, for example, there were 746 companies with more than 2,000 employees covered by the legislation of 1976, together with a further 50 companies covered by the coal, iron and steel legislation (Calvo et al. 2008:241). These numbers are declining due to restructuring and, in coal, iron and steel, a contraction of the industries, but the coverage remains wide-ranging, as illustrated by the most recent figures of 640 companies applying the *Mitbestimmungsgesetz* (1976) (Ehrenstein 2014) and 1,500 companies covered by the *Drittelbeteiligungsgesetz* (2004) (Bayer 2009). In contrast, in Norway and Denmark, where the arrangements for board-level employee representation have to be triggered by the workforce, the coverage is estimated to be about 50 per cent of all eligible companies with higher densities recorded among the larger companies (Hagen 2008:9; Lavesen and Kragh-Stetting 2011:16).

In addition to the sixteen national situations, board-level employee representation also applies transnationally in the form of SEs. The 2001 Regulation and Directive on the European Company Statute[7] entered into force in 2004 after Member States had transposed them into national legislation, with the consequence that companies with cross-border activities could choose a European legal status instead of a national equivalent. Three points explain the restrictions to the coverage of board-level employee representation. First, companies can, but are not obliged to, adopt the SE statute, which has been designed as an optional provision open to voluntary choice from the management and/or shareholders. Second, the lack of a size threshold should not lead to the conclusion that any company can adopt the SE statute.[8] The activities of the company must have a cross-border component. In addition, an SE can be formed by any one of the following means and not from scratch: the merger of two joint stock companies from (at least) two different Member States; the creation by joint-stock and/or limited liability companies from (at least) two different Member States of a joint holding company; the creation by any type of company from (at least) two different Member States of a joint subsidiary; the conversion of a joint-stock company, if for at least two years it has had a subsidiary in a Member State other than that of its registered and head offices (Stollt and Wolters 2011). Third, employee representation at board level is not automatically present, because it depends both on the outcome of negotiations and on the application of a 'before and after' principle. Inspired by the flexible approach developed in European works council directive, employee involvement institutions in an SE covering information, consultation and representation at the board level are determined by a negotiated agreement, which is a prerequisite for the legal registration of the SE and allows for tailor-made arrangements. To avoid that self-regulation leads to the weakening or circumvention of acquired rights, a second principle, the 'before and after' principle, was adopted, according to which pre-existing national rights to employee representation at board level should be safeguarded, although there is no obligation to agree on provisions related to board-level employee representation if none existed in any of the companies participating in the establishment of the SE. As a consequence, board-level employee representation is unlikely to be set up in SEs whose constituent companies did not have employee representatives on the board prior to the adoption of the European Company Statute. In practice, this leads to a very limited coverage, with only 54 SEs having employee representatives on the board, which, according to the SE regulation, can either be a board of directors or a supervisory board (ETUC and ETUI 2014:106).

For the same reasons, the proportion or number of employee representatives varies between SEs because board-level employee representation follows the pattern of the national situation in place prior to the adoption of the European Company Statute.[9]

FORMAL SUPPORT FOR ARTICULATION IN SELECTION PROCEDURES

This section examines the formal links established in the selection procedures between board-level employee representatives and institutions internal to the company, such as works councils and trade union branches, and external to the company, such as trade unions, where dual systems of industrial relations operate. In addition, the electorate of the board-level employee representatives is identified. The section thus establishes the formal basis that underpins the articulation of board-level employee representation with other representative institutions. Chapter 1 demonstrated that the articulation of board-level employee representatives is central to the purposes of this study on three counts. First, a concern within many labour movements is that if board-level employee representatives become isolated from other institutions representative of labour within the company, they will be incorporated and, thus, act on behalf of management. Second, articulation with other labour institutions is prerequisite if board-level employee representatives are to undertake a communication function between the board and worker representatives within the company. Third, only if board-level employee representatives are articulated with employees will they be able to forward the views of employees to other members of the board. The second and third of these issues are viewed as essential to both the efficiency enhancing and the democratising arguments associated with board-level employee representation (Aoki 2001; Blair 1995). The procedures involved in the selection of board-level employee representatives are presented in Table 2.2 together with information on the duration of the terms of office of board-level employee representatives.

The analysis of selection procedures starts from the distinction between single-channel and dual systems of industrial relations. In single-channel systems, trade unionists undertake collective bargaining functions outside of the company together with bargaining and representative functions within the company, whereas in dual systems the external trade union collective bargaining function is formally separate from the conduct of representative functions, which are usually undertaken by works councils or their equivalent operating within the company. In drawing this distinction it is acknowledged that the presence of works councils does not necessarily confirm the presence of a dual system. In Hungary and Spain, for example, trade unions and works councils coexist at the workplace, often in competition, and in France trade unions have a monopoly in making nominations

Table 2.2 How Are Board-Level Employee Representatives Selected?

Country	Nomination	Eligibility Criteria	Electorate	Term of Office
Austria	Works council	Works council member having a right to vote (so employee of the company)	Works council	4 years
Czech Republic	Private sector companies: management board and trade union/works council or at least 10% of workforce	Employee or (external) trade union official	Workforce	Up to 5 years
	State enterprises: electoral regulations agreed between employer and trade union	Employee of company	Workforce	Up to 5 years
Denmark	Not specified in law	Employee of company	Workforce	4 years
Finland	Trade unions: personnel groups where several unions are present	Employee of company	Trade unions through the personnel groups, or election by the workforce if no agreement among the former	1 up to 3 years
France	Trade union(s) or a minimum quota (at least 5%) of employees (in privatised companies) or employee representatives (in state enterprises)	Employee of company	Workforce	5 years in state enterprises. Up to 6 years in private (privatised) companies

(Continued)

Table 2.2 (Continued)

Country	Nomination	Eligibility Criteria	Electorate	Term of Office
Germany	Coal, iron and steel: trade union and works council	Employee of company and (external) trade union official, plus an extra member who is neither an employee nor a trade union official	Shareholders' meeting	Up to 5 years
	Other sectors: employees, works council and/or trade union	Employee of company and (external) trade union official	Workforce; in companies with 8,000 or more delegates of employees at an electoral college	Up to 5 years
Greece	By law the workforce, in practice the trade unions	Employee of company	Workforce and then approved by responsible minister	Up to 6 years
Hungary	Works council with a duty to consult trade union(s)	Employee of company	Shareholders' meeting	Up to 5 years
Ireland	Trade union(s) or representative organisations recognised for collective bargaining	Employee of company	Workforce and then approved by responsible minister	4 years
Luxembourg	Staff representatives, trade unions (in iron and steel sector)	Employee of company in all sectors except iron and steel where trade unions appoint 3 employee representatives who must not be employed by the company	Staff representatives, employee delegates	Up to 6 years
Norway	Company trade union branch	Employee of company	Workforce	2 years
Poland	Not specified in law	No legal stipulation	Workforce	Up to 5 years

Slovakia	Private-sector companies: trade unions or 10% of workforce	No restrictions	Workforce	Up to 5 years
	State enterprises: not specified in law	Employee of company; trade union member for the trade union seat	Workforce, and direct appointment of one member by trade union (if any)	Up to 5 years
Slovenia	Works council	Employee of company	Works council	Up to 6 years
Spain	Trade union(s)	No restriction	Trade union(s)	Up to 6 years
Sweden	Company trade union branch(es)	'Should' be employee of company (i.e. no formal restriction)	Company trade union branch(es)	Up to 4 years

Sources: Büggel (2010); Calvo et al. (2008); Fulton (2013a); HBS and ETUI (2004); Kluge and Stollt (2006, 2009 updated by Conchon in 2015); SDA and ETUI (2005); authors' own research with the support of the members of the SEEurope network (http://www.worker-participation.eu/European-Company-SE/SEEurope-network/Network-members).

for the first round of voting in elections for works councils (Fulton 2013a). The distinction between single-channel and dual systems of representation also 'cuts across' the divide between LMEs and CMEs. In particular, some CMEs operate with a single channel of representation (Denmark, Finland, Norway, Sweden) whereas others rely on dual systems (Austria, Germany). Chapter 6 examines whether the variation in systems of representation within CMEs influences the character and efficacy of the articulation of board-level employee representatives.

Table 2.2 shows that in countries where single-channel systems operate, the nomination of candidates to serve as board-level employee representatives rests principally with trade unions (Finland, Ireland, Norway, Sweden). In countries where more than one trade union may be present within the company, procedures agreed by the unions usually influence the nomination procedure. In Sweden, for example, agreements concluded by the unions with membership in the company usually decide the composition of employee representation on the board, with trade union membership numbers being the key criterion in the allocation of seats on the board. In the countries with dual systems the nomination of persons to stand as board-level employee representatives rests primarily with works councils. In Austria and Slovenia, for example, the works council has the sole nomination right. Elsewhere, the works council shares the nomination right with trade unions (Czech Republic, Germany) or the workforce (Germany) or has a duty to consult with the trade union(s) (Hungary).

Turning to the eligibility criteria and the electorate of board-level employee representatives reveals further differences between countries operating with single-channel and dual systems of representation. In countries with single-channel systems, board-level employee representatives tend to be employees of the company elected by the workforce (Denmark, Greece, Ireland, Norway). In Finland, Spain and Sweden the trade union has a more prominent position insofar as the electorate in these countries is restricted to trade unionists, a position qualified in Spain, where there is no restriction on who is eligible to stand as a board-level employee representative. In countries operating with dual systems there is greater variation in the configurations of eligibility criteria and electorate. Employees and trade union officials may serve as board-level employee representatives in three countries (Czech Republic, Germany, Luxembourg), although the electorate varies from the workforce (Germany, with employee delegates comprising the electoral college in companies with more than 8,000 employees) to staff representatives (Luxembourg) or shareholders (Germany). In Hungary the shareholders' meeting also formally approves the nominated board-level employee representatives. The works council is the electorate in Austria and Slovenia. In Austria board-level employee representatives must be selected from the works council, and while there are no formal restrictions, many board-level employee representatives are drawn from works councils in Slovenia.

The formal arrangements for the selection of board-level employee representatives in countries in which dual systems operate raise two further questions regarding articulation. First, can trade unions and/or works councils ensure that their members are elected to serve as board-level employee representatives, thereby facilitating articulation whether it is internal or external to the company? Second, do board-level employee representatives hold other representative positions in the company thereby facilitating articulation? In Austria, for example, a candidate must be a works councillor in order to stand for election as a board-level employee representative and must relinquish his/her seat on the board if no longer a member of the works council. By this means articulation between the board and works council may be sustained through personal involvement. In Ireland, institutional means to facilitate articulation were implemented. The Worker Participation (State Enterprises) Act 1988 created opportunities for employee participation arrangements to be established at levels below the board within more than 30 public-sector companies to facilitate articulation between the board and the workforce in the absence of any other employee participation arrangements. Chapter 3 establishes whether board-level employee representatives typically hold multiple mandates, while Chapter 6 questions whether informal means are deployed to the same effect elsewhere.

As mentioned earlier, variation between countries is reflected in SEs insofar as national arrangements influence board-level practices concerning the nomination, electorate and eligibility criteria of employee representatives on SE boards, which, in consequence, vary markedly from one SE to another. These elements are either freely defined and laid out in the SE agreement on employee involvement or, if there are none, follow the provisions specified in the standard rules. According to the standard rules, it is up to the transnational works council of the SE to allocate board seats according to the proportion of employees in each Member State. The nationally transposed laws determine the manner in which these seats are filled. Variety is again a key feature as no fewer than five different appointment procedures, derived from national arrangements, can be identified from the transpositions of the directive's standard rules: appointment by the national body of employee representation, be it works councils or staff representatives (Austria, Ireland, Luxembourg), appointment by the works council of the SE (France, Hungary, Slovenia), election by the workforce (Czech Republic, Denmark, Poland, Slovakia), appointment according to the same procedure as that which governs appointment of the SE works council members (Sweden), and appointment according to the same procedure as that which governs appointment of the members of the special negotiating body (Finland, Germany, Greece, Norway, Spain) (Stollt and Wolters 2011).[10]

The final column of Table 2.2 specifies the length of one term of office of a board-level employee representative. Irrespective of whether a single-channel or a dual system is in operation, a term of office of either four or five years is the legal norm. The shortest legally defined terms of office are the two years available in Norway and the one to three years set in Finland, while the longest is six years in French privatised companies, Greece, Luxembourg, Slovenia, Spain and SEs. In countries where the term of office is defined as a range rather than a fixed value, the trade unions determine the term (Sweden), or more commonly, it varies according to company statutes. In none of the sixteen countries and SEs is appointment renewal specifically forbidden, so employee representatives can serve several terms of office, similarly to other board members. A further research question arises in this context: Do board-level employee representatives effectively become ensconced in their positions and serve multiple terms of office in succession? If this is the case, what are the implications in terms of the support required by board-level employee representatives and made available by trade unions and works councils?

THE CONSTITUTION OF THE BOARD

The majority of the measures examined hitherto originate in industrial relations legislation directed towards some form of industrial democracy. This section assesses aspects of the constitution of the board and thus shifts attention towards company law or codes of corporate governance. The objective is to establish some of the parameters within which employee representatives operate at the board and to assess how these impinge on the conduct of their duties as board members and as representatives of labour. Codes of corporate governance principally compose 'soft law' recommendations, in contrast to the 'hard law' of industrial relations legislation and company law. Referencing the issues that originate in codes of corporate governance enables an assessment of the extent to which soft law recommendations are implemented in practice from the perspective of board-level employee representatives. The section thus introduces further research questions for examination in subsequent chapters. The data are presented in Table 2.3.

In eight countries the rights and obligations of employee representatives differ from those of other members of the board, although this point is legally specified in only two countries. In three of the eight countries (Denmark, Finland, Sweden) employee representatives are excluded from discussions at the board level on collective disputes and industrial action, thus conforming to rules intended to avoid board members confronting a conflict of interests. In Austria and Finland employee representatives do not participate in, or have no decision-making power on, decisions concerning the appointment or dismissal of senior managers. Other differences in the rights and obligations of employee representatives are country specific and relate to remuneration (Austria, French state enterprises) and informing the shareholders' meeting in the absence of a consensus at the board (Czech Republic, Hungary, Slovakia). Two points arise here that are pertinent to the subsequent analysis. First, because only two of the sixteen national legislative frameworks

Table 2.3 The Constitution of the Board

Country	Are the rights and obligations of employee representatives the same as other board members?	How do they differ?	Is there a duty of confidentiality?	Frequency of meetings	Voting procedure[1]	Regulations to promote the involvement of women on boards
Austria	Yes, as specified in law	But, legal treatment differs insofar as employee representatives, amongst other things, receive no director's fee and have no decision-making rights regarding the appointment/dismissal of management board	Yes, on confidential information obtained as a board member, the disclosure of which would harm the company	At least quarterly	Simple majority	Private sector: corporate governance code recommends that 'reasonable attention' is paid to the representation of both genders. State enterprises: federal government committed to a 35% quota (amongst state appointees) by 2018
Czech Republic	Yes, as specified in law	But, employee representatives enjoy greater rights than their counterparts on the board insofar as their diverging opinion (if any) must be reported to the shareholders' meeting	Yes, duty not to disclose information if such disclosure would harm the company	No legal provision. Corporate governance code recommends a monthly meeting	Simple majority	None

(Continued)

Table 2.3 (Continued)

Country	Are the rights and obligations of employee representatives the same as other board members?	How do they differ?	Is there a duty of confidentiality?	Frequency of meetings	Voting procedure[1]	Regulations to promote the involvement of women on boards
Denmark	Yes, as specified in law	Employee representatives are equally subject to rules on conflict of interest. Hence, they cannot take part in discussions and decisions relating to collective disputes and collective agreement negotiations	Yes, on information obtained as a board member	'When necessary', as stated in hard law	Simple majority	Private sector: a 'flexible' quota obliges some companies to self-define a target and report progress on its achievement State enterprises: a 33% up to 40% quota (depending on the type of company)
Finland	No	The law specifies that employee representatives shall have the same rights and duties, except that they cannot take part in decisions relating to management appointment/dismissal/terms of contract and in decisions concerning industrial actions	Yes, on information presented as 'business secret' and whose disclosure would harm the company	'When necessary', as stated in hard law	Simple majority	Private sector: corporate governance code recommends the representation of both gender on the board State enterprises: state appointees must comprise an equitable proportion of both women and men

France	Yes in private (privatised) companies. No in state enterprises	In state enterprises employee representatives receive no director's fee, hence have a reduced liability	Yes, on confidential information presented as such by the chairman of the board	No legal provision. Corporate governance code recommends the frequency of meetings to be such that it allows 'in-depth review and discussion of the matters subject to the board's authority'	Simple majority	A 40% gender quota to be reached by 2017 applies to listed, large joint stock companies
Germany	Yes		Yes, on confidential information and secrets obtained as a board member and whose disclosure would harm the company	Quarterly. Non-listed companies may restrict to a meeting every six months	Simple majority	No regulation at the time of writing, but ongoing discussions following a government commitment to adopt a gender quota. Corporate governance code recommends having 'an appropriate degree of female representation'

(Continued)

Table 2.3 (Continued)

Country	Are the rights and obligations of employee representatives the same as other board members?	How do they differ?	Is there a duty of confidentiality?	Frequency of meetings	Voting procedure[1]	Regulations to promote the involvement of women on boards
Greece	Not specified in (hard or soft) law		No legal provision. The corporate governance code specifies a duty to protect the confidentiality of information that has not been disclosed to the public	No legal provision. 'The board should meet sufficiently' according to the corporate governance code	Simple majority	Private sector: corporate governance code recommends that 'optimum diversity' be pursued, 'including gender balance' State enterprises: a 33% quota amongst state appointees
Hungary	Yes, as specified in law	But, employee representatives enjoy greater rights than their counterparts on the board insofar as their diverging opinion (if unanimous) must be reported to the shareholders' meeting	Yes, on business secrets[2]	No legal provision. Corporate governance code recommends the board to meet 'regularly'	Simple majority	None

Ireland	Yes	No legal provision. The corporate governance code for state enterprises specifies a duty of non-disclosure of privileged or confidential information	No legal provision. Corporate governance code for state enterprises recommends the board to meet 'regularly'	Simple majority	No quota based on hard law, but a commitment to have a target of 40% female state appointees
Luxembourg	Yes	Yes, on information obtained as a board member and whose disclosure would harm the company	No legal provision. Corporate governance code recommends at least quarterly meeting	Simple majority	No legal provision. Corporate governance code recommends an 'appropriate representation of both genders'
Norway	Yes	No legal (nor soft law) provision	No legal (nor soft law) provision	Simple majority	40% quota for joint stock companies
Poland	Yes	Yes, although indirectly (i.e. derived from general rules in absence of legal or soft law provision)	Not specified for state enterprises and limited liability companies. At least 3 times a year for joint stock companies	Simple majority	No legal provision. Corporate governance code recommends 'a balanced proportion of women and men'

(Continued)

Table 2.3 (Continued)

Country	Are the rights and obligations of employee representatives the same as other board members?	How do they differ?	Is there a duty of confidentiality?	Frequency of meetings	Voting procedure[1]	Regulations to promote the involvement of women on boards
Slovakia	Yes	But, in private companies, employee representatives enjoy greater rights than their counterparts on the board do insofar as their diverging opinion could be reported to the shareholders' meeting, if so requested.	Yes, on confidential information whose disclosure would harm the company	No legal (nor soft law) provision	Simple majority	None
Slovenia	Yes		Yes, on 'business secret'	At least quarterly	Simple majority	Private sector: corporate governance code recommends that boards 'adhere to the principle of equal representation of both sexes' State enterprises: a 40% quota amongst state appointees

Spain	Yes, as specified in law		Yes, on information obtained as a board member	At least quarterly	Simple majority	40% quota for large 'market' companies. Corporate governance code recommends that listed companies with few women on their boards actively seek out female candidates
Sweden[1]	Yes	Employee representatives are equally subject to rules on conflict of interest. Hence, they cannot take part in discussions and decisions relating to collective disputes, collective agreement negotiations and any other issue for which a workplace trade union has a substantial interest which may conflict with that of the company	No legal (nor soft law) provision	'When necessary', as specified in hard law	Simple majority	No legal provision. Corporate governance code recommends 'to strive for equal gender distribution'

Sources: Büggel (2010); Calvo et al. (2008); European Commission (2012b); Gahleitner (2013); Gerner-Beuerle et al. (2013); Köstler et al. (2013); Lavesen and Kragh-Stetting (2011); PTK (2011); Senčur Peček (2011); Skupień (2011); authors' own research with the support of the members of the SEEurope network (http://www.worker-participation.eu/European-Company-SE/SEEurope-network/Network-members) as well as of personal communications from Antonio Martin Antilles, Niklas Bruun, Wolfgang Greif, Anders Kjellberg and Helena Ysas.

Notes:

1. The specification is that applying in normal circumstances.

2. Since the survey was conducted, a new company law entered in force in 2014 in which board members' duty of confidentiality is no longer mentioned.

specify a different status, employee representatives generally have the same general rights and obligations as other board members. The SE directive is explicit on this point in stating that every board-level employee representative 'shall be a full member with the same rights and obligations as the members representing the shareholders, including the right to vote' (Part 3 of the Annex). In practice, therefore, employee representatives should have access to the same information within the same timescale as other board members and should participate in discussions on all agenda items on an equal footing as other board members. These propositions are examined in Chapter 4. Second, support in the form of training, analyses of information and access to networks of other board-level employee representatives is essential if employee representatives are to participate meaningfully across the range of issues discussed by the board, particularly as many issues are technical, such as law and accountancy, and may necessitate an expertise not required by the employee representatives in their day-to-day work for the company or in undertaking other representative duties. Chapter 6 identifies the type, quality and source of support utilised by board-level employee representatives.

In most countries with a system of board-level employee representation, a requirement for confidentiality is usually based in company law, as illustrated by the case of SEs for which the duty of confidentiality is defined within the regulation.[11] The requirement for confidentiality is placed on all board members, irrespective of their constituency. Greece, Ireland, Norway and Sweden are the exceptions to this general schema insofar as there is no legal requirement for confidentiality placed on board members, but compliance with recommendations in codes of corporate governance by companies may impose such a requirement. In the context of this study three questions arise from the almost universal requirement for confidentiality. First, is the requirement for confidentiality interpreted in such a manner as to apply to all agenda items discussed by the board or to specific items? Second, how and by whom is the requirement for confidentiality enforced within the company? Third, does the requirement for confidentiality impinge on the capacity of employee representatives to articulate their activities with other institutions of labour representation and, if so, to what extent and with which consequences? In Hungary, for example, the requirement for confidentiality is attached to an obligation placed on board-level representatives to inform the workforce through the works council of decisions taken by the board as a means of facilitating articulation. Chapters 4 and 6 examine these questions.

There is considerable variation in the manner in which the frequency of board meetings is determined and the frequency at which board meetings take place. The law sets the frequency of meetings in four countries (Austria, Germany, Slovenia, Spain), whereas in eleven countries (Czech Republic, Denmark, Finland, France, Greece, Hungary, Ireland, Luxembourg, Norway, Slovakia, Sweden) the law remains silent or vague on this issue. The situation in SEs is ambivalent insofar as the regulation sets a minimum frequency for the board of directors to meet quarterly but is not specific when it comes to the supervisory board in dual systems (Articles 41 and 44 of the SE Regulation). In two countries, the lack of a specific legal provision is counterbalanced by soft law recommendations grounded in corporate governance codes, advising boards to meet as often as monthly in the Czech Republic or quarterly in Luxembourg. Elsewhere the law is silent, and corporate governance recommendations are imprecise on the frequency of meetings, effectively leaving the matter to be determined within the company. Irrespective of the manner in which the frequency of meetings is determined, the frequency of meetings ranges from monthly to twice a year. In practice, therefore, the intensity of participation of board-level employee representation varies across a considerable range. Such variation raises a question for subsequent analysis. In most countries there is no legal minimum requirement regarding the frequency of board meetings, which is determined by voluntary mechanisms internal to the company.

Turning to the voting procedure reveals a uniform position, which is also shared by SEs: a simple majority among the board members is required to reach a decision in normal circumstances. Particular decisions may require alternative voting requirements. A two-thirds majority, for example, is required in German companies covered by the *Mitbestimmungsgesetz* (1976) in decisions to appoint or dismiss members of the management board or the chair and vice-chair of the supervisory board. In this context another question arises for subsequent examination. Given that board-level employee representatives are in an absolute or a technical minority in most circumstances, it is necessary for them to enter into alliances with other board members in order to secure a majority, raising the questions: With which parties are alliances concluded? and On what agenda items are alliances necessary?

Finally, Table 2.3 presents details on regulations to promote the involvement of women at the board level. The situation in SEs with regard to this matter is not reported in Table 2.3, given that it is determined by national regulatory frameworks, in particular by that of the country of the SE's registered and head offices. In eight of the sixteen countries there are no hard law provisions to promote the number of women board members, although in some of these countries there is a political debate on the issue. More common and more recent is the introduction of gender friendly recommendations in corporate governance codes which specifically apply to private-sector companies, as is the case in eight countries (Austria, Finland, Germany, Greece, Luxembourg, Poland, Slovenia, Sweden). In another eight countries specific regulations have been introduced since 2000 to increase the number of women at the board level in private-sector companies (Denmark, France, Norway, Spain) or state-owned companies only (Austria, Greece, Ireland, Slovenia). Where specific legislation has been introduced it is usually based on a quota system with targets set for particular dates. It remains unclear whether sanctions, if extant, will be imposed should targets not be met.

Chapter 3 establishes the proportion of women that serve as board-level employee representatives, as well as the presence of other women on the board, while Chapter 7 contrasts the views of women board members with those of their male counterparts.

CONCLUSION

The legal perspective of the corporate governance literature predicts consistent differences arising from the distinction drawn between common law and civil law systems. This review of the national and SE regulations that underpin board-level employee representation confirms that such an appraisal is overstated on at least two counts. First, institutional diversity is so wide ranging that discrepancies between countries are manifest and are independent of whether a common law or a civil law system is in operation. Furthermore, the legal perspective tends to treat a national legal framework as one coherent body of law. The findings of Chapter 2 suggest that this reading requires refinement insofar as the philosophy and approach of board-level employee representation in the field of labour law may differ from that pursued in the field of company law within a single country. In the Nordic countries, for instance, provisions relating to board-level employee representation support industrial democracy insofar as coverage of the regulation is extensive. In contrast, company law provisions tend to restrict the influence of board-level employee representatives as they are excluded from discussions and votes on some social issues discussed at the board.

Second, the legal perspective within corporate governance literature underestimates the dynamics and potential change within both common and civil law systems. It is apparent from this review of the coverage of national and SE regulations that rights are not static but evolving, to such an extent that a country could move from one analytical group to another, whatever the underpinning classification criteria. Several factors account for recent developments in national regulation. In particular, the weak position of labour, in terms of declining trade union membership, strike activity and political leverage, has been linked to the effects of exogenous pressures and shocks. Furthermore, some suggest that neo-liberal political responses will promote changes in corporate governance and the nature of coordination within the firm to the detriment of labour (Block 2007; Boyer 2000; Duménil and Lévy 2004). This chapter has shown that where board-level employee representation is restricted to the public sector, privatisation has tended to narrow its coverage, with the noticeable exception of France. Similarly, in CEE, shifts in corporate governance towards neo-liberal practices contrast markedly with the institutions of board-level employee representation established after 1988, suggesting that the position of employee representatives is far from secure. Furthermore, the coverage of board-level employee representation in practice within CEE tends to be markedly narrower than intended *de jure*. Elsewhere increasing international competition, greater concentration of ownership, repeated bouts of company restructuring and changing relations between companies and banks have generated debates in some countries on the reform of systems of corporate governance (Deeg 1999; Engelen and Konings 2010; van Apeldoorn and Horn 2007). While these developments have not led to the abandonment of board-level employee representation, they constitute substantial changes to the circumstances that prevailed when board-level employee representation was introduced and suggest that the practices of employee representatives and their relations with other board members are likely to be subject to change.

Central to the sociological perspective in the corporate governance literature is the concept of institutional complementarity. Within this framework, CMEs, MMEs and EMEs operate with systems of board-level employee representation, the scope of which is assumed to be strong in CMEs, weaker in MMEs and even more restricted or fragile in EMEs. As expected, board-level employee representation is more prevalent in CMEs where it operates with a relatively broad scope and coverage. This strength is called into question, however, by restrictions based in company law, which exclude board-level employee representatives from discussions on some board issues in the Nordic countries. In addition, the lack of legal guidelines regarding the frequency of board meetings in the same countries leaves a key element of board practice open to negotiation. It is also noteworthy that in only three CMEs (Norway, state enterprises in Austria, Denmark) is the involvement of women as board members promoted by hard law. The two MMEs (France, Luxembourg) do not have much in common regarding both the constitution of the board and the coverage of the regulations, not least because they did not belong to the same analytical group with regard to the latter until 2013 when the new law moved France to the same category as Luxembourg, in which all state enterprises and private-sector companies above a certain employment size threshold are covered. Contrasting situations also prevail among EMEs with restricted or fragile regulations in place in Poland, Czech Republic and Slovakia, while in Hungary and Slovenia widespread rights are in place in contrast to theoretical expectations. All EMEs provide either the same rights to employee representatives as those available to shareholder representatives or even greater rights, with employee representatives having the possibility of submitting a minority report to shareholders' meetings. The strength of these rights constitutes a further challenge to theoretical assumptions, as such privileged positions would be expected to be found in CMEs.

Within the industrial relations literature, countries are divided into those with single channel and those with dual systems of representation, suggesting different approaches to both internal and external articulation with other institutions of labour representation. This binary distinction is reflected in the formal support of articulation, which is to be seen through the way employee representatives are selected and later appointed to the board. Trade unions, along with the workforce in most cases, play a key role in countries in which a single-channel system is in place, as illustrated by the Nordic CMEs. Correspondingly, works councils are directly involved in the selection procedure of board-level employee representation in countries in which a dual system prevails. These variations, as well as many other national differences, are reflected in the case of SEs, as no fewer than five selection procedures are laid out in each of the national transposition laws.

Chapter 2 has demonstrated that diversity best characterises the legal position of board-level employee representation across Europe, be it diversity between nations, diversity between national and SE regulations or diversity between theoretical assumptions and reality. Subsequent chapters deepen the understanding of employee representation at board level by questioning the, now expected, variation between the *de jure* intention described in this chapter and the *de facto* practices in different contexts.

NOTES

1. With 'participation' understood as meaning board-level employee representation, Article 17 of the 1989 Community Charter reads as follows: 'Information, consultation and participation of workers must be developed along appropriate lines, taking account of the practices in force in various Member States. This shall apply especially in companies or groups of companies having establishments or companies in two or more Member States of the European Community'.
2. With 'co-determination' understood as meaning board-level employee representation, Article 153 (1) of the Treaty on the Functioning of the European Union reads as follows: 'The Union shall support and complement the activities of the Member States in the following fields: [. . .] (f) representation and collective defence of the interests of workers and employers, including codetermination'.
3. In the context of the SE regulation, board-level employee representation is referred to as 'participation', with the following definition being attached to this terminology: ' "Participation" means the influence of the body representative of the employees and/or the employees' representatives in the affairs of the company by way of: the right to elect or appoint some of the members of the company's supervisory or administrative organ; or the rights to recommend and/or oppose the appointment of some or all of the members of the company's supervisory or administrative organ' (Article 2 (k) of Directive 2001/86/EC of 8 October 2001 supplementing the Statute for a European Company with regard to the involvement of employees).
4. Source: the European Company Database [ECDB], which can be accessed at http://ecdb.worker-participation.eu/.
5. The Worker Participation (State Enterprises) Act 1977 enabled board-level employee representation at Bord na Móna (peat), Córas Iompair Éireann (public transport), Electricity Supply Board, Aer Lingus, B&I Line (sea transport), Siúicre Éireann (sugar), and Nítrigen Éireann (fertilisers). To these companies were added An Post and Bord Telecom in 1984 and, following the Worker Participation (State Enterprises) Act 1988, Aer Rianta (airport management),

National Rehabilitation Board, Teagasc (Agriculture and Food Development Agency), Coillte (Forestry Board), Legal Aid Board, FAS (Employment and Training Authority) and Great Southern Hotels. Board-level employee representation at the B&I Line was withdrawn on privatisation and at Siúicre Éireann and Nítrigen Éireann has been diluted on privatisation. It should also be noted that the 1988 legislation allowed employee participation at sub-board levels in a more than 30 further companies within the state sector (Carley 1996:12).

6. Single-shareholder companies of the State Treasury operate with the state as the sole shareholder.
7. The SE statute is regulated by two inseparable and complementary legal texts: the Council Regulation 2157/2001 on the Statute for a European Company (which is referred to as the SE Regulation and deals with company law elements, i.e. provisions related to legal registration, structure of managerial bodies, accounts, capital requirement and so on) and the Council Directive 2001/86/EC supplementing the Statute for a European Company with regard to the involvement of employees: that is, employee information, consultation and board-level representation.
8. It should be noted that a threshold exists, which is linked to the size of the capital. The SE regulation states that an SE shall have a capital of at least 120,000 euros.
9. Board-level employee representation in SEs is arranged as follows. As with European works councils a special negotiation body (SNB) has to be set up to convene negotiations on employee involvement in the SE, prior to its formal registration. If the SNB is able to reach an agreement with management, both parties can freely decide on its content. However, for such an open agreement to be allowed to reduce or eliminate the application of pre-existing national rights to board-level employee representation, the support of a majority of two-thirds of the SNB members is required in situations in which pre-existing rights covered at least 25 per cent of employees (in case of the constitution by a merger) or 50 per cent (in case of the formation of a holding company or of joint subsidiaries). Where an SE is formed by means of a conversion, the SNB cannot decide to reduce pre-existing rights. If the SNB and management agree, or if they fail to reach an agreement within the stipulated time frame, the standard rules provided as an annex to the SE directive apply. Regarding employee representation at board level, the standard rules state that, in the case of an SE established by conversion, pre-existing rights, if any, continue to apply. In all other cases, the 'higher' pre-existing right (equal to the highest proportion of employee representatives on the board to be found in the participating companies) is safeguarded, as long as it covers at least 25 per cent of the employees of an SE formed by a merger, or at least 50 per cent of the employees of an SE formed as a holding company or joint subsidiaries.
10. The SE directive has been transposed into the national laws of 31 countries, a number that includes three countries from the European Economic Area (EEA) and all Member States of the EU. The countries listed here are those covered by this study, thus excluding EU Member States and countries within the EEA that have no formal system of board-level employee representation, and the three EU Member States excluded from this study for the reasons outlined in Appendix A.
11. The SE regulation specifies that '[t]he members of an SE's organ (the board) shall be under a duty, even after they have ceased to hold office, not to divulge any information which they have concerning the SE the disclosure of which might be prejudicial to the company's interests, except where such disclosure is required or permitted under national law provisions applicable to public limited-liability companies or is in the public interest' (Article 49).

3 The Morphology of Board-Level Employee Representation

Chapter 2 focused on the *de jure* intention of board-level employee representation in sixteen countries and the SEs. This preliminary analytical step is important insofar as the legal framework conditions the morphology of employee participation in terms of the scope, board composition and the profile of employee representatives. With regard to some variables, *de facto* practices arising from the implementation of the legislation reflect *de jure* intention. Regarding the legal status of the company, for example, the survey records no difference between law and practice. Although legislation conditions the extent and shape of board-level employee representation, it does not necessarily determine practice. The workforce threshold above which a company must introduce board-level employee representation constitutes a minimum and is not sufficient to determine the actual distribution of companies with employee representation on the board. There is thus a need to complement an analysis of the legislation with knowledge of the manner in which it is implemented in order to assess the reality of employee representation at the board.

Prior to the investigation of the activities, power and articulation of board-level employee representatives, this chapter establishes what employee representation at board level looks like in practice, thereby making a threefold contribution to the analysis. First, the survey findings deliver first-hand knowledge about the demographics of companies and boards on which employee representatives sit, as well as their individual characteristics. Apart from a few national surveys covering Germanic countries (Brachinger 2004; Jürgens et al. 2008), Nordic countries (Hagen 2010; Lavesen and Kragh-Stetting 2011; Sairo 2001), France (Conchon 2009) and Slovenia (Gostiša 2001) and a small survey involving nine countries with 285 respondents (Carley 2005; O'Kelly 2006), very little is known about board-level employee representatives and the boards and companies within which they operate. This chapter seeks to fill this knowledge gap. Second, on empirical grounds the chapter challenges some of the assumptions concerning the supposed correlation between the presence of employee representatives and the structure of the board. Among these correlations are the assumed inflationary effect of board-level employee representation on the size of the board (Bermig and Frick 2011, Nygaard Thorkildsen and Haugland Gaure 2013), its impediment to board independence (Davies and Hopt 2013) and its limitation to only dual corporate governance structures (Roth 2010). This latter point was at the core of the 1970s debates on the reform of the structure of companies in France and the UK (Bullock 1977; Sudreau 1975). Third, Chapter 3 compares the features of European corporate boards open to employee representation with the profiles of board structure and directors across Europe based on the analysis of more than 400 listed companies (Heidrick & Struggles 2011).

For the purpose of this and subsequent chapters, the data are analysed by reference to five country clusters, the composition of which is derived from the literature and legal provisions: a *Germanic* cluster (Austria, Germany), a *Nordic* cluster (Denmark, Finland, Norway, Sweden), a *Francophone* cluster (France, Luxembourg), a *New Member States* cluster (Czech Republic, Hungary, Poland, Slovakia, Slovenia) and a final *IGS* cluster (Ireland, Greece, Spain). According to sociological perspectives on corporate governance (see Chapter 1), the Germanic and Nordic clusters are classified as CMEs, the Francophone countries as MMEs and the New Member States as EMEs (Hall and Soskice 2001a, Hancké et al. 2007). A restricted coverage of the right to board-level employee representation is common to Ireland, Greece and Spain, the clustering of which echoes the 'GIIPS' category (see Schweiger 2014). In addition to the results for the five country clusters, each table presents an 'All Country Clusters' column, which refers to the aggregate results of 'all' respondents from sixteen countries.

Responses from employee representatives on the boards of SEs are treated separately and are excluded from the 'all' data on the grounds that SEs cannot be attached to a single cluster or type of capitalism. An SE can be registered anywhere within the European Economic Area (EEA), the 28 Member States of the European Union plus Iceland, Lichtenstein and Norway, and, hence, in any of the sixteen countries within which the survey was distributed. In practice, however, SEs with board-level employee representation are found in a limited number of countries and are concentrated in companies of German origin. No fewer than 44 of the 54 SEs (81.5 per cent) with board-level employee representation are registered in Germany (ETUC and ETUI 2014). The distribution of survey respondents follows this pattern insofar as 81.6 per cent indicate that they sit on the board of an SE with headquarters in Germany. Analysis of SE data thus focuses on the similarities with responses from within the Germanic cluster. To achieve these purposes the chapter comprises three further sections, which analyse the structural characteristics of the companies and the boards on which board-level employee representatives sit, the key individual characteristics of employee representatives, and the constituencies, nomination mechanisms and appointment procedures of board-level employee representatives.

THE FEATURES OF COMPANIES AND BOARDS WITH EMPLOYEE REPRESENTATION

The institutional diversity of board-level employee representation in Europe may be assessed by reference to four variables: the characteristics of the companies covered by the national legislation; the characteristics of the board; the manner in which employee representatives are appointed to the board; and the rules governing the implementation of the legal provisions, for example, by means of specific trigger mechanisms (Kluge and Stollt 2009). This section focuses on the first two of these variables. The characteristics of the companies with board-level employee representation are assessed in terms of the size of the companies, their sector of activity and their organisational level; that is, whether the company is a single independent entity, a holding company or a subsidiary. The characteristics of the board are usually explained in terms of monistic or dual corporate governance structures, coupled with analyses of the composition and duties of the board (Kluge and Stollt 2009). The analysis of board duties is presented in Chapter 4. This section elaborates the structure, size and composition of boards.

Company Characteristics

Large variations in the size of companies with board-level employee representation are expected given the diversity of legally defined workforce thresholds for board-level employee representation. As Chapter 2 demonstrated, such thresholds range from 25 to 1,000 employees depending on the national legal framework. The economic landscape of board-level employee representation in Europe thus is predicted to comprise small, medium-sized and large companies. Survey results draw a somewhat different picture characterised by the predominance of large companies.

Data from the 'all' column of Table 3.1 reveal that board-level employee representation is a feature of large to very large (XXXL) companies, with 65.5 per cent of respondents indicating that the company on whose board they sit employs more than 250 employees in their country and 71.2 per cent reporting that the company employs more than 250 employees at the global level. More specifically, very large companies with more than 2,000 employees head the ranking 'globally' and 'in your country'. Regarding both the national and global situation, however, a significant proportion of respondents report that they sit on the board of a medium-sized firm: 21.2 per cent when considering the size of the global workforce or 25.8 per cent by reference to the national workforce.

The ranking of companies based on their employment size reveals marked discrepancies between country clusters. In a first category composed solely of IGS, the national and global rankings are equivalent to that of the 'all' data, although the prevalence of very large (XXXL) companies is more pronounced and the presence of medium-sized companies is slightly

Table 3.1 What Is the Size of the Company/Group of Companies for Which You Have Board-Level Responsibilities?

Number of Employees[1]		All Country Clusters N = 3,902–4,045 %	CMEs: Germanic N = 1,487–1,489 %	CMEs: Nordic N = 1,751–1,886 %	MMEs: Francophone N = 146 %	EMEs: New Member States N = 490–496 %	Ireland, Greece and Spain N = 28 %	SEs N = 38 %
Globally	1–9 (micro)	1.4	2.1	1.1	0.7	0.6	/	/
	10–49 (small)	6.2	2.4	11.5	0.7	0.6	10.8	/
	50–249 (medium)	21.2	4.6	32.7	9.5	34.5	14.3	/
	250–499 (large)	8.7	4.0	10.3	4.8	18.6	7.1	/
	500–999 (XL)	8.9	6.5	9.1	15.8	13.5	/	5.3
	1,000–1,999 (XXL)	8.6	8.2	7.7	25.3	8.1	7.1	7.9
	More than 2,000 (XXXL)	45.0	72.2	27.6	43.2	24.1	60.7	86.8
In your country	1–9 (micro)	2.0	2.2	2.1	0.7	1.0	/	/
	10–49 (small)	6.7	1.8	12.5	0.7	1.0	10.8	/
	50–249 (medium)	25.8	4.4	41.7	9.5	35.3	14.3	2.5
	250–499 (large)	11.5	6.2	13.8	5.5	20.6	7.1	5.3
	500–999 (XL)	11.4	10.1	10.7	17.1	16.9	/	5.3
	1,000–1,999 (XXL)	9.7	10.6	8.1	23.3	9.7	7.1	23.7
	More than 2,000 empl. (XXXL)	32.9	64.7	11.1	43.2	15.5	60.7	63.2

Note:
Respondents were asked to provide an approximate figure for the number of employees. Responses were then grouped into categories following the European classification of companies by size with regard to SMEs (see Recommendation 2003/361/EC which distinguishes micro, small and medium-sized companies) and the four extra categories, which were included to disaggregate the otherwise to loose category of 'large companies' with more than 250 employees according to the European classification.

1. The global employment data include the employees employed 'in your own country'.

lower but still ranked second. A second category consists of the MMEs and the Germanic CMEs in which board-level employee representation is marginal in small and medium-sized enterprises (SMEs) and is concentrated in large to very large XXXL companies. SEs follow the same pattern in a more pronounced form as, at the global level, almost all SE respondents sit on the board of very large (XXXL) companies. The legal framework plays a major role in shaping such distributions insofar as the workforce thresholds triggering board-level employee representation are particularly high in Luxembourg (1,000 employees) and in Germany (500 employees for one-third co-determination and 2,000 employees for parity co-determination). In France board-level employee representation is primarily a feature of state-owned companies, which explains the high proportion of extra-large companies, as French public-sector companies are traditionally very large.[1] In these two categories, differences are not significant between the global and national distribution of companies according to their size. The opposite is the case for the third category comprising the EMEs and Nordic CMEs. With regard to the global workforce, the highest proportion of respondents belonging to this third group are those that sit on the board of medium-sized companies and the second-highest proportion includes respondents that sit on the boards of very large companies with more than 2,000 employees. The legal framework thus appears to determine this configuration because, with the exception of Austria, the lowest workforce thresholds are found in the EMEs and the Nordic CMEs. National legislation sets workforce threshold as starting from 25 employees in Sweden, 30 employees in Norway, 35 employees in Denmark and 50 employees in Slovenia, Slovakia and Czech Republic. Data on the size of companies at country level illustrate this legal influence. In EMEs and the Nordic CMEs very large XXXL companies do not appear second in the ranking, but are replaced by large companies with between 250 and 499 employees for 'in your country' data. In consequence, a majority of Nordic and NMS respondents sit on the board of a medium or large company (55.5 and 55.9 per cent, respectively).

The capacity of board-level employee representatives to exert power over strategic corporate decisions depends on several factors including the constitution and duties of the board (Kluge and Stollt 2009). The latter varies, *inter alia*, according to the organisational level at which the board is located. The board of a single company or of a holding company enjoys considerable strategic power, whereas the decision-making capacity of a board within a subsidiary company is likely to be limited by decisions made at higher levels within the group. Respondents were asked whether the board on which they sit is a single company; a parent company of a group; a first-tier subsidiary, a subsidiary directly owned by a parent company; or an indirect subsidiary, a subsidiary owned by another subsidiary of a parent company. Table 3.2 shows the results, which are analysed based on the distinction between independent companies (single or holding companies) and controlled companies (subsidiaries).

Table 3.2 Is The Company on the Board of Which You Sit . . . ?

		CMEs		MMEs	EMEs		
	All Country Clusters %	Germanic %	Nordic %	Franco-phone %	New Member States %	Ireland, Greece and Spain %	SEs %
A single company	21.9	9.3	20.5	45.2	56.3	50.0	5.3
A parent or holding company	30.2	33.9	30.8	24.7	17.9	41.7	57.9
A subsidiary, directly owned by a holding company	39.3	45.4	41.0	27.4	19.6	8.3	31.5
A subsidiary, owned by another subsidiary of the holding company	8.6	11.4	7.7	2.7	6.2	/	5.3
	N = 4,063	N = 1,500	N = 1,889	N = 146	N = 504	N = 24	N = 38

There is a balanced distribution of independent and controlled companies according to the 'all' data with 52.1 per cent of respondents reporting that they operate within independent companies and 47.9 per cent are based in controlled companies. Results for the Nordic CMEs show no significant difference with the 'all' data. The distribution between independent and controlled companies is also balanced in the Germanic CMEs, although the proportion of controlled companies is slightly higher (56.8 per cent) than that of independent firms (43.2 per cent), whereas the opposite is the case in the Nordic CMEs. The predominance of independent companies is obvious in the MMEs (69.9 per cent), EMEs (74.2 per cent) and IGS (91.7 per cent). More specifically, the single company is the most frequent organizational level reported by board-level employee representatives in these three clusters. Independent companies are also predominant among SEs (63.2 per cent), although the most common organizational level at which respondents are located is that of a parent or holding company. SEs and all country clusters are uniform in that a relatively small proportion of respondents is active on the board of an indirect subsidiary.

Respondents were asked to indicate the principal sector of activity of the company within which they sit on the board. The 'all' data in Table 3.3 show that 'industry' is by far the most common sector of activity of companies with employee representatives on their board, followed by 'private-sector services' and then by 'agriculture, mining, quarrying and other activities'. 'Transportation and storage activities' are only marginally represented, as are 'public-sector services' and 'construction'. The aggregate situation regarding 'public-sector services' and 'construction' is common to all country clusters. Examination of the disaggregated data illustrates that the rank and values of the three most common sectors in CMEs and in the SEs are similar to those of the 'all' data. In contrast, the situation in MMEs, EMEs and IGS differ markedly from that of the 'all' data. Although 'industry' is also the most represented sector in EMEs, the rank order of 'private-sector services' and 'agriculture, mining, quarrying and other activities' differs from that of the 'all' data. 'Agriculture, mining, quarrying and other activities' are ranked second whereas 'private-sector services' and 'transportation and storage' together occupy the third position. As opposed to the other country clusters, 'industry' does not occupy first place in the Francophone and IGS clusters. Board-level employee representation is more commonly found in 'private-sector services' in MMEs (42.2 per cent as opposed to 22.5 per cent for 'all') and in 'private-sector services', 'transportation and storage', and 'agriculture, mining, quarrying and other activities' in IGS.

Characteristics of the Boards

Having looked at the characteristics related to companies with board-level employee representation, the analysis now turns to the characteristics of the board, with emphasis initially placed on the structure of the board before the size and composition of the board are assessed.

The Structure of the Board. National legislation obliges companies to adopt a specific corporate governance structure, which could be monistic, comprising a single board of directors, or a dual structure composed of a supervisory board and a management board. In some countries, companies may choose between these options (see Chapter 2). The legal framework is thus expected to influence the corporate governance structure on which board-level employee representatives sit. Soft law recommendations, such as those contained in national codes of corporate governance, may also play a role, as such codes where monistic structures prevail usually recommend that the CEO is not concurrently the chair of the board of directors. Table 3.4 illustrates the distribution of these structures across the country clusters. The 'all' data in Table 3.4 report the majority of respondents as sitting on monistic boards with 54.7 per cent of board-level employee representatives sitting on either 'a board of directors and a CEO' or 'a board of directors and a chair of the board separate from the executive officer'. This finding refutes the contention that board-level employee representation is a feature of only dual-board structures (Roth 2010). The dual structure appears as the second most common form with 'a management group' and 'other' of only marginal importance.

Table 3.3 What Is The Main Sector of Activity of the Company?

		CMEs		MMEs	EMEs		
	All Country Clusters %	Germanic %	Nordic %	Franco-phone %	New Member States %	Ireland, Greece and Spain %	SEs %
Industry	44.2	47.6	44.5	23.8	40.9	14.3	39.5
Construction	5.1	2.1	7.5	/	6.3	3.6	18.4
Private-sector services	22.5	22.9	23.3	42.2	12.4	28.6	18.4
Public-sector services	4.6	5.4	4.3	4.8	3.1	/	5.3
Transportation and storage	7.6	6.7	5.9	14.2	13.9	28.6	/
Agriculture, mining, quarrying and other activities	16.0	15.3	14.5	15.0	23.4	24.9	18.4
	N = 4,098	N = 1,500	N = 1,914	N = 147	N = 509	N = 28	N = 38

Note:
The survey question contained 22 items based on the NACE Revision 2 classification as well as an extra 'other' item. The items 'construction' and 'transportation and storage' were retained as stand-alone categories. The 20 other items were grouped into four broader categories as follows:

- *Industry*: automobile, manufacture of motor vehicles (NACE C29); chemicals (NACE C20); clothing and textiles (NACE C13); food and beverages (NACE C10-C11); manufacture of computer and electronic products (NACE C26); other manufacturing (NACE C32); electricity, gas and water supply (NACE D and E)
- *Private-sector services*: whole sale and retail trade (NACE G); accommodation and food service activities (NACE I); information and communication (NACE J); real estate activities (NACE L); financial and insurance activities (NACE K); professional, scientific and technical activities (NACE M); administrative and support service activities (NACE N); arts, entertainment and recreation (NACE R)
- *Public-sector services*: public administration and defence, compulsory social security (NACE O); education (NACE P); human health and social work activities (NACE Q);
- *Agriculture, mining, quarrying and other activities*: agriculture (NACE A); mining and quarrying (NACE B); other.

Results disaggregated by the country clusters, which allow a single corporate governance structure show no deviation from the legal framework. The vast majority of board-level employee representatives in IGS define the corporate governance structure of the company as monistic, whereas a similarly high proportion of Germanic respondents indicate a dual structure. As

Table 3.4 What Is the Corporate Governance Structure of the Company?

		CMEs		MMEs	EMEs	Ireland, Greece and Spain	
	All Country Clusters %	Germanic %	Nordic %	Francophone %	New Member States %	%	SEs %
A board of directors and a CEO	21.3	6.4	29.8	40.6	27.7	28.6	5.3
A board of directors and a chair of the board separate from the executive officer	33.4	2.1	61.6	44.8	16.3	67.8	5.3
A supervisory board and a management board	38.7	86.7	2.1	12.5	42.4	3.6	84.1
A management group	1.7	0.5	2.9	/	0.9	/	5.3
Other	4.9	4.3	3.6	2.1	12.7	/	/
	N = 4,080	N = 1,508	N = 1,899	N = 143	N = 502	N = 28	N = 38

more than one configuration is allowed, variations arise in the remaining country clusters. In both the Nordic and Francophone countries, the monistic structure dominates in spite of the freedom granted to companies in two of the Nordic countries and both of the Francophone countries to choose either a monistic or a dual structure. These findings might be explained by a path dependency resting on the recent introduction of a freedom of choice in Luxembourg (in 2006) and in Denmark (in 2010), where monistic boards were previously required, and by the reluctance of French executives to adopt the dual structure for fear of a reinforcement of control over their actions (Hollandts 2010). Specific results recorded in EMEs reflect the significant proportion of respondents who replied 'other', and the balanced distribution among those who define the corporate governance structure as monistic (44.0 per cent) and those who indicate a dual structure (42.4 per cent). Although the option of a monistic board structure is available only in Hungary and Slovenia, the peculiarity of the EMEs arises from the large majority of Slovak and Czech respondents (83.9 and 87.6 per cent, respectively) that classify themselves as operating within a monistic governance structure. Confusion may have arisen in the Czech and Slovak contexts because national company law allows a single person to constitute the management board. In such cases, the difference between a monistic structure composed of 'a board of directors and a CEO' and a dual structure composed of a single-person management board together with a supervisory board may not be obvious.

One of the alleged motives for management to adopt the SE statute is to enjoy flexibility regarding corporate governance structure, as the SE statute allows for a choice between dual or monistic systems, irrespective of the country of registration. This argument is said to be particularly appealing to German companies, which otherwise are bound to the dual structure (Ernst & Young 2009). In practice, 47 out of the 147 'normal' German-based SEs, that is, SEs with a genuine business activity and at least five employees, have opted for a monistic structure (Pütz 2014). With the single exception of Puma SE, none of these 47 companies is (nor was) subject to board-level employee representation because of national legislation. The scarcity of employee representation on monistic boards within SEs is confirmed by the survey results, which show that the majority of SE respondents (84.2 per cent) sit on a supervisory board, thus replicating the same pattern as required in Germany.

The Size and Composition of the Board. Debate about board size is important among corporate governance scholars. Early authors within this perspective argued that 'small is beautiful' and viewed the optimal board size as about eight members (Jensen 1993; Lipton and Lorsch 1992). This argument has been sustained by empirical evidence from econometric studies, which focus on the link between board size and company performance (Yermack 1996; Bennedsen et al. 2008), and has been used by opponents of board-level employee representation, who argue that such representation would unduly increase the size of the board and put company performance at risk (see for Germany, Bermig and Frick 2011; for Norway, Nygaard Thorkildsen and Haugland Gaure 2013). German quantitative research, however, finds no evidence that large boards impede the formulation of corporate strategy (Gerum and Debus 2006). The 'all' results from Table 3.5 show that the average size of the board, including employee representatives, is 8.8 members. This number is smaller than the average board size of European listed companies, which is reported as 12.1 members overall, or 11.5 members if calculated on the basis of the nine countries covered by both studies (Heidrick & Struggles 2011:37).[2]

Average board sizes in IGS, NMS and the Germanic and Nordic CMEs are all below the corresponding average board size mentioned in the Heidrick & Struggles report. The respective figures from the survey and the Heidrick & Struggles report are 11.1 compared to 14.3 reported by board-level employee representatives in IGS, 5.5 compared to 8.2 in NMS, 12.2 compared to 14.3 in the Germanic cluster, and 6.2 compared to 9.1 in the Nordic cluster. It is only in the Francophone cluster that the average

Table 3.5 The Size of the Board and Presence of Employee Representatives

		CMEs		MMEs	EMEs		
	All Country Clusters N = 4,024–4,048	**Germanic** N = 1,466–1,468	**Nordic** N = 1,877–1,903	**Francophone** N = 146–147	**New Member States** N = 503–507	**Ireland, Greece and Spain** N = 27–28	**SEs** N = 38
Total number of board members[1] *Mean in absolute value [min.–max. values]*	8.8 [2–32]	12.2 [3–30]	6.2 [2–30]	16.8 [2–32]	5.5 [2–30]	11.1 [4–22]	11.1 [6–18]
Proportion of employee representatives[2] *Mean in % [min.–max. values]*	37.2 [3–50]	43.4 [3–50]	33.6 [4–50]	27.0 [3–40]	34.2 [3–50]	20.0 [8–50]	43.8 [33–50]
Number of employee representatives *Mean in absolute value [min.–max. values]*	3.6 [1–20]	5.6 [1–20]	2.5 [1–20]	4.8 [1–17]	2.03 [1–12]	2.2 [1–5]	5.0 [1–9]

Notes:

1. Employee representatives included.
2. The proportion of employee representatives was calculated by dividing the number of board members who represent the employees by the total number of board members, as reported by the respondents (themselves included).

board size (16.8 members) is greater than that of the Heidrick & Struggles report (14.2). Nevertheless, Francophone boards with employee representatives remain smaller than the legally defined maximum size of 18 board members. Boards could be larger in the case of state-owned companies, a point that would explain why the largest board size of 32 members is found in the Francophone cluster. Such large boards with employee representatives also exist in other country clusters. Boards of 30 members are the maximum size in the EMEs and the CMEs, while in the Germanic countries the law stipulates that the board size increases with the company size. It is thus possible to find very large boards on which employee representatives sit, but the inflationary effect of board-level employee representation on board size has been overstated.

Regarding the composition of boards, Table 3.5 also illustrates the proportion and number of employee representatives. Again, the legal framework is expected to determine the actual extent of employee representation at board level. National legislation usually stipulates fixed rules in this regard. The exceptions are Finland; monistic boards in Hungary, where the number of employee representatives is subject to negotiation; and the Czech Republic, Slovakia and Slovenia, where the company articles of association can set higher levels to those set in law. The comparison between these legally defined proportions (see Table 2.1) and those reported by respondents (Table 3.5) reveals no significant differences. In descending order, the highest average proportion of employee representatives (43.4 per cent) is that of the Germanic CMEs, which include the German one-third, parity and Montan co-determination systems. EMEs and Nordic CMEs appear next in the ranking with averages of 34.2 and 33.6 per cent of employee representatives on the board. These two results are consistent with the corresponding national legal provisions, but bring into question the use of the option in the Czech Republic, Slovakia and Slovenia to choose to go beyond the legal requirement to have up to 50 per cent of the board composed of employee representatives. MMEs occupy the third position with more than a quarter of the board composed on employee representatives, which corresponds to the coexistence of various legally based proportions in France and Luxembourg, the legal maximum being 33 per cent. The lowest average proportions are to be found in IGS, where employee representatives hold, on average, 20 per cent of the board seats. Using the data on the average number of board members and that on the average proportion of employee representatives on the board, suggests that the number of board-level employee representatives ranges from about two in Nordic CMEs, EMEs and IGS to about five in MMEs and Germanic CMEs. In brief, the data from the country clusters shows that board-level employee representatives comprise 37.2 per cent of board members and that an average of 3.6 employee representatives sit on each board.

In some cases, the presence of employee representatives within boardrooms could be larger than suggested in Table 3.5 as a result of legal provisions, which allow for the attendance of other employee representatives. In France and Sweden additional employee representatives are invited to attend board meetings in a consultative capacity without the right to vote. In France the works council sends these additional representatives, whereas in Sweden they are the deputies of the board-level employee representatives. Additional employee representation may also arise in companies that have decided, either voluntarily or in application of a legal obligation, to grant one or several board seats to representatives of employee shareholders, as in France. In this context the situation in France is unique in that three-quarters of Francophone respondents report that works council delegates attend the board meeting, whereas 78.0 per cent of 'all' respondents indicate either that there is no participation of additional employee representatives on the board or that the question is irrelevant in their national situation.

The situation in SEs appears almost identical to that in the Germanic cluster on all variables presented in Table 3.5. The average board size in SEs is comparable to that of Germanic countries (11.1 and 12.2 members, respectively), as is the average proportion of employee representatives (43.8 per cent in SEs compared to 43.4 per cent in Germanic countries), as well as the average number of employee representatives on the board (5.0 in SEs, 5.6 in Germanic countries). These findings signal a transfer of German practices once a company has adopted the SE statute.

THE INDIVIDUAL CHARACTERISTICS OF BOARD-LEVEL EMPLOYEE REPRESENTATIVES

The survey provides first-hand and comparative knowledge of the individual characteristics of a largely unknown population of employee representatives. It thus allows for an investigation of some issues raised by corporate governance scholars in relation to the composition of boards and by industrial relations scholars concerning the representative capacity of employee representatives.

When corporate governance became subject to soft law during the 1990s, a 'good practices' recommendation that was frequently stated was the introduction of independent non-executive directors who were expected to challenge CEOs or executive-dominated boards. Two decades later empirical criticisms of the added value of 'independent' board members (Bhagat and Black 2002; Volonté 2015), led to a shift in emphasis with greater attention paid to the concept of 'board diversity' at the expense of the 'pro-independence' rhetoric. The 'board diversity' discourse, as employed extensively by the European Commission (2012a), intends to tackle directly the issues arising from the demographic and socioeconomic homogeneity of boardrooms.[3] While gender has received most attention, the concept of diversity is multidimensional and encompasses demographic and cognitive attributes (Jackson et al. 1995; Engelen et al. 2012). Although some argue that diversity would increase coordination costs related to boards and slow down decision-making because of the higher probability of conflicts (Knyazeva et al. 2013), the recent political trend at EU level emphasises, *inter alia*, the benefits of diversity (European Commission 2012b). From a resource dependence perspective, such diversity increases the variety of information resources at the disposal of problem solving (Pfeffer and Salancik 1978) and the quality of decisions due to the integration of a wider range of perspectives (Milliken and Martins 1996). From a behavioural and socio-psychological perspective, which conceives boardrooms as decision-making teams, diversity enables avoidance of the 'groupthink' bias of homogeneous groups (Janis 1972).

In the field of industrial relations, scholars link the study of indirect forms of employee representation to two related issues. First, the representativeness of employee representatives is conceived more as a matter of coverage of the represented population, rather than as a matter of 'demographic' representativeness, in the sense that representatives have to constitute a representative sample of the represented population in terms of age, gender, qualification and the like (Dachler and Wilpert 1978; Globerson 1970; McBride 2001).[4] This point is associated with the nature of the constituency, which could comprise the entire workforce, trade unions or elected employee representation bodies in dual systems of industrial relations. The third section of this chapter addresses these themes. A second issue in the industrial relations literature is the autonomy of interest representation from management, or alternatively its incorporation: and autonomy vis-à-vis constituents, as a certain distance from them is required for employee representatives to exercise a 'filtering and prioritizing of multiple, fragmentary and often contradictory grievances and aspirations' (Hyman 1997:310).

Depending on the perspective adopted, the main questions regarding the individual profile of board-level employee representatives concern knowing if and how they contribute to board diversity, knowing if and how they are distant enough from the management and if they are involved in the labour movement? To address these questions, the first part of this section identifies the gender composition of employee representatives, while the second addresses the question of their activism by looking at their degree of involvement in employee representation activities beyond their board-level mandate.

Gender Distribution as a Demographic Characteristic

Gender balance on boards is a topical issue in Europe with discussions underway on a proposal for a directive, which, if adopted, would set a 40 per cent quota for women in non-executive positions of boards of large listed companies to be met by 2018 and in private-sector companies to be met by 2020. Although the European legislative process is stalled because of a lack of political agreement at the Council, there is an ever growing body of evidence that gender quotas established at national level have been more efficient than soft law mechanisms in raising the proportion of women on board positions (Fagan et al. 2012). As seen in Chapter 2, three of the surveyed countries enacted hard law that set such quotas for the boards of private- and public-sector companies (Norway, France, Spain), and five others did the same with reference to state-owned companies (Austria, Denmark, Finland, Greece, Slovenia). Linked to the issue of the impact of legislation on practice is the question of whether these quotas apply to board positions occupied by employee representatives: Are they included in the quota of female board members? The quota of the proposed EU directive covers employee representatives insofar as they are included in the calculation of the proportion of each sex on boards. Due to the institutional diversity of board-level employee representation in Europe, the proposed directive leaves it up to Member States to define the practical procedures required regarding this particular case. Whether the Danish and Spanish quotas are meant to include board positions occupied by employee representatives is not specified in the corresponding law. Elsewhere, however, board seats occupied by employee representatives are excluded from the gender quota, which applies only to board members elected by the annual general meeting or appointed by the state (Austria, Finland, France, Greece, Norway, Slovenia). In France and Norway the gender distribution of employee representatives is subject to a specific regulation. When board-level employee representatives are appointed by means of an election in France, the list of candidates must comprise candidates of both sexes listed alternately, and on each of these lists, the difference between the number of candidates of each sex cannot be greater than one. In Norway, when two or more employee representatives are to be appointed, both sexes must be represented, except in companies in which one sex represents less than 20 per cent of the workforce. Until a legal quota was adopted in Germany in the spring of 2015, the 2004 act on one-third co-determination stated that men and women 'should' be represented on the board in proportion to the composition of the workforce. This provision was not legally binding, but the Deutscher Gewerkschaftsbund (DGB), which was in favour of a statutory quota, committed itself and its affiliates at its 2010 congress to support a more rigid application of this rule and to extend it to all co-determined companies. In addition, inspired by rules in force in the metal and service sectors' unions, the DGB went further in 2014 and resolved that at least one of the seats reserved for external trade union officials should be occupied by a member of the under-represented sex. Taking into account the situation in France, Norway and Germany, it is expected that the feminisation of board-level employee representatives will be greater in the CMEs and MMEs.

With regard to the proportion of female directors on the boards on which respondents sit, the 'all' data in Table 3.6 indicate an average of 18.4 per cent, from which the average rates within country clusters do not differ markedly. Feminisation in the Nordic CMEs and the EMEs is most developed at 24.1

Table 3.6 The Gender Distribution among All Board Members and among Employee Representatives

		CMEs		MMEs	EMEs		
	All Country Clusters N = 4,077–4,133 Mean in %	Germanic N = 1,002–1,547 Mean in %	Nordic N = 1,283–1,903 Mean in %	Francophone N = 121–147 Mean in %	New Member States N = 347–506 Mean in %	Ireland, Greece and Spain N = 22–28 Mean in %	SEs N = 17–38 Mean in %
Proportion of female directors[1]	18.4	10.4	24.1	17.3	22.3	12.8	5.7
Proportion of female directors being employee representatives[2]	53.1	70.3	43.5	44.7	44.9	4.5	31.4
Proportion of employee representatives being women[3]	21.8	16.9	24.9	24.3	25.8	2.7	5.6

Notes:

1. The proportion of total board members being women was calculated by dividing the number of women on the board by the total number of board members as reported by the respondents (including themselves if relevant).
2. The proportion of female directors being board-level employee representatives was calculated by dividing the number of women being employee representative by the total number of women on the board as reported by the respondents (including themselves if relevant).
3. The proportion of board-level employee representatives being women was calculated by dividing the number of women being employee representative by the total number of employee representatives on the board as reported by the respondents (including themselves if relevant).

per cent and 22.3 per cent, respectively, and the Germanic CMEs record the lowest proportion of female directors at 10.4 per cent. Thanks to the data collection undertaken by Directorate General (DG) Justice, the survey data can be compared with that of the EC database of 'men and women in key decision-making positions' for 2009 to 2013 when the survey distribution was conducted. Reference to the 'all' data shows that boards with employee representatives are more feminised at 18.4 per cent, whereas 15.4 per cent of board members are women at the large listed companies included in the EC database. Employee representatives, if present, are included in the EC database calculation. There are, however, great differences between the survey results and the EC database when considering the disaggregated data. The proportion of female directors on the boards on which sit respondents to the survey is lower than that covered by the EC database in the CMEs: 10.4 per cent female directors in Germanic countries in the survey compared to 13.1 per cent in the EC database, and 24.1 compared to 28.2 per cent in the Nordic countries. The reverse is found in the other country clusters with female directors being more frequent on the boards of respondents in IGS, 12.8 per cent compared to 8.9 per cent in the EC database; MMEs, 17.3 per cent compared to 13.1 per cent; and EMEs, 22.3 per cent compared to 13.5 per cent.

The 'all' data in the second row of Table 3.6 show that employee representatives make a significant contribution to the feminisation of boards, as somewhat more than half of female directors are employee representatives. The data disaggregated by country clusters reveal extreme variations, with almost three-quarters of women board members in the Germanic CMEs serving as employee representatives, whereas only 4.5 per cent of women occupy the same position in IGS. The situation is closer to that of 'all' in the other country clusters, which demonstrates that there is no correlation between the feminisation of employee representatives and the proportion of employee representatives on the board. The outcome of a comparison of the survey results with the Heidrick & Struggles report on listed companies is that female directors are much more likely to be employee representatives in the companies covered by the survey than reported within the listed companies. The proportions of women board members who are employee representatives mentioned in the Heidrick & Struggles report (2011:40) are lower than that of the survey evidence. The survey data indicate a proportion of 53.1 per cent compared to 18.8 per cent reported by the Heidrick & Struggles report. This situation is replicated for each country cluster: 70.3 per cent compared to 61.5 per cent in Germanic CMEs;[5] 43.5 per cent compared to 26.5 per cent in Nordic CMEs; 44.7 per cent compared to 1.0 per cent in MMEs; 44.9 per cent compared to 15.0 per cent in EMEs; 4.5 per cent compared to zero in IGS. Not only do employee representatives contribute to the feminisation of boards, but they do so in a more significant way than implied by the study of listed companies alone as well. It should be stressed, however, that comparisons between the survey data, the EC database and the Heidrick & Struggles report have to be treated with caution, given that the scope of covered companies is dissimilar and only a minority of the companies on the board of which respondents sit are listed on the stock exchange.

The final row of Table 3.6 provides information on the proportion of employee representatives that are women. The 'all' data suggest that there is about one woman for every five board-level employee representatives. The ratio is higher and closer to one in four in MMEs, EMEs and Nordic CMEs, whereas it is lower than the 'all' average and closer to one in six in the Germanic CMEs.[6] The IGS respondents stand apart, with fewer than 3.0 per cent women. As no fewer than 86.1 per cent of survey respondents are unionised, the findings confirm that women are under-represented in trade union leadership and representative positions, despite the growing number of women trade unionists (Ledwith 2012).[7]

The presence of women on SE boards appears precarious, for both the proportion of female directors (5.7 per cent), the proportion of serving female directors that are employee representatives (31.4 per cent) and the proportion of women employee representatives (5.6 per cent) are significantly lower than the 'all' and country cluster results, with the exception of the IGS cluster. Whereas the *de facto* position of board-level employee representation in SEs looks very similar to that of the Germanic countries on a number of points, disparity emerges when considering the gender distribution of board members, in general, and of employee representatives on boardrooms, in particular.

Activism-Related Characteristics

Examining the activist features of board-level employee representatives elaborates differences between their characteristics and those of other board members, their contribution to board diversity and their degree of autonomy and representative capacity. The point under investigation is less that of knowing whether board-level employee representatives are active, than that of revealing how committed they are to the labour movement. The extent of their activism is beyond question insofar as 53. 8 per cent of board-level employee representatives devote one day per month to board activities and 24.7 per cent devote two days per month to board duties, accounting for an overall average of 10.3 hours per month, a figure that rises to 17, 26 and 30 hours in EMEs, MMEs and IGS, respectively. A key question addressed by this study is the articulation of board-level employee representation with other employee representation bodies and trade unions within the company. The contribution of board-level employee representatives to collective action is all the more relevant given that 86.1 per cent of respondents are trade unionists. Marked variations are noted between the very high unionisation rates among board-level employee representatives in the SEs and the Germanic cluster, 100 per cent and 94.5 per cent, respectively, which are closely followed by unionisation rates in among IGS, Nordic and Francophone respondents, 89.3 per cent, 87.7 per cent and 74.8 per cent, respectively. The lowest unionisation rate of respondents is reported in the NMS at 57.8 per cent, signalling potential differences in the degree of activism and the distance vis-à-vis company management. While Chapter 6 deals with articulation between the various institutions of labour representation more extensively, some preliminary information related to respondents' individual characteristics can inform this problematic by assessing the extent to which board-level employee representatives are members of other company-level bodies of employee representation.

The 'all' data in Table 3.7 demonstrate that only one-quarter of board-level employee representatives currently hold no other representative position, a proportion that rises to one-third in IGS and close to a half in the EMEs, further questioning the activist ethos of the latter. The most extreme situation is that of the Francophone MMEs where 76.2 per cent of board-level employee representatives do not hold any other mandate. The French result is explained by reference to the specific legal rule of 'incompatibility', which forbids board-level employee representatives from holding any other representative position within the company, such as that of works councillor, trade union representative or trade union officer. Similar 'incompatibility' rules can only be found in Poland, where legal provisions prohibit employee representatives on the board of 'commercialised' companies from carrying out trade union activities and, no doubt, contribute to the result recorded for the EMEs.[8]

The three most common representative positions held in addition to the board mandate are, in the descending order of the 'all' results, trade union representative, member of the works council and health and safety representative. Proportions related to the other four potential representative positions are marginal and account for 10 per cent or fewer of the board-level employee representatives. The distribution of respondents over the four marginal positions does not differ from that of the 'all' data in the Nordic CMEs, EMEs and IGS. In contrast, no fewer than one-fifth of the Germanic board-level employee representatives are staff representatives, a proportion that is similar to the proportion that are members of the group works council. This latter response is linked to the extremely high proportion of Germanic respondents who are also members of the works council, which could partially be attributed to the eligibility criteria set in Austrian law and the effectiveness of trade unions/works councils in the two countries in supporting candidates. Works council membership is far lower in the other country clusters, where respondents are more likely to be trade union representatives, particularly in the single-channel Nordic cluster. SE respondents look very similar to their Germanic counterparts, with the same three popular mandates held by the majority of SE respondents. This result confirms previous qualitative findings showing that board-level employee representatives are also members of the SE works council in the majority of SEs (Rehfeldt et al. 2011).

Table 3.7 Do You Hold/Have You Held Any Other Representative Positions within the Company?

			CMEs				MMEs	
	All Country Clusters %		Germanic %		Nordic %		Francophone %	
	Currently	Previously	Currently	Previously	Currently	Previously	Currently	Previously
Shop steward, union/office representative	41.5	17.1	20.2	8.2	63.0	22.8	8.2	25.9
Member of the works council[1]	38.6	18.5	72.5	30.8	16.7	7.8	4.8	42.2
Health and safety representative	25.2	14.2	36.3	14.5	22.5	15.4	1.4	19.7
Member of the group works council	10.0	7.6	18.7	14.8	5.5[3]	2.6[3]	/[4]	19.0[4]
Staff representative	9.0	7.3	22.5[2]	14.7[2]	n. a.	n. a.	6.1	46.3
Member of the European works council	7.7	3.9	10.0	6.4	7.6	2.8	0.7	3.4
Other	8.7	7.4	4.6	4.5	12.2	8.5	9.5	8.8
None	24.3	35.9	16.0	26.8	21.9	40.0	76.2	29.3
	N = 4,155		N = 1,554		N = 1,917		N = 147	

(Continued)

Table 3.7 (continued) Do You Hold/Have You Held Any Other Representative Positions within the Company?

	EMEs					
	New Member States %		Ireland, Greece and Spain %		SEs %	
	Currently	Previously	Currently	Previously	Currently	Previously
Shop steward, union/office representative	35.6	19.4	35.7	39.3	23.7	18.4
Member of the works council[1]	27.3	13.2	32.1	32.1	68.4	50.0
Health and safety representative	9.2	7.1	10.7	17.9	10.5	13.2
Member of the group works council	3.5[5]	1.4[5]	3.6[6]	7.1[6]	52.6	18.4
Staff representative	2.4[5]	0.6[5]	3.6[7]	7.1[7]	7.9	5.3
Member of the European works council	3.5	0.6	/	3.6	63.2	5.3
Other	7.5	11.4	10.7	10.7	7.9	7.9
None	43.6	50.9	35.7	28.6	18.4	21.1
	N = 509		N = 28		N = 38	

Notes:
Respondents could tick more than one box for this question hence the sum of the percentage data is more than 100 per cent.

1. Responses to the item 'member of the works council' integrate responses to the following country-specific items: 'member of the blue-collar workers' works council', 'member of the white-collar workers' works council' (both Austria-specific) and 'member of the young workers'/trainees' representative body' (Austria and Germany).

These two questions were adapted to national situations. As a consequence, some items were excluded from questionnaires related to countries where not all the six representative positions are statutorily or conventionally foreseen. In particular, see the following notes.

2. The ‘staff representative’ item only appeared in the German questionnaire, not in the Austrian one.
3. The ‘member of the group works council’ option only appeared in the Danish and Norwegian questionnaires, not in the Swedish and Finnish versions.
4. The ‘member of the group works council’ option only appeared in the French questionnaire, not in the Luxembourgian version.
5. The options ‘member of the group works council’ and ‘staff representative’ only appeared in the Hungarian and Slovenian questionnaires, not in the Czech, Polish and Slovak questionnaires.
6. The option ‘member of the group works council’ only appeared in the Greek and Spanish questionnaires, not in the Irish version.
7. The option ‘staff representative’ only appeared in the Spanish questionnaire, not in the Irish and Greek versions.

The comparison between the current and past situations with regard to the 'all' data reveals that the activism of respondents has increased over time. In the past, one-third of the respondents did not hold other representative positions whereas currently a quarter of the respondents do not hold other positions. A higher proportion of board-level employee representatives currently hold each of the other mandates than previously was the case. Results from board-level employee representatives in CMEs, EMEs and SEs replicate this pattern. In the MMEs, however, this situation is reversed, as on accepting the mandate to serve on the board French board-level employee representatives are obliged by law to resign from other posts. The trend in IGS is similar to that of the MMEs with respondents holding more posts previously than currently. The statistical variations between the past and current situations are not significant.

Irrespective of the timeline, Table 3.7 sheds light on the activism of board-level employee representatives in showing how many extra mandates they may hold, which, in turn, is an indicator of articulation achieved through personal engagement. Using the sum of the percentage data presented in Table 3.7, excluding responses to 'none', as a proxy measure for the multiplicity of current mandates held by board-level employee representatives reveals some similarities between country clusters. 'All' respondents hold on average 1.4 additional mandates. Respondents in the Germanic and Nordic CMEs follow the same pattern as they hold more than one other representative position within the company (1.8 and 1.3, respectively). SE respondents are even more active when it comes to employee representation because they hold an average of 2.3 other representative mandates within the company. In contrast, respondents from EMEs and IGS hold one other mandate (0.9 and 1.0) and the extreme situation in MMEs is confirmed in that Francophone board-level employee representatives hold 0.3 other mandates. These findings demonstrate existing multiple personal connections between board-level employee representatives and other institutions of labour representation. With the exception of the MMEs, the likelihood of 'incorporation' is reduced in that board-level employee representatives tend to be members of other interest representation bodies, which is the case of all country clusters with the exception of MMEs. While these findings suggest that articulation through personal contact is a feature of board-level employee representation, they do not confirm the case as multiple mandate holders could either serve as 'disseminating' actors who foster information exchange between different institutions or they could function as autonomous agents. These points are further explored in Chapter 6.

THE CONSTITUENTS OF BOARD-LEVEL EMPLOYEE REPRESENTATION

The suggestion that board-level employee representatives aim to represent employees might be considered an oversimplification if the variety of legally defined nomination and appointment mechanisms presented in Chapter 2 are taken into account.[9] This variation raises the question of a potential multiplicity of constituencies for board-level employee representatives, such as individuals, groups or institutions. The question is of importance in relation to the articulation between board-level employee representatives and with their constituents. This section assesses the potential gap between legal rules and actual practices based on the variation in legal context. In this context the sixteen participating countries can usefully be grouped into four categories according to the number of actors (the constituents) involved in the nomination and appointment processes. In a first group of six countries, a single actor nominates and appoints employee representatives to the board, which is the trade union (Luxembourg [the iron and steel sector], Spain, Sweden), the works council (Austria, Slovenia), personnel groups within the company (Finland) or staff representatives (Luxembourg with the exception of the iron and steel sector). In a second group of three countries (Greece, Ireland, Norway) nomination and appointment are linked to two distinct actors: nomination by trade unions and election by employees. In a third group of five countries, more than two actors are involved, with the possibility of multiple alternative sources of nomination (trade unions, employees, works council), not least in situations of trade union pluralism (Czech Republic, France, Germany, Hungary, Slovakia). In Denmark and Poland, which constitute a fourth group, the number of constituents is not stipulated as a consequence of the lack of specific legal provisions to regulate the nomination decision. This section comprises two stages, which, in turn, identify the actors involved in the nomination process and those involved at the appointment stage of survey respondents.

Table 3.8 identifies those who initially nominated and presented the application of the respondent to serve on the board. Reference to the 'all' data shows that trade unions, and, in particular, trade unions at the workplace rather than national confederations, play a key role in the nomination of more than half of board-level employee representatives (54.1 per cent). Another half of respondents declares that their nomination was supported either by the works council (25.1 per cent) or by the employees (26.6 per cent). The practical involvement of other potential supporting actors is marginal, as confirmed by the disaggregated data. The data also show variations between country clusters, which are partially explained by the legal framework, particularly in countries in which only one actor is involved in the nomination process. In IGS, more than eight respondents in ten are nominated by trade unions, with the highest rate of involvement of national union confederations. The majority of Nordic board-level employee representatives are nominated by trade unions, and more particularly by local trade unions. Employees, however, nominated more than a third of Nordic board-level employee representatives. Denmark accounts for a large proportion of this group, as Danish legislation does not specify any particular nomination procedure. The absence of specific nomination procedures tends to lead to nomination primarily by employees rather than any other actors, as is also the case in Poland, where slightly more than half of respondents report that they were nominated by employees. The

Table 3.8 Who Initially Nominated You to Serve on the Board?

		CMEs		MMEs	EMEs		
	All Country Clusters %	Germanic %	Nordic %	Franc-phone %	New Member States %	Ireland, Greece and Spain %	SEs %
Sectoral/ industrial national trade union	15.6	34.4	3.5	23.1	1.6	14.3	31.6
Trade union at the workplace	36.8	15.4	51.1	60.5	40.3	57.1	15.8
National trade union confederation	1.7	1.1	2.5	0.7	0.4	14.3	/
Works council	25.1	54.7	2.5	5.4	26.5	10.7	55.3
Other employee representatives	8.4	3.5	12.6	17.0	5.3	3.6	7.9
Employees	26.6	10.3	37.4	8.2	41.3	25.0	7.9
Other organisations	1.7	1.7	2.1	/	0.6	/	7.9
Another method of nomination	3.3	1.9	3.5	5.4	6.1	10.7	5.3
TOTAL %	119.2	123	115.2	120.3	122.1	105.7	131.7
	N = 4,155	N = 1,554	N = 1,917	N = 147	N = 509	N = 28	N = 38

Note:
Respondents could tick more than one box for this question; hence, the sum of the percentage data is more than 100 per cent.

Polish situation contributes significantly to the 41.3 per cent of board-level employee representatives in the EMEs who report that employees nominated them. The situation in EMEs is also specific in that works councils nominated a high proportion of board-level employee representatives (26.5 per cent) and sectoral/industrial trade unions nominated a small proportion (1.6 per cent). Two factors explain this distribution. First, nomination is a duty of the works council in Hungarian and Slovenian law. Second, workplace trade unionists, works councils and/or employees may be involved in the nomination process in the Czech Republic and Slovakia, which may account for the limited involvement of sectoral/industrial trade unions. This not to argue that trade unionists are excluded from nomination processes as workplace unions nominated 40.3 per cent of board-level employee representatives. The MMEs illustrate that the potential for a multiplicity of nominating actors does not always act to the expense of trade union involvement. Although employees can nominate candidates to the board in France, trade unions, particularly at the workplace, nominated the vast majority of board-level employee representatives. The legal context is also influential in the MMEs insofar as other employee representatives, specifically staff representatives in Luxembourg, nominated one-sixth of board-level employee representatives. In the Germanic CMEs, two main actors nominated board-level employee representatives, the works council (54.7 per cent) and the trade union at sectoral/industrial or workplace level (49.8 per cent), with a particular involvement of sectoral/industrial trade unions as required by German legal provisions. Information reported by SE respondents reflect the influence of the Germanic patterns in that the works council (55.3 per cent) and the trade union at sectoral/industrial or workplace level (47.4 per cent) are the two major actors in nominations. Involvement of employees, however, is under-represented compared to their role envisaged in German legal provisions on parity co-determination. Such under-representation may result from the exclusion of non-unionised board-level employee representatives from this co-determination system within the questionnaire distribution (see Appendix A).

In terms of the range of actors involved, the legal provisions that regulate the appointment of board-level employee representatives vary more narrowly than those that govern nomination. With the exception of Slovak state-owned companies and the Luxembourgian companies in the iron and steel sector, where two different actors are involved in the appointment procedure, a single actor or institution is usually responsible for the appointment of board-level employee representatives. These actors or institutions, however, differ within national legislation. In nine countries, employees vote for board-level employee representatives in a direct election (Czech Republic, Denmark, France, Germany [one-third and parity systems] Greece, Ireland, Norway, Poland, Slovakia). In two countries (Hungary, Germany [Montan system]), formal appointment is a duty of shareholders. The appointment decision is in the hands of the works council in two countries (Austria, Slovenia), in those of the trade unions in two countries (Spain, Sweden), in those of the personnel groups in Finland, and of the staff representatives in Luxembourg. Given that each national law specifies clear rules as to the actor or institution in charge of the appointment decision, it is expected that only minor departures from the legal framework would emerge from the survey results.

The 'all' data in Table 3.9 confirm that the direct election by employees is by far the most common appointment mechanism of board-level employee representatives. The other appointment procedures and actors involved in them are much less frequent with fewer than 15 per cent of board-level employee representatives appointed by trade unions, by employee representatives and by the works council. Two other methods of appointment are exceptional: by shareholders or by another method. The variety of national legal situations is reflected in the survey insofar as the ranking of appointment procedures in the 'all' data is not reproduced in any of the country clusters. In all country clusters, however, employees are responsible for the appointment of the largest group of board-level employee representatives. In the SEs, however, the SE works council is most influential. This result is consistent with the provisions of SE agreements, which tend to afford a major role to the SE works council in appointing board-level employee representatives (Rose and Köstler 2014).

Returning to the country clusters, differences arise as to the coexistence and nature of a second actor in the appointment process. In Germanic CMEs and EMEs, the works council is the second actor in appointing board-level employee representatives, which is expected from German, Austrian and Slovenian legal provisions. In contrast, the second important appointing actor in Nordic CMEs and IGS is the trade union, again in accord with Finnish, Swedish and Spanish legislation. Only 3 per cent of Hungarian respondents mention shareholders as the source of their appointment, and none of the respondents from the German Montan co-determination system does so, which underestimates the role specified in the law for these actors and implies that respondents may not consider shareholders as one of their constituents, although shareholders appoint them to the board.

Table 3.9 How Were You Appointed/Elected to the Board?

		CMEs		MMEs	EMEs		
	All Country Clusters %	Germanic %	Nordic %	Franco-phone %	New Member States %	Ireland, Greece and Spain %	SEs %
Direct election by employees	58.8	57.1	56.1	89.1	65.0	67.9	21.1
Elected/ appointed by employee representa-tives	11.6	13.5	12.9	4.1	3.7	3.6	10.4
Elected/ appointed by the works council	11.9	22.0	1.4	0.7	25.0	/	55.3
Appointed by trade union	14.5	4.0	27.2	4.1	0.8	17.8	5.3
Elected/ appointed by shareholders	0.9	0.6	0.3	/	4.1	7.1	/
Another method of appointment	2.3	2.8	2.1	2.0	1.4	3.6	7.9
	N = 4,118	N = 1,523	N = 1,911	N = 147	N = 509	N = 28	N = 38

CONCLUSION

Comparative analysis of the morphology of board-level employee representation in Europe maps the topic in three areas. First, Chapter 3 drew a picture of board-level employee representation as it is implemented, thereby moving beyond *de jure* descriptions. Second, the findings allow for an initial commentary on aspects of the corporate governance and industrial relations points of departure. Third, some of the key variations between country clusters have been identified, and the regulatory influence of the legal framework assessed.

Based on the situation reported by board-level employee representatives from sixteen countries, board-level employee representation in Europe tends to be located in companies with more than 2,000 employees or medium-sized companies, which may be independent or controlled. These companies are most likely to be found in 'industry' or 'private-sector services' and to operate with a monistic corporate governance structure. The boards on which board-level employee representatives sit are relatively small, comprising nine members of which one-third are employee representatives with the right to vote. On average, boards with employee representation are more feminised than boards of listed companies, with female employee representatives comprising about half of the female directors, although only one-fifth of employee representatives are women. The average board-level employee representative is a member of a trade union, holds more than one but less than two other representative positions within the company and has two main constituents, the trade union, which nominated him or her for the board and the employees that elected him or her.

Chapter 3 clarifies several points regarding the corporate governance and industrial relations points of departure. In particular, several of the arguments advanced by proponents of the finance or principal–agency model within corporate governance to deny the legitimacy of board-level employee representation within the private sector are brought into question (Davies and Hopt 2013; Jensen and Meckling 1979). Chapter 3 shows that board-level employee representation is not confined to very large companies in public-sector services. It is also a feature of the private sector and is to be found in SMEs in the Nordic countries and NMS in particular. Board-level employee representation is also not only a feature of dual systems of corporate governance. Among survey respondents a greater proportion of board-level employee representation is found within monistic systems. Furthermore, the presence of employee representatives does not necessarily lead to increases in board size as feared by the proponents of the finance model. Some of the founding assumptions of the finance model are thus brought into question. In addition, Chapter 3 confirms a significant contribution of board-level employee representatives to board diversity in terms of demographics, particularly regarding gender, and diversity in terms of their experience and knowledge of the company established over time as both employees of the company and as employee representatives within the company (Duran and Pull 2014). Board-level employee representatives may enrich the working of the board with their in-depth knowledge of the internal processes, organisation, dynamics and politics of the company developed, on average, over 23 years of service with the company (Jürgens et al. 2008).

Chapter 3 also raises issues concerning sociological perspectives within corporate governance. Board-level employee representation in Germanic and Nordic CMEs shares some common features regarding organisational level and the main sector of activity. There are, however, marked variations on some key variables, such as company size, the prevalent corporate governance structure and the proportion of employee representatives on the board. Board-level employee representation in EMEs is very particular, whereas commonalities may be identified between MMEs and IGS on some company-related characteristics, including the predominance of independent, large and very large companies located in private-sector services, and the prevalence of monistic structures of corporate governance.

Industrial relations scholars emphasise the risk of the incorporation of board-level employee representatives, a point related to the autonomy of board-level employee representatives from management in undertaking their representative duties (Clark 1977; Hyman 1975). This risk is exacerbated given that, with the exception of MMEs, no other employee representatives sit on the board beside those with a right to vote. With the exception of the EMEs, the high unionisation rates reported among board-level employee representatives, coupled with their extensive and long-standing experience in other representative positions, suggest that the risk of incorporation is limited. Board-level employee representatives whose appointment is subject to approval at the AGM tend to undervalue the role of shareholders as one of their constituents, again suggesting a limit to the risk of incorporation. Furthermore, in assuming that the constituents of board-level employee representatives monitor their activities, it is reasonable to argue that constituents are likely to act as a guardian against incorporation. Chapter 6 explores these arguments in more detail.

Very different national legal provisions underpin board-level employee representation. In consequence, considerable institutional variation characterises board-level employee representation in Europe, which is reflected in the differing characteristics of the country clusters. Chapter 3 shows that the legal framework determines the morphology of board-level employee representation on several variables specifically addressed by national laws including company size, corporate governance structure and composition, the status of employee representatives, the holding of other representative positions, nomination and appointment. It is only on the gender distribution among board-level employee representatives that the legislative environment tends to play no or only a minor role. The outcome of this legal diversity is marked differences between the country clusters. Some commonalities are noticeable. This is the case between the Germanic and Nordic CMEs on some of the characteristics related to companies, boards and employee representatives. Board-level employee representation in Germanic and Nordic CMEs, for example, is a feature of both independent and controlled companies from industry and private-sector services. The profile of Germanic and Nordic board-level employee representatives is also similar with reference to their occupancy of other representative positions. Nevertheless, differences between Germanic and Nordic CMEs rest on key variables, which may suggest significant variations in the practice of board-level employee representation. Board-level employee representation is essentially a feature of very large companies in Germanic CMEs whereas in Nordic CMEs it is also a phenomenon of medium-sized companies. Board-level employee representatives sit on supervisory boards in Germanic CMEs and on monistic boards of directors in Nordic CMEs, where the proportion of employee representatives is lower. The works council is the second most important nominating actor in the Germanic dual system of industrial relations, whereas it plays no role in the Nordic countries characterised by a single-channel system. Chapter 3 also shows that board-level employee representatives in the SEs, which are primarily registered in Germany, share many practices with their Germanic counterparts, suggesting that a transfer of domestic practices to the transnational level has taken place. In this context, however, differences are noted, with women under-represented on SE boards compared to Germanic boards. Similarly, the SE works council occupies the position of principal constituent in both nomination and appointment procedures, whereas in Germanic board-level employee representation employees undertake a more influential role. Similarities are also apparent regarding the characteristics of companies and boards in the MMEs and IGS, but the profiles of board-level employee representatives differ markedly. Board-level employee representatives in EMEs are characterised by comparatively low rates of unionisation raising questions about the nature of support that they may receive from, and their articulation with, trade unions in the context of relatively immature systems of board-level employee representation. Chapter 4 opens the 'black box' that is the board by examining the board agenda and processes, thereby simultaneously extending the analysis of the impact of the law and introducing the agenda items of importance to board-level employee representatives.

NOTES

1. This statement is valid for the timeframe within which the survey was conducted, 2009 to 2013. A new law was adopted in 2013, which introduced compulsory board-level employee representation in large private-sector companies with a minimum of 5,000 employees in France or 10,000 employees worldwide (see Appendix B.)
2. Seven of the sixteen countries included in the survey are not covered by the Heidrick & Struggles report (Luxembourg, Slovenia, Slovakia, Czech

Republic, Hungary, Ireland, Greece). The comparative exercise with data from MMEs, EMEs and IGS is thus limited to the data in the Heidrick & Struggles report for France, Poland and Spain. This remark applies to all the comparative use of the Heidrick & Struggles data throughout Chapter 3.

3. 'Diversity of competences and views of the members of administrative, management and supervisory bodies of undertakings facilitates a good understanding of the business organisation and affairs of the undertaking concerned. It enables members of those bodies to constructively challenge management decisions and to be more open to innovative ideas, addressing the similarity of views of members, also known as the 'group-think' phenomenon. It contributes thus to effective oversight of the management and to successful governance of the undertaking' (recital No. 18 of Directive 2014/95/EU, which amends Directive 2013/34/EU as regards disclosure of non-financial and diversity information by certain large undertakings and groups).
4. Emphases are changing in this regard because recently several trade unions have established 'proportionality' as the basis of representativeness, particularly regarding gender and sexuality (McBride 2001).
5. According to Weckes (2015), the two figures would be closer nowadays with almost 60 per cent of female board members in co-determined German companies being board-level employee representatives as of December 2014.
6. The situation in Germanic countries may have improved, as research on large companies in Austria indicate that, as of January 2015, one board-level employee representative in five is a woman: 20.7 per cent compared to 16.9 per cent in all Germanic countries in our survey data. The Austrian data still demonstrate a greater feminisation of employee representatives than of shareholder representatives on Austrian supervisory boards, where only 14.3 per cent are women (AK Wien 2015).
7. The figure of 86.1 per cent for the unionisation rate of survey respondents is almost certainly an over-statement of the rate of unionisation among board-level employee representatives in Europe. This overstatement arises from the manner in which the survey was distributed (see Appendix A).
8. In Poland privatised companies in which the state remains the sole shareholder are referred to as 'commercialised' companies.
9. In this context nomination refers to the persons or institution that supports the application to the board of a candidate, and appointment refers to the institution/procedure through which candidates are selected to serve on the board.

4 The Board Agenda and Processes

National legislators justified the introduction of board-level employee representation in terms of practices concerned with both corporate governance and industrial relations. By reference to corporate governance, board-level employee representation was justified as broadening the range of stakeholders engaged in strategic corporate decision-making and, in consequence, improving the quality of decision-making at the board. Within industrial relations, board-level employee representation was viewed as a component of industrial democracy that supplemented forms of workplace participation with workers' involvement in strategic company decision-making. From both the corporate governance and industrial relations points of departure, the content of the agenda of board meetings and the priorities of board members are indicators of whether the purpose of board-level employee representation is being achieved. This chapter examines the agenda of board meetings from the perspective of employee representatives as a means to establish their priorities within the board. The extent and character of their influence on, or power over, decisions made at the board is the subject of Chapter 5.

From the corporate governance point of departure arise a range of expectations based on the characteristics of the economy within which board-level employee representatives operate. From within the sociological perspective, for example, the distinction drawn between CMEs, MMEs and EMEs assumes differences in the density of the networks established by board-level employee representatives, which, in turn, is viewed as having an impact on the quality of the agenda of the board and the influence at the board of the employee representatives (Molina and Rhodes 2007; Mykhnenko 2007). In terms of the framework developed here, differences in the quality of the agenda would thus be expected to vary between the Germanic and Nordic CMEs, the Francophone MMEs and the EMEs of the NMS. Within political perspectives on corporate governance, emphasis is placed on differences in interests between employee representatives, shareholder representatives and managers (Roe 2003). Arising from this view is thus the expectation that employee representatives will emphasise issues of direct concern to employees while downplaying shareholder and managerial concerns. Advocates of financial or principal–agency perspectives within the corporate governance literature develop similar arguments, insofar as they view the separation of ownership and control as promoting different priorities between shareholders and managers. Advocates of financial perspectives argue that employee representatives should be excluded from the board on the grounds that such representatives would not be committed to maximising the value of the company, defined in terms of shareholder value (Fama 1980; Jensen and Meckling 1976). By extension, the inclusion of employee representatives would thus introduce a further stakeholder interest to the board, which would pursue priorities that may differ from those of shareholders and managers. As with political perspectives, the expectations arising from within the financial perspective assume the pursuit of different priorities by employee representatives, shareholder representatives and managers.

Those within industrial relations view board-level employee representation as an element of industrial democracy, albeit in circumstances in which workers and their representatives form a constituency in permanent opposition and never in government (Clegg 1951, 1960; Pateman 1970). A key question that arises from within industrial relations is: can board-level employee representatives inject items of concern to the workforce onto the agenda of board meetings? In addressing this question, some argue that board-level employee representatives are inclined to focus on industrial relations issues, their area of expertise, to the relative exclusion of issues concerning company performance and strategy (Jackson et al. 2005). Some employers who oppose board-level employee representation also take this view by arguing that the presence of board-level employee representatives leads to issues that are inappropriate or not central for board-level discussions appearing on the agenda of the board (Bullock 1977: Minority Report).

Industrial relations perspectives also prompt examination of the agenda of board meetings as an indicator of the intensity of participation (Knudsen 1995). A wide-ranging agenda at the board constitutes the potential for an intensity of participation that may allow board-level employee representatives to influence strategic decision-making within the company. In contrast, a narrow board agenda restricts the possibility of an appropriate level of intensity of participation and, thus, board-level employee representatives influencing decision-making at the board. An associated point concerns incorporation. If the agenda of the board is restricted to items of concern only to the efficient financial operation of the company or to the interests of shareholders to the exclusion of issues of concern to board-level employee representatives and the workforce, the possibility of incorporation is raised, that is, board-level employee representatives participating in pursuit of management and shareholder interests rather than workforce interests. Conversely, adversarial positions adopted by board-level employee representatives would be reflected in the pursuit of interests relevant to the workforce and wide-ranging interventions at board meetings intended to further these interests.

Common to the corporate governance and industrial relations points of departure is that *de jure* positions are likely to come under increasing pressure *de facto* as international competition intensifies, financialisation becomes more prominent, and companies embark on repeated restructuring initiatives. In practice, these developments suggest an increasing tension between the requirements of stakeholder participation in decision-making at board level and demands arising from economic efficiency: circumstances that contrast markedly with those that prevailed when board-level employee representation was introduced in Western Europe.

It is worth noting from the outset that this study deals with a lively institution insofar as board-level employee representatives report their regular attendance at board meetings that take place every three months on average. Board-level employee representatives report an average attendance rate of 91.8 per cent. This point challenges a common misconception that boards with employee representation are likely to meet less frequently to enable decisions to be made informally elsewhere in the absence of board-level employee representatives (Batstone et al. 1983). Similarly, a significant proportion (70.1 per cent) of 'all' board-level employee representatives consider other board members as viewing them as skilled partners in board decision-making, and almost a half (48.5 per cent) of board-level employee representatives think that senior company managers and shareholder representatives appreciate their knowledge of the company and use this knowledge as a resource in decision-making. The assumption of the finance perspective to corporate governance that board-level employee representatives will weaken decision-making at the board is thus brought into question.

In the light of these findings, Chapter 4 is composed of three further sections that examine the issues arising from both the corporate governance and industrial relations points of departure. The first section identifies the content of the agenda of board meetings, the importance attached to agenda items by board-level employee representatives and the influences they perceive on the selection of agenda items for the board meeting. The second section examines the provision of information made available to board-level employee representatives for board meetings and assesses the confidentiality provisions associated with the processes of the board. The third section establishes the character of interventions made by employee representatives at the board. The chapter argues that variation in the content of the agenda is relatively narrow between the different country clusters. The priorities of board-level employee representatives and the extent and character of their interventions at the board meeting, however, vary markedly between the country clusters.

THE AGENDA OF THE BOARD

Analysis of the agenda of the board proceeds in two stages. Drawing on the content of legislation regarding the issues appropriate for the board agenda, the first stage examines the importance attached by board-level employee representatives to items that appear on the agenda of the board and thus identifies their priorities and, by inference, the range of agenda items handled at boards. The first stage thus assesses whether the agenda at the board allows board-level employee representatives the opportunity to generate an appropriate intensity of participation, which is prerequisite to them influencing strategic company decision-making (Knudsen 1995). Agenda items that refer to company strategy and finance are contrasted with those on which board-level employee representatives are viewed as having relatively greater expertise and concern, such as human resources and corporate social responsibility. The second stage locates the key influences on the content of the agenda of the board and assesses the extent to which the impact of legislation on the content of the agenda of board meetings is supplemented by that arising from other board procedures.

From the outset it is noteworthy that the importance attached to an agenda item by board-level employee representatives does not necessarily reflect the views of other stakeholders on the board. Political perspectives on corporate governance anticipate that board-level employee representatives will emphasise issues of direct concern to employees to the relative exclusion of shareholder and managerial interests (Roe 2003), whereas industrial relations scholars argue that board-level employee representatives will emphasise matters concerning employment relations as their background and expertise lie in this field (Cressey 1992; Jackson et al. 2005). To examine these arguments two approaches were adopted. The first asked board-level employee representatives to indicate the most important agenda items discussed at the board. Table 4.1 presents the results. The second approach identifies the extent to which the agenda of the board meeting is determined by the legal underpinning that was outlined in Chapter 2.

What Are the Most Important Agenda Items?

Table 4.1 expresses the importance of issues discussed at the board by reference to broad categories. Initially, it should be noted that the category 'other' is cited by relatively few board-level employee representatives, indicating that the broad categories 'capture' the range of issues discussed at the board.

The 'all' column of Table 4.1[1] shows that 'human resources' and 'finance' are regarded as the most important issues discussed at the board, suggesting that board-level employee representatives prioritise both the social and economic dimensions of the company in their board-level decision-making and that these two issues are clearly interlinked. This result supports earlier findings showing that board-level employee representatives define their duties as serving the interests of the company (Hassel and Rehder 2001), where the company is treated as an institution comprising social and economic realms rather than as a nexus of contracts (Conchon and Waddington 2011). This result thus contradicts arguments based on the assumption that board-level employee representatives emphasise issues of direct concern to employees to

Table 4.1 As a Board-Level Employee Representative, Which Are the Most Important Issues Discussed at the Board?

	All Country Clusters %	CMEs: Germanic %	CMEs: Nordic %	MMEs: Francophone %	EMEs: New Member States %	Ireland, Greece and Spain %	SEs %
Human resources[1]	55.8	64.9	52.2	34.7	48.1	46.4	76.3
Finance	48.3	38.3	47.8	58.5	76.0	75.0	44.7
Structure and organisation of the company	35.2	33.2	42.5	36.1	14.0	21.5	42.1
Market policy	30.2	27.7	28.1	44.2	40.3	50.0	10.6
Corporate social responsibility	8.9	8.6	10.0	8.9	6.3	/	18.4
System of corporate governance	8.3	6.4	9.5	8.8	10.5	7.2	7.9
Other	1.2	0.6	1.9	1.4	0.6	/	/
	N = 4,155	N = 1,554	N = 1,917	N = 147	N = 509	N = 28	N = 38

Notes: Respondents were asked to rank their answers to the question 1, 2, 3 and so on. The reasons ranked at position 1 and 2 in the ranking are reported here; hence, the percentage data add up to more than 100 per cent.

1. The complete titles used for each category were 'human resources': employment situation, vocational training, industrial relations and working conditions; 'finance': annual accounts or report, dividends, capital increase, loans and credits; 'structure and organisation of the company': mergers, acquisitions, plans sales/closures; 'market policy': products, research and development, investment policy; 'corporate social responsibility': environment, gender and equality policies; and 'system of corporate governance': appointment, dismissal, remuneration of managers and management board.

the relative exclusion of financial and performance priorities (Cressey 1992; Jackson et al. 2005). 'Finance', 'structure and organisation of the company' and 'market policy' occupy positions 2, 3 and 4 in the ranking of Table 4.1, confirming that the defence of the company by board-level employee representatives necessitates attention being directed towards issues which are usually regarded as the sole domain of shareholder representatives and managers (Adams et al. 2011). The sensitivity of board-level employee representatives to the demands of market competition bring into question those criticisms of board-level employee representation that argue that it results in inappropriate items appearing on the agenda of boards to the exclusion of issues of strategic importance to the company.

Corporate social responsibility (CSR) is defined in terms of companies assuming responsibilities vis-à-vis environmental and social issues on a voluntary basis that go beyond statutory obligations (Banerjee 2007; Mückenberger 2011). Board-level employee representatives attach little importance to CSR compared to issues of 'human resources' and 'finance', suggesting that new approaches to corporate governance that embrace CSR are, at best, second-level issues. Similarly, little importance is attached to the 'system of corporate governance', indicating either that current arrangements are not particularly controversial among board-level employee representatives or that board-level employee representatives do not have a great deal of influence in this area. It is perhaps surprising that so few Germanic board-level employee representatives assign importance to the 'system of corporate governance', given that legislation introduced in 2009 (VorstAG) in Germany made the review of managerial remuneration a duty of the full board. A subcommittee of the board previously handled executive remuneration. The legal change introduced immediately prior to the survey introduced a new practice, which enabled employee representatives to become more directly involved in decisions regarding executive remuneration.

Differentiating the data by country clusters reveals some marked variations in emphasis. Board-level employee representatives in Germanic and Nordic CMEs and in the SEs, for example, prioritise 'human resources' above all other issues. In contrast, in Francophone MMEs and the EMEs of the NMS greatest importance is attached to 'finance'. 'Market policy' is also viewed as more important in these countries than in the CMEs. In other words, board-level employee representatives in CMEs and the SEs are much more likely to prioritise issues relating to 'human resources' whereas in Francophone countries and in the NMS, issues relating to company performance and finance hold centre stage. Board-level employee representatives in IGS replicate the emphases of the Francophone and NMS group, thereby consolidating the notion of two distinct approaches to the issues discussed at the board.

A second approach to the importance of agenda items from the perspective of board-level employee representatives asked respondents to indicate the five most important agenda items from a list comparable to that employed in Table 4.1, but with the broad categories disaggregated into individual agenda items.[2] On this basis, the 'adoption/review of accounts and balance sheets' is at the head of the ranking. Because this item is specifically mentioned in most national legislation as a key duty of the board, it is not surprising that it is prioritised. Issues of company strategy and finance tend to appear towards the top of the ranking. The 'sale/closure of plants, relocation of production', 'investment in technology, real estate, etc.' and 'acquisitions or mergers', for example, appear at positions 2, 4 and 6 in the ranking with more than 35 per cent of board-level employee representatives treating each of these items as among the five most important discussed at the board. That issues concerned with company restructuring are prominent reflects the high rate of corporate restructuring prevalent in Europe following the establishment of the single European market (*Acquisitions Monthly* various; Buiges 1993). The 'employment situation' and 'health and safety' occupy the third and fifth positions in the ranking, illustrating that board-level employee representatives treat these issues as priorities. 'Industrial relations' and 'vocational training', however, appear in the lower reaches of the ranking, bringing into question the argument that board-level employee representatives prioritise those items on which they have expertise.

Assessment of the variation between the country clusters and the SEs on the disaggregated basis reveals some marked differences in emphasis, although the rank order of the importance attached to agenda items is broadly similar throughout and is particularly so at the top of the ranking. There are no significant differences between CMEs, MMEs and EMEs regarding the prioritisation of issues concerning company strategy and finance. In particular, 'adoption/review of accounts and balance sheets' and 'investment in technology, real estate, etc.' exhibit no consistent differences between CMEs, MMEs and EMEs. Board-level employee representatives in Francophone MMEs and the EMEs of the NMS attach greater importance to the 'profit distribution, dividends or settlement of losses' than their counterparts in the CMEs and SEs, suggesting a greater concern on the distributive role implicit in board decision-making. Within the IGS, however, this issue is considered relatively unimportant. Board-level employee representatives in CMEs and the SEs, particularly Germanic CMEs, treat company restructuring as consistently more important than their counterparts in MMEs and EMEs. In the SEs, for example, the 'sale/closure of plants, relocation of production' and 'acquisitions or mergers' occupy the top two positions in the ranking. In contrast, Francophone board-level employee representatives downplay the importance of the 'sale/closure of plants, relocation of production', and those from the NMS attach relatively little importance to 'acquisitions and mergers' and the 'purchase/sale of subsidiaries'. The impact of board-level employee representatives on corporate restructuring is examined in greater detail in Chapter 5.

The 'employment situation' appears in the higher reaches of the ranking in all the country clusters and the SEs, although, in relative terms, Nordic and IGS board-level employee representatives tend to downplay the issue. The importance attached to the 'employment situation' confirms the centrality of the issue to the strategic approach taken by board-level employee representatives. Turning to the issues on which board-level employee representatives have specific expertise again reveals no consistent differences between the country clusters. Board-level employee representatives in Nordic CMEs and the EMEs of the NMS, for example, attach greater importance to 'health and safety' than do their counterparts in Germanic CMEs, the SEs and Francophone MMEs. 'Industrial relations' is a more important agenda item in Francophone MMEs and the EMEs of the NMS than in the Germanic or Nordic CMEs and the SEs. 'Environmental matters' are also downplayed by Germanic, SE and NMS board-level employee representatives compared to their counterparts elsewhere. The importance attached to the oversight of management by the board also shows no consistent variation by country clusters. Board-level employee representatives from Germanic CMEs and Francophone MMEs, for example, treat 'remuneration/compensation of senior managers' as more important than their counterparts from Nordic CMEs and the EMEs of the NMS.

What Influences the Content of the Agenda?

Chapter 2 demonstrated that systems of board-level employee representation are underpinned by legislation, which also stipulates the purpose and duties of the board and, by inference, aspects of the content of the agenda of board meetings (Büggel 2010). This stage of the assessment of the agenda of board meetings investigates the extent to which the requirements of the law are supplemented by other procedures in determining the agenda of the board. The potential impact of board-level employee representatives is thus assessed as the legal framework could grant them rights to include topics of the agenda of the board. The results are shown in Table 4.2.

Table 4.2 What Is the Most Important Influence on the Selection of Agenda Items for the Board Meeting?

		CMEs		MMEs	EMEs		
	All Country Clusters %	Germanic %	Nordic %	Francophone %	New Member States %	Ireland, Greece and Spain %	SEs %
Law	30.7	43.0	19.9	48.3	30.1	28.6	43.2
Manual of board procedures	25.4	29.8	24.5	13.1	19.9	21.5	27.1
Company's statute, articles of association	22.6	12.9	26.0	27.6	34.8	35.7	18.9
Negotiation between board members	11.0	11.1	12.2	7.6	7.9	7.1	8.1
Other	10.3	3.2	17.4	3.4	7.3	7.1	2.7
	N = 3,976	N = 1,437	N = 1,858	N = 145	N = 508	N = 28	N = 37

The 'all' column of Table 4.2 shows that although the law is the single most important influence on the content of the agenda, it is by no means the only influence. Procedures within the company are, in combination, more influential than the law: 'the manual of board procedures' combined with the 'company's statute, articles of association', for example, are viewed by board-level employee representatives as more influential than the law on the selection of agenda items for board meetings. Furthermore, 11.0 per cent of board-level employee representatives report that negotiation rather than formal procedures is the most influential factor on the selection of agenda items for the board meeting, indicating that informal processes remain influential on setting the agenda of the board.

There is considerable variation between country clusters in the influences that determine the content of the board agenda that is consistent with differences in industrial relations traditions rather than distinctions between market economies that characterise sociological approaches to corporate governance. Within the juridified industrial relations systems that characterise the Germanic CMEs and the SEs, for example, the impact of the law is pronounced and supplemented by that arising from the formal 'manual of board procedures'. Because Austrian and German company law provisions can be interpreted as granting each board member the right to include an item on the agenda of the board (Gahleitner 2013; Köstler et al. 2013), these findings suggest that Germanic and SE board-level employee representatives enjoy some flexibility in law while advancing their positions at the board. Similarly, the legal underpinning in the Francophone MMEs results in the law being the most influential factor, supplemented in these countries by the impact of the 'company's statute, articles of association'. In the Francophone countries, however, board-level employee representatives find themselves in a more uncertain position by comparison with their Germanic and SE counterparts as the right of an individual board member to include an item on the agenda of the board is not recognised in national legislation. The law in the Francophone cluster considers this a collective right, which requires all board-level employee representatives to address their demand collectively to have an item included on the agenda of the board.[3]

In contrast, within the terms of the Nordic tradition that places greater reliance on agreements concluded between the social partners, the impact of the law is secondary compared to that of formal procedures originating at company level based on 'company's statute, articles of association' and the 'manual of board procedures'. The inclusion of an item on the agenda of the board is thus flexible and dependent on understandings that are specific to the company. In the EMEs of the NMS the influence of the 'company's statute, articles of association', which are defined by shareholder representatives, is greater than that of the law and that of the manual of board procedures, the latter of which is usually defined by the board. Board-level employee representatives thus have limited room for manoeuvre to extend the agenda of the board to items of their specific concern.

In summary, there is no country cluster in which the board agenda is so narrow that it precludes an appropriate intensity of participation and, hence, an influence on the outcome of board-level decision-making. In a few instances it is difficult for all board members, including board-level employee representatives, to broaden the agenda of the board beyond the items specified in the law or in the statutes of the company. In general, however, there are opportunities to extend the agenda of board meetings beyond any formal requirements. Board-level employee representatives demonstrate sensitivity to the demands of market competition in assigning importance to agenda items, while ensuring that 'human resources' and the 'employment situation' are prioritised throughout. The next section of the chapter turns to the views of board-level employee representatives on the information made available to them to conduct the business of the board.

THE PROVISION OF INFORMATION

The provision of information to employee representatives is key to any system of employee participation. Provision in this context refers to the timeliness, adequacy and confidentiality of information. The initial focus is on issues of timeliness in examining the provision of information to board-level employee representatives in relation to the board meeting. The data are concerned with the formal provision of information for board meetings. It is acknowledged, of course, that informal channels of information may supplement the formal provision of information that is examined here. The section next assesses whether board-level employee representatives think that sufficient information is made available to them to enable them to fulfil their board-level employee responsibilities. Finally, the determinants of, and approaches to, confidentiality are examined to establish the extent to which the legal provisions identified in Chapter 2 influence board processes.

Is the Provision of Information Timely?

The timeliness of information provision is examined in Table 4.3, together with an assessment of issues excluded from the ambit of board-level employee representatives. Two points are noteworthy from the data on exclusions. First, it is apparent that almost all board-level employee representatives are adequately informed about their brief. In all countries, for example, the monitoring of company finances is included in the brief of board-level employee representatives and only 0.7 per cent of all respondents indicate that this issue is either 'not a board duty' or 'BLERs [board-level employee representatives] do not participate on this issue'. Second, there is marked variation within the country clusters in the practices of boards according to board-level employee representatives. To illustrate, 16.7 per cent of Nordic and 20.5 per cent of Francophone board-level employee representatives are not involved at the board level on the 'system of corporate governance' whereas 83.3 per cent and 79.5 per cent, respectively, of their counterparts are so engaged.

Table 4.3 Typically, How Long before the Board Meeting Is Information/Documentation Made Available to You?

				CMEs						MMEs		
	All Country Clusters $N = 3,964–4,054$			Germanic $N = 1,426–1,480$			Nordic $N = 1,872–1,895$			Francophone $N = 139–144$		
Information on	Index[1]	Not a board duty %	BLERs do not participate on this issue[2] %	Index	Not a board duty %	BLERs do not participate on this issue %	Index	Not a board duty %	BLERs do not participate on this issue %	Index	Not a board duty %	BLERs do not participate on this issue %
Company finances	3.70	0.2	0.5	4.15	/	0.3	3.41	0.3	0.6	3.19	0.7	0.7
Structure and organisation of the company	3.50	1.3	1.9	3.82	0.5	0.7	3.24	1.8	2.7	3.09	2.1	0.7
Human resource issues	3.45	7.2	2.8	3.82	3.6	1.4	3.11	10.3	3.8	3.18	12.1	6.4
Corporate social responsibility	3.43	7.6	3.6	3.71	6.4	3.5	3.19	8.0	3.5	3.19	7.9	4.3
Market policy of the company	3.39	2.1	2.5	3.62	0.7	1.8	3.18	3.3	3.1	3.12	3.6	1.4
System of corporate governance	3.35	5.7	6.7	3.65	1.0	5.9	3.07	9.3	7.4	2.95	9.9	10.6

Table 4.3 (Continued) Typically, How Long before the Board Meeting Is Information/Documentation Made Available to You?

	EMEs								
	New Member States $N = 498–507$			Ireland, Greece and Spain $N = 27–28$			SEs $N = 36–38$		
Information on	Index	Not a board duty %	BLERs do not participate on this issue %	Index	Not a board duty %	BLERs do not participate on this issue %	Index	Not a board duty %	BLERs do not participate on this issue %
Company finances	3.64	0.2	0.8	2.71	/	/	3.92	2.6	/
Structure and organisation of the company	3.69	1.6	2.8	2.96	/	/	3.84	2.6	/
Human resource issues	3.61	5.4	2.2	2.63	3.6	/	3.62	8.1	/
Corporate social responsibility	3.62	10.0	4.2	2.57	/	/	3.76	8.3	/
Market policy of the company	3.60	1.8	2.4	2.75	/	/	3.69	2.7	/
System of corporate governance	3.56	4.8	5.2	2.70	/	/	3.64	5.3	/

Notes:

1. The index data were calculated in two stages. In stage 1 the number of respondents who indicated that an issue was 'not a board duty' and 'BLERs do not participate on this issue' was subtracted from the value of *N*. In stage 2, points were awarded on a five-point scale: five points were awarded to respondents who answered that information was available 'more than two weeks' before the board meeting, four points when the answer was 'between one and two weeks', three points for 'between three days and one week', two points for 'within three days', and one point awarded where information was presented 'at the board meeting'. Points awarded on this basis were summed and divided by the value of *N* calculated in stage 1 to produce an average score. In practice, therefore, the higher the index score, the greater the time before the board meeting that the information was available.
2. 'BLERs' refers to board-level employee representatives.

The index column of Table 4.3 reports the timeliness of the information provision and reveals considerable variation in the time before board meetings that information is made available. The average index score for the 'all' column is 3.47, suggesting that information is generally made available 'between three days and one week' and 'between one and two weeks' before the board meeting. Board-level employee representatives thus have some time to prepare their positions for presentation at board meetings. The range of index scores for 'all' respondents varies from 3.35 for 'systems of corporate governance' to 3.70 for 'company finances'. Possible explanations of the variation in timeliness by topic that are not mutually exclusive include a recognition that different periods are required to assess information on different topics, hence variation in distribution dates, or that different timelines may reflect that some material is distributed on a 'for information' basis and is thus distributed later than the material requiring detailed analysis. A further explanatory factor may relate to the importance attached by board-level employee representatives to topics discussed at the board. Table 4.1 for example, showed that board-level employee representatives attached greatest importance to topics concerned with 'human resources', 'finance' and 'structure and organisation of the company'. Information on these three issues may be distributed earlier, or perceived as such, than that on other issues viewed as less important by board-level employee representatives. In other words, the importance of the issue to board-level employee representatives may influence the timing of the distribution of information on the topic or the perception thereof. This explanation of the variation in the timing of the availability of information, however, would have been more strongly supported had the highest index scores been attached to 'human resource issues', which were ranked as the most important issues discussed at the board by board-level employee representatives (see Table 4.1).

Comparing the average index scores for the country clusters also reveals considerable variation in practice. The lowest average index score is in IGS (2.72) and is consistent with Greek and Spanish legal provisions, which require agenda-related documents to be sent to board members at least two days prior to the meeting. The situation in Germanic CMEs, where an average index score of 3.80 is reported, confirms the impact of the legal framework insofar as Austrian and German law is read as requiring a minimum of one week between the distribution of information and the board meeting (Gahleitner 2013; Köstler et al. 2013). German board-level employee representatives report that they are generally satisfied with the timeliness of the information provision (Gerum 2007). The presence of a dual board structure is also associated with timeliness in the SEs and NMS, where the average index scores are 3.75 and 3.62, respectively. The lower index scores reported in the clusters where neither hard nor soft law rules and where monistic boards prevail support the argument that timeliness is influenced by the regulatory framework and the structure of corporate governance.

The average index scores in the Nordic (3.20) and Francophone (3.12) clusters, for example, are lower than elsewhere.

The average index scores regarding timeliness are thus not consistent with the sociological distinction between CMEs, MMEs and EMEs. No single country cluster replicates the ranking of index scores reported by 'all' respondents, further indicating wide-ranging variation in practices between country clusters. In the Germanic and Nordic CMEs, the SEs and in Francophone MMEs, for example, the highest index score is recorded for 'company finances'. Elsewhere, the highest index score is reported for the 'structure and organisation of the company' (NMS and IGS).

Is Sufficient Information Provided?

A second aspect of the provision of information is the adequacy of the information provided for the purposes of conducting the business of the board. The issue here is that if information is made available in a timely manner yet is insufficient in content, the board-level employee representative cannot be expected to engage adequately in decision-making. To explore this issue, board-level employee representatives were asked to indicate whether the information they received for board meetings is sufficient. Table 4.4 presents the results.

The 'all' column of Table 4.4 shows that fewer than 25 per cent of board-level employee representatives 'always' receive sufficient information for board meetings. That a minority of board-level employee representatives 'always' receive sufficient information lends further support to the argument that shortcomings in the provision of information may impair the performance of board-level employee representatives. Fewer than 10 per cent of board-level employee representatives, however, report that they 'rarely' or

Table 4.4 Do You Think That Information Received for Board Meetings Is Sufficient?

		CMEs		MMEs	EMEs		
	All Country Clusters %	Germanic %	Nordic %	Francophone %	New Member States %	Ireland, Greece and Spain %	SEs %
Always	22.8	22.6	20.7	11.8	34.1	21.5	31.5
Often	51.9	53.2	51.8	48.6	48.6	57.1	42.1
Sometimes	16.7	16.7	17.3	27.1	12.8	10.7	21.1
Rarely	6.9	6.7	7.5	11.1	3.5	10.7	/
Never	1.7	0.8	2.7	1.4	1.0	/	5.3
	N = 4,063	N = 1,478	N = 1,905	N = 144	N = 508	N = 28	N = 38

'never' receive sufficient information for board meetings, suggesting that only a small minority of board-level employee representatives is in practice excluded from participating meaningfully in board meetings.

There is also variation in the pattern of information provision in the different country clusters. Combining the 'always' and 'often' scores, for example, produces a range of results for the CMEs varying from 72.5 per cent for the Nordic countries to 75.8 per cent for the Germanic countries. The result for the Germanic cluster is consistent with previous empirical findings that show a high degree of satisfaction among German board-level employee representatives regarding the quality of the information provision (Jürgens et al. 2008). Similar data for the other country clusters fall outside of this range: NMS, 82.7 per cent; IGS, 78.6 per cent; and the Francophone MMEs, 60.4 per cent, although the SEs, at 73.6 per cent, are within the limits reported from the CMEs. The low score recorded for the Francophone countries suggests that more adversarial industrial relations practices are more likely to be associated with the provision of insufficient information. Furthermore, board-level employee representatives from Francophone countries are also the most likely to report sufficient information being available only 'rarely'. The relatively high combined 'always' and 'often' scores for the Germanic countries and the NMS confirms a positive impact of juridification and the presence of a dual board structure on the practices associated with the provision of information.

How Is Confidential Information Treated?

A third aspect of the provision of information concerns confidentiality. The confidentiality of information is a contested issue. Assessments of the practices of European works councils (EWCs), for example, show that managements attempt to widen the scope of confidentiality, hence restricting the distribution of information beyond the members of the EWC. In contrast, EWC representatives strive to limit confidentiality in order to facilitate the distribution of information released at EWCs to interested parties beyond the EWC (Hume-Rothery 2004; Gold and Rees 2013). In the context of board practices, similar tensions are anticipated insofar as board-level employee representatives may wish to liaise with other representative institutions within the company and trade unions in order to assess and respond to information provided at the board. Furthermore, some critics of board-level employee representation argue that employee representatives lack discretion and fail to treat material as confidential even though a legal duty of confidentiality may exist (Davies and Hopt 2013). This view illustrates how the assumption of managerial prerogative remains entrenched as contested aspects of confidentiality are downplayed. A recent Danish legal case, for example, confirmed the legality of board-level employee representatives consulting with union officers on issues that have arisen at the board on the condition such information disclosure is necessary for the satisfactory performance of the duties of the board-level employee representative (Lavesen and Kragh-Stetting 2011). This Danish case demonstrates that respect of the duty of confidentiality can be concurrent with a capacity of board-level employee representatives to articulate their activities with those of other institutions of labour representation (Hamskär 2012). To address these issues the determination of what is confidential is examined followed by an assessment of how confidentiality is treated in practice.[4]

Table 2.3 demonstrated that, with the exceptions of Greece, Ireland, Norway and Sweden, the law intervenes in the determination of confidentiality in the countries covered by this study. It is thus surprising that when asked who or what determines what is confidential only 43.7 per cent of 'all' board-level employee representatives regard 'hard law, legal texts' as determining what is confidential.[5] Although 'hard law, legal texts' are most influential in determining confidentiality, the point remains that a majority of board-level employee representatives fail to recognise a primary influence arising from legislation. National legislation on confidentiality may underpin an explanation of the differences between country clusters, insofar as most national legislation provides only a general definition of confidentiality rather than specifying detailed requirements on each topic, with the exception of information relating to the possibility of insider trading in listed companies.[6] There is thus some leeway in the manner in which board-level employee representatives can interpret confidentiality. General principles may be laid out in legislation, but these have to be implemented in practice, suggesting some scope for variation regarding the determination of confidentiality. The results presented in Table 4.5 apply to two types of statement. The views of board-level employee representatives towards documents in general are reported in the upper panel of Table 4.5 while the lower panel identifies views on documents with a specific subject matter.

Reference to the data on documents in general confirms that confidentiality is contested in a manner similar to that within EWCs. Only 59.1 per cent of board-level employee representatives, for example, treat 'documents marked confidential' as such. In other words, more than 40 per cent of board-level employee representatives do not treat documents marked as confidential in such a manner. These results downgrade the importance of the determinants of confidentiality insofar as they suggest that board-level employee representatives do not universally respect the status 'confidential', as assigned by management, and may assess confidentiality according to other criteria. An example of another criterion explicitly recognised in the legal definition of confidentiality in four countries (Czech Republic, Finland, Luxembourg, Slovakia) and the SEs concerns whether information disclosure is detrimental to the interests of the company (see Table 2.3). The leeway in the interpretation of general principles of confidentiality laid out in national legislation does not seem to create a great deal of difficulty in practice, as only 5.7 per cent of board-level employee representatives treat no document as confidential irrespective of the status of the document.

Table 4.5 What Is Defined as Confidential and Non-Communicable Regarding the Affairs of the Board?

		CMEs		MMEs	EMEs		
	All Country Clusters %	Germanic %	Nordic %	Franco-phone %	New Member States %	Ireland, Greece and Spain %	SEs %
Documents marked confidential	59.1	47.7	66.0	46.9	71.5	60.7	71.1
Every document	27.9	21.8	35.3	34.0	15.7	50.0	18.4
No document is confidential	5.7	3.2	6.4	10.9	8.8	7.1	2.6
Information about the strategic plan of senior management	42.8	47.7	41.4	31.3	37.1	32.1	60.5
Information about the budget/ financial circumstances of the company	31.2	33.3	32.1	17.7	25.1	35.7	42.1
Information about investment budgets	24.3	23.0	27.8	16.3	17.5	21.4	39.5
	N = 4,155	N = 1,554	N = 1,917	N = 147	N = 509	N = 28	N = 38

Note:
Respondents could tick more than one box for this question; hence, the sum of the percentage data is more than 100 per cent.

Board-level employee representatives were not asked whether they thought that documents marked confidential were worthy of that status, so it is not possible to ascertain whether the failure to respect the status 'confidential' was a rejection of confidentiality *per se* or of the decision of those who marked the document confidential.

The extent to which confidentiality of documents marked as such is respected is pronounced in the EMEs (71.5 per cent), the SEs (71.1 per cent) and the Nordic CMEs (66.0 per cent). The processes underpinning confidentiality in these three clusters differ, however, with 'hard law, legal texts' being the most influential in the EMEs and SEs, whereas in the Nordic

CMEs the 'chair of the board' and the 'CEO' are influential determinants of confidentiality.[7] In contrast, in the Francophone MMEs and the Germanic CMEs 'documents marked confidential' are less likely to be treated as confidential by board-level employee representatives. The adversarial industrial relations that characterise the Francophone countries may contribute to an explanation of why Francophone board-level employee representatives are suspicious of confidentiality provisions that are subject to a marked influence from the 'chair of the board'. That 10.9 per cent of Francophone board-level employee representatives treat no documents as confidential further supports this argument. Explaining the situation in the Germanic CMEs is far from straightforward as it is 'hard law, legal texts' and 'the board procedures' that are the principal determinants of confidentiality, yet only 47.7 per cent of Germanic board-level employee representatives treat documents marked as confidential as such. A partial explanation may lie in the wording of the legal definition of the duty of confidentiality, which in Austria and Germany allows for interpretation to the extent that a 'confidential' stamp on a document is less important than knowing whether the disclosure of information could harm the company (Gahleitner 2013; Köstler et al. 2013). A further contributory factor to an explanation of this situation may lie in the possibility of information exchange between board-level employee representatives and other institutions of employee representation within the company, primarily the works council. This tendency may be enhanced as no fewer than 72.5 per cent of Germanic board-level employee representatives hold positions on works councils (see Chapter 3). In Austria and Germany confidentiality provisions laid out in the Companies Act apply to board-level employee representatives, yet the information right granted to the works council allows board-level employee representatives the possibility of exchanging and discussing information with works councillors (Gahleitner and Preiss 2003:40; Köstler et al. 2013). Irrespective of the explanation of the treatment of confidentiality by Germanic board-level employee representatives, it is acknowledged that their practice conforms with legal requirements because there are very few cases of confidentiality violation in Germany (Raabe 2005).

Turning to the specific documents mentioned in Table 4.5, the 'all' data indicate that no topic is treated as confidential by more than half of the board-level employee representatives. There is a clear hierarchy of respect for confidentiality with 'information about the strategic plan of senior management' more likely to be respected than 'information about the budget/financial circumstances of the company', which, in turn, is more likely to be respected that 'information about investment budgets'. Only in IGS is this rank order changed, with 'information about the budget/financial circumstances of the company' most likely to be viewed by board-level employee representatives as confidential.

In summary, although information is regularly available a week before the board meeting, there is a marked variation in the timing of the distribution of information dependent on the topic, with information on topics viewed as important by board-level employee representatives tending to be distributed earlier. The adequacy of information is broadly satisfactory, although only 22.8 per cent of board-level employee representatives report 'always' to be in receipt of sufficient information. Confidentiality is a contested issue within the board. A large number of board-level employee representatives do not respect on all occasions the status 'confidential' as marked on documents. Many board-level employee representatives base their understanding of confidentiality on other criteria. Interpretation of what is confidential varies between country clusters with the influence of management on confidentiality being particularly marked in the Nordic CMEs.

INTERVENTIONS MADE BY BOARD-LEVEL EMPLOYEE REPRESENTATIVES AT THE BOARD

Incorporation and contestation are among the themes that resonate throughout this study. The objective of this section is to examine aspects of these two themes in the context of the interventions made by board-level employee representatives at the board. The incorporation theme originates in industrial relations literature and, as evidenced in Chapter 1, is cited within several European trade union movements as the reason why board-level employee representation is considered an inappropriate strategy. To examine whether extant board-level employee representatives are subject to incorporation, this section assesses the character of their interventions at the board. Earlier in this chapter it was established that board-level employee representatives pursue a set of objectives that originate in the interests of their constituents and, regarding confidentiality, these interests do not necessarily overlap with those of other stakeholders, with the consequence that processes and decisions at the board level may be contested.

Interventions made by board-level employee representatives at the board are indicators of the extent of incorporation and contestation within the board. Put bluntly, if board-level employee representatives are incorporated, very few interventions would be anticipated, and those that take place would not have a significant impact. Similarly, the more contested decision-making is at the board, the greater the likelihood of interventions from board-level employee representatives to delay decision-making or to refer decision-making elsewhere. Table 4.6 lists seven forms of intervention that can be made by board-level employee representatives.

The data in Table 4.6 indicate that board-level employee representatives intervene with very different frequencies on the different forms of intervention. More than 70 per cent of 'all' board-level employee representatives, for example, had 'required a topic to be included on the board's agenda' compared to only 2.8 per cent that had 'called an extraordinary shareholder meeting'. No fewer than 27.0 per cent of board-level employee

Table 4.6 Interventions Made by Board-Level Employee Representatives at the Board

				CMEs						MMEs		
	All Country Clusters N = 4,007–4,086			Germanic N =1,472–1,519			Nordic N = 1,848–1,886			Francophone N = 141–145		
Have you . . .	Yes %	No %	I do not have the possibility to do so %	Yes %	No %	I do not have the possibility to do so %	Yes %	No %	I do not have the possibility to do so %	Yes %	No %	I do not have the possibility to do so %
Required a topic to be included on the board's agenda?	72.0	27.0	1.0	71.6	28.1	0.3	73.0	26.1	0.9	55.9	36.5	7.6
Requested a report on company affairs?	58.5	40.1	1.4	64.2	35.3	0.5	51.1	47.4	1.5	35.2	58.5	6.3
Delayed a board decision?	42.5	54.3	3.2	58.0	40.3	1.7	34.0	63.1	2.9	43.4	46.3	10.3
Prevented a decision being made by the board (e.g. when unanimity is required)?	21.7	71.5	6.8	26.3	66.3	7.4	17.3	77.1	5.6	20.3	66.4	13.3
Called an extraordinary board meeting?	15.6	79.8	4.6	25.1	72.1	2.8	8.5	87.0	4.5	13.9	72.9	13.2
Prevented a board decision from being implemented?	13.6	78.7	7.7	18.6	73.4	8.0	9.7	84.6	5.7	5.6	74.3	20.1
Called an extraordinary shareholder meeting?	2.8	83.9	13.3	1.9	82.4	15.7	3.2	86.7	10.1	2.8	71.7	25.5

Note:
Respondents were asked to indicate 'yes', 'no' or 'I do not have the possibility to do so'. The sum of the figures for each intervention is thus 100 per cent.

Table 4.6 (Continued) Interventions Made By Board-Level Employee Representatives at the Board

	EMEs								
	New Member States N = 508–509			Ireland, Greece and Spain N = 27			SEs N = 38		
Have you . . .	Yes %	No %	I do not have the possibility to do so %	Yes %	No %	I do not have the possibility to do so %	Yes %	No %	I do not have the possibility to do so %
Required a topic to be included on the board's agenda?	73.2	25.0	1.8	88.9	11.1	/	65.8	34.2	/
Requested a report on company affairs?	74.1	23.6	2.3	81.5	18.5	/	65.8	34.2	/
Delayed a board decision?	26.9	66.8	6.3	55.6	37.0	7.4	50.0	44.7	5.3
Prevented a decision being made by the board (e.g. when unanimity is required)?	23.6	69.1	7.3	44.4	44.4	11.2	23.7	68.4	7.9
Called an extraordinary board meeting?	14.1	79.2	6.7	11.1	63.0	25.9	13.2	81.5	5.3
Prevented a board decision from being implemented?	14.4	75.6	10.0	29.6	55.6	14.8	18.4	68.4	13.2
Called an extraordinary shareholder meeting?	4.3	81.8	13.9	/	70.4	29.6	5.3	73.6	21.1

representatives, however, had not even 'required a topic to be included on the board's agenda', indicating a failure to intervene at the board among a substantial minority of board-level employee representatives. In contrast, some wide-ranging interventions are also apparent. More than 13 per cent of board-level employee representatives had 'prevented a board decision from being implemented' and 'called an extraordinary board meeting', and more than 21 per cent had 'prevented a decision being made by the board'.

In terms of incorporation and contestation the 'all' evidence presented in Table 4.6 is thus far from straightforward. The passivity of more than a quarter of board-level employee representatives in not inserting items on to the agenda of the board certainly suggests an absence of contestation at the board and, at the very least, the absence of independent strategies, if not incorporation, among some board-level employee representatives. Conversely, it is also apparent that those board-level employee representatives who make more substantial interventions are not incorporated and are prepared to contest board-level decision-making.

The variation between the country clusters in the processes associated with the board is also apparent in the character of the interventions made by board-level employee representatives. Only the board-level employee representatives in the Germanic cluster, for example, replicate the rank order illustrated by the 'all' data. Elsewhere particular issues are either accentuated or downplayed.

The average 'yes' score for the interventions made by 'all' board-level employee representatives is 32.4 per cent. The average 'yes' scores for the country clusters reveals a pattern that is not consistent with the distinctions drawn in sociological approaches to corporate governance, but can be partially explained by reference to the industrial relations traditions emphasised within the different country clusters. In descending order, the average 'yes' scores for the country clusters are: IGS, 44.4 per cent; Germanic cluster, 37.9 per cent; NMS 33.0 per cent; Nordic cluster 28.1 per cent; and the Francophone countries, 25.3 per cent. The average 'yes' score for the SEs is in the middle of the range exhibited within the national clusters at 34.6 per cent. There are thus marked differences in the average 'yes' scores between the CMEs. Furthermore, the adversarial industrial relations characteristic of IGS and the Francophone countries are associated with both the highest and the lowest average 'yes' scores.

The relatively low average 'yes' score for the Nordic cluster, however, may result from the long-standing reliance in Nordic industrial relations on reaching agreements and shared positions between the social partners. If an agreement or a shared position is reached within the board there is no tactical advantage to be gained by board-level employee representatives, for example, in intervening by precluding the board from making or implementing decisions or by referring issues to further meetings. In other words, it is the perceived purpose of board-level employee representation that may contribute to the low average 'yes' scores in the Nordic countries.

The low average 'yes' scores in Francophone countries suggest a relatively superficial engagement by board-level employee representatives compared with counterparts in the other country clusters. Francophone board-level employee representatives may make relatively few interventions of the type listed in Table 4.6 because they take the view that such interventions are unlikely to have much impact and, thus, there is little point in making them. Alternatively, the low level of intervention by Francophone board-level employee representatives may be the result of Francophone board-level employee representatives making different forms of intervention to those listed in Table 4.6.[8] The relatively low rate of intervention by Francophone board-level employee representatives, however, is associated with less adequate information provisions (see Table 4.4) and information available in an untimely manner compared to the other country clusters (see Table 4.3), suggesting that Francophone board-level employee representation has a different character to that practiced elsewhere. These issues are addressed in more detail in Chapter 5.

The pattern of intervention by board-level employee representatives within the Germanic cluster and in SEs is broadly similar with about a half of the representatives reporting that they had 'delayed a board decision'. While this result may be influenced by the adoption of SE status by companies that were initially registered in Germany, it also reflects a degree of maturity within the SEs. By comparison within the EMEs in the NMS fewer than 25 per cent of board-level employee representatives have 'delayed a board decision', lower than in any other cluster and suggesting that the recent establishment of board-level employee representation in these countries may impinge on the pattern of intervention.

CONCLUSION

Chapter 4 has identified the practices undertaken during the board meeting and assessed arguments arising from the corporate governance and industrial relations points of departure in the light of these practices. Five points arise from the examination of the agenda and processes of board meetings. First, the agenda of the board and the provision of information in all the country clusters and the SEs comprised sufficient breadth and quality to sustain an appropriate intensity of participation, which, in turn, suggests that there is potential for, at least, partial participation in each of the country clusters and in the SEs. Second, 'human resources' and the 'employment situation' figure prominently as priority agenda items pursued by board-level employee representatives. Coupled with the widespread possibilities of including agenda items of interest to board-level employee representatives these results confirm the view that board-level employee representatives are able to ensure that issues of their central concern are raised at the board. Third, board-level employee representatives are sensitive to the demands of market competition in their priorities for the board insofar as they display an awareness of issues concerning company strategy and finance. Accusations that board-level employee representatives are solely concerned with the defence of sectional interests at the board are thus misplaced. Fourth, the duty of confidentiality is not problematic for most board-level employee representatives who either respect documents marked as confidential or apply an interpretation of confidentiality that ensures information that would harm the company is not released. A small minority of respondents (5.7 per cent), however, treats no documents as confidential. Fifth, practices within the Nordic CMEs differ from these in the Germanic CMEs insofar as the influences on the setting of the agenda of the board are more likely to come from within the company in the Nordic CMEs and the pattern of interventions made at the board differ. Both of these variations may result from the contrast between the juridification of Germanic practices and the reliance on the social partners reaching agreements and shared positions in the Nordic CMEs.

The implications of these findings for the corporate governance literature are wide-ranging. Political perspectives on corporate governance argue that board-level employee representatives will pursue different interests from those that represent managerial and shareholder interests (Roe 2003). By implication, advocates of financial perspectives would agree that the inclusion of employee representatives on the board would introduce an additional stakeholder interest and further dilute the concern of the board with shareholder interests; thus, the exclusion of employee representatives is key to corporate success (Fama 1980; Jensen and Meckling 1976). The expectations of both political and financial perspectives are partially met insofar as 'human resources' are the most important priorities of board-level employee representatives. Issues relating to company performance and finance, however, are also assigned considerable importance by board-level employee representatives, indicating that the one-dimensional pursuit of the interests of the workforce suggested by political and financial perspectives within the corporate governance literature is well wide of the mark in practice.

Sociological approaches to corporate governance draw distinctions between the intensity of the interlinkages between and within companies in identifying CMEs, MMEs and EMEs as categories within which board-level employee representation may be implemented. Advocates of the sociological approach to corporate governance thus argue that different board practices and outcomes should be associated with the distinction between CMEs, MMEs and EMEs. With reference to the agenda of the board this expectation was largely fulfilled insofar as board-level employee representatives in Germanic and Nordic CMEs were more likely to assign 'human resources' a greater importance that their counterparts in the MMEs and EMEs. Although Francophone board-level employee representatives were the least likely to intervene at board meetings, their counterparts in the EMEs of the NMS were comparable in their rates of intervention at the board meeting to

Germanic and Nordic board-level employee representatives, contrary to the expectations of sociological approaches.

From within industrial relations literature, opposition to board-level employee representation is expressed in terms of the likely incorporation of employee representatives into processes directed towards the achievement of managerial and shareholder objectives rather than representing the interests of the workforce (Clarke 1977). There is no evidence to suggest the incorporation of extant board-level employee representatives has occurred on a large scale. To the contrary, the agendas of board meetings address issues relevant to the workforce *and* to the challenges faced by companies in an increasingly internationalised economy. Discussions at the board level are thus not exclusively concerned with the interests of management and shareholders. By inference, of course, these findings confirm the tension faced by board-level employee representatives in attempting to reconcile social and economic dimensions within the company. Similarly, the rate and the pattern of interventions made by board-level employee representatives suggest the pursuit of an independent agenda rather than a dependence on management for strategic direction. Also central to the industrial relations literature are the issues of the intensity of participation, the nature of participation and industrial democracy. The breadth of the agenda of board meetings, coupled with the capacity of board-level employee representatives to ensure that issues of their central concern are raised at board meetings, confirms the potential for an appropriate intensity of participation. The objective of Chapter 5 is to assess whether board-level employee representatives realise this potential in exerting power at board meetings.

NOTES

1. Following the convention established in Chapter 3 the data in the 'all' column refer to all the country clusters and exclude the data from the SEs.
2. The complete list of disaggregated individual agenda items in the order they appeared from 'all' respondents is 'adoption/review of accounts and balance sheets', 'sale/closure of plants, relocation of production', 'employment situation (likely trends)', 'investment (technology, real estate, etc.)', 'health and safety', 'acquisitions or mergers', 'product market policy', 'appointment/removal of management board/executive committee/senior managers', 'profit distribution, dividends or settlement of losses', 'research and development', 'purchase/sale of subsidiaries', 'industrial relations (collective bargaining and trade unions)', 'taking out of loans and credits', 'environmental matters', 'remuneration/compensation of senior managers', 'increase/reduction in the company's share capital', 'gender policy, promotion of women' and 'appointment/removal of auditors'.
3. In Luxembourg, for example, where employee representatives comprise a third of the board when present, the labour code specifies that the chair of the board is obliged to open the agenda to any item on the proviso that it is proposed by a third of the board members (Article L426–11).

4. Chapter 6 explores in detail the issues associated with the articulation of the activities of board-level employee representatives with those of other institutions of labour representation and how approaches to confidentiality impinge on processes of articulation.
5. This figure is taken from responses to a question otherwise unreported in this volume. The complete range of 'all' responses to the question 'who or what determines what is confidential?' are as follows: 'hard law, legal texts', 43.7 per cent; 'the board procedures', 39.3 per cent; 'chair of the board', 34.5 per cent; 'board members through negotiation', 19.1 per cent; 'CEO, if different from the chair', 15.2 per cent; 'each board member acting individually', 14.0 per cent; 'soft law, recommendations or guidelines', 11.7 per cent; and 'other', 3.4 per cent.
6. 'Inside information' is defined by Regulation 596/2014 on market abuse as 'information of a precise nature, which has not been made public relating directly or indirectly to one or more issuers, or to one or more financial instruments, and, which, if it were made public, would be likely to have a significant effect on the prices of those financial instruments or on the price of related derivative financial instruments' (Article 7.1 (a)).
7. This statement is based on the results from the question referred to the note 6, disaggregated into the different country clusters.
8. Other forms of intervention not listed in Table 4.6, for example, may involve leaving the board meeting or presenting a joint statement prepared by all board-level employee representatives.

5 The Exercise of Power at the Board

Chapter 4 established that board-level employee representatives have the potential to exert power within the board insofar as issues they consider important appear on the agenda of the board meeting; they receive sufficient information, much of it in a timely manner; and many intervene at board meetings. This chapter establishes whether board-level employee representatives exercise power at the board and thus change the character and content of strategic decision-making at the board. That is, do board-level employee representatives convert the potential arising from the intensity of participation generated in the board agenda and processes to the co-determination of strategic decision-making, thereby achieving *de facto* what was intended *de jure*? It is acknowledged from the outset that an analysis of the exercise of power by board-level employee representatives involves more than a consideration of their activities at the board, the sole sphere of concern of corporate governance. Chapter 6 thus assesses the extent to which the activities of board-level employee representatives are articulated with those of other representative industrial relations institutions within and outside of the company as a means of exerting power.

Expectations on issues of power are in relatively short supply within the corporate governance literature. Sociological approaches to corporate governance, for example, draw the key distinction between an LME and a CME in terms of the presence of representation at board level rather than the power exerted by board-level employee representatives at the board (Hall and Soskice 2001a). Sociological explanations focus on the presence or absence of institutions rather than the manner in which members of the board interact. Although specific expectations on power exercised within the board are absent from sociological approaches to corporate governance, the participation of board-level employee representatives in subcommittees established from within the board and in pre-meetings with management would be anticipated to take place at a higher rate when coordination is developed compared to the Francophone MMEs and the EMEs of the NMS, where coordination is not as sophisticated. Similarly, political perspectives acknowledge differences in the priorities of different stakeholder groups on the board but do not speculate as to how these may be manifest in terms of the power exerted by board-level employee representatives within the board (Roe 2003). In short, within the corporate governance literature there is little consideration of 'if' and 'how' board-level employee representatives exert power.

From within the industrial relations perspective board-level employee representation is an element of industrial democracy. As participants in industrial democracy, board-level employee representatives would be anticipated to exercise power over the outcome of board decision-making processes. Chapter 4 demonstrated a potential for the exercise of power by board-level employee representatives insofar as the agenda of the board was sufficiently wide ranging to allow for the generation of an intensity of participation (Knudsen 1995:8–13). Similar to the corporate governance literature, industrial relations scholars have focused on the presence, and the form of board-level employee representation rather than the processes through which power is exercised. Likert (1961), for example, treats participation and power as unified insofar as the two processes are incorporated in practice.

In a development of Likert's formulation, distinctions were drawn between pseudo-participation, partial participation and full participation (Pateman 1970:67–84). Pseudo-participation refers to circumstances where management exploit participatory mechanisms to generate the impression among employee representatives of participation, even though the latter have neither power nor influence over decision-making. In contrast, partial participation refers to circumstances in which employee representatives do not have power equal to that of management and thus cannot co-determine decision-making but are in a position to influence the outcome of decision-making thanks to either information or consultation procedures. Consultation, for example, allows a board-level employee representative to present an opinion, which may have an impact, but not necessarily so. Finally, full participation assumes equality of power among the parties to determine the outcome of decision-making.

Early studies that explicitly addressed board-level employee representation and power are far from conclusive but question whether employee representatives exert power over strategic decisions (Cordova 1982; Mulder 1971). Board-level employee representation may result in a capacity to change managerial strategic decision-making, but is not certain to do so, thus highlighting a theoretical distinction between board-level employee representation and power (Lund 1980). The same author argued that drawing a distinction between scope and degree facilitates the analysis of power: where scope refers to the number of areas in management's activity where board-level employee representatives participate and degree refers to the number of managerial decision-making stages in which worker representatives within the company participate. Chapter 4 has shown that the scope of board-level employee representation is generally viewed as satisfactory by representatives. Although Chapter 6 does not assess the number of managerial decision-making stages in which workers participate, it examines the articulation between board-level employee representatives and their counterparts within the company who sit on other representative bodies.

More recent analyses of influence and power exerted by board-level employee representatives over strategic corporate decision-making rely on either country case studies or comparative research and are far from conclusive. In Sweden, for example, board-level employee representatives were shown to have influenced local decisions and conditions but were much less successful in changing the strategic decisions of corporations (Wheeler 2002). Substantiating this position are findings showing that Swedish board-level employee representatives have limited influence over agenda setting and a growing proportion do not receive requested information, thus restricting their capacity to exert power over strategic decision-making (Movitz and Levinson 2013). Similarly, in Finland a majority of board-level employee representatives were able to exert some influence on issues such as 'monitoring the business' and 'improving cooperation between management and employees', but only small minorities were able to exert much influence on 'strategic decision-making' (12 per cent) and the 'organisation of production' (3 per cent) (Sairo 2001). In contrast, almost 30 per cent of Danish board-level employee representatives thought that they had 'much influence' over strategic decision-making compared to 7 per cent who viewed themselves as having 'no influence' (Rose 2008). The Danish situation is almost reproduced in Norway where 30 per cent of board-level employee representatives have 'much or very much influence' and 15 per cent have 'little or no influence' (Hagen 2011:135).

Moving beyond the Nordic countries, Polish research concluded that the capacities of board-level employee representatives 'to influence the position of the board are limited' (Skupień 2011:157), and in Slovenia, board-level employee representatives 'behave more as a firm's shareholders than its stakeholders, suggesting a degree of incorporation (Prašnikar and Gregorič 2002:289). Although French data do not suggest incorporation, they demonstrate that more than 90 per cent of board-level employee representatives participate at the board by means of information or consultation and are thus unable to exert power over strategic corporate decision-making (Conchon 2013a). In contrast, recent developments within the German system of corporate governance have enhanced the proactive role of the supervisory board in strategic decision-making, thus ensuring that employee representatives now have more influence over strategic corporate decision-making than when legislation was adopted in the 1970s (Gerum 2007; Jürgens et al. 2008).

Comparative interview evidence reports that the influence exerted by twenty board-level employee representatives is qualified while also demonstrating that they thought early involvement in strategic decision-making processes improves the quality of decision-making by introducing the views and interest of labour (Gold 2011). Similarly, a more wide-ranging study based on 282 questionnaire responses from board-level employee representatives in nine countries concludes that they do not believe their influence to be great, although very few felt that they had no influence, and that the extent of influence varied by topic with influence being most marked in health and safety, the environment and industrial relations (Carley 2005; O'Kelly 2006).

Although the approach adopted here allows assessment of these case study and comparative findings in the light of more detailed evidence, two further approaches to power inform the analysis of the survey data. Institutional power is the focus of the first approach. The support for the institution of board-level employee representation may vary in terms of the content of legislation (see Chapter 2), employer attitudes for or against, and the degree of embeddedness of board-level employee representation with other institutions of worker representation within or outside the company. An objective of this investigation is to establish whether the institutional power of board-level employee representation has been 'hollowed out' as part of the neo-liberal project (Crouch 2004, 2011). In this context, the deployment of power resources by board-level employee representatives is key. Such power resources may take the form of communicative power, whereby board-level employee representatives are able to posit alternatives to the strategic choices made by management (Munck 2000; Urban 2012); collaborative power resources, in the form of allies within the board who, of course, may vary on an issue-by-issue basis (Gourevitch and Shinn 2005); and strategic power resources, requiring the use of scarce resources to best effect (Ganz 2000; Gumbrell-McCormick and Hyman 2013). These aspects of power are examined in Chapter 5 by reference to tactical manoeuvring within the board and in Chapter 6 in terms of articulation.

A second approach to power utilised here builds on the observation that power relations are not based solely on participation in decision-making processes (Dahl 1961). Board-level employee representatives, for example, may exclude themselves from involvement in particular decisions on the recognition that involvement may have adverse political consequences. Board-level employee representatives have also been shown not to criticise management because they wish to demonstrate loyalty to management (Lund 1980). Furthermore, managers and shareholder members of the board may meet together before the plenary meeting of the board to establish a common or shared position before meeting employee representatives, thereby avoiding the release of sensitive information to employee representatives (Charkham 2005). These examples illustrate the 'latent power' of management in shaping circumstances to mitigate or preclude a challenge to their self-perceived strategic decision-making prerogative and suggest that 'non-decisions' are as important as decisions in an assessment of power (Bachrach and Baratz 1962, 1963). Taking this argument still further, Lukes argues that a complete analysis of power requires the integration of an examination of the structure of the roles of actors as well as their roles in practice in order to understand how systems 'prevent demands from becoming political issues or even from being made' (1974:38). To operationalise this approach to any decision-making process is extremely complex (Lukes 1974:46–56). In the context of board-level employee representation, however, this chapter examines where, from the perspective of board-level employee representatives, board decisions are made in practice and whether board-level employee representatives engage with senior management in pre-meetings to establish joint positions that may subsequently be taken to the plenary board meeting.

To examine these issues the chapter is composed of three sections. The first section assesses the priorities of board-level employee representatives when companies restructure and the influence that they consider themselves as bringing to bear on such events. The second section further establishes the character of the power that board-level employee representatives exert on decision-making and identifies where board-level employee representatives think strategic company decision-making takes place. The third section identifies the extent of coordination among board-level employee representatives and between board-level employee representatives and senior managers prior to the plenary board meeting.

Chapter 5 also includes bivariate analyses. Some survey questions relating to the power of board-level employee representatives are cross-tabulated with the following independent variables: board size; board composition, as measured by the proportion of employee representatives on the board; the organisational level at which the board is located, either a controlled or an independent company in the language used in Chapter 3; and the sector of activity of the company. Previous empirical studies demonstrated the influence of these variables on the practices of board-level employee representation (Jansen 2013; Jürgens et al. 2008). Three other variables are also used in these bivariate analyses. First, employment size is used, because it is a critical variable within the corporate governance perspective regarding the extent of board-level employee representation (see Hagen 2014) and within the industrial relations perspective regarding the practices of worker involvement (see Eurofound 2015). In addition, gender and the structure of the board, defined in terms of whether it is monistic or dual, are used as variables on the grounds that the relationship between gender and corporate governance is of current importance to policymaking in the field and that different expectations regarding the practices of the board are anticipated to arise from its structure (see Chapter 3). As a rule, the results of the bivariate tests are reported only when a significant correlation is established.[1]

The chapter argues that a substantial minority of board-level employee representatives are effectively precluded from exercising power over board decision-making and those who can exert power do so in different ways dependent on the country cluster within which they are based.

BOARD-LEVEL REPRESENTATION AND COMPANY RESTRUCTURING

Levels of transnational corporate restructuring involving companies with European interests have been pronounced since the 1980s when proposals for the single European market were mooted and legislation to promote such a market adopted by the EU (Buiges 1993; *Acquisitions Monthly*, various). Furthermore, the norms characteristic of LMEs are increasingly influential on the process of corporate restructuring in Europe (Edwards 2004; Pulignano 2006). The EC cited the then anticipated scale of company restructuring as a reason for the introduction of EWCs as a means of allowing worker representatives the opportunity to influence the terms on which transnational company restructuring takes place. Most EWCs have not influenced company restructuring as worker representatives have neither been informed nor consulted in a timely manner (Waddington 2011:102–107). Board-level employee representatives, however, are, in theory, in better positions to influence company restructuring as the decision to restructure either is made or is ratified by the board. Furthermore, legislation in many countries requires the board to agree to a major restructuring proposal before the policy is implemented. In other words, board-level employee representatives should be close to the decision to restructure if not directly involved. An examination of the priorities pursued by board-level employee representatives during company restructuring and the influence they exert over company restructuring is thus a 'test' of board-level employee representation as a means to influence corporate decision-making at a moment of considerable uncertainty vis-à-vis employment levels and changes to terms and conditions of employment among those represented by employees who sit on the board.

To examine these issues this section comprises two stages. The first stage establishes the priorities of board-level employee representatives when restructuring takes place. The second stage ascertains the views of board-level employee representatives on their influence over decisions made to restructure. The data show that board-level employee representatives assign greater priority to the protection of employees and the company than any other interests during restructuring. The influence of board-level employee representatives during restructuring, however, is restricted.

The Priorities of Representatives during Restructuring

Chapter 4 demonstrated that aspects of company restructuring are frequently addressed at board meetings and that board-level employee representatives attach considerable importance to company restructuring (see also Hagen 2011; Movitz and Levinson 2013). Arising from these findings is the question of what emphases do board-level employee representatives place during restructuring: Do they prioritise a concern for the company during restructuring because such events entail risks for the company, or do they prioritise a concern for employees because restructuring introduces uncertainties for employees? Of course, these questions are not mutually exclusive, but they are at the heart of the key tension in the role of the board-level employee representative: Can board-level employee representatives represent the interests of the employees that elect them without assigning a greater priority to the interests of the company? Table 5.1 presents the results.

The 'all' column of Table 5.1 shows that board-level employee representatives prioritise the interests of 'employees' over those of 'the company' during restructuring. Although there is a difference of almost 20 percentage points between 'employees' and 'the company', 72.3 per cent of board-level employee representatives report 'the company' to be one of their top two priorities during corporate restructuring. This result suggests that during restructuring board-level employee representatives take into account both the social and economic dimensions of the company, thus confirming Polish (Wratny and Bednarski 2005, quoted in Skupień 2011), Danish (Rose 2008) and Swedish (Movitz and Levinson 2013) evidence. The emphasis placed on the interests of the company contradicts the expectations of the financial perspective within the corporate governance literature, which excludes board-level employee representation on the grounds that employee representatives would only be interested in protecting jobs and raising wages

Table 5.1 If Restructuring to Improve Economic Performance Should Entail Job Losses, When The Final Decision Has to Be Made What Are Your Priorities?

		CMEs		MMEs	EMEs		
To protect	All Country Clusters %	Germanic %	Nordic %	Francophone %	New Member States %	Ireland, Greece and Spain %	SEs %
Employees	90.4	89.2	90.8	98.0	90.8	89.3	100.0
The company	72.3	74.2	71.5	54.4	74.5	71.4	84.2
Local labour market	11.1	7.6	12.8	23.8	12.0	10.7	7.9
Wider society	7.8	5.7	10.5	14.2	2.2	17.9	5.3
Shareholders	3.4	1.0	3.0	/	13.3	10.7	/
Another interest	0.6	0.7	0.2	/	0.6	/	/
	N = 4,155	N = 1,554	N = 1,917	N = 147	N = 509	N = 28	N = 38

Note: Respondents were asked to rank their answers to the question 1, 2, 3 and so on. The reasons ranked at position 1 and 2 in the ranking are reported here; hence, the percentage data add up to more than 100 per cent.

(Fama and Jensen 1983, 1985). It is also apparent that the range of other interests listed in Table 5.1 is, at best, second level compared to 'employees' and 'the company'. 'Shareholder' interests, for example, are one of the two top priorities for only 3.4 per cent of board-level employee representatives.

Reference to the data disaggregated by country clusters shows that 'employees' are the top priority everywhere and are one of the two primary priorities among at least 89.2 per cent of board-level employee representatives. The argument that German employee representation is now a means to improve corporate competitiveness rather than represent the interests of labour would thus appear to be overstated (Boyer 2005). Every board-level employee representative in SEs thinks that 'employees' are one of the two principal priorities during corporate restructuring. Similarly, 'the company' always appears at position two in the ranking, albeit with greater variation between the country clusters than reported for 'employees'. There are also no consistent differences between CMEs, MMEs and EMEs. The most marked variation, however, is the downplaying of the interests of 'the company' by the board-level employee representatives based in the Francophone countries, where adversarial industrial relations prevail (Goyer and Hancké 2005). These representatives also entirely dismiss the interests of 'shareholders' during company restructuring in placing greater emphasis on the 'local labour market'. Board-level employee representatives in the SEs also entirely dismiss the interests of 'shareholders' but emphasise 'the company' more than their counterparts in the national clusters. Board-level employee representatives in the NMS are more likely than their counterparts elsewhere to emphasise the interests of 'shareholders', suggesting a concern that extends beyond the immediate well-being of the company. Although board-level employee representatives in IGS rank the 'wider society' as third in the ranking, the issue is generally downplayed.

The Influence of Employee Representatives on Company Restructuring

The second stage of the analysis assesses the extent to which board-level employee representatives thought that they influenced the process of company restructuring. Table 5.2 presents the results. From the outset, it is noteworthy that only 28.4 per cent of board-level employee representatives report that 'no restructuring has taken place over the past two years', suggesting that the wave of corporate restructuring that commenced during the 1980s is still underway.

Reference to the 'all' column shows that more board-level employee representatives report that they were 'not very influential' or 'not at all influential' than report having an influence on restructuring. As a consequence, the index score is minus 9.2. Three points arise from this observation. First, the minus index score suggests that the capacity of board-level employee representatives to secure positions for employee and the company consistent

Table 5.2 If Your Company Has Restructured over the Past Two Years, How Influential Were You on the Process?[1]

		CMEs		MMEs	EMEs		
	All Country Clusters %	Germanic %	Nordic %	Francophone %	New Member States %	Ireland, Greece and Spain %	SEs %
Very influential	6.7	6.0	7.7	2.0	6.4	5.3	3.8
Influential	25.0	27.0	25.0	20.8	18.4	42.1	29.6
Intermediate	27.4	32.1	23.8	28.7	27.5	15.8	33.3
Not very influential	24.6	27.0	21.4	33.6	27.9	31.5	25.9
Not at all influential	16.3	7.9	22.1	14.9	19.8	5.3	7.4
Index score	–9.2	–1.8	–10.9	–25.7	–22.8	+10.5	0
	N = 2,975	N = 1,094	N = 1,463	N = 101	N = 298	N = 19	N = 27

Note: The index score was calculated by subtracting the sum of the percentage scores recorded for 'not very influential' and 'not at all influential' from the sum of the percentage scores recorded for 'very influential' and 'influential'.

1. Respondents were also given the opportunity to report that 'no restructuring has taken place over the past two years'. In 'all country clusters' 28.4 per cent reported no restructuring, hence the values of *N* are lower than reported elsewhere.

with their interpretation of events is limited in practice. Second, the limited influence brought to bear on restructuring by board-level employee representatives brings into question their capacity to convert the intensity of participation of board-level representation into influence in practice. Third, it is apparent that for many board-level employee representatives, the 40.9 per cent who were either 'not very influential' or 'not at all influential', for example, participation on the board is akin to partial participation. In combination the second and third points suggest that many board-level employee representatives may carry a collective responsibility for board decisions, because they are members of the board, even though they had no or very little influence on the decisions reached by the board.

Although a zero score is recorded in the SEs, it is only in IGS that a positive index score is reported. The positive index score reported for IGS may be associated with the peculiarities of public sector board-level representation, which characterises these three countries. The index scores for the Germanic and Nordic CMEs are not as negative as were those for the Francophone MMEs and the EMEs of the NMS, suggesting that the more wide-ranging systems of participation characteristic of CMEs allow board-level employee representatives to exert more influence. Even in the CMEs, however, only one-third of Germanic and Nordic respondents (33.0 and 32.7 per cent, respectively) regarded themselves as either 'very influential' or 'influential' on restructuring.

The relationship between the influence attained by board-level employee representatives during company restructuring and the composition of the board can be further assessed by reference to the three systems of board-level representation found in Germany. In practice, a direct relationship exists between the perceived influence of board-level employee representatives and the strength of their constitutional position on the board. To illustrate, in one-third co-determination 4.3 per cent of board-level employee representatives think that they were 'very influential' on decisions to restructure compared to 6.6 per cent and 13.3 per cent in parity and Montan co-determination. Similarly, the index score in one-third co-determination is minus 2.4 whereas in parity and Montan codetermination index scores of plus 5.0 and plus 13.3, respectively, are recorded.[2] These results suggest that the impact of the extent of coordination within a society on board-level decision-making is supplemented by that arising from the institutional power of the employee representatives on the board.

Although the composition of the board in Germany has a marked effect on the influence exerted by board-level employee representatives during restructuring, there is no statistically significant relationship between the proportion of the board composed of board-level employee representatives and their influence on restructuring decisions throughout the sixteen countries as a whole, indicating that the constitutional position of employee representation is not the only variable at play in this context. Furthermore, sector, company size, board size, corporate governance structure and the sex of board-level employee representatives have no statistically significant relation with the influence exerted by board-level employee representatives on restructuring decisions. Statistical significance is attained, however, when comparing the influence of board-level employee representatives in independent companies (single or holding companies) with their counterparts in controlled companies (subsidiaries), with the latter exerting far less influence than the former: 46.3 per cent of the board-level employee representatives on the board of a controlled company report being either 'not very influential' or 'not at all influential' whereas 35.6 per cent of their counterparts on the board of independent companies expressed the same view ($\chi^2 = 35.61$, $df = 4$, $p < 0.01$).

In summary, board-level employee representatives prioritise the interest of employees during company restructuring. As in the case of the agenda, there is also sensitivity to the situation of the company during restructuring. In an environment where board-level employee representatives report high rates of company restructuring, they also report having limited influence on the outcome of restructuring events, although there are marked variations between country clusters and the SEs. The extent of influence over restructuring is most limited in the Francophone MMEs and the EMEs of the NMS, further suggesting that it is within CMEs that board-level employee representation is at its most influential. Nowhere is this clearer than in Germany, where there is a direct relationship between the influence of board-level employee representatives and the proportion of the board that they comprise. To explore this issue further the next section assesses the power exercised by board-level employee representatives within the board generally, rather than just in the particular circumstances of company restructuring.

DO EMPLOYEE REPRESENTATIVES EXERT POWER OVER BOARD DECISION-MAKING?

The limited influence exerted by board-level employee representatives over the process of company restructuring raises questions about the role undertaken by employee representatives at the board. Put bluntly, the assumption underpinning the corporate governance literature is that board-level employee representatives exert a stakeholder power on board-level decision-making, while the industrial relations literature assumes that employee representatives exercise power at the board thus contributing to industrial democracy. Both literatures assume that board-level employee representatives exert some power over strategic long-term company decision-making. Both literatures also acknowledge that present economic and political circumstances differ markedly from those prevailing when systems of board-level employee representation were implemented in Western Europe (Lazonick and O'Sullivan 2000; Williams 2000). The change in these circumstances raises questions concerning the extent to which *de jure* positions are under pressure *de facto* as international competition intensifies (Hagen 2011; Movitz and Levinson 2013). This section examines these propositions in two stages. First, it assesses the form of power exerted by board-level employee representatives by reference to the actual practices of the board. Second, it identifies where the main decisions taken by the board are made and the extent to which board-level employee representatives are excluded from these decisions.

How Is Power Exerted on Board Decision-Making?

Power is at the core of the study of the participation of workers. In the classic literature on participation influence and power are treated as points on a continuum of involvement in decision-making, usually expressed with polar positions of no involvement, where management has the sole responsibility for decision-making, and self-management, where decision-making rests in the hands of workers. The 'influence power continuum', for example, identifies five points: no involvement, information, consultation, joint decision-making and self-management (Heller 1971). This formulation has underpinned many of the subsequent analyses of workers involvement, albeit often expressed with different numbers of, and titles for, the points on the continuum (Boxall and Purcell 2011; Briefs 1989; Dachler and Wilpert 1978; Knudsen 1995; Marchington et al. 1992; Strauss 1998). In practice, situations of no involvement mean that workers are excluded from the decision-making process and thus have neither influence nor power. Where information disclosure or consultation takes place workers may have some influence, although decision-making rests solely in the hands of management. Information and consultation are thus the two lower rungs on a continuum of involvement. In this context, information and consultation correspond to a situation of partial participation (Pateman 1970) or 'participation to take part' (Lund 1980). Joint decision-making, which is classically associated with collective bargaining, co-determination and self-management assumes that workers have sufficient power to ensure that their preferences are incorporated into the outcome of the decision-making process (Heller et al. 1988:17).

By definition, board-level employee representation comprises some involvement, and thus, the category no involvement is excluded from the analysis that follows. The two lower rungs on the continuum employed here 'are informed, but have little opportunity to discuss matters' (hereafter, informed) and 'are consulted, but the final decision rests with other board members' (hereafter, consulted) are drawn directly from the influence power continuum. A third position corresponds to joint decision-making, assumes that employee representatives have some power and is expressed here as 'discuss matters with other board members until a shared position is reached' (hereafter, reach a shared position). In addition to these three positions on a continuum of involvement, two further positions are identified in Table 5.3: 'control the management through supervision' and 'co-manage the company by participating in the preparation of decisions' (hereafter co-manage the company). In dual-board systems a key brief of the supervisory board is to oversee the activities of the management board. The inclusion of the variable to 'control the management through supervision' is thus intended to 'capture' a particular form of involvement, implicit to which is that management takes initiatives that are then rejected, refined or accepted by the board-level employee representatives on the supervisory board. This approach should be most pronounced where dual-board systems operate. 'Co-manage the company' is included in recognition that the involvement of workers in the various stages of decision-making ensures greater influence or power within the decision-making process than involvement to discuss a decision already reached by management (Heller et al. 1988:4). Table 5.3 presents the results in the form of a hierarchy of involvement in ascending order of influence or power afforded to board-level employee representatives.

Table 5.3 shows that 45.6 per cent of 'all' board-level employee representatives are 'informed' or are 'consulted' at board meetings and thus have, at best, restricted opportunities to influence strategic company decision-making. In other words, more than 45.0 per cent of board-level

Table 5.3 Regarding the Actual Practices of the Board, Do You . . .

	All Country Clusters %	CMEs: Germanic %	CMEs: Nordic %	MMEs: Francophone %	EMEs: New Member States %	Ireland, Greece and Spain %	SEs %
Co-manage the company by participating in decision-making	12.4	11.6	14.6	0.7	10.4	7.1	10.5
Discuss matters with other board members until a shared position is reached	20.2	15.8	23.5	7.5	22.8	35.7	13.2
Control the management through supervision	21.8	31.5	11.0	10.9	38.4	28.6	21.1
Are consulted, but the final decision rests with other board members	29.4	28.9	30.2	60.5	19.5	14.3	39.5
Are informed, but have little opportunity to discuss matters	16.2	12.2	20.7	20.4	8.9	14.3	15.8
	N = 3,971	*N* = 1,386	*N* = 1,902	*N* = 147	*N* = 508	*N* = 28	*N* = 38

employee representatives can do no more than influence board-level decision-making. For these board-level employee representatives the position *de facto* differs markedly from the *de jure* intention, insofar as they are members of the board and thus carry responsibility for board decisions, but they are unable to exercise power over the content of these decisions. The situation reported in national studies is thus reproduced throughout Europe, with a substantial minority of board-level employee representatives unable to exert power at the board (e.g. Hagen 2011; Prašnikar and

Gregorič 2002; Skupień 2011). In contrast, just under one-third (32.6 per cent) of board-level employee representatives have some power over decision-making insofar as their agreement with a decision is sought to 'reach a shared position' or they 'co-manage the company'. A further 21.8 per cent of board-level employee representatives view themselves as in a position of 'controlling the management through supervision'.

Treating the two points on the continuum that indicate no more than influence ('informed' and 'consulted') as one, and adopting the same procedure for the two points that suggest power ('reach a shared position' and 'co-manage the company') reveals some marked differences between the country clusters. No fewer than 80.9 per cent of Francophone respondents view their position as no more than influential, confirming earlier French findings (Conchon 2013a). The situation in the Francophone countries also suggests that factors beyond the institutional setting affect the practices of the board. The adversarial industrial relations that characterise Francophone MMEs are thus associated with employee representatives exerting little board-level power and an inability to affect strategic board-level decision-making. Based on this, Francophone systems comprise no more than partial participation and allow 'management considerable unilateral control over business strategy and corporate reorganisation' (Goyer and Hancké 2005:173). Furthermore, this result confirms that the 'transformation of the French model of shareholding and management' (Morin 2000) has not been accompanied by an increase in influence among Francophone board-level employee representatives. In contrast, in the Nordic CMEs 38.1 per cent of board-level representatives define themselves as in positions of power, in a manner consistent with 'a political consensus between the labour movement and the major capital owners' (Agnblad et al. 2001) or a 'negotiated solidarism' (Swenson 2002). It is noteworthy, however, that 50.9 per cent of Nordic board-level employee representatives regard themselves as having, at best, only an influence over decision-making. The adversarial relations of the Francophone countries thus appear relative ineffectual compared to the consensus seeking or solidaristic approaches that characterise Nordic industrial relations practices. That more than half of Nordic board-level employee representatives can at best, influence board decisions, however, suggests that the terms on which management and labour cooperate are skewed and may reflect the diminution of the power of Nordic labour as reported elsewhere (Rothstein 2001; Swenson and Pontusson 2000).

As anticipated, in dual systems 'control the management through supervision' is the most prevalent form of participation: 31.5 per cent of Germanic and 38.4 per cent of NMS board-level employee representatives define their participation in this manner. Other forms of participation, however, are also present. Almost one-third (33.2 per cent) of NMS board-level employee representatives and more than a quarter (27.4 per cent) of Germanic respondents, for example, report that they either 'co-manage the company' or 'reach a shared decision'. The finding for the Germanic cluster confirms that compromise-oriented board decision-making is common in German companies, in particular those with parity co-determination (Jansen 2013; Jürgens et al. 2008). Differentiating German results by the type of board-level employee representation reveals marked differences in practice dependent on the constitutional position of the employee representatives on the board. More than half (54.0 per cent) of board-level employee representatives on boards with one-third co-determination, for example, are only 'informed' or 'consulted' compared to 33.9 per cent and 31.6 per cent within parity and Montan co-determination, respectively. Similarly, in Montan co-determination 44.7 per cent of board-level employee representatives report that they 'control the management through supervision' whereas 33.8 per cent in parity co-determination and 24.3 per cent in one-third co-determination report the same circumstance. In contrast to the statistical analyses, these results demonstrate the stronger the constitutional position of board-level employee representatives, the more power they can exercise on board-level decision-making.[3]

Apart from the Francophone respondents, it is also apparent that board-level employee representatives in SEs are the most likely to participate based on either 'information' or 'consultation' and are the least likely to exercise power over board decision-making. Given that many SEs are Germanic in origin, this situation constitutes a marked loss of power for board-level employee representatives in SEs compared to their counterparts based in companies that retain a Germanic legal identity.

Power is correlated with the organisational level of the board on which the employee representative sits. In independent companies (single or holding companies) 37.9 per cent of board-level employee representatives indicate that they are either 'informed' or 'consulted' on board decisions, whereas 54.2 per cent of their counterparts on the boards of controlled (subsidiary) companies report the same situation ($\chi^2 = 137.09$, $df = 4$, $p < 0.01$). The capacity of board-level employee representatives within controlled companies to exert power is thus much reduced compared to their counterparts in independent companies.

Are Employee Representatives Present When Board Decisions Are Made?

The previous stage showed that a large proportion of board-level employee representatives participate at board level only by means of information and consultation and thus are unable to exercise power over board decision-making in a strategic manner. Furthermore, an extensive literature drawn primarily from that on corporate governance argues that European stakeholder systems of board-level employee representation are coming under increasing pressure as Anglo-Saxon or LME practices become more pervasive within corporate governance (Renaud 2007; Poutsma and Braam 2005), leading some to question whether board-level employee representation has any meaning when neo-liberal ideologies are dominant (Höpner 2001). Furthermore, recent Swedish data demonstrate a marked increase between 1999 and 2009 in the proportion of board-level employee representatives that thinks board decisions are made outside of the board in their absence (Movitz and Levinson 2013). In combination, these points raise a further question; namely, are efforts made to exclude board-level employee representatives from decision-making within the board, thereby ensuring that managerial and shareholder interests exert an unqualified power over board-level decision-making and further ensuring that *de facto* practice differs from *de jure* intention? A measure of exclusion is thus a further indicator of an absence of power. Table 5.4 examines the views of board-level employee representatives as to where the main board decisions are made and whether the board-level employee representatives are party to these decisions.

It is apparent from the 'all' column of Table 5.4 that only a minority (40.3 per cent) of board-level employee representatives think that major decisions are taken at formal board meetings. Assuming that board-level employee representatives attend meetings of the board and subcommittees, and, by definition, are present 'during meetings outside of the board involving employee representatives', the data suggest that between 50.6 per cent and 70.2 per cent of board-level employee representatives are engaged in the principal decisions taken by the board.[4] In contrast, the only circumstances when shareholder representatives are definitely excluded, 'during meetings outside of the board excluding shareholder representatives', are cited by only 2.2 per cent of board-level employee representatives.

Reference to the country clusters shows that the pattern of decision-making is not consistent with sociological approaches to corporate governance. The proportion of meetings at which the main decisions of the board are made and attended by board-level employee representatives in Germanic and Nordic CMEs is 47.7 to 77.3 per cent and 50.3 to 61.3 per cent, respectively. The maximum rate of exclusion of Nordic board-level employee representatives is thus 49.7 per cent, which is lower than the 77 per cent of Swedish board-level employee representatives who report board decisions as made outside of the board meeting (Movitz and Levinson 2013). In contrast, the situation reported from within the Germanic cluster is broadly consistent with previous research that showed that 40 per cent of board-level employee representatives operating within parity co-determination think that board decisions are always or often made outside of the plenary board meeting (Jürgens et al. 2008). This finding might be attributed to the frequent practice of convening preliminary meetings in German codetermined companies between management and shareholder representatives (see the following discussion). In turn, such practices explain why there is a correlation between corporate governance structure and the location of board decision-making as perceived by board-level employee representatives ($\chi^2 = 243.02$, $df = 15$, $p < 0.01$). Board-level employee representatives who sit on a supervisory board are much more likely than their counterparts who sit

Table 5.4 In Your View, Where Are the Main Decisions on Board-Level Issues Really Made?

		CMEs		MMEs	EMEs	
	All Country Clusters %	Germanic %	Nordic %	Franco-phone %	New Member States %	Ireland, Greece and Spain %	SEs %
During board meetings	40.3	31.6	42.0	13.6	64.8	57.1	33.4
During meetings outside the board excluding employee representatives	29.8	22.7	38.7	45.6	12.7	14.3	19.4
During meetings outside the board involving shareholder representatives	17.4	27.8	8.3	29.9	19.1	3.6	22.2
During meetings outside the board involving employee representatives	6.7	8.9	6.6	0.7	2.2	17.9	11.1
During subcommittee meetings	3.6	7.2	1.7	4.1	0.6	7.1	8.3
During meetings outside the board excluding shareholder representatives	2.2	1.8	2.6	6.1	0.6	/	5.6
	N = 3,982	N = 1,412	N = 1,887	N = 147	N =508	N = 28	N = 36

on a monistic board to report that board decisions are made at meetings outside of the board involving shareholder representatives (26.3 per cent compared to 11.7 per cent).

In the SEs, board-level employee representatives attend between 52.7 per cent and 80.6 per cent of meetings at which decisions are made. By comparison the same range for the EMEs of the NMS is between 67.6 and 87.3 per cent. In other words, the rate of exclusion of board-level employee representatives from meetings at which the main decisions of the board are made tends to be lower in the NMS than in Germanic and Nordic CMEs and the SEs. As with the practices of the board, the outlying cluster is the Francophone MMEs. Between 18.4 per cent and 54.4 per cent of board-level employee representatives attend the meetings at which the main board decisions are made. The minimum rate of exclusion is thus 45.6 per cent, and the maximum, 81.6 per cent.

Examination of the character of participation that takes place when the main decisions of the board are taken 'during meetings outside the board meetings excluding employee representatives' reveals the efficacy of exclusion as a means to limit the influence of employee representatives. Table 5.3, for example, shows that 45.6 per cent of 'all' board-level employee representatives are only either 'informed' or 'consulted' during the board meetings and thus exert, at best, an influence on board decision-making. This proportion rises to 67.2 per cent among 'all' board-level employee representatives who regard the main decisions of the board to be taken 'during meetings outside the board meetings excluding employee representatives'. Furthermore, similar rises are recorded for each of the country clusters: Germanic, 41.1 to 58.7 per cent; Nordic, 50.9 to 70.7 per cent; Francophone, 80.9 to 92.5 per cent; and the NMS, 28.4 to 48.5 per cent. In other words, if management and shareholder representatives create circumstances in which the main decisions of the board are made at meetings from which the board-level employee representatives are excluded, a greater proportion of these representatives view their involvement in terms of only information and consultation and thus as lacking power over strategic company decision-making.

The strength of the constitutional position of the board-level employee representatives within the German system is inversely related to their exclusion from decision-making. Within Montan codetermination, for example, board-level employee representatives attend between 68.5 per cent and 97.4 per cent of meetings at which the main decisions of the board are made, whereas in parity and one-third codetermination the ranges of attendance are 53.5 to 82.6 per cent and 40.3 to 70.3 per cent.[5] Again this result suggests that the stronger the institutional power of the board-level employee representatives, the more *de facto* practice mirrors *de jure* intention

The organisational level at which the board is located again plays a distinctive role insofar as 29.2 per cent of board-level employee representatives that sit on the board of a controlled company (subsidiary) think that board decisions are made during board meetings whereas 49.7 per cent of board-level employee representatives that sit on the board of an independent company share the same view ($\chi^2 = 206.88$, $df = 5$, $p < 0.01$). Practices differ also significantly depending on the sector of activity of the company ($\chi^2 = 74.93$, $df = 25$, $p < 0.01$). In particular, informality is more prevalent in private-sector services and industry, where 35.6 per cent and 37.0 per cent of board-level employee representatives, respectively, report that board meetings are the locus of decision-making, whereas 51.4 per cent of their counterparts in the public sector express the same opinion. Board-level employee representatives are thus more likely to be excluded from board-level decision-making in marketised services, confirming the limitations of labour representation in these segments of the economy (Dølvik and Waddington 2005).

A substantial minority of board-level employee representatives in the country clusters and in the SEs are involved at the board only in terms of 'information' or 'consultation' and are thus unable to exert power over long-term strategic company decision-making. Furthermore, a substantial minority of board-level employee representatives are excluded from the meetings at which the main decisions of the board are made. Where power is exerted, the manner of its exercise varies. In Nordic single-channel systems, board-level employee representatives are most likely to 'reach a shared solution', whereas in Germanic and NMS dual systems influence is more likely to take the form of 'control the management through supervision'. In the Germanic and NMS clusters, together with the SEs, a substantial minority of board-level employee representatives are only either 'informed' or 'consulted'. In contrast, in the Nordic and Francophone clusters the majority of board-level employee representatives are involved at board-level in these modes, suggesting that they are only able to influence, rather than exert power, over strategic board-level decision-making.

TACTICAL MANOEUVRING WITHIN THE BOARD

Chapter 1 identified coordination as one of the themes that resonate throughout this study. The objective of this section is to examine aspects of coordination in the context of the tactical manoeuvring within the board. A degree of coordination is a feature of all the economies covered by this study. It is accepted that the character of coordination varies between country clusters. Two aspects of coordination are examined here: the involvement of board-level employee representatives in subcommittees formed by board members and the extent to which pre-meetings are convened exclusively for board-level employee representatives or alternatively for board-level employee representatives and senior managers. The objective of this section is thus to establish whether and, if so, to what extent, board-level employee representatives coordinate with one another and with senior management prior to the plenary board meeting.

The Involvement of Board-Level Employee Representatives in Subcommittees

The establishment of subcommittees allows examination of specific agenda items in detail by a small, select group of board members, who may subsequently table recommendations to the entire board. Subcommittees were initially established in the application of soft law recommendations originating in codes of corporate governance. As practices of corporate governance were subject to increased criticism, some of these recommendations became law. At present, for example, listed companies are required to set up an audit subcommittee, whereas banks and investment firms must establish nomination and remuneration committees in addition to audit subcommittees.[6] The development of subcommittees is thus a key and distinctive feature of the recent evolution of corporate governance from which companies with board-level employee representation are not excluded (Gerum 2007). The shift of preparatory work to subcommittees raises concerns about the location of board-level decision-making (Jürgens et al. 2008). Although Table 5.4 showed that only 3.6 per cent of board-level employee representatives take the view that board decisions are taken within subcommittees rather than at the plenary board meeting, the risk is considered to be so high that public authorities explicitly warn against such a practice.[7] When subcommittees restrict their role to making recommendations to the full board, for example, the full board is likely to accept such recommendations without further discussion (Davies et al. 2013). Furthermore, some subcommittees may be granted decision-making powers. In Germany the supervisory board can delegate decision-making power to subcommittees in some fields. The appointment or remuneration of management is explicitly excluded from this form of delegation (Roth 2013). Similarly, in Austria the code of corporate governance recommends that subcommittees have the right to make decisions on behalf of the full board in emergency situations (Point 39 of the January 2015 edition).

The involvement of board-level employee representatives in any established subcommittee is thus key to their engagement in strategic decision-making. From the outset it is important to acknowledge that of 'all' board-level employee representatives, only 42.7 per cent report that at least one subcommittee had been formed by the board. The 3.6 per cent of board-level employee representatives who regard board decisions as taken within subcommittees thus constitute almost 10 per cent of board-level employee representatives who operate in the presence of subcommittees. Furthermore, there is marked variation between the country clusters in the proportion of board-level employee representatives indicating the presence of subcommittees: NMS, 20.2 per cent; Nordic, 30.5 per cent; Germanic, 62.4 per cent; Francophone, 65.3 per cent; and IGS, 71.4 per cent. Subcommittees are more widespread in the SEs, where 81.6 per cent of board-level employee representatives report their presence. The low level at which board decisions are made by subcommittees in the NMS and Nordic countries (see Table 5.4) is thus a function of the low rate of establishment of subcommittees in these country clusters. Table 5.5 shows the involvement of board-level employee representatives in subcommittees in companies where the board had set up, at least, one subcommittee.

Table 5.5 The Participation of Board-Level Employee Representatives in Subcommittees

					CMEs							
	All Country Clusters $N = 1,774$				Germanic $N = 970$				Nordic $N = 585$			
Subcommittee	Full member, invited to each meeting %	Guest member, invited to some meetings %	Not a member, never inviting %	This subcommittee does not exist %	Full member, invited to each meeting %	Guest member, invited to some meetings %	Not a member, never inviting %	This subcommittee does not exist %	Full member, invited to each meeting %	Guest member, invited to some meetings %	Not a member, never invited %	This subcommittee does not exist %
Strategy	10.7	3.6	18.6	67.1	7.6	0.8	14.8	76.8	14.2	7.5	24.3	54.0
Investment	8.1	2.4	19.7	69.8	9.3	0.8	16.8	73.1	6.7	4.3	25.3	63.7
Audit/accounting	20.9	3.8	33.9	41.4	28.0	2.6	27.1	42.3	6.8	4.6	41.4	47.2
Nomination/ appointment	8.7	1.9	32.2	57.2	12.0	1.0	25.5	61.5	4.8	2.6	48.0	44.6
Remuneration/ compensation	14.7	1.5	33.4	50.4	22.7	0.7	30.2	46.4	5.7	2.2	38.1	54.0

Note: Respondents were initially asked to indicate whether subcommittees of the board existed at all within their company. The data reported in Table 5.5 are those from respondents who indicated that one or more subcommittees were in operation.

Table 5.5 (Continued) The Participation of Board-Level Employee Representatives in Subcommittees

	MMEs				EMEs							
	Francophone N = 96				New Member States N = 103				Ireland, Greece and Spain N = 20			
Subcommittee	**Full member, invited to each meeting %**	**Guest member, invited to some meetings %**	**Not a member, never inviting %**	**This subcommittee does not exist %**	**Full member, invited to each meeting %**	**Guest member, invited to some meetings %**	**Not a member, never inviting %**	**This subcommittee does not exist %**	**Full member, invited to each meeting %**	**Guest member, invited to some meetings %**	**Not a member, never invited %**	**This subcommittee does not exist %**
Strategy	20.8	4.2	26.0	49.0	7.8	5.8	11.6	74.8	20.0	10.0	40.0	30.0
Investment	7.3	/	17.7	75.0	4.8	6.8	13.6	74.8	10.0	10.0	40.0	40.0
Audit/ accounting	26.0	6.3	52.1	15.6	31.1	7.8	33.0	28.1	10.0	10.0	60.0	20.0
Nomination/ appointment	/	/	25.0	75.0	6.8	6.8	12.6	73.8	15.0	10.0	30.0	45.0
Remuneration/ compensation	3.1	/	51.1	45.8	2.9	4.8	14.6	77.7	10.0	10.0	60.0	20.0

Table 5.5 (Continued) The Participation of Board-Level Employee Representatives in Subcommittees

	SEs $N = 31$			
Subcommittee	**Full member, invited to each meeting %**	**Guest member, invited to some meetings %**	**Not a member, never invited %**	**This subcommittee does not exist %**
Strategy	6.4	/	9.7	83.9
Investment	3.2	/	12.9	83.9
Audit/ accounting	35.5	3.2	35.5	25.8
Nomination/ appointment	9.7	3.2	35.5	51.6
Remuneration/ compensation	22.6	/	32.2	45.2

It is immediately apparent from Table 5.5 that the formation of subcommittees is very much a minority event. If the board-level employee representatives that report no subcommittees in operation are added to those indicating that 'this subcommittee does not exist', 79.7 per cent of board-level employee representatives indicate that there is no 'strategy subcommittee'. Corresponding figures for the other subcommittees are 'investment', 80.9 per cent; 'nomination', 75.5 per cent; 'remuneration', 72.6 per cent; and 'audit', 68.7 per cent. In other words, it is only audit subcommittees that more than 30 per cent of board-level employee representatives report being operational, confirming that audit committees occupy a key position in current European corporate governance arrangements (Enriques and Volpin 2007). The small proportion of board-level employee representatives that report the presence of subcommittees may result from the low levels of participation in the survey by employee representatives based in companies traded on the stock exchange.[8]

The participation of board-level employee representatives at the subcommittees that are in place reveals a pattern of widespread exclusion. The sum of the proportion of board-level employee representatives who report being a 'full member, invited to each meeting' (hereafter, full member) and those who report being a 'guest member, invited to some meetings' (hereafter, guest member) is a lower figure than that reported for 'not a member, never invited' (hereafter, not a member) for each of the subcommittees, suggesting a pronounced rate of exclusion of board-level employee representatives, which, in turn, implies restrictions on the capacity of board-level employee representatives to engage in strategic decision-making with the board. Furthermore, the highest rate of participation as 'full members' is recorded for the audit subcommittee, which primarily has a monitoring rather than a strategic function.

In addition to the variation between the country clusters in the presence of subcommittees noted earlier, there is variation in the patterns of establishment of subcommittees and of excluding board-level employee representatives from subcommittees. Audit subcommittees are most likely to be established in the Germanic, Francophone, NMS and IGS country clusters and in the SEs, while in Nordic countries nomination subcommittees are almost as common as audit committees. In contrast, those subcommittees with explicit strategic functions are less likely to be established. Investment subcommittees, for example, are one of the two subcommittees least likely to be established in the Germanic, Nordic, Francophone, NMS and IGS country clusters, together with the SEs. Similarly, strategy subcommittees are one of the two least likely subcommittees to be established in the SEs and the Germanic, Nordic and NMS clusters. Strategy committees are a more frequent occurrence in the Francophone and IGS clusters. In practice, of course, the lower rate of establishment of subcommittees with a strategic brief implies that decisions on strategic issues are more likely to rest with the full board, irrespective of the presence of board-level employee representatives.

The data on the exclusion of board-level employee representatives from subcommittees where such committees are in place suggest, from the perspective of promoting the involvement of board-level employee representatives in strategic decision-making, that the establishment of subcommittees has a negative effect and that it is preferable that board decision-making remains within the jurisdiction of the full board or that the presence of board-level employee representatives in subcommittees is either legally underwritten, as is the case in only three countries (Austria, Slovenia, Sweden), or is acknowledged by case law, as in Germany.[9] To illustrate, where a subcommittee exists more than half of board-level employee representatives engage as either 'full members' or a 'guest members' in Germanic and SE audit subcommittees and subcommittees on strategy, audit and nomination in the NMS. More than half of board-level employee representatives are not engaged in any subcommittee in the Nordic, Francophone and IGS countries. In short, a considerable number of board-level employee representatives are effectively excluded from subcommittees in all the country clusters.

The Participation of Board-Level Employee Representatives in Pre-Meetings

Pre-meetings are a further feature of the engagement of board-level employee representatives in board processes and, as such, constitute an additional indicator of coordination. Two forms of pre-meeting are addressed here: pre-meetings involving only board-level employee representatives (panel 1, Table 5.6) and pre-meetings between board-level employee representatives and senior management (panel 2, Table 5.6). The pre-meetings examined here are thus those in which company insiders participate. Pre-meetings involving only board-level employee representatives are indicative of efforts to establish agreed positions among board-level employee representatives to take to meetings with other stakeholders. The structure of unionism in the Nordic and Francophone countries ensures that pre-meetings involving only board-level employee representatives are more likely to bring together members of different trade unions than in the other country clusters, which may necessitate more pre-meetings in order to establish agreed positions. Although pre-meetings involving board-level employee representatives and senior managers also constitute attempts to identify positions and establish agreed positions, where possible, prior to meetings with other stakeholders, the composition of such meetings may also reflect attempts to avoid the airing of positions contested by board-level employee representatives and senior managers in front of other stakeholders, particularly shareholder representatives.

Table 5.6 Are Pre-Meetings of Board-Level Employee Representatives Held before the Formal Board Meeting?

PANEL 1

		CMEs		MMEs	EMEs		
	All Country Clusters %	Germanic %	Nordic %	Franco-phone %	New Member States %	Ireland, Greece and Spain %	SEs %
Always	37.4	72.2	17.7	34.2	12.8	7.1	60.5
Often	11.8	10.3	12.4	23.3	10.8	10.8	13.2
Sometimes	14.5	5.8	19.9	13.7	19.0	25.0	5.3
Rarely	12.5	4.6	18.0	8.2	16.1	7.1	13.2
Never	16.0	3.5	23.4	19.2	23.0	25.0	5.3
I am the only BLER on the board	7.8	3.6	8.6	1.4	18.3	25.0	2.5
	N = 4,061	N = 1,473	N = 1,905	N = 146	N = 509	N = 28	N = 38

Are Pre-Meetings of Board-Level Employee Representatives and Senior Management Held before the Formal Board Meeting?

PANEL 2

		CMEs		MMEs	EMEs		
	All Country Clusters %	Germanic %	Nordic %	Franco-phone %	New Member States %	Ireland, Greece and Spain %	SEs %
Always	20.3	37.9	9.6	30.3	7.7	10.7	39.3
Often	9.7	12.4	7.0	17.3	11.0	3.6	13.2
Sometimes	15.6	14.7	13.6	12.4	25.5	28.6	13.2
Rarely	17.7	12.3	21.1	13.8	21.0	25.0	13.2
Never	36.7	22.7	48.7	26.2	34.8	32.1	21.1
	N = 4,041	N = 1,456	N = 1,903	N = 145	N = 509	N = 28	N = 38

Almost half of the board-level employee representatives 'always' or 'often' hold pre-meetings among themselves prior to the formal meeting of the board, suggesting widespread coordination between board-level employee representatives for board activities. In contrast, 16.0 per cent of board-level employee representatives 'never' engage in pre-meetings with other board-level employee representatives, and a further 7.8 per cent report that they are 'the only BLER on the board'. Almost a quarter of board-level employee representatives are thus relatively isolated in conducting duties associated with the board.

Turning to the country clusters shows that pre-meetings involving board-level employee representatives are convened at different rates. Contrary to expectations multi-unionism in the Francophone and Nordic countries does not result in particularly high rates of pre-meetings involving only board-level employee representatives. Such meetings are much more likely in the Germanic countries where multi-unionism is exceptional. No fewer than 72.2 per cent of Germanic board-level employee representatives 'always' convene a pre-meeting before the plenary meeting of the board, suggesting that the principal purpose of such pre-meetings is to establish positions to present to other stakeholders rather than to address differences between unions. This Germanic idiosyncrasy also illustrates how influential soft law can be on practice, as among the sixteen countries within which the survey was distributed it is only in Germany that the conduct of pre-meetings is regulated by recommendations with their origin in the national code of corporate governance.[10] In all other country clusters pre-meetings of board-level employee representatives are infrequent compared to the Germanic countries, with more than a third of board-level employee representatives reporting pre-meetings as 'always' taking place only in Francophone countries (34.2 per cent). In the SEs, however, 60.5 per cent of board-level employee representatives 'always' convene pre-meetings, confirming the retention of Germanic practices in these companies. In contrast, the 'always' frequency in IGS (7.1 per cent), NMS (12.8 per cent) and the Nordic countries (17.7 per cent) is markedly lower. The absence of consistency among the CMEs regarding the frequency at which pre-meetings take place is reproduced when the extent of isolation of board-level employee representatives is assessed. Only 8.1 per cent of Germanic board-level employee representatives indicate that pre-meetings were 'never' or 'rarely' held compared to 41.4 per cent of Nordic board-level employee representatives. Similarly, board-level employee representatives in IGS (32.1 per cent) and the NMS (39.1 per cent) indicate that pre-meetings were 'never' or 'rarely' held, although in these two country clusters, there is the highest likelihood of the board-level employee representative being the one employee representative on the board. While the Nordic result may be partially explained in terms of the small number of board-level employee representatives that are present within each small and medium-sized enterprise, this explanation cannot apply to the NMS.

Reference to the 'all' data in Panel 2 of Table 5.6 shows that pre-meetings between board-level employee representatives and senior managers are less frequent that those involving only board-level employee representatives. For example, 49.2 per cent of board-level employee representatives either 'always' or 'often' hold pre-meetings with other board-level employee representatives compared with 30.0 per cent who participate at the same frequency in pre-meetings with senior managers. Indeed, there are more board-level employee representatives that 'never' participate in pre-meetings with senior managers than are 'always' or 'often' involved. Board-level employee representatives 'always' participate in pre-meetings with senior management at a greater frequency than 'never' participate only in the Germanic and Francophone clusters and in the SEs. Elsewhere pre-meetings with senior management 'never' happen compared to 'always' happen at ratios as high as 5.1:1 in the Nordic countries and 4.5:1 in the NMS.

Combining the 'never' and 'I am the only BLER on the board' scores from panel 1 and the 'never' scores from panel 2 reveals the proportion of board-level employee representatives who participate in neither form of pre-meeting. Based on this, 16.9 per cent of 'all' board-level employee representatives engage in neither form of pre-meeting. Corresponding data for the country clusters are Germanic, 5.5 per cent; Nordic, 24.0 per cent; Francophone, 11.0 per cent; NMS, 24.2 per cent; IGS, 28.6 per cent; and the SEs, 5.9 per cent. Two points are apparent from these data. First, the majority of those who either 'never' participate in pre-meetings with other board-level employee representatives or are 'the only BLER on the board' also 'never' participate in pre-meetings with senior managers. Second, the pattern of attendance at pre-meetings varies between country clusters in a manner that is not consistent with the distinction between CMEs, MMEs and EMEs. Tests were also conducted to establish whether the practices of the board influenced the patterns of pre-meetings. These tests indicate that 42.1 per cent of Nordic board-level employee representatives who 'discuss matters with other board members until a shared position is reached' do not attend pre-meetings with senior managers, suggesting that the practices of the board reduced the requirement for such pre-meetings, because the plenary board meeting is the location at which the board members express their views. In contrast, only 17.3 per cent of Germanic board-level employee representatives who state that they 'control the management through supervision' 'never' hold pre-meetings with senior managers. Arguments concerning the impact of the practices of the board on the convening of pre-meetings, however, would have been more strongly supported had the pattern of pre-meetings in the NMS, where to 'control the management through supervision' is also dominant (see Table 5.3), replicated that of the Germanic countries. This is not the case: 32.7 per cent of board-level employee representatives from the NMS who state that they 'control the management through supervision' do not hold pre-meetings with senior management.

CONCLUSION

The priorities of board-level employee representatives during company restructuring are consistent with those expressed for the agenda, insofar as protecting the interests of employees and those of the company head the ranking. The capacity of board-level employee representatives to convert the potential for an appropriate intensity of participation, available from the agendas of board meetings, is brought into question in the context of company restructuring. In most country clusters the index score for the influence of board-level employee representatives on the process of company restructuring is negative, indicating a very limited overall influence.

The character of the power exerted by board-level employee representatives at board meetings varies markedly. More than 45.0 per cent of 'all' board-level employee representatives report that they are either 'informed' or 'consulted' at the board with the consequence that they are unable to bring power to bear on strategic company decision-making. These board-level employee representatives are only able to influence strategic decision-making. Nowhere is the lack of power over strategic company decision-making more marked than in the Francophone MMEs where a clear majority of board-level employee representatives (80.9 per cent) are either 'informed' or 'consulted'. Furthermore, Francophone board-level employee representatives consider that most board decisions are taken during meetings outside of the board from which they are excluded. In practice, therefore, by shifting the location of decision-making away from the plenary meetings of the board, management has effectively limited the capacity of board-level employee representatives to exert power over strategic decision-making. There is a tendency for the manner in which board-level employee representatives exert power to vary with industrial relations institutions. In single-channel Nordic CMEs with monistic board arrangements and a dominant position afforded to the conclusion of collective agreements in industrial relations, to 'reach a shared position' is the principal means whereby board-level employee representatives secure power, whereas in the dual-board systems of the Germanic CMEs and the EMEs of the NMS board-level employee representatives are more likely to 'control the management through supervision'.

Bivariate analyses highlight that the capacity of board-level employee representatives to exert power over strategic decisions is, in part, dependent on the power of the board, which, in turn, is influenced by the location of the board. Boards located at the level of independent companies are more powerful than boards located in controlled companies. Company size, board size, gender, sector of activity and corporate governance structure have no statistically significant relationship with the power exerted by board-level employee representatives, although the latter two variables influence whether the full board is the locus of decision-making. The relationship between the constitutional position of Germanic board-level employee representatives and the power they can exert is not reproduced across Europe. This suggests that the proportion of the board comprising employee representatives is a necessary, but not sufficient, condition for the exercise of power. Chapter 6 explores a further aspect of this dynamic in the form of the articulation of board-level employee representatives.

Associated with variation in the manner and extent to which board-level employee representatives exert power in the different country clusters and the SEs is the pattern of participation in subcommittees and pre-meetings. In the Nordic and NMS clusters, subcommittees are far less likely to be convened than elsewhere, suggesting different forms of internal board coordination. In all country clusters where subcommittees are formed, however, a greater number of board-level employee representatives are excluded from participation in the subcommittee than participate either as a full or guest member. Marked differences between the country clusters are also in evidence regarding pre-meetings. In particular, board-level employee representatives in the Germanic cluster, in SEs and, to a lesser extent, in the Francophone cluster are more likely than their counterparts elsewhere to convene exclusive pre-meetings and pre-meetings with senior managers, although the latter are less frequent than the former.

The implications of these findings for the corporate governance and industrial relations literatures are profound on three counts. First, for a significant minority of representatives participation at the board is not accompanied by the possibility of exercising power to coordinate within companies or to facilitate industrial democracy. The *de jure* intention of board-level employee representation is not matched by *de facto* practice. Second, where board-level employee representatives are able to exercise power over board decision-making they do so using a variety of approaches, thereby demonstrating that coordination within companies and industrial democracy are by no means monolithic categories. Third, contrary to the expectations of the finance or principal–agency perspective of corporate governance almost three-quarters of board-level employee representatives regard the interests of the company to be one of their two principal concerns during restructuring, thereby bringing into question the assumption of proponents of the finance perspective that employee representatives will only act to protect the specific interests of workers rather than the general interest of the company (Fama and Jensen 1983, 1985).

A further point has implications for the analysis that follows. The increasing internationalisation of the global economy has been associated with greater pressure to adopt practices characteristics of companies with origins in LMEs. If companies that function with board-level employee representation are to adopt such practices, managements have two options that are not mutually exclusive: campaign to change the legislation that underpins board-level employee representation or change the manner in which board-level decision-making is made to facilitate the achievement of objectives that they consider appropriate to current circumstances. Initiatives concerned with the first option were discussed in Chapter 1. The data presented here demonstrate that many board-level employee representatives are excluded from strategic company decision-making in that decisions are taken at meetings where employee representatives are not present, the form of participation is limited to information or consultation and board-level employee representatives may be excluded from subcommittee meetings.

The cross-sectional data presented here do not allow comment as to whether the rate of exclusion has increased over time but do raise questions about relations within the board between employee representatives and other stakeholders. Chapter 6 examines these relations.

Finally Chapter 5 allows further specification of the character of participation and the power of board-level employee representatives. It is apparent that many board-level employee representatives are unable to convert the intensity of participation demonstrated in Chapter 4 to exercise power within the board. Those board-level employee representatives who participate at the board through only information or consultation are reduced to partial participation. Similarly, the board-level employee representatives who exert no or little influence on company restructuring decisions fall short of partial participation. The disaggregated German data, however, demonstrate that institutional power derived from the constitutional provisions attached to the board, influence the power resources available to board-level employee representatives and enable those operating within Montan systems to exert more power than those in parity and one-third systems. The development of collaborative power resources varies across the country clusters with Germanic, Francophone and SE board-level employee representatives being markedly more likely than their counterparts elsewhere to caucus and to engage in pre-meetings with senior management before plenary meetings of the board. This suggests that power derived from articulation is dependent on the character of relations generated by board-level employee representatives within the company. These relations are examined in Chapter 6.

NOTES

1. The same approach is used in Chapter 6, where bivariate analyses are used to assess the impact of the same group of variables on the networking and articulation of board-level employee representatives.
2. The complete range of influence within the three German systems of codetermination is as follows:

	One-third co-determination, %	Parity co-determination, %	Montan co-determination, %
Very influential	4.3	6.6	13.3
Influential	28.7	29.7	23.3
Intermediate	31.6	32.3	40.1
Not very influential	28.2	24.2	23.3
Not at all influential	7.2	7.2	/
Index score	–2.4	+4.9	+13.3
	N = 209	N = 712	N = 30

3. The form of influence exerted by board-level representatives within the three German systems is as follows:

	One-third co-determination %	Parity co-determination %	Montan co-determination %
Co-manage the company by participating in decision-making	9.7	14.2	15.8
Discuss matters with other board members until a shared position is reached	12.0	18.1	7.9
Control the management through supervision	24.3	33.8	44.7
Are consulted, but the final decision rests with other board members	38.7	23.5	21.1
Are informed, but have little opportunity to discuss matters	15.3	10.4	10.5
	N = 300	N = 855	N = 38

4. The range of attendance of board-level representatives at board meetings where the main decisions are made is calculated as follows. The minimum figure in the range is calculated by summing the proportion of respondents that cited 'during board meetings', 'during meetings outside the board involving employee representatives' and 'during subcommittee meetings'. The maximum figure is calculated by subtracting the proportion of respondents that mentioned 'during meetings outside of the board excluding employee representatives' from 100.0 per cent.
5. The complete results disaggregated by the form of codetermination in Germany are as follows:

	One-third co-determination, %	Parity co-determination, %	Montan co-determination, %
During board meetings	33.3	31.7	50.0
During meetings outside the board excluding employee representatives	29.7	17.4	2.6

	One-third co-determination, %	Parity co-determination, %	Montan co-determination, %
During meetings outside the board involving shareholder representatives	28.3	27.0	23.6
During meetings outside the board involving employee representatives	4.0	12.1	13.2
During subcommittee meetings	3.0	9.7	5.3
During meetings outside the board excluding shareholder representatives	1.7	2.1	5.3
	N = 300	N = 849	N = 38

6. These two obligations are based in European regulation: the 2006/43/EC Directive on statutory audits of annual accounts and consolidated accounts, as amended by Directive 2014/56/EU and Directive 2013/13/EU on access to the activity of credit institutions and the prudential supervision of credit institutions and investment forms.
7. See, for example, the following position of European institutions: 'the creation of these committees is not intended, in principle, to remove the matters considered from the purview of the (supervisory) board itself, which remains fully responsible for the decisions taken in its field of competence' (Point 6.1 of Commission recommendation 2005/162/EC).
8. Only 23.5 per cent of respondents reported that they sit on the board of a company traded on the stock exchange.
9. In Austria one-third co-determination also applies to the composition of subcommittees, thereby ensuring the participation of employee representatives, although board-level employee representatives cannot take part in regular meetings covering management contracts and remuneration. Board-level employee representatives, however, can take part in specific meetings on issues relating to the appointment of managers, their dismissal or the granting of stock options (Gahleitner 2013). In Slovenia and Sweden board-level employee representatives are granted by law one seat on subcommittees (Senčur Peček 2011; PTK 2011), while in Germany the Federal Court of Justice called for an 'adequate representation of employees on each board sub-committee' (Roth 2013).
10. The German code of corporate governance states that 'in supervisory boards with codetermination, representatives of the shareholders and of the employees can prepare for the supervisory board meetings separately, possibly with members of the management board (Point 3.6 of the June 2014 English version).

6 The Articulation of Board-Level Employee Representation

Chapter 5 focused on the influence and power exerted by board-level employee representatives. Chapter 6 shifts the focus to three themes, which address aspects of the articulation between board-level employee representatives and agencies external to the board, including other institutions of labour representation within the company, and the parties that represent interests that differ from those of labour. The three interrelated themes concern issues such as training and expertise, articulation and networking, and enterprise coalitions. Examinations of the data based on these themes allow for further analyses of the power resources available to board-level employee representatives insofar as communicative power relies on robust articulation with other institutions of labour representation (Munck 2000; Urban 2012), collaborative power depends on alliances formed within the board and elsewhere (Gourevitch and Shinn 2005), and strategic power requires board-level employee representatives to acquire support from institutions within and outside of the company to strengthen their position (Ganz 2000; Gumbrell-McCormick and Hyman 2013:30–31).

Critics of board-level employee representation cite the lack of appropriate training and expertise among employee representatives as a reason for curtailing or not implementing arrangements for employee representation at board level (Bullock 1977: Minority Report; Davies and Hopt 2013; Mertens and Schanze 1979). In particular, critics argue that shortfalls in training and expertise among board-level employee representatives may delay decision-making and/or result in weaker decision-making at the board. There is no doubt that the skills and expertise that underpinned the initial employment with the company of many board-level employee representatives are different from those required to participate and influence board-level decision-making. No fewer than 62.1 per cent of board-level employee representatives surveyed, for example, completed elementary or upper-secondary education or obtained vocational training in their area of specialism as their highest level of qualification, thereby confirming the findings of earlier studies that the majority of board-level employee representatives do not have formal training beyond that of a vocational qualification (Gold 2011). Furthermore, some have argued that the need for additional training and expertise for board-level employee representatives has been exacerbated by the increased pressure on company boards arising from the post-2007 economic crisis (Paris et al. 2012).

Some national legislative arrangements that underpin board-level employee representation include reference to training provisions.[1] Company and/or industry level agreements may supplement statutory training provisions. In addition, most codes of corporate governance recommend induction programmes and regular training sessions for all board members, including board-level employee representatives. A review of national training arrangements available through either of these means in France, Germany and the Netherlands shows that their content varies according to national traditions and practices but tend to focus on the terms of national legislation (Paris et al. 2012). Extant research also suggests that a majority of board-level employee representatives attend training courses at different levels to acquire expertise in areas such as law, accountancy and finance; that is, board-level employee representatives supplement their vocational education and training with specialist and technical training for their board-level activities (Gold 2011).

Personal acquisition of the expertise required to participate at board level and to interpret the information available at the board is no straightforward task for many board-level employee representatives. Access to such expertise is available from external agencies, such as trade unions and consultancies, thereby reducing the pressure on board-level employee representatives to acquire knowledge in a range of technical specialisms. Some trade unions, for example, have established support departments that provide analyses of company and industry information for unionised board-level employee representatives. In consequence, the manifestoes of many unionists standing for election as a board-level employee representative refer to the support that the union will provide and cite this support as advantageous compared to the situation of non-unionists who are unable to access such support.

A second theme of Chapter 6 concerns articulation and networking. Systems of information and consultation tend to be viewed as being effective from the perspective of labour when the component parts of such systems are articulated; that is, there are inter-linkages between the different components, which ensure flows of information between the institutions that comprise the system (Streeck 1995; Svensson and Öberg 2005). In the context of board-level employee representation articulation has a range of components both within and external to the company. Within the company, board-level employee representatives may be articulated with other institutions of labour representation, including European works councils; other board members, whether they represent labour, management or shareholders; employees; and managers. Chapter 5 identified marked differences between board-level employee representatives operating in different country clusters regarding their capacity to exert power over long-term strategic corporate decisions. Chapter 6 extends this analysis by reference to the intensity of articulation achieved by board-level employee representatives within the company. Articulation external to the company may involve trade unions and networks of board-level employee representatives drawn from different companies, the former of which may *inter alia* provide specialist expertise as discussed earlier.

Three further introductory remarks apply to both internal and external components of articulation. First, the parties involved in articulation are likely to vary between country clusters, not least because of the wide variation in the constituencies of board-level employee representatives (see Chapter 3). Second, articulation arrangements with trade unions, in part, are dependent on whether there is a single channel or a dual system of representation in place. In single-channel systems, articulation with trade unions can be both internal and external to the company. Third, Chapter 3 showed that articulation between institutions of labour representation may be sustained through personal involvement and the holding of multiple representative positions within the company and/or trade union. French board-level employee representatives, however, are prohibited by law from holding trade union positions and seats on the works council in the company in which they serve on the board. Again, therefore, variation is anticipated between the country clusters.

A third theme of Chapter 6 concerns enterprise coalitions. To exert influence within the board many employee representatives recognise that enterprise coalitions may enhance their political position. Where investors seek improved corporate disclosure arrangements vis-à-vis managerial decision-making and strategy, for example, board-level employee representatives and other representatives of labour within the company may benefit in terms of greater managerial transparency. In these circumstances a 'transparency coalition' between investor representatives and board-level employee representatives may yield mutual benefits (Gourevitch and Shinn 2005:65–66 and 208–210). Similar trade-offs may be available to board-level employee representatives through enterprise coalitions with other stakeholders (Aguilera and Jackson 2003; Aoki 1994). Irrespective of the composition and character of enterprise coalitions involving board-level employee representatives, three issues underpin the position of labour in such coalitions. First, to varying degrees employees are tied to the company by specific characteristics such as skills, pay and pensions. External institutions including national education, training and welfare systems influence the nature of these characteristics. Second, the character of industrial relations institutions, traditions and practices, particularly views held within the trade union movement, are likely to influence the attitude of board-level employee representatives towards specific coalition partners. Adversarial relations between managers and worker representatives in French workplaces, for example, may promote the seeking of different coalition partners by board-level employee representatives compared to their Nordic counterparts, where the character of relations between managers and worker representatives differs markedly. Third, enterprise coalitions may be issue-specific, as in the case of the 'transparency coalition' mentioned earlier or may be broader in scope. There is no expectation, however, that enterprise coalitions will necessarily be long-standing. In short, there is no reason to anticipate uniformity in the approaches of board-level employee representatives towards enterprise coalitions.

While the composition, character and longevity of enterprise coalitions vary both within and between country clusters, two general forms of enterprise coalition have been identified that involve investors, management and employees: a 'corporatist compromise' between employees and management that has dominated continental Western European corporate governance since 1945 and an 'investor model' dependent on an enterprise coalition between management and investors that is characteristic of the UK and the US (Gourevitch and Shinn 2005:96–131). Based on the same three actors, several typologies of enterprise coalitions have been formulated (Gourevitich and Shinn 2005; Jackson 2005). Jackson proposed a typology of enterprise coalitions comprising class coalitions, insider–outsider coalitions and accountability coalitions (2005:296–297). A class coalition is essentially similar to the investor model, whereas an insider–outsider coalition corresponds to the corporatist compromise insofar as the parties in coalition are identical in both pairs. Accountability coalitions comprise investors and labour acting in alliance against management. Identifying similar categories in terms of the relationships involved within each coalition Gourevitch and Shinn (2005) label the coalitions as class, sector and voice. The data presented here are examined by reference to the latter typology because it is drawn directly from the political approach to corporate governance. In the context of this study the issue is to identify whether board-level employee representatives have established, or seek closer, relations with management or shareholder representatives. Given the recent changes in the pattern of corporate governance in continental Western Europe noted in Chapter 1, the parties with which board-level employee representatives have or are prepared to enter into coalition may indicate either the resilience of Western European forms of corporate governance or the extent to which these forms have changed.

Sociological approaches to corporate governance are relatively silent on issues of articulation, although implicitly such approaches assume that in CMEs where coordination is more sophisticated than in the Francophone MMEs and the EMEs of the NMS articulation should be more intense. Evidence from Sweden, for example, shows that non-market mechanisms of power and trust are integral to coordination (Svensson and Öberg 2005). Similarly, to include an element of industrial democracy within industrial relations frameworks, the expectation is that board-level employee representation will be articulated with other institutions of labour representation within and outside of the company.

To examine these themes Chapter 6 includes four further sections. The first section identifies the resources available to board-level employee representatives and their source. The second section analyses the support available to unionised board-level employee representatives by trade unions and the additional forms of support that unionised board-level employee representatives would prefer trade unions to provide. The third section assesses the reporting activities of board-level employee representatives in terms of its frequency and the persons or institutions to which the board-level employee representatives report back. The fourth section examines the articulation and networking of board-level employee representatives by reference to relationships, meetings and preferences for more intense contact. In essence, the argument advanced in Chapter 6 is that board-level employee representatives are articulated by a variety of means with a wide range of institutions of labour representation, other board members and management. The pattern of this articulation varies between the country clusters in a manner that is consistent with neither political nor sociological approaches to corporate governance.

THE RESOURCES AVAILABLE TO BOARD-LEVEL EMPLOYEE REPRESENTATIVES

This section traces the resources available to board-level employee representatives and the origin of these resources. An examination of the support available to board-level employee representatives contributes to the understanding of articulation insofar as it allows the identification of the intensity of relations between board-level employee representatives and the parties that provide them with services and support. The results are presented in Table 6.1. The source 'other' refers primarily to the range of consultancies that offer support and services. It should be acknowledged that several consultancies that provide support to board-level employee representatives are closely related to trade unions and often act as service providers on behalf of trade unions. The distinction drawn between 'trade unions' and 'other' is thus not necessarily clear-cut.

In terms of resources received by board-level employee representatives, the 'total' column of the 'all' data indicates that all the listed resources are available to a majority of board-level employee representatives. 'Training' and 'communications facilities' are available to more than 85 per cent of board-level employee representatives, while about three-quarters also benefit from 'reimbursements of travel' and 'advice from experts'. Analysis by country clusters, however, highlights sharp discrepancies. Germanic board-level employee representatives are found to be in a comparatively better position when it comes to resources related to expert advice. Germanic, NMS and SE board-level employee representatives are the most likely to receive a 'director's fee', while Germanic board-level employee representatives are most likely to receive 'liability insurance'. Contributing to the latter result is the incorporation of Austrian board-level employee representatives in the Germanic cluster as they are covered by the group insurance policy that the *Österreichischer Gewerkschaftsbund* (ÖGB) has contracted for their benefit (Gahleitner 2013). Board-level employee representatives from the NMS and IGS are the least equipped in terms of 'training' and, for the latter, in terms of 'reimbursements of travel', although a majority of board-level employee representatives in both clusters benefit from these resources. The most precarious position is that of the Francophone respondents who receive the lowest level of resource provision on no less than five of the seven items listed in Table 6.1. In particular, only 25.2 per cent of Francophone board-level employee representatives benefits from a director's fee. Legal provisions in France preclude employee representatives with seats on the board of state-owned companies from receiving such fees.

The 'all' data in Table 6.1 also show that the key distinction in the origin of resources is between trade unions and employers. Trade unions are the principal, but not the sole, suppliers of 'training' and 'advice from experts', while employers occupy the same position for 'secretarial/administrative', 'communications', 'reimbursement for travel', 'director's fee' and 'liability insurance'. For each resource, however, a substantial proportion of board-level employee representatives obtain the support from a source other than the principal provider. To illustrate, 54.1 per cent of board-level employee representatives have received 'training' from 'employers', 'works councils' or 'other' in addition to the 65.2 per cent of unionists who have received 'training' from their trade union. Neither trade unions nor employers approach universal coverage when they are the principal supplier of a resource. In several instances the relatively low level of coverage is noteworthy. It is surprising, for example, that only 55.9 per cent of unionised board-level employee representatives have received 'advice from experts' that originates in their union and only 47.5 per cent of board-level employee representatives are in receipt of 'secretarial/administrative' support provided by the employer.

Three points are immediately apparent from these results. First, board-level employee representatives are reliant on external agencies for support in conducting their duties at the board. Second, board-level employee representation is to a degree subsidised by the employer beyond the payment of a 'director's fee', 'reimbursement for travel' and 'liability insurance', which are provided to all board members if they are available to employee representatives. In particular, employers subsidise 'communications' and 'secretarial/administrative' support. Third, 'works councils' and 'other' provide support to relatively few board-level employee representatives. Only the provision of 'training' and 'secretarial/administrative' support from 'works councils', for example, reaches more than 10 per cent of board-level employee representatives from either of these two sources.

Turning to the country clusters shows that the support available to board-level employee representatives varies markedly between clusters, as does the source

Table 6.1 The Resources and Their Source Provided to Board-Level Employee Representatives

Support	All Country Clusters N = 3,243–4,155					CMEs: Germanic N 1,468–1,554					CMEs: Nordic N = 1,005–1,917					MMEs: Francophone N 110–147				
	Total %	Employer %	Trade union[1] %	Works council[2] %	Other %	Total %	Employer %	Trade union[1] %	Works council %	Other %	Total %	Employer %	Trade union[1] %	Works council[2] %	Other %	Total %	Employer %	Trade union[1] %	Works council %	Other %
Training	86.4	37.1	65.2	11.3	5.7	88.9	22.4	78.1	18.1	6.3	88.9	44.2	63.2	2.5	4.5	81.0	57.8	43.6	3.4	3.4
Communi-cations	85.1	72.0	12.5	11.1	3.8	85.5	61.1	19.3	21.1	3.7	86.1	80.3	6.8	0.6	3.3	70.7	66.0	7.3	0.7	2.7
Reimbursements of travel	78.1	72.5	5.0	2.4	1.9	80.6	75.4	3.1	4.4	0.8	77.8	72.5	6.7	/	2.1	76.9	71.4	6.4	/	2.0
Advice from experts	73.3	23.9	55.9	8.0	9.5	82.2	19.8	70.4	11.6	8.0	69.6	24.2	49.1	1.9	10.0	54.4	12.9	38.2	9.5	7.5
Secretarial/ administrative	69.4	47.5	13.2	15.9	4.9	75.5	38.5	15.5	31.0	5.0	63.6	49.7	12.1	1.3	5.0	51.7	35.4	10.0	2.0	9.5
Director's fee	67.2	60.7	2.1	0.5	5.0	72.5	70.1	2.5	0.8	0.8	62.5	52.6	2.1	0.1	8.3	25.2	17.0	2.7	/	6.1
Liability insurance/ legal aid insurance	66.9	47.1	21.3	0.8	4.8	75.9	52.3	29.6	1.1	2.1	64.0	46.7	16.9	/	4.4	51.0	36.7	16.4	1.4	2.7

Notes:

1. The column headed trade union contains only responses from trade union members. The lower values of *N* are those for trade union members alone.
2. Swedish respondents are excluded from these two columns, because there is no possibility of establishing a works council in Sweden.

Table 6.1 (Continued) The Resources and Their Source Provided to Board-Level Employee Representatives

Support	EMEs														
	New Member States N = 294–509					Ireland, Greece and Spain N = 25–28					SEs N = 38				
	Total %	Employer %	Trade union[1] %	Works council %	Other %	Total %	Employer %	Trade union[1] %	Works council %	Other %	Total %	Employer %	Trade union[1] %	Works council %	Other %
Training	71.7	49.1	26.5	10.8	8.8	71.4	35.7	36.0	3.6	7.1	89.5	47.4	71.1	13.2	10.5
Communi-cations	84.3	76.6	10.5	4.7	6.1	78.6	64.3	24.0	/	3.6	89.5	68.4	18.4	7.9	5.3
Reimbursements of travel	72.3	65.0	6.1	1.8	4.5	64.3	57.1	4.0	/	7.1	94.7	94.7	5.3	/	/
Advice from experts	65.8	38.7	31.6	8.6	12.8	60.7	28.6	20.0	7.1	7.1	78.9	21.1	60.5	7.9	5.3
Secretarial/ administrative	77.4	69.4	9.2	3.7	3.5	71.4	53.6	16.0	/	3.6	68.4	42.1	18.4	26.3	7.9
Director's fee	80.7	75.6	0.3	0.6	5.1	60.7	50.0	4.0	/	7.1	89.5	84.2	2.6	/	2.6
Liability insurance/ legal aid insurance	55.6	35.4	10.2	1.6	15.1	60.7	53.6	/	/	7.1	86.8	63.2	31.6	2.6	7.9

from which the support originates. Only Germanic, Nordic and SE board-level employee representatives report the same distribution of support between employers and trade unions as for the 'all' data, in that the trade union is the principal source of 'training' and 'advice from experts' whereas employers are the primary source for the other forms of support. Even within these parameters, however, it is noteworthy that Germanic trade unions are more likely to support board-level employee representatives with 'training' and 'advice from experts' than are Nordic trade unions, whereas Nordic board-level employee representatives are more reliant than their Germanic counterparts on employers for support in the form of 'communications', 'secretarial/administrative' and 'training'.

Elsewhere there are variations in the relationship between trade unions and employers regarding the provision of support. In the Francophone countries, for example, the employer provides more board-level employee representatives with support than trade unions on all issues with the single exception of 'advice from experts', while in the NMS employers provide resources to more board-level employee representatives than trade unions in every form listed in Table 6.1. Articulation between board-level employee representatives and trade unions is thus less intense in these two country clusters than in the Germanic and Nordic CMEs.

Works councils in the Germanic countries are more effective providers of support than their counterparts in the Nordic, Francophone and IGS clusters. Articulation between board-level employee representatives and works councils in the Germanic countries is thus underpinned by a relatively intense servicing relationship. The relatively weak servicing relationship between Nordic board-level employee representatives and works councils is, of course, anticipated as Nordic countries operate with single-channel systems of representation where the union club rather than a works council is the principal means of workplace representation.[2] While support from the 'works council' in the NMS reaches fewer board-level employee representatives than in the Germanic countries, it is more wide ranging in its coverage than elsewhere. This suggests that the relative immaturity of the industrial relations and corporate governance systems in the NMS, coupled with the scarcity of resources available to trade unions and with 'works councils' in the NMS, have yet to allow the provision of support available in the Germanic countries, although the Germanic model is the basis on which several of the industrial relations and corporate governance systems in the NMS are being developed.

In summary, most board-level employee representatives are reliant on support from both trade unions and employers, with only those from the Germanic countries in receipt of wide-ranging support from works councils, suggesting more intense articulation between board-level employee representatives and institutions of labour representation. There is little evidence to suggest variation consistent with the categories based on sociological approaches to corporate governance, although there are indications that support systems available to board-level employee representatives in the NMS are in a process of development that could be construed as 'emerging'.

TRADE UNIONS: PROVIDING ADDED VALUE?

Trade unions are only moderately influential on the decision-making of board-level employee representatives.[3] Furthermore, only 26.2 per cent of unionised board-level employee representatives thought trade unions to be one of the two most important sources of information in undertaking their duties at the board level.[4] In contrast, vast numbers of union members standing for election as a board-level employee representative cite in their election manifestoes the benefits of the support they may receive from trade unions and the advantages that will accrue to the electorate from voting for a unionised candidate. Similarly, literature generated by trade unions mentions the influence that unions may wield through the organisation of networks of board-level employee representatives within both companies and industries, and use reference to this influence as justification for the maintenance of departments that provide support to board-level employee representatives.

The purpose of this section is to examine the forms of support provided to unionised board-level employee representatives by trade unions and the additional support from trade unions that board-level employee representatives encourage. Throughout the section attention is directed only to unionised board-level employee representatives on the assumption that non-unionised board-level employee representatives would be unable to access support from trade unions on the same scale as their unionised counterparts. As noted in Chapter 3 the rate of unionisation among board-level employee representatives in the sample is for all, 86.1 per cent; Germanic, 94.5 per cent; Nordic, 87.7 per cent; Francophone, 74.8 per cent; NMS, 57.8 per cent; IGS, 89.3 per cent; and SEs, 100.0 per cent.[5] The unionisation rate among board-level employee representatives is thus higher than the national rates for all employees, particularly in IGS and the Germanic and Francophone countries, indicating the efficacy of union campaigns during elections and the appeal of unionised board-level employee representatives to electorates.

The forms of support examined in Table 6.2 are primarily of a servicing character: information, training, and expertise provided by trade unions and sought by board-level employee representatives. Two of these forms of support, however, encompass more than servicing or differ in character to servicing: 'access to networks of BLERs' and 'informed political advice'. While the provision of 'access to networks of BLERs' certainly has an element of the servicing function, it may also enable board-level employee representatives to mobilise both within and across companies. 'Informed political advice' from trade unions suggests that board-level employee representatives may seek political leadership from unions. As such, this form of support is beyond that of a servicing agenda.

Table 6.2 outlines the support available from trade unions and the proportion of unionised board-level employee representatives seeking these different forms of support. It is immediately apparent that only one form of support, 'a means to consult in specific circumstances' (hereafter, 'a means

Table 6.2 How Are Union Members Supported by Their Trade Union?

Support provided	All Country Clusters %	CMEs		MMEs	EMEs	Ireland, Greece and Spain %	SEs %
		Germanic %	Nordic %	Francophone %	New Member States %		
A means to consult in specific circumstances	50.9	61.4	43.1	25.5	53.1	40.0	47.4
'Technical' training (accounting, finance, etc.)	48.0	68.9	36.4	28.2	20.1	16.0	60.5
Access to experts (lawyers, accountants, etc.)	41.4	61.9	23.5	42.7	41.8	40.0	55.3
Access to networks of BLERs	33.3	44.3	26.7	40.9	15.3	12.0	55.3
Early access to relevant information	32.1	39.2	24.0	38.2	40.8	36.0	31.6
Analyses/interpretation of information	29.2	49.6	12.9	29.1	20.4	24.0	39.5
Better access to more wide-ranging information	28.4	44.1	13.4	27.3	35.0	48.0	52.6
Informed political advice	26.0	45.2	10.5	51.8	8.8	32.0	47.4
Access to trade union organisations at European level	15.5	24.4	7.6	19.1	15.6	8.0	57.9
Other	13.2	12.6	14.0	2.7	16.7	8.0	21.1
	N = 3,578	N = 1,468	N = 1,681	N = 110	N = 294	N = 25	N = 38

Note:

Only the responses from trade union members are provided above and the question specifically requested that only unionists respond. Respondents could tick as many boxes as were appropriate; hence, the sum of the percentage figures is more than 100 per cent.

to consult'), reaches more than half of 'all' unionised board-level employee representatives. That consultation with trade unions heads the list of support utilised by board-level employee representatives suggests that articulation with unions remains in place for a substantial number of board-level employee representatives and that trade unions may act as 'sounding boards' for board-level employee representatives. Technical support in the form of both 'training' and 'access to experts' appears at positions two and three in the ranking, confirming that board-level employee representatives seek support on matters on which they are unlikely to have received formal education. One-third of board-level employee representatives are supported by their union through gaining 'access to networks of BLERs'. 'Access to trade union organisations at European level' is a form of support that is utilised by relatively few board-level employee representatives. This is not the case in the SEs, however, where almost 58.0 per cent of board-level employee representatives indicate that they benefit from 'access to trade union organisations at European level'.

The location of the board-level employee representative influences the extent of support available from trade unions. Using the 'all' data, for example, demonstrates that board-level employee representatives based in subsidiaries are more likely than their counterparts in single or holding companies to receive all the forms of support listed in Table 6.2, with the single exception of 'early access to relevant information'. Only for 'technical training', however, was the relationship statistically significant. Although sector had no effect on the support available from trade unions, board-level employee representatives in companies with 2,000 or more employees are more likely to be in receipt of trade union support than those in smaller companies, confirming the view that unions struggle to support representation at smaller sites (Fairbrother and Griffin 2002; Phelan 2007). The gendered nature of many trade unions is also confirmed insofar as men receive moderately more support than women on all the items listed in Table 6.2, with the exception of 'a means to consult'. Policies intended to increase the proportion of women board members clearly constitute a challenge for unions to ensure equality in the provision of support.

Two points are immediately apparent from the data disaggregated by the country clusters. First, there is marked variation between country clusters in the forms of support received by board-level employee representatives from trade unions, which is illustrated by variation in the most widespread form of support available. 'A means to consult' heads the ranking in the Nordic countries and the NMS. Elsewhere 'technical training' (Germanic countries, SEs), 'informed political advice' (Francophone countries) and 'better access to more wide-ranging information' (IGS) were the most frequently provided trade union support. Second, using the sum of the percentage data presented in Table 6.2 as a proxy measure for the intensity of articulation between trade unions and board-level employee representatives regarding the provision of support illustrates entirely different patterns of articulation ranging from the Germanic countries, where, on average, each board-level employee representative received 4.51 forms of support, to the Nordic countries, where the corresponding figure was 2.12. The intermediary figures for the other country clusters are Francophone countries, 3.06; NMS, 2.68; and IGS, 2.64. Two of the archetypical CMEs thus occupy the polar positions regarding the intensity of support sought from trade unions by board-level employee representatives. Only by examining the country clusters can the extent of the variation between them be elaborated. Board-level employee representatives within the SEs, however, received 4.69 forms of support from trade unions, making them the most supported.

Not surprisingly in the light of the second point mentioned earlier, Germanic board-level employee representatives receive above average rates of support on all issues listed in Table 6.2. Particularly large proportions of Germanic board-level employee representatives seek technical support in the form of either 'training' or 'access to experts'. These proportions are not matched in any other country cluster or in the SEs. Similarly, relatively large proportions of Germanic board-level employee representatives seek 'early access to relevant information', 'analyses/interpretation of information' and 'better access to more wide-ranging information'. In combination, these findings suggest that trade unions in the Germanic countries are adept in the provision of information and expertise to unionised board-level employee representatives. Furthermore, given the relatively dense networks between Germanic board-level employee representatives and works councils noted earlier, it would appear that articulation is well developed in the form of dense networks with institutions of labour representation both within and external to the company. Germanic board-level employee representatives are also not averse to seeking 'informed political advice' from their unions, suggesting that trade unions may generate policies for board-level employee representatives to implement and/or may provide some form of political leadership. Articulation in the Germanic countries thus comprises both service-oriented and political elements.

The relationship between Nordic board-level employee representatives and the provision of support from trade unions is the polar opposite to that in the Germanic countries. Nordic board-level employee representatives are the least articulated with trade unions in the context of support, with below average rates at which support is provided on every issue mentioned in Table 6.2. Furthermore, the rate of provision of 'access to experts', 'early access to relevant information', 'analyses/interpretation of information', 'better access to more wide-ranging information' and 'access to trade union organisation at European level' to Nordic board-level employee representatives is the lowest among the country clusters and the SEs. These results show that Nordic board-level employee representatives are relatively independent from union organisation whether it is within or external to the workplace. Furthermore, Nordic board-level employee representatives do not seek 'informed political advice' from trade unions in large numbers, indicating that Nordic trade unions do not provide political leadership to board-level employee representatives on the same scale as Germanic trade unions. In combination, these results lend support to recent Swedish data that suggest board-level employee representation is an underutilised resource, particularly within private-sector services (Berglund et al. 2013).

A possible explanation for the low levels of support available through Nordic trade unions to representatives is that the coverage of board-level representation extends to relatively small organisations, where trade union representation and support are unsophisticated compared to that at larger workplaces (see Chapter 3). To test this proportion the Nordic data were divided into categories consistent with the German legislation; that is, categories of 499 or fewer employees and 500 or more employees.[6] For seven of the nine forms of support listed in Table 6.2 Nordic board-level employee representatives operating at larger companies were more likely to be in receipt than were their counterparts at smaller workplaces. The proposition that trade unions are unable to support representatives at smaller companies at the same intensity as they do at larger companies is thus confirmed. It is also apparent from the Nordic data disaggregated by size that board-level employee representatives at larger companies receive support at a lower rate than elsewhere as recorded by the 'all' data of Table 6.2. The relative independence of Nordic board-level employee representatives from trade union support is thus a feature of the Nordic system of board-level representation rather than a result of the extensive coverage of the Nordic system.

The pattern of support received by Francophone board-level employee representatives differs from that received by their Germanic and Nordic counterparts insofar as 'informed political advice' is the key priority and is available to more than half of Francophone board-level employee representatives. While the extent to which 'informed political advice' is prioritised by Francophone board-level employee representatives suggests that trade unions may provide some form of political leadership or may generate policies for board-level employee representatives to implement, two other factors are likely to influence the Francophone situation. First, French union confederations are divided by political outlook and affiliation. Seeking 'informed political advice' may reflect a perceived need to retain politically differentiated positions. Second, the adversarial character of Francophone industrial relations may prompt board-level employee representatives to seek 'informed political advice' in contesting issues with management and shareholder representatives at the board. This argument is lent further support by the large numbers of Francophone board-level employee representatives that benefit from 'access to networks of BLERs' through trade unions, which suggests that collective organisation may be used to consolidate the position of board-level employee representatives in contesting issues at the board. Only 25.5 per cent of Francophone board-level employee representatives receive support in the form of 'a means to consult' from trade unions, which is a lower proportion than in any other country cluster and suggests that Francophone trade unionists view their unions through a political lens rather than as a 'sounding board'.

Board-level employee representatives in the NMS are the least likely to seek 'informed political advice' but are provided with support in the form of 'a means to consult', 'access to experts' and 'early access to relevant information'. The trade union emphasis in the NMS is thus on the servicing function rather than the provision of political leadership. Both a servicing function and political leadership are available from trade unions in IGS. In IGS, Francophone countries and the NMS, board-level employee representatives are more likely to seek 'access to experts' rather than 'technical training'. This situation is the reverse of that found in the Germanic and Nordic countries. In the IGS, Francophone countries and NMS it appears that there is a greater reluctance to acquire technical skills and a greater reliance on external expertise provided by experts made available through trade unions.

The analysis now turns to the additional support sought by unionised board-level employee representatives from trade unions. Reference to the 'all' column of Table 6.3 reveals that the percentage figures tend to be smaller than those of Table 6.2, indicating that the existing support from trade unions satisfies many unionised board-level employee representatives. The rank order in which additional support is required differs from that indicating the support that is already available. In particular, 'access to networks of BLERs' rises to head the ranking, although 'training' and 'as a means to consult' remain prominent as requirements from trade union despite these two items heading the ranking on the support that is already provided (see Table 6.2). There is no wide-ranging demand for additional 'informed political advice' or 'access to trade union organisations at European level'.

There is a marked transformation in the data documenting the additional support required compared to that on available support. This is most apparent among Germanic board-level employee representatives who, on average, require an additional 1.48 forms of support compared to Nordic, 1.79; SEs, 1.84; Francophone, 1.85; NMS, 2.20; and IGS, 2.52. In other words, Germanic board-level employee representatives currently receive the most forms of support and require the least additional forms of support. Furthermore, the relatively even distribution of the results from the Germanic cluster in Table 6.3 indicates that Germanic board-level employee representatives do not have any particular priorities regarding additional support.

Nordic board-level employee representatives emphasise 'technical training', 'access to networks of BLERs', 'access to experts' and 'a means to consult' as the additional support they require from trade unions. More than 20 per cent of Nordic board-level employee representatives require these additional forms of support. There is no single issue on which 20 per cent of Germanic board-level employee representatives require additional support. Furthermore, the proportion of Nordic board-level employee representatives that receive support in the form of 'access to networks of BLERs' is

Table 6.3 What Additional Support Do Union Members Want from Their Trade Union?

		CMEs		MMEs	EMEs		
Additional support required	**All Country Clusters %**	**Germanic %**	**Nordic %**	**Francophone %**	**New Member States %**	**Ireland, Greece and Spain %**	**SEs %**
Access to networks of BLERs	21.9	18.3	26.0	28.2	13.3	24.0	15.8
'Technical' training (accounting, finance, etc.)	21.8	13.6	27.8	14.5	31.3	24.0	34.2
A means to consult in specific circumstances	22.1	16.8	26.3	24.5	22.8	36.0	21.1
Analyses/interpretation of information	19.4	18.5	18.9	20.0	25.2	28.0	23.7
Early access to relevant information	17.0	14.8	17.0	18.2	25.5	36.0	15.8
Better access to more wide-ranging information	16.4	14.6	16.1	16.4	26.9	20.0	10.5
Access to experts (lawyers, accountants, etc.)	22.3	19.7	21.9	29.1	34.0	32.0	34.2
Informed political advice	11.6	13.1	9.9	19.1	9.9	20.0	5.3
Access to trade union organisations at European level	9.6	10.8	6.0	14.5	20.1	28.0	15.8
Other	8.1	7.4	8.9	/	10.5	4.0	7.9
	N = 3,578	N = 1,468	N = 1,681	N = 110	N = 294	N = 25	N = 38

Note:
Only the responses from trade union members are provided, and the question specifically requested that only unionists respond. Respondents could tick as many boxes as were appropriate; hence, the sum of the percentage figures is more than 100 per cent.

almost matched by the proportion that seek additional support in this area. Demands on trade unions from Nordic board-level employee representatives are thus more intense than those lodged by their Germanic counterparts.

Francophone, NMS and SE board-level employee representatives prioritise additional 'access to experts' from trade unions. In Francophone countries this demand is significantly greater than that for 'technical training' confirming the preference in this cluster for external expertise rather than each board-level employee representative acquiring a broader range of personal skills through training. In contrast, respondents based in SEs would welcome additional support in the form of 'access to experts' and a more developed offer in terms of 'technical training'. Francophone board-level employee representatives also seek greater 'access to networks of BLERs'. The emphasis on this point among Francophone board-level employee representatives is anticipated because they require such networks to effectively contest board-level decision-making. Relatively large numbers of NMS board-level employee representatives also seek additional support in information provision and interpretation. Although this finding confirms the strong servicing function in the articulation between board-level employee representatives and trade unions in this cluster, it also raises questions of resource allocation within trade unions.

Trade unions provide added value to unionised board-level employee representatives in the form of support services and, in some country clusters, political leadership. There is marked variation in the extent to which board-level employee representatives are articulated with trade unions though the support that they receive. In particular, articulation between Germanic board-level employee representatives and trade unions is sophisticated regarding its scale and both its servicing and political elements. In contrast, articulation between Nordic board-level employee representatives and trade unions is relatively weak, whereas in the Francophone countries political leadership occupies a more prominent position than elsewhere.

ARTICULATION BY MEANS OF REPORTING BACK

A second element of articulation concerns the frequency at which board-level employee representatives report affairs of the board back to institutions of labour representation and the workforce that compose their electorate. Whereas the support available through trade unions is not unidirectional in that unions may provide different forms of support and board-level employee representatives may seek support from unions, the initiative for reporting back lies principally with board-level employee representatives. It should be acknowledged, however, that a persistent failure to report back may result in a refusal to nominate by the relevant parties or electoral defeat at subsequent elections. The frequency at which reporting back takes place is also an indicator of the isolation from, or engagement with, institutions of labour representation and the workforce within the company. Board-level employee representatives that are isolated are more likely to be subject to incorporation (Levinson 2000; Pistor 1999). What is or is not reported back is dependent to a degree on approaches to confidentiality taken by board-level employee representatives. As was noted in conjunction with Table 4.5, board-level employee representatives handle confidentiality very differently between country clusters.

Reference to the 'all' data in Table 6.4 shows that more than 37 per cent of board-level employee representatives 'never' report back to 'employees' and to 'trade unions', while 36.2 per cent 'never' report back to the 'works council'. No fewer than 14.6 per cent of 'all' board-level employee representatives 'never' report back to the three parties. A substantial minority of board-level employee representatives are thus isolated from institutions of labour representation and their electorates. The extent to which board-level employee representatives are isolated from institutions of labour representation and employees varies markedly between the country clusters. The Nordic countries occupy one polar position in that 16.5 per cent of board-level employee representatives indicate that they 'never' report back to the 'works council', 'trade union' or 'employees'. Elsewhere the results for the same analysis are NMS, 12.6 per cent; SEs, 10.8 per cent; Germanic, 8.1 per cent; Francophone, 7.5 per cent; and IGS, 7.1 per cent. In all country clusters and the SEs, a minority of board-level employee representatives, thus, is isolated from institutions of labour representations and employees. While the size of companies covered by the legislation on board-level employee representation in the Nordic countries influences the situation, it does not explain why so many Nordic board-level employee representatives 'never' report back to the three parties. In companies in which 499 or fewer people are employed, for example, 17.8 per cent of Nordic board-level employee representatives 'never' report back to the three parties whereas 13.0 per cent of their counterparts employed at companies with 500 or more employees 'never' report back. In short, even at the larger companies a larger proportion of Nordic board-level employee representatives 'never' report back than in the other country clusters and the SEs.

Turning to 'all' board-level employee representatives that report back, 48.2 per cent report back to the 'works council', 38.6 per cent to 'employees' and 47.1 per cent to the 'trade union' at least once every three months. In other words, more board-level employee representatives report back at least once every three months to the works council, employees and trade union than 'never' do so. This finding also suggests a link between the frequency at which board activities are reported back and the frequency of board meetings. Only a minority of board-level employee representatives report back as frequently as 'monthly', 'every two weeks' or 'weekly' (11.7 per cent to works councils, 9.9 per cent to employees and 17.4 per cent to trade unions). Bearing in mind that 69.1 per cent of 'all' board-level employee representatives indicate that the board meets on average once every three

Table 6.4 Typically, How Frequently Do You Report Back the Activities of the Board?

				CMEs						EMEs		
	All Country Clusters			Germanic			Nordic			Francophone		
	Report to works council[2] %	Report to employees %	Report to trade union[1] %	Report to works council %	Report to employees %	Report to trade union[1] %	Report to works council[2] %	Report to employees %	Report to trade union[1] %	Report to works council %	Report to employees %	Report to trade union[1] %
Never	36.2	37.3	37.7	12.2	37.6	41.9	74.6	39.5	39.3	57.3	32.8	9.0
Every six months	15.6	24.1	15.2	21.6	34.1	18.4	5.4	17.0	12.6	7.3	14.9	9.0
Every three months	36.5	28.7	29.7	53.1	25.8	29.4	14.5	30.3	29.3	30.0	44.5	46.0
Monthly	10.0	7.8	13.7	10.9	2.3	8.2	4.8	9.7	13.8	5.4	7.8	32.0
Every two weeks	0.7	1.3	2.1	1.2	0.2	0.4	0.3	2.5	3.7	/	/	1.0
Weekly	1.0	0.8	1.6	1.0	/	1.7	0.4	1.0	1.3	/	/	3.0
	N = 2,614	*N* = 3,628	*N* = 3,143	*N* = 1,352	*N* = 1,323	*N* = 1,238	*N* = 764	*N* = 1,695	*N* = 1,512	*N* = 110	*N* = 128	*N* = 100

Notes:

1. Only the responses from trade unionists are reported in the column headed 'report to trade union' on the assumption that non-members would not generally report the outcome of board meetings to a trade union.

2. Swedish respondents are excluded from these two columns, because there is no possibility of establishing a works council in Sweden.

Table 6.4 (Continued) Typically, How Frequently Do You Report Back the Activities of the Board?

	EMEs								
	New Member States			Ireland, Greece and Spain			SEs		
	Report to works council %	Report to employee %	Report to trade union[1] %	Report to works council %	Report to employees %	Report to trade union[1] %	Report to works council %	Report to employees %	Report to trade union[1] %
Never	37.3	29.8	21.1	53.9	26.9	20.0	25.0	47.2	54.3
Every six months	18.0	24.6	17.5	3.8	15.4	4.0	16.7	36.1	11.4
Every three months	25.1	27.4	30.2	/	11.5	8.0	47.2	13.9	20.0
Monthly	17.7	15.4	28.0	30.8	30.8	40.0	11.1	2.8	14.3
Every two weeks	0.3	0.6	1.7	/	3.9	20.0	/	/	/
Weekly	1.6	2.2	1.5	11.5	11.5	8.0	/	/	/
	N = 362	N = 456	N = 275	N = 26	N = 26	N = 25	N = 36	N = 36	N = 35

months, the results suggest that the largest group of board-level employee representatives tend to report back on the occasion of every board meeting.[7] The disaggregated data tend to confirm this argument. In IGS, boards meet monthly on average and the proportion of board-level employee representatives who report back their activities 'monthly' is greater than that of those who report back 'every two weeks' or 'weekly', irrespective of whether the reporting back is to the 'works' council', 'employees' or 'trade union'. In the other country clusters and in the SEs, the board is most likely to meet 'every three months', which is the same frequency at which the largest single group of board-level employee representatives report back.

Analysis of the relationship between board-level employee representatives and the actors or institutions to which reporting back occurs suggests a second connection, namely, that between board-level employee representatives and the parties that nominate them for the position (see Table 3.8). In the SEs and the Germanic cluster a substantially larger proportion of board-level employee representatives report back the affairs of the board to the 'works council' at least once every three months than 'never' report back (SEs, 55.2 per cent compared to 25.0 per cent; Germanic cluster, 66.2 per cent compared to 12.2 per cent). These findings consolidate earlier results that demonstrate a more articulated relationship between Germanic board-level employee representatives and works councils than elsewhere. In contrast, however, more SE and Germanic board-level employee representatives 'never' report back to trade unions than do so at least 'every three months' (SEs, 54.3 per cent compared to 34.3 per cent; Germanic cluster, 41.9 per cent compared to 39.6 per cent). These results are not surprising given that works councils undertake prominent roles in the nomination of SE and Germanic board-level employee representatives. A similar pattern can be observed in the Nordic, Francophone, NMS and IGS clusters, where trade unions are the main party to which reporting back is addressed and are responsible for the nomination of the board-level employee representatives. More Nordic, Francophone, NMS and IGS board-level employee representatives report back to the trade union at least 'every three months' than 'never' report back: Nordic cluster, 48.1 per cent compared to 39.5 per cent; Francophone cluster, 82.0 per cent compared to 9.0 per cent; NMS, 61.4 per cent compared to 21.1 per cent; IGS, 76.0 per cent compared to 20.0 per cent. With the exception of the NMS, the converse is the case for the proportions of board-level employee representatives that 'never' report back to the 'works council', which are greater than the proportions who report back at least 'every three months': Nordic, 74.6 per cent compared to 20.0 per cent; Francophone, 57.3 per cent compared to 35.4 per cent; IGS, 53.9 per cent compared to 30.8 per cent.

The reporting-back relationship between board-level employee representatives and employees is less developed than that between board-level employee representatives and the parties that nominated them. This is not to argue that board-level employee representatives do not report back to employees. The proportion of board-level employee representatives that 'never' report back to employees falls within a relatively narrow range of 26.9 per cent (IGS) to 47.2 per cent (SEs). The country cluster data show that reporting back to employees is less frequent than to works councils in the Germanic clusters and SEs (66.2 per cent of Germanic board-level employee representatives report to the works councils at least 'every three months' compared to 28.3 per cent who report to employees: in SEs the same comparison is 58.3 per cent compared to 16.7 per cent). Elsewhere similar relationships are found in the frequency of reporting back to trade unions and employees: Nordic, 48.1 per cent compared to 43.3 per cent; Francophone, 82.0 per cent compared to 52.3 per cent; NMS, 61.4 per cent compared to 45.6 per cent; IGS, 76.0 per cent compared to 57.7 per cent. In brief, the party that nominates the board-level employee representative, rather than the party that appoints or elects them is key to explaining the marked variation between the country clusters in reporting back practices.

To summarise, the character of articulation between board-level employee representatives and institutions of labour representation and employees in terms of reporting the affairs of the board back varies between country clusters. For Germanic board-level employee representatives it is important to report back to the works council, whereas for their Francophone, NMS and IGS counterparts the trade union is the most important interlocutor. Substantial minorities of board-level employee representatives 'never' report back to works councils, employees and trade unions. In combination these findings highlight two issues. First, the extent to which there is variation within the country clusters with large proportions of board-level employee representatives answering either than they 'never' report back or regularly do so, suggests that confidentiality provisions are not uniformly applied by board-level employee representatives. Second, there is clearly a political dimension to reporting back. In particular, Germanic board-level employee representatives focus their reporting back activities on the works council as the principal institution of labour representation within the company and the institution that is extremely influential on their subsequent re-election when their term of office expires, whereas in the NMS, Francophone countries and IGS the attention of board-level employee representatives in reporting back is directed towards the trade union, which is more influential than the works council. In this context, board-level employee representation in the Germanic countries is more 'in-company' than in the NMS, Francophone countries and IGS.

SEEKING COALITIONS WITHIN THE BOARD

Board-level employee representatives may establish relationships with other representative groups within the company and with parties that represent interests other than labour at the board to exert greater power at the board. Relationships within the board may be short term and issue specific or may develop into long-term coalitions that influence the character of board politics (Gourevitch and Shinn 2005; Jackson 2005). In the context of the country clusters identified here three forms of such long-term coalition should be in evidence if the explanation of corporate governance founded on political perspectives is to be supported (for details, see Gourevitvch and Shinn 2005:95–276). First, the Nordic approach is designated as a 'class model' in which labour competes with capital, in the form of owners and managers acting in alliance. Second, a 'sector model' envisages elements of labour and management acting in coalition against external investors and is exemplified by Germanic practices. Third, a 'voice model' assumes that labour seeks working relationship with external investors to protect pensions and employment levels from initiatives taken by management. Among others, France is regarded as an exemplar of the voice model.[8]

This section identifies how board-level employee representatives perceive relations with other parties in two stages. The first stage assesses how board-level employee representatives perceive their relationship with parties within and outside the board. Entering into working relationships with these parties may enable board-level employee representatives to exert greater power at the board and should vary as outlined above if they are consistent with political approaches to corporate governance. The second stage traces the frequency at which board-level employee representatives meet other parties outside of the board meeting and the extent to which board-level employee representatives wish to meet these parties more frequently. The argument advanced is that there is no clear-cut distinction between the sector, class and voice models in terms of the relationships established by board-level employee representatives. There are, however, differences in emphasis in the relationships established by board-level employee representatives in the various models proposed from within the political perspective that confirm that the character of working relationships established by board-level representatives vary between country clusters.

Cooperation or Conflict in Extant Relationships

The first approach to assessing the character of relations established by board-level employee representatives identifies the extent to which they perceive relations to be cooperative or conflictual. The results are presented in Table 6.5 in the form of an index, where a score of five indicates a very cooperative relationship, together with a 'no relationship' measure. From the outset it is apparent that 'no relationship' is reported in substantial numbers by 'all' board-level employee representatives for three relations: with 'other trade unions in the company', 'shareholder representatives' and 'works councillors'. The absence of relationships between the two institutions of labour representation and board-level employee representatives is, in no small part, due to peculiarities within two country clusters. The high 'no relationship' score for 'other trade unions in the company', for example,

Table 6.5 How Would You Describe Your Relationship With . . .

	All Country Clusters $N = 2,930–3,997$		CMEs: Germanic $N = 1,297–1,468$		CMEs: Nordic $N = 858–1,901$		MMEs: Francophone $N = 110–147$		EMEs: New Member States $N = 294–508$		Ireland, Greece and Spain $N = 21–28$		SEs $N = 29–38$	
	Index	No relationship %	Index	No relationship %	Index	No relationship %	Index	No relationship %	Index	No relationship %	Index	No relationship %	Index	No relationship %
Other board-level employee representatives	4.49	7.9	4.57	2.3	4.51	11.1	4.25	1.4	4.28	13.7	4.00	8.7	4.59	/
Works councillors[1]	4.40	14.1	4.64	0.6	4.18	35.5	4.06	8.9	3.98	17.8	4.08	/	4.55	/
Your trade union at the workplace (if you are a member)	4.38	3.6	4.23	2.0	4.49	5.6	4.57	0.9	4.43	0.7	4.56	/	4.29	/
Employee representatives throughout the company	4.33	6.1	4.41	0.9	4.33	10.3	4.19	2.7	4.15	6.5	4.22	/	4.47	/
Other trade unions in the company	3.81	35.3	3.34	59.0	4.11	21.2	3.42	8.2	3.53	28.9	3.89	14.3	3.95	24.1
Other board members	3.80	7.0	3.53	9.5	3.97	6.2	3.45	6.8	4.00	3.2	3.79	/	3.89	15.6
Senior managers of the company	3.72	1.5	3.53	0.5	3.86	2.5	3.25	0.7	3.82	1.2	3.82	/	3.66	/
Shareholder representatives	3.67	21.7	3.40	7.2	3.98	35.5	3.16	17.1	3.74	12.0	3.71	14.3	3.65	10.5

Notes:

Respondents were asked to specify whether their relationship was 'very cooperative/consensual', 'fairly cooperative/consensual', 'intermediate', 'fairly conflictual', 'very conflictual' or that there was 'no relationship'. The 'no relationship' scores were excluded from the calculation of the index. The index was created by assigning a response 'very cooperative/consensual' 5 points and a response 'fairly cooperative/consensual' 4 points and so on. The range of the index is thus between 1 and 5.

1. Swedish respondents are excluded from this row, because there is no possibility of establishing a works council in Sweden. The values of *N* are thus 2,930 for 'all' and 858 for the Nordic cluster.

is heavily influenced by the situation in the Germanic cluster where the presence of more than one union within a company is exceptional by comparison with the other country clusters. Similarly, the score attained in the single-channel Nordic cluster influences the absence of relationships with 'works councillors'.

As all the index scores are greater than three, the first point to emerge from Table 6.5 is that in no circumstances is a 'fairly conflictual' or 'very conflictual' relationship reported in any of the country clusters or the SEs between board-level employee representatives and the listed parties. Relationships with four other forms of labour representation head the index ranking for 'all' board-level employee representatives. For these relationships the index score is between four and five suggesting that where such relationships exist they are cooperative and that within labour in the company there is a relatively high degree of consensus. Three of the four relationships at the foot of the ranking are those involving parties that represent interests other than labour. Board-level employee representatives do not view these relationships as conflictual, each receives an index score of between 3.67 and 3.80, but they are not as cooperative as those among labour.

Within the political approach to corporate governance the sector model assumes that Germanic board-level employee representatives generate cooperative relations with managers. The proportions of board-level employee representatives from this cluster that report 'no relationship' with 'senior managers of the company' are lower than those reported within the Nordic class model and the Francophone voice model and certainly suggest that establishing relationships with managers is a priority. The frequency of pre-meetings between senior managers and board-level employee representatives in the Germanic cluster further supports this position (see Table 5.6). The index score for the Germanic cluster is higher than that reported for the Francophone countries but, and contrary to the expectations of the political approaches, is lower than that reported by Nordic board-level employee representatives. Furthermore, in the NMS, IGS and SEs the index scores for the relationship with 'senior managers of the company' are higher than that in the Germanic cluster. The lower level of cooperation in the Germanic cluster is contrary to the expectations of the sector model. In the Germanic cluster, relations between board-level employee representatives and shareholders are less cooperative than those between board-level employee representatives and managers by reference to the 'no relationship' and index scores. This situation, however, is present in all country clusters rather than being a feature of the sector model. A feature unique to the Germanic cluster is the extent of cooperation between board-level employee representatives and works councils, a relationship that receives the highest index score only in the Germanic cluster.

The expectation of the class model is met within the Nordic cluster insofar as the extent of cooperation between board-level employee representatives and their trade unions, other trade unions and employee representatives exceeds that between board-level employee representatives and either managers or shareholders. This is not a distinguishing feature of the Nordic cluster as the class model predicts, in that it is reproduced in most country clusters. The proportion of Nordic board-level employee representatives that report 'no relationship' with either 'senior managers' or 'shareholder representatives', however, is high relative to most country clusters and does not differ markedly between companies of different size.

The anticipated relatively cooperative relationship between board-level employee representatives and 'shareholder representatives' within the Francophone voice model does not appear in Table 6.5. To the contrary, the index score of 3.16 is the lowest among all the country clusters, indicating the least cooperative relationship. Furthermore, relations between board-level employee representatives and 'other board members' and 'senior managers' are also the least cooperative compared to other country clusters. While these latter results are not inconsistent with the voice model they tend to confirm that the adversarial character of Francophone industrial relations pervades relationships at the board level, although the relationships between representatives of capital in the form of senior managers and shareholder representatives and board-level employee representatives are not reported as conflictual with index scores greater than three.

Bivariate analyses substantiate the limitations of the class, sector and voice differentiation. The role played by some basic variables is overlooked in this differentiation, although they have considerable explanatory power. In particular, the size of the company and the size of the board exert a marked influence on the quality of the relationship between board-level employee representatives and both shareholder and management representatives: the smaller the board, the more cooperative the relationship with shareholder representatives ($\chi^2 = 179.47$, $df = 24$, $p < 0.01$), with other board members ($\chi^2 = 183.23$, $df = 24$, $p < 0.01$) and with senior managers ($\chi^2 = 130.65$, $df = 24$, $p < 0.01$); the smaller the company, the more cooperative the relationship with other board members ($\chi^2 = 97.21$, $df = 24$, $p < 0.01$). These findings suggest that smaller companies and boards are likely to lead to informal and cooperative relationships, irrespective of the class, sector and voice differentiation.

Developing Relationships outside the Board Meeting

A second means whereby the relationships entered into by board-level employee representatives can be examined is to assess the frequency at which they meet other parties outside of the board meeting and the extent to which they would prefer to meet these parties more frequently. Tables 6.6 and 6.7 present the data on these topics.

The 'all' data of Table 6.6 reproduce earlier tables insofar as the frequency of meetings involving board-level employee representatives outside of the board is most pronounced with other representatives of labour. Also

Table 6.6 How Often Do You Meet the Following outside of the Board Meeting?

	All Country Clusters N = 2,895–3,922		CMEs: Germanic N = 1,285–1,375		CMEs: Nordic N = 886–1,881		MMEs: Francophone N = 124–145		EMEs: New Member States N = 476–504		Ireland, Greece and Spain N = 26–28		SEs N = 36–37	
	Index	Never %	Index	Never %	Index	Never %	Index	Never %	Index	Never %	Index	Never %	Index	Never %
Employee representatives throughout the company	2.83	10.0	3.13	2.9	2.64	15.5	2.78	7.0	2.65	9.7	2.75	7.7	2.97	5.4
Works councillors[1]	2.76	21.3	3.09	7.0	2.24	43.0	2.62	20.6	2.39	23.1	2.83	7.7	3.03	2.7
Trade union officials with responsibilities within the company	2.58	23.1	2.74	8.7	2.40	36.9	2.75	13.2	2.52	14.5	2.71	11.1	2.50	16.7
Senior managers of the company	2.44	8.9	2.61	3.8	2.28	12.7	2.15	15.2	2.58	7.1	2.68	/	2.39	10.8
CEO	2.42	8.6	2.47	4.2	2.39	10.6	2.01	19.8	2.51	10.7	2.36	/	2.26	16.2
Trade union officials with no direct responsibility within the company	2.05	32.6	1.87	24.4	2.22	39.9	2.26	34.6	1.94	27.2	2.12	37.0	1.76	32.4
Chair of the board	1.85	20.2	1.84	15.7	1.73	25.0	1.85	27.2	2.26	13.4	2.35	17.9	1.93	21.6
BLERs from other companies	1.80	41.8	1.93	24.6	1.64	52.4	2.04	43.8	1.70	49.4	2.05	32.1	1.59	27.0
Other experts, external to your trade union (accountants, lawyers, etc.)	1.76	29.1	1.89	9.4	1.50	47.3	1.67	33.6	1.98	15.3	2.00	7.1	2.00	8.1
Shareholder representatives	1.77	42.4	1.72	28.8	1.80	55.2	1.67	58.1	1.88	30.0	1.74	32.1	1.73	40.5

Notes:

Respondents were asked to specify whether they meet the specified persons 'always', 'often', 'sometimes, 'rarely' or 'never'. The 'never' responses are reported in the table and the index was created by assigning a response 'always' 4 points, a response 'often' 3 points and so on. The range of index scores is thus between 1 and 4.

1. The Swedish respondents are excluded from this row with the consequence that the values of *N* for 'all country clusters' is 2,895 and for the Nordic cluster is 886.

replicating earlier tables is the relatively large proportion of board-level employee representatives (21.3 per cent) that 'never' meet 'works councillors', which, as expected, is heavily influenced by responses from the single-channel Nordic cluster. Almost a quarter of board-level employee representatives 'never' meet 'trade union officials with responsibilities within the company' outside of the board meeting, although for those board-level employee representatives that engage in such meetings, they are among the most frequent. 'Trade union officials with no direct responsibility within the company' and 'BLERs from other companies' are two of the three parties with which board-level employee representatives are most likely 'never' to meet outside of the board meeting, suggesting that the perspective of board-level employee representatives is largely restricted to affairs within their own company rather than embracing a broader political perspective.

Turning to the parties that represent interests other than labour illustrates a varied frequency pattern of meetings outside of the board meeting. In particular, and continuing the theme of in-company meetings, fewer than 9 per cent of board-level employee representatives 'never' meet the 'senior managers of the company' and the 'CEO', and those who engage in such meetings do so at a higher frequency than board-level employee representatives engage in meetings with labour representatives from outside the company. A smaller proportion of board-level employee representatives engage in meetings with 'shareholder representatives' than with any other party listed in Table 6.6. Furthermore, the board-level employee representatives who engage in meetings with 'shareholder representatives' do so at a low frequency, suggesting a greater distance between board-level employee representatives and 'shareholder representatives' than between board-level employee representatives and 'senior management'.

Reference to the country clusters again illustrates a mixed picture vis-à-vis the political approach to corporate governance. Germanic board-level employee representatives confirm the absence of any intense working relationships with 'shareholder representatives' in that the index score appears at the foot of the ranking. Furthermore, the 'never' score for 'shareholder representatives' is the highest reported within the Germanic cluster, although it is low compared to the SEs and all other country clusters. There is thus a distance between Germanic board-level employee representatives and 'shareholder representatives', as suggested by the sector model, but this distance is present elsewhere. Large numbers of Germanic board-level employee representatives also 'never' meet 'trade union officials with no direct responsibility within the company' and 'BLERs from other companies' confirming the centrality of in-company relations to board-level employee representatives. Germanic board-level employee representatives also report lower index scores for 'senior managers of the company' and the 'CEO' than for 'trade union officials with direct responsibilities within the company', confirming articulation between board-level employee representatives and trade unions. The two highest index scores recorded by board-level employee representatives within the Germanic cluster, however, are for 'works councillors' and 'employee representatives throughout the company' thus confirming the centrality of articulation with these parties within the sector model.

For seven of ten of the relationships listed in Table 6.6, 25 per cent or more Nordic board-level employee representatives report 'never' engaging in meetings outside of the board meeting. This figure compares with one in ten for Germanic board-level employee representatives. Fewer board-level employee representatives are networked in the Nordic cluster than elsewhere. Disaggregating the Nordic results by company size does not alter this position substantially insofar as 25 per cent or more Nordic board-level employee representatives employed at companies with 499 or fewer employees report 'never' engaging in meetings outside of the board meeting for seven out of ten of the relationships compared to six out of ten of the relationships for Nordic board-level employee representatives working at companies where 500 or more are employed.[9] A feature of the Nordic results pertinent in the context of the political approach to corporate governance is that the index scores for 'shareholder representatives' are broadly comparable with those recorded by Germanic board-level employee representatives as would be expected from within the political approach, where both the sector model and the class model anticipate a political distance between board-level employee representatives and 'shareholder representatives'. The index scores reported by Nordic board-level employee representatives for 'senior managers in the company', 'CEO' and 'chair of the board' are also lower than those reported in the Germanic cluster, again meeting the expectations of the political approach. In some instances regarding these relationships, however, the differences between the sector model and the class model scores are not marked, suggesting that there is a greater degree of overlap than implied in the political differentiation of the two models.

Francophone board-level employee representatives report higher index scores for 'trade unions officials with responsibilities within the company', 'employee representatives throughout the company' and 'works councillors' than for the three parties associated with management. Uniquely, the index scores for 'trade union officials with no direct responsibility within the company' also indicate more frequent meetings than those with the three parties associated with management. The coalition between Francophone board-level employee representatives and other representatives of labour is thus more wide ranging than elsewhere. Contrary to the expectations of the voice model, however, Francophone board-level employee representatives report the highest 'never' score and the lowest index score for 'shareholder representatives' indicating that no special relationship, as measured by the frequency of meetings, has been established that unites board-level employee representatives and shareholders. Indeed, there is greater distance between board-level employee representatives and shareholders than between board-level employee representatives and managers in the Francophone cluster.

Finally, the survey examined whether board-level employee representatives would prefer to meet some parties more frequently than at present in order to improve their performance at the board. Table 6.7 presents the results using the same categories as employed in Table 6.6. Reference to the 'all' data is unambiguous insofar as they demonstrate that board-level employee representatives would prefer more frequent contact with those that represent interests other than labour rather than more intense contact with labour representatives. While it may be argued that more contact with the 'chair of the board' is about securing tactical advantages within the terms of operation of the board, more contact with 'senior managers in the company', 'CEO' and 'shareholder representatives' is clearly about entering into more wide-ranging discussions with parties that represent interests that may compete with labour and are likely to exert more power over board decisions. The absence of any wide-ranging desire to meet representatives from labour more frequently may also imply a degree of satisfaction with extant relationships.

The desire for more contact within the sector model replicates the 'all' results in that securing tactical advantages through more contact with the 'chair of the board' is the key priority for Germanic board-level employee representatives. Contrary to the expectations of the sector model, Germanic board-level employee representatives also prioritise more contact with 'shareholder representatives' in preference to that with 'senior managers of the company' and the 'CEO', thus suggesting that diluting the alliance with managers, that is at the core of the sector model, is not beyond the realms of possibility from the perspective of Germanic board-level employee representatives. Two further issues arise from the Germanic results. First, although unionised Germanic board-level employee representatives are the most likely to receive support from trade unions in the form of access to experts (see Table 6.2), they emphasise access to 'other experts external to your trade union', which is not common in practice (Jürgens et al. 2008). Two explanations of this result that are not mutually exclusive are available. The first explanation is that Germanic board-level employee representatives, who place great value on advice from experts, simply want more such advice and are not overly concerned about the source, while a second explanation suggests that they would prefer additional expert advice to come from a source other than trade unions. A second issue arising from the preferences of Germanic board-level employee representatives for more meetings concerns 'BLERs from other companies'. The preference for more such meetings places the onus on trade unions to convene the meetings and suggests that Germanic board-level employee representatives may be prepared to endorse broader alliances that embrace activity beyond the company.

The class model that characterises Nordic board-level employee representation is also subject to pressure from the preferences of board-level employee representatives for more contact. In particular, Nordic board-level employee representatives seek more frequent contact with the 'chair of the

Table 6.7 With Whom Would You Like to Have More Frequent Contact in Order to Improve Your Performance as a Board-Level Employee Representative?

		CMEs		MMEs	EMEs		
	All Country Clusters %	Germanic %	Nordic %	Francophone %	New Member States %	Ireland, Greece and Spain %	SEs %
Chair of the board	34.3	34.9	37.0	20.4	26.7	21.4	28.9
Senior managers in the company	27.6	21.0	29.6	35.4	36.7	42.9	34.2
CEO	24.3	14.6	34.3	19.7	16.9	28.6	21.1
Shareholder representatives	21.9	27.5	14.0	21.1	34.6	25.0	15.8
BLERs from other companies	21.4	22.3	22.0	29.9	15.1	10.7	13.2
Other experts external to your trade union (accountants, lawyers, etc.)	19.0	25.2	13.0	39.5	17.1	10.7	31.6
Employee representatives throughout the company	12.0	7.3	16.1	7.5	12.2	21.4	26.3
Trade union officials with responsibilities for the company	6.4	6.7	6.1	7.5	6.3	14.3	5.3
Works councillors[1]	5.1	3.5	6.8	5.4	6.5	3.6	7.9
Trade union officials with no direct responsibility for the company	3.9	5.2	3.8	2.0	1.0	/	/
	N = 4,155	*N* = 1,540	*N* = 1,917	*N* = 147	*N* = 509	*N* = 28	*N* = 38

Notes:

Respondents could tick up to two options; hence, the sum of the percentage figures is more than 100 per cent.

1. Swedish respondents are excluded from this row with the consequence that the value of *N* for 'all country clusters' is 3,243 and that for the Nordic cluster is 1,005.

board', the 'CEO' and 'senior managers of the company', suggesting a move from the class model towards the sector model, which encompasses closer relations with management. Furthermore, there is no wide-ranging desire among Nordic board-level employee representatives for closer relations with 'shareholder representatives', indicating their exclusion from any closer coalition between management and board-level employee representatives.

Francophone board-level employee representatives are the only group that regards more frequent contact with 'other experts external to your trade union' as the primary priority. This view is consistent with the desire of Francophone board-level employee representatives for greater 'access to experts' provided through the union (see Table 6.3) and suggests a shortfall within the cluster, even though 42.7 per cent of Francophone board-level employee representatives are already in receipt of this form of support from trade unions (see Table 6.2). Contrary to the expectations of the voice model, Francophone board-level employee representatives would prefer more contact with 'senior managers in the company' than with 'shareholder representatives'. Given that the index score for the Francophone cluster for 'senior managers in the company' was lower than elsewhere (see Table 6.6), the desire for more contact suggests that management may be resisting closer relations with board-level employee representatives in Francophone countries; that is, management is adversarial. Consolidating the impact of adversarial industrial relations on Francophone board practices is the preference of board-level employee representatives for more frequent contact with 'BLERs from other companies', thereby expressing a desire to extend alliances and generating the prospect of mobilisation, beyond the company.

The results from this section demonstrate that distinctions among the sector, class and voice models of corporate governance are not clear-cut, as suggested by the political approach to corporate governance. This is not to argue, however, that the clustered exemplars of these models examined here are similar in terms of working relationships, the degree of cooperation/conflict and relationships outside of the board meeting. The section has shown that the pattern of relationships established by board-level employee representatives is unique to each country cluster and this substantiates earlier arguments that board-level employee representation is not a monolithic institution but is varied, and within each variant board-level employee representatives express particular priorities in terms of the relationships they develop.

CONCLUSION

The pattern of articulation between board-level employee representatives, other parties represented on the board, and agencies external to the board varies between the country clusters. The variation in the pattern of articulation is not consistent with either sociological or political perspectives on corporate governance, although some of the expectations from both approaches are realised in practice. The pattern of articulation within the Francophone

MMEs, for example, varies markedly from that in the Germanic and Nordic CMEs. The source of the Francophone variation is borne of industrial relations: in particular, the adversarialism evident in the attitudes of board-level employee representatives and in their views of the attitudes of management. Similarly, in the EMEs there is evidence of new systems of corporate governance and industrial relations 'emerging' in the form of institutional development and the practices of board-level employee representatives, but these have yet to reach the 'maturity' of the CMEs. Contrary to sociological approaches, however, is the variation between CMEs. Articulation involving Germanic board-level employee representatives is wide ranging, both within the board and with external agents, whereas articulation in the Nordic cluster is narrower in scope. In all country clusters and in the SEs articulation between board-level employee representatives and other institutions of labour representation, coupled with the support provided by trade unions, suggests that incorporation for the majority of board-level employee representatives is unlikely. For a minority of isolated board-level employer representatives who are unable to exert either power or influence at the board, however, incorporation cannot be ruled out.

Given the differences in the exercise of power between the Germanic and Nordic clusters noted in Chapter 5, it would appear that within the CMEs there are two distinct systems of board-level employee representation. A Germanic system reliant on the control of management through supervision, coupled with extensive articulation between board-level employee representatives and other institutions of labour representation, particularly works councils. Integral to the Germanic system is communicative power and strategic power resources whereby board-level employee representatives are key to networks of labour representation within the company and are in receipt of wide-ranging support from trade unions with no formal role within the company. In contrast, in the Nordic system power is exercised though co-management or discussions culminating in a shared position or 'negotiated solidarism' (Swenson 2002) between board-level employee representatives and management in circumstances where articulation with institutions of labour representation is narrower in scope and trade union support is less prevalent. Collaborative power resources at the board meeting are thus available to Nordic board-level employee representatives. These collaborative power resources are not complemented by communicative and strategic power resources to the same degree as they are in the Germanic cluster. Although articulation by means of non-market mechanisms and trust are regarded as a feature of Swedish industrial relations (Svensson and Öberg 2005), the Germanic system is more intensely articulated.

In all country clusters, relations between board-level employee representatives and shareholder representatives are less cooperative than those between board-level employee representatives and managers. Similarly, the extent of cooperation between board-level employee representatives and other representatives and institutions of labour exceeds that between board-level employee representatives and either managers or shareholder representatives. The uniformity of these relationships is contrary to the expectations of the political approach to corporate governance, which anticipates variation rather than uniformity in these relationships. The variation that exists, however, would appear to be as much a function of industrial relations institutions and practices, coupled with the structural characteristics of the company and the board, as political differentiation. The extent of cooperation between board-level employee representatives and works councils in the sector model, for example, is also a feature of dual systems of workplace representation. Similarly, relations between board-level employee representatives and managers are the least cooperative in the Francophone cluster, meeting the expectation of the voice model but also confirming the adversarial character of Francophone industrial relations.

NOTES

1. Notable exceptions where training is not specified in the legislation that underpins board-level employee representation include Austria, Czech Republic, Denmark, Germany and Luxembourg.
2. In Sweden it is not possible to establish works councils; hence, the Swedish data are excluded in this chapter from all the options where works councils are mentioned. In Denmark, Finland and Norway it is possible to establish workplace councils or institutions that resemble works councils, but they are by no means the majority form of workplace representation. As a consequence, the Nordic data refer only to these three countries.
3. Responses to the question, 'What sources of information influence your board-level decision-making?' for 'all' respondents are as follows:

	All, N = 3,055–3,942	
Your network/contact	**Index**	**I do not have such networks/contacts, %**
With employees in general	3.73	2.0
With other BLERs in the company	3.60	11.6
Within your trade union	3.44	10.0
Within the works council[1]	3.41	18.6
With managers in the company	3.38	5.7
Within the board	3.32	5.4
With experts, external to a trade union	2.67	25.6
Other networks	2.38	39.9
With BLERs in other companies	2.33	36.3

Notes:

Respondents were asked to specify whether a network/contact was 'very influential', 'fairly influential', 'intermediate', 'not very influential' or 'not at all influential'. The index was calculated by assigning a response 'very influential', 5 points; 'fairly influential', 4 points; and so on.

1. The data for 'within the works council' exclude Swedish respondents.

4. Responses to the question 'what is the importance of information sources that influence board-level employee representatives' are as follows:

Your network/contacts	All Country Clusters, %
With managers in the company	43.0
With employees in general	34.2
Within the board	29.6
Within your trade union	26.2
With other BLERs in the company	21.0
Within the works council	17.7
With experts, external to a trade union	4.5
With BLERs in other companies	3.4
Other networks	1.3
	N = 4,155

Notes:
Respondents were asked to rank the sources of information that influence them, putting the most important influence first in the ranking, the second most important second in the ranking and so on until the sources of information were no longer influential. The data presented in the preceding table include the responses at positions one and two in the ranking; hence, the percentage values are greater than 100 per cent. For the option 'within your trade union' only the responses from trade union members were considered; hence, the values of *N* are less than those stated.

5. These data are almost certainly an exaggeration of the situation in practice as the identification of individuals to whom questionnaires were sent relied mostly on information from trade unions and, in four cases (Austria, Germany, Denmark, Finland), on databases of board-level employee representatives exclusively maintained by trade unions (see Appendix A).
6. The complete range of Nordic data disaggregated by the size of the company are as follows:

Support provided	Nordic BLERs in companies with 499 or fewer employees, %	Nordic BLERs in companies with 500 or more employees, %
A means to consult in particular circumstances	42.1	45.7
'Technical' training (accounting, finance, economics)	33.7	42.8
Access to experts (lawyers, accountants etc.)	21.1	27.9
Access to networks of BLERs	24.3	31.8
Early access to relevant information	24.5	22.9

(*Continued*)

Table (Continued)

Support provided	Nordic BLERs in companies with 499 or fewer employees, %	Nordic BLERs in companies with 500 or more employees, %
Analyses/interpretation of information	13.3	12.3
Better access to more wide-ranging information	13.1	13.7
Informed political advice	8.0	15.6
Access to trade union organisations at European level	5.7	11.9
Other	14.4	12.9
	N = 1,135	*N* = 519

7. Respondents were asked to indicate whether the board typically meets 'weekly', 'every two weeks', 'monthly', 'every three months' or 'every six months'. From the results to this question an index was calculated by awarding points to responses on a five-point scale, with 5 points awarded to responses indicating that the board meets 'weekly' and 1 point to a response indicating that the board meets 'every six months'. The higher the index score, the greater the frequency at which the board meets. Results for each category used here are as follows: 'all', 1.98; Germanic, 1.77; Nordic, 2.03; Francophone, 2.16; NMS, 2.33; IGS, 3.39; and SEs, 1.74.
8. Gourevitch and Shinn (2005:205–276) also treat Chile, the US and the UK as exemplars of the voice model.
9. The complete range of Nordic results disaggregated by company size is as follows:

	Nordic BLERs in companies with 499 or fewer employees, *N* = 1,135		Nordic BLERs in companies with 500 or more employees, *N* = 519	
	Index	Never, %	Index	Never, %
Employee representatives throughout the company	2.60	17.5	2.72	10.4
Trade union officials with responsibilities within the company	2.33	40.8	2.56	27.8
Works councillors[1]	1.96	49.0	2.05	31.3

	Nordic BLERs in companies with 499 or fewer employees, $N = 1{,}135$		Nordic BLERs in companies with 500 or more employees, $N = 519$	
	Index	Never, %	Index	Never, %
Senior managers of the company	2.30	13.2	2.26	10.9
CEO	2.41	10.8	2.37	9.3
Trade union officials with no direct responsibility within the company	2.19	44.2	2.31	31.0
Chair of the board	1.73	25.8	1.73	22.4
BLERs from other companies	1.61	58.6	1.69	37.4
Shareholder representatives	1.82	54.6	1.78	57.1
Other experts, external to your trade union (accountants, lawyers, etc.)	1.48	52.1	1.53	36.4

1. The data for 'works councillors' exclude the Swedish data: the values for *N* are 745 for the companies with 499 employees or fewer and 260 for companies with 500 or more employees.

7 Conclusion
What Does All This Mean?

Board-level employee representation is the principal formal mechanism whereby representatives of labour can bring direct, participatory influence to bear on strategic company decision-making. While the period over which board-level employee representation has been in operation and the scope of its coverage vary between nations, in the SEs and in fifteen of the sixteen countries included in this study legislation underpins board-level employee representation. A first specific question addressed by this study was thus: is there variation between the content of the legislation on board-level employee representation and the manner in which it is implemented in practice? This question does not have a constant temporal element insofar as the legislation that underpinned national board-level employee representation when the survey distribution took place was enacted between 1951 in Germany and 1993 in Slovenia. Given that much of the legislation on board-level employee representation in Western Europe was implemented during the 1970s when labour was more strongly positioned than at present, a second specific question arises concerning the spirit and intention of the legislation; namely, does the legislation enable board-level employee representatives to exert power over strategic decision-making within the company as was intended within the rubric of industrial democracy? Implicit in board-level employee representation practices is the notion of articulation. Articulation can be between board-level employee representatives and employees and other institutions of labour representation within the company, while external to the company articulation most notably involves trade unions, but may also embrace consultancies and agencies of the state. A failure of board-level employee representatives to articulate may result in their isolation and incorporation. Similarly, a failure to articulate may deprive the board-level employee representatives of power, of information, of access to expertise and of allies. A third specific question raised at the outset of the study thus took the following form: what is the nature and the intensity of articulation involving board-level employee representatives?

More generally, the study set out to identify the practices of board-level employee representation in Europe from the perspective of the employee representatives that sit on the board. In this context three broad questions resonated throughout the study. What are the forms of board-level employee representation found in Europe? What are the implications of the survey findings for the competing positions on corporate governance and industrial relations within the academic literature? What are the implications of the study for policy makers at national and European level? To formulate and present answers to both these specific and general questions, Chapter 7 comprises three further sections. The first section identifies the features of the systems of board-level employee representation found in each of the five country clusters and in the SEs, thus establishing the similarities and the variation in practice within the phenomenon. Attention is also directed here to whether extant systems and practices of board-level employee representation meet the expectations of the policymakers and legislators who generated and implemented the legislation that underpins board-level employee representation. The second section assesses the implications of the variation in practice in board-level employee representation for the corporate governance and industrial relations literatures that formed the initial points of departure for the study. The third section briefly examines the policy issues at national and European level that arise from these findings.

THE CHARACTER OF BOARD-LEVEL EMPLOYEE REPRESENTATION WITHIN THE COUNTRY CLUSTERS

This section presents the principal features of the different clustered systems of board-level employee representation and highlights the variation between these systems. To a degree, these presentations are caricatures insofar as no attempt is made to include all the details of each system. The objective of the section, however, is to compare the situation *de jure* and *de facto* and to assess the nature and intensity of articulation within the different country clusters.

Germanic Cluster

Germanic board-level employee representation is a feature of very large independent and controlled companies based in industry or private-sector services, which rely on dual board structures. On average, board-level employee representatives comprise 43.4 per cent of a twelve-member supervisory board. The 'typical' Germanic board-level employee representative is male, is unionised and holds an average of 1.8 other representative positions within the company, which are often based in the works council.

The largest single group of Germanic board-level employee representatives regard their role on the board as 'controlling management through supervision' (31.5 per cent) and a further 27.4 per cent either 'co-manage the company by participating in decision-making' or 'discuss matters with other board members until a shared position is reached', suggesting some overlap between the situation *de jure* and *de facto*. No fewer than 41.1 per cent of Germanic board-level employee representatives, however, define their role at the board in terms of merely receiving information or engaging in consultation, rather than exerting power over strategic decision-making. Furthermore, similar proportions of Germanic board-level employee representatives think that they had little or no influence over company restructuring (34.9 per cent) and think that they influenced the outcome of restructuring processes (33.0 per cent). A substantial minority of Germanic board-level employee representatives thus report that their board level engagement does not meet the expectations of the policymakers and legislators who drew up the legislation on board-level employee representation, insofar as these representatives do not exert power over but influence strategic company decision-making.

This absence of power is not explained by reference to the information provision in that Germanic board-level employee representatives report that they are content with the timing and the quality of information. The absence of power is also not explained by reference to the activities at the board of Germanic employee representatives, the majority of whom intervene at the board by requiring a topic to be included on the agenda, by requesting reports on company affairs or by delaying board decisions. Contributing to the absence of power, however, is the shift in the location of board decision-making. Between 22.7 and 52.3 per cent of Germanic board-level employee representatives think that board decisions are made at meetings from which they are excluded and 35.0 per cent 'never' or 'rarely' participate in pre-meetings with senior managers. Furthermore, the participation of Germanic board-level employee representatives in subcommittees is mixed with larger proportions of employee representatives reporting that they are not members of extant subcommittees than those who report they are invited to participate.[1] A further factor that influences the exercise of power by Germanic board-level employee representatives is the positive correlation between power and the proportion of employee representatives on the board. This confirms earlier research showing that the greater the constitutional strength of board-level employee representatives, the greater the power they exert over strategic company decision-making (Greifenstein and Kißler 2010).

By comparison with their counterparts elsewhere, Germanic board-level employee representatives are intensely articulated within the company and with institutions of labour representation external to the company. Within the company, Germanic board-level employee representatives almost always convene preparatory meetings involving only employee representatives before the formal board meeting. In addition, works councils, which nominate most board-level employee representatives and include most board-level employee representatives as members, have cooperative/consensual relations with board-level employee representatives and receive regular report backs from board-level employee representatives on events at the board. Overlapping mandates between board and works council allows articulation between the two institutions while also respecting confidentiality provisions. External articulation for Germanic board-level employee representatives is primarily through the trade union, which provides training in specific technical skills, access to experts and a means to consult in specific circumstances. Only a small proportion of Germanic board-level employee representatives require additional support from trade unions. Articulation with trade unions thus complements that with works councils. Germanic board-level employee representatives have thus developed intensely articulated relations with other institutions of labour representation within and external to the company. This articulation reinforces their capacity to act at the board. Communicative power and strategic power resources are thus key to networks of labour representation within Germanic companies, integral to which is wide-ranging support from trade unions with no formal role within the company. Although relationships between Germanic board-level employee representatives and parties that represent interests other than labour are not conflictual, they are less intense than relations with institutions of labour representation. In particular, relations with shareholder representatives and other board members, including the chair, are more distant, although Germanic board-level employee representatives express a desire to narrow the gap with these parties.

Nordic Cluster

Nordic board-level employee representation is more likely than its Germanic counterpart to be a feature of small and medium-sized companies, although, similarly to the Germanic situation, both independent and controlled companies are represented. Also similar to the Germanic cluster, industry and, to a lesser extent, private-sector services are the largest sectors of operation of Nordic companies with board-level employee representation. Linked to the size of company is the point that Nordic boards are about half the size of those in the Germanic countries (6.2 members compared to 12.2 members), with about one-third of board members being employee representatives. The prevalence of monistic board structures within the Nordic cluster results in 'a board of directors with the chair of the board separate from executive officers' being the dominant board arrangement. Although more likely to be female than a Germanic board-level employee representative, the majority of Nordic board-level employee representatives are male. Similarly to their Germanic counterparts, the vast majority of Nordic board-level employee representatives are unionised but hold fewer representative positions additional to that of employee representative on the board (1.3 compared to 1.8). Reflecting the dominant single-channel system in Nordic countries, the mandate held most commonly concurrent with that of board-level employee representative is shop steward.

Nordic board-level employee representatives are most likely to exert power at the board meeting by either 'discussing matters with other board members until a shared position is reached' (23.5 per cent) or to 'co-manage the company by participating in decision-making' (14.6 per cent). Nordic board-level employee representatives thus exert power over strategic board decision-making in a different manner to their Germanic counterparts. The proportion of Nordic board-level employee representatives who report that they are only in receipt of information or engage in consultation but that decision-making rests with other board members (50.9 per cent), however, belittles the proportion that exerts power over strategic board decision-making. A small majority (50.9 per cent) of Nordic board-level employee representatives, thus, have no power over decision-making at the board but can only exercise influence. Furthermore, and contrary to the situation in the Germanic cluster, a larger proportion of Nordic board-level employee representatives think that they had little or no influence over company restructuring (43.5 per cent) than those who think that they influenced the outcome of restructuring processes (32.7 per cent). For a large number of Nordic board-level employee representatives the situation *de facto* thus differs markedly from the situation intended *de jure*.

Similar to their Germanic counterparts, Nordic board-level employee representatives are generally satisfied with the timing and the content of information provisions, confirming that it is not an information shortfall that precludes the involvement of Nordic board-level employee representatives in board decision-making. The absence of power over board decision-making for half of Nordic board-level employee representatives is partially explained by their activities at the board. Although the level of interventions made by Nordic board-level employee representatives is limited compared to their Germanic counterparts, three-quarters of Nordic board-level employee representatives have required a topic to be included on the agenda of the board, and half of them have also requested a report on company affairs. The exclusion of Nordic board-level employee representatives from the location of decision-making is a more likely explanation of their absence of power. Between 38.7 and 49.7 per cent of Nordic board-level employee representatives think that they are excluded from the meetings at which board decision-making takes place. Furthermore, the vast majority of Nordic board-level employee representatives 'rarely' or 'never' hold pre-meetings with senior management and are only exceptionally full members of the relatively few subcommittees convened in Nordic companies.

Contrary to their Germanic counterparts, Nordic board-level employee representatives do not convene pre-meetings with other board-level employee representatives, although relations between employee representatives on the board are consensual as are relations with the trade union at the workplace. Whereas Germanic board-level employee representatives are articulated primarily with works councils within the company, Nordic board-level employee representatives are articulated with trade unions, as befits Nordic single-channel systems. Nordic trade unions are primarily responsible for the nomination of employee representatives wishing to sit on the board. Articulation between board-level employee representatives and trade unions is not as developed as in the Germanic cluster. Although observance of confidentiality provisions does not prevent Nordic board-level employee representatives from reporting back the affairs of the board to trade unions, the reporting back process is not as anchored as in the Germanic cluster: 48.1 per cent of Nordic board-level employee representatives report back to the trade union at least quarterly compared to the 66.2 per cent of Germanic respondents who report back to the works council. Nordic trade unions also provide fewer board-level employee representatives with training than Germanic unions (63.2 per cent compared to 78.1 per cent) and advice from experts (49.1 per cent compared to 70.4 per cent). Germanic trade unions are also more proficient than their Nordic counterparts 'as a means to consult in specific circumstances' and in the provision of 'analyses/interpretation of information', 'better access to more wide-ranging information' and 'informed political advice'. With the exceptions of 'informed political advice' and 'access to trade union organisation at European level', more Nordic board-level employee representatives than Germanic board-level employee representatives want their trade union to provide more support in these areas. In short, within the company Nordic board-level employee representatives downplay their relations with the trade union compared to the relationship between the works council and Germanic board-level employee representatives. The wider coverage by employment size of Nordic board-level employee representation offers only a partial explanation of the variation between the Nordic and Germanic systems insofar as in Nordic companies with 500 or more employees articulation with the trade union is not as intense as that with the works council in the Germanic cluster. In short, Nordic systems of board-level employee representation are more reliant on collaborative power resources at the board meeting than are their Germanic counterparts. These collaborative power resources, however, are not consolidated by communicative and strategic power resources to the same degree as in the Germanic cluster.

Compared to the Germanic cluster, relationships with parties that represent interests other than labour are more likely in the Nordic cluster. Relationships with senior managers are more frequent and are viewed as more cooperative/consensual. There is also a greater willingness for more extensive contacts with both senior managers and other board members. It is only in relationships with shareholder representatives than Nordic board-level employee representatives are more distant than their Germanic counterparts, although, even in this case, the relationship is not seen as conflictual.

Francophone Cluster

Employee representation at board level in the Francophone cluster is associated with very large companies, which operate as independent entities. Compared to the CMEs, board-level employee representation in industry in the Francophone cluster is rare. Although companies in the Francophone cluster may choose between a monistic or a dual board structure, it is clear that the majority have chosen monistic systems with either 'a board of directors and a CEO' or 'a board of directors and a chair of the board separate from the executive officer'. Company boards in the Francophone countries are the largest (average 16.8 members) among the country clusters, are composed of about a quarter of board-level employee representatives on average, and are the most likely to be attended by members of the works council with consultative voice.[2] Characteristically, a Francophone board-level employee representative is male, is unionised and is unlikely to hold other representative positions within the company.

More than 80 per cent of Francophone board-level employee representatives define their participation at the board in terms of information or consultation rather than more powerful forms of participation. Furthermore, in the Francophone countries is the largest proportion of board-level employee representatives who think that they had no influence over company restructuring. In brief, the situation *de facto* in the Francophone countries is distant from the intention *de jure*.

A range of board processes explains the lack of development within Francophone systems of board-level employee representation. In particular, Francophone board-level employee representatives are among the least likely to receive timely information and are more likely than their counterparts elsewhere to regard the information they receive to be inadequate. Francophone board-level employee representatives also record the lowest level of activity and regard themselves as having little possibility to intervene by any of the means listed in Table 4.6. Confirming the absence of power among Francophone board-level employee representatives is the observation that 45.6 per cent of them report that the principal decisions of the board are made 'during meetings outside the board excluding employee representatives'. Although there are many subcommittees established by Francophone boards, only a small minority of board-level employee representatives are involved in them as full members. The many pre-meetings held between Francophone board-level employee representatives and senior managers do not serve to pre-define board decisions, but rather address questions of clarification regarding the agenda or issues not directly related to the affairs of the board.

Francophone board-level employee representatives organise more meetings involving other board-level employee representatives than their Nordic counterparts but fewer meetings than are convened in the Germanic cluster. Similarly to Nordic board-level employee representatives, Francophone board-level employee representatives emphasise the influence and importance of the trade union rather than the works council, the former playing a key role in the nomination of candidates for vacancies on the board. Relationships between Francophone board-level employee representatives and workplace trade unions are more developed in terms of the reporting back of board affairs and are more cooperative than they are with works councils. This finding lends further weight to the argument that compliance with confidentiality provisions is not incompatible with the articulation of labour representation within the company, although a greater proportion of Francophone board-level employee representatives than from any other country cluster are prepared to treat no document presented at the board as confidential.

Furthermore, and unique among the country clusters, a key mechanism whereby board-level employee representatives and trade union are articulated in the Francophone countries is the provision of political leadership by trade unions. Articulation between Francophone works councils and board-level employee representatives is not as intense as in the Germanic cluster but is by no means non-existent. The legislation that precludes works council members from also serving as board-level employee representatives, no doubt, contributes to the distance between the works council and the employee representative on the board. The frequency at which works council members attend the board in a consultative capacity may act to mitigate the impact of this legislation with the consequence that articulation with the works council may complement that with trade unions. Articulation and alliances with parties that represent interests other than labour are unlikely in the Francophone countries, reflecting the influence of adversarial industrial relations. No other country cluster exhibits relationships between board-level employee representatives and senior management, other board members and shareholder representatives which are more infrequent and of lower quality.

New Member States

Similarly, to Nordic CMEs, but differing from the situation in the Germanic and Francophone clusters, large numbers of board-level employee representatives in the NMS sit on boards of medium-sized companies, most of which are independent single companies. A majority of these companies operate in 'industry' or 'agriculture, mining, quarrying and other activities'. A dual board structure is the most frequently occurring form. Average board size is the smallest (5.5 members) in the NMS and, associated with this, the number of board-level employee representatives on the board is also the lowest (2.0) among the country clusters, although board-level employee representatives comprise a similar proportion of the board to the European average at 34.2 per cent. A 'standard' board-level employee representative in the NMS is male, unionised, and, on average, holds less than one (0.9) other representative position within the company. The concurrent mandates are usually that of shop steward or member of the works council. Contrary to the situation elsewhere, employees play a prominent role in the nomination and the appointment of board-level employee representatives in the NMS. Trade unions are also influential on nomination processes.

To a greater extent than their Germanic counterparts, board-level employee representatives in the NMS define their role as 'controlling the management through supervision' (38.4 per cent compared to 31.5 per cent). In addition, a further 22.8 per cent of board-level employee representatives in the NMS think that they 'discussed matters with other board members until a shared position is reached', reflecting diversity within the countries covered by the cluster. Around a quarter (28.4 per cent) of board-level employee representatives in the NMS report that they only received information or are consulted, but are not involved in final decision-making, which is less than in either the Germanic (41.1 per cent), Nordic (50.9 per cent) or Francophone (80.9 per cent) clusters. Board-level employee representatives in the NMS, however, are not as influential as their Germanic and Nordic counterparts are on restructuring. In short, although there is a minority of board-level employee representatives in the NMS that are excluded from strategic company decision-making, this minority is relatively small, which suggests that the intended situation *de jure* is fairly consistent with the situation *de facto*.

Several processes within the board in the NMS contribute to an explanation of the positive situation of board-level employee representation reported by representatives. Similar to the Germanic system, the timing and quality of information is generally regarded as satisfactory. The level of activity of board-level employee representatives in the NMS is mixed with interventions at the board, primarily comprising requests for items to be added to the agenda or reports on the affairs of the company. Board-level employee representatives in the NMS are the most likely to report that the principal decisions of the board are taken at board meetings and the least likely to report that board decisions are made in their absence. These findings suggest that the relatively rare pre-meetings with senior management may not be an impediment to the involvement of board-level employee representatives in strategic decision-making. This argument is further supported by the observation that relocation of decision-making to subcommittees is very infrequent.

Systems of articulation within which board-level employee representatives in the NMS operate, however, are relatively unsophisticated compared to the Germanic cluster. The organisation of pre-meetings among board-level employee representatives is rare and the resources provided by trade unions are of lesser value than those provided by the employer. While board-level employee representatives in the NMS do receive some support from trade unions, it is far less developed than that received by their Germanic counterparts. The relative absence of trade union support, no doubt, contributes to an explanation of why more than 30.0 per cent of board-level employee representatives in the NMS require more support from trade unions in the form of 'access to experts' and 'technical training'.

Contrary to Germanic practices and more akin with those in the Nordic and Francophone clusters, articulation within companies in the NMS primarily involves the trade union. Relationships between board-level employee representatives and trade unions are generally cooperative/consensual and are marked by more representatives reporting back to the trade union 'at least quarterly' (61.4 per cent) than those 'never' reporting back (21.1 per cent). Again, the extent of articulation suggests that respect for the duty of confidentiality, which is relatively high in the NMS, is not a barrier to articulation. Similar to the other country clusters, articulation with trade unions is not exclusive of that with works councils, but is more intense.

Board-level employee representation in both the NMS and IGS share the distinctive feature that articulation with parties that represent interests other than labour is as developed as that with personnel and institutions that represent labour. Board-level employee representatives in the NMS report more cooperative relationships with other board members than with the works council and as many contacts outside of the board with senior managers and the CEO as they have with labour representatives. Furthermore, the proportion of board-level employee representatives who require more contact with parties representing interests other than labour is greater than that requiring more contact with labour representatives. Articulation is the NMS is thus a phenomenon involving board-level employee representatives, other representatives of labour and the representatives of other interests within the company.

Ireland, Greece and Spain

The overwhelming majority of companies with board-level employee representation in IGS are very large, state-owned and operate as either a single company or as a parent/holding company with a monistic board in which 'the chair of the board is separate from the executive officer'. Employee representatives compose the lowest proportion of board members in IGS compared to the other country clusters. On average, there are two board-level employee representatives on relatively large boards composed of eleven members. Board-level employee representatives in IGS are overwhelmingly male, are unionised and hold one other representative position within the company, usually as a shop steward or member of the works council. Nomination procedures are most strongly influenced by trade unions, whereas appointment is usually through a direct election by employees.

A minority of board-level employee representatives in IGS (28.6 per cent) are excluded from having power over strategic company decision-making in that their engagement at the board level is only by means of information and consultation. This minority is smaller than that found in the Germanic, Nordic and Francophone clusters and is comparable to that in the NMS. A relatively small proportion (14.3 per cent) of board-level employee representatives in IGS also report that the principal decisions of the board are taken at meetings from which they are excluded. Relatively large proportions of board-level employee representatives in IGS define their engagement at the board in terms of 'discussing matters with other board members until a shared position is reached' (35.7 per cent) and 'controlling the management through supervision' (28.6 per cent), again reflecting the different board arrangements within the cluster. More board-level employee representatives in IGS think that they were influential on company restructuring decisions than think they had little or no influence, a situation not replicated in the other country clusters. There is thus a relative convergence between the intended situation *de jure* and the situation *de facto*.

The nature of board processes certainly contributes to the relatively positive assessment of board-level employee representatives from the IGS cluster. Although information supplied on board topics is delivered to a shorter time frame than elsewhere, board-level employee representatives are generally satisfied with the quality of the information. The majority of board-level employee representatives effectively participate in strategic decision-making in that they are present at the meetings where decisions are made. In addition, board level employee representatives in IGS are the most active in requiring topics to be added to the agenda of the board, reports on the affairs of the company and in preventing the board from making a decision.

The situation in IGS regarding articulation follows the same pattern as exhibited in other country clusters insofar as board-level employee representatives are most likely to articulate their actions with the party responsible for their nomination: the trade union in the IGS cluster. The relationship between board-level employee representatives and trade unions at the workplace is the most cooperative internal relationship reported in the IGS cluster. Furthermore, no fewer than 68.0 per cent of board-level employee representatives report back the affairs of the board to the trade unions 'at least monthly' compared to 42.3 per cent who report back to the works council at the same frequency and 46.2 per cent who do so to employees. Trade unions, however, make available a modest support provision compared to that available in the other country clusters, particularly regarding training. Although not conflictual, relationships with parties that represent interests other than labour are less developed than those with institutions of labour representation. In consequence, no fewer than 42.9 per cent of board-level employee representatives in IGS would prefer more frequent contact with senior managers who they 'rarely' or 'never' meet prior to the formal board meeting.

European Companies

Board-level employee representation in SEs is principally a phenomenon of parent or holding companies with more than 2,000 employees. Although 39.5 per cent of board-level employee representatives in SEs are based in 'industry', there are substantial minorities in 'construction', 'private-sector services' and 'agriculture, mining, quarrying and other activities'. No fewer than 81.6 per cent of board-level employee representatives in SEs report that the headquarters of the company is in Germany, reflecting the origins of most SEs. These origins are influential insofar as board-level employee representatives in SEs report most frequently operating in the presence of supervisory and management boards. Furthermore, the proportion of employee representatives on the supervisory board of a SE is comparable to that in the Germanic cluster, as is the average number of board-level employee representatives and the average size of the board. The influence of the works council in SEs is also similar to that in the Germanic cluster regarding the concurrent holding of works council and board-level positions. The works council is the key influence on the nomination of board-level employee representatives in the Germanic cluster and in SEs. Unlike the situation in the Germanic cluster, however, board-level employee representatives in SEs were most likely to be appointed by the works council and to serve on the European works council. The boards of SEs comprise the lowest proportion of women directors and, with the exception of IGS, women constitute the smallest proportion of board-level employee representatives in the SEs. The typical SE board-level employee representative is male and a trade unionist.

Similar to their counterparts in the Germanic cluster, board-level employee representatives based in SEs are most likely to 'control the management through supervision' (21.1 per cent). A further 23.7 per cent of these board-level employee representatives either 'co-manage the company by participating in decision-making' or 'discuss matters with other board members until a shared position is reached', suggesting diffuse approaches to the exercise of power. Replicating the situation in most country clusters, however, is the presence of large numbers of board-level employee representatives in SEs that engage at the board only by means of information or consultation (55.3 per cent). While engagement at the board by means of information or consultation demonstrates an inability to exert power, board-level employee representatives in the SEs are more positive about their capacity to influence restructuring than their counterparts in the country clusters, with the single exception of the IGS.

The absence of power for many board-level employee representatives in the SEs is explained neither by shortfalls in information, which is both timely and of adequate quality, nor by exclusion from meetings at which decisions are made, as Germanic, Nordic and Francophone board-level employee representatives are more likely to be excluded from such meetings. In addition, the degree of activity at board meetings by SE board-level employee representatives is comparable to that of their Germanic counterparts, suggesting that this is also not an explanation for the absence of power.

In terms of articulation, board-level employee representatives in the SEs chart a course very similar to their counterparts in the Germanic cluster. In particular, board-level employee representatives in the SEs engage in large numbers of pre-meetings with other board-level employee representatives and with senior management, rely on trade unions for 'technical training' and 'access to experts' and are more likely to report back to the works council than to trade unions. The proximity of the relationship with works councils is no surprise, given that large numbers of board-level employee representatives based in SEs are also works councillors, who meet fellow works councillors regularly outside of the board meeting. The European dimension is predictably accentuated by board-level employee representatives in the SEs in that they are more likely than their counterparts in the country clusters to gain 'access to trade union organisations at European level' through national trade unions.

Four principal points emerge from this review of board-level employee representation within the five country clusters and the SEs. First, the personal characteristics of board-level employee representatives are similar across the country clusters. Second, the form of board-level employee representation and the nature of the relationships between the parties involved in the process are unique to each country cluster and the SEs. Board-level employee representation is thus not monolithic but ensures that board-level employee representatives operating under the various systems experience the phenomenon differently. Third, in every country cluster there is a proportion of board-level employee representatives that is excluded from having power over strategic company decision-making and is limited to influencing it, contrary to the intentions of policymakers and legislators. The proportion of board-level employee representatives prevented from exercising power over board decisions varies from cluster to cluster and is a majority in the Francophone and Nordic clusters and in the SEs. Fourth, the nature and intensity of articulation of board-level employee representatives within and externally to the company also varies between country clusters. Board-level employee representatives are more intensely articulated, however, with the party responsible for their nomination. In terms of the country clusters, Germanic board-level employee representatives are the most intensely articulated.

THE IMPLICATIONS FOR THE ACADEMIC POINTS OF DEPARTURE

Chapter 1 contrasted the emphases of the corporate governance literature with those of the industrial relations literature to highlight two points of departure for the study of board-level employee representation. In essence, corporate governance is principally concerned with relationships between capital and management (Gospel and Pendleton 2005; Gourevitch and Shinn 2005; Roe 2003), whereas industrial democracy, coupled with the intensity and quality of participation, figures large in analyses grounded in industrial relations (Hyman 1975; Müller-Jentsch 1986). This section takes the features of these two points of departure and assesses them in the light of the findings of this study.

The Corporate Governance Point of Departure

Three elements of the corporate governance literature are examined here: finance or principal–agency models, the political perspective and sociological approaches. The survey data are shown to offer qualified support to aspects of the political perspective and sociological approaches. The assumptions that underpin finance or principal-agency models, particularly the exclusion of labour from the analytical framework, are brought into question by the survey data.

Finance or principal–agency models of corporate governance are primarily concerned with issues arising from the separation of ownership and control and, hence, relationships between shareholders and managers. In terms of the essence of the corporate governance literature, finance or principal–agency models are partial in that labour is excluded from the analysis. Chapter 1 highlighted a further limitation to finance models in demonstrating that the theoretical position of employees is similar to that of shareholders insofar as both groups have claims against the firm that are dependent on the performance of the firm.

Although advocates of finance models exclude labour as a primary actor within systems of corporate governance, they have advanced three interlinked arguments that have been deployed against board-level employee representation. First, there is wide-ranging support among advocates of principal–agency models for the argument that boards perform best when they are small: eight board members, or thereabouts, being viewed as the optimal size (Jensen 1993: Lipton and Lorsch 1992). Second, and building on the first observation, a series of largely econometric studies presented evidence that a movement away from the optimal size of the board, particularly when this movement leads to an increase in the size of the board, is associated with the deteriorating economic performance of the firm (Bennedon et al. 2008; Yermack 1996). Third, proponents of the finance model argue that board-level employee representatives will prioritise concerns of exclusive interest to labour in preference to the well-being of the company (Fama 1980; Jensen and Meckling 1976). These studies, in turn, have been cited by opponents of board-level employee representation who argue that the presence of employee representatives on the board will lead to an increased number of board members and, thus, a weaker economic performance (Bermig and Frick 2011). Chapter 3, however, demonstrated that the average size of boards covered by the survey is 8.8 members, that is, within the margin of error of the calculations for the optimum board size. The general prediction arising from the finance model that the size of boards will necessarily rise to unmanageable proportions when board-level employee representation is in place, thus is rejected. Similarly, Chapter 4 demonstrated that board-level employee representatives do not exclusively prioritise concerns of interest only to labour. In practice, issues of 'company finance', 'structure and organisation of the company' and 'market policy' are considered as important agenda items by substantial numbers of board-level employee representatives, suggesting a wider ambit of concern than that assumed from within the finance models of corporate governance. Chapter 5 confirmed this position in showing that board-level employee representatives prioritise the interests of employees and those of the company.

A further area in which the results presented here impinge on the finance model concerns the agenda of the board. The finance model is primarily built around perceived competition for control between shareholders and managers. The model accepts that the interests of these two groups need not necessarily overlap entirely. In excluding labour from the analysis, advocates of the finance model assume that labour has no specific contribution to make and that the interests of labour are separate from the board. This study demonstrates that there are at least two areas where the finance model fails to adequately theorise the nature of activity at the board of companies in Europe. First, labour has vested interests that rest on the performance of the firm. These interests may be long-term, such as pensions, retirement provisions and job security, or variable in duration, such as promotion, training or health and safety. Second, the character of employment relations may also affect the performance of the firm. Indeed, a central tenet of the burgeoning human resource management literature is that 'bundles' of employment relations practices can be deployed in specific circumstances to improve the performance of the firm (Boselie 2013; Delery and Doty 1996). In this context, there is no reason to anticipate that shareholder representatives have any specific expertise in either of these areas. The study shows that board-level employee representatives make a substantial contribution to the agenda of the board in the areas that the human resource management literature assumes may contribute to the improved economic performance of the company. The findings presented here do not allow us to argue that the presence of board-level employee representatives extends the scope of the agenda of the board, because no comparators are drawn from boards where board-level employee representation is absent. The data, however, support the argument that board-level employee representatives bring an expertise to agenda items covered by the board, which may contribute to company performance. The presence of this expertise also ensures that the scope of board-level discussions incorporates the interests of labour, which most scholars accept as a key element of corporate governance. Furthermore, the majority of board-level employee representatives report that other board members regard them as 'skilled partners able to participate fully in board meetings'. In short, the analytical omission of board-level employee representation constitutes a fundamental limitation of the finance model as it excludes labour from the analysis, which is a central component of attempts to enhance economic performance by intensifying links between human resource management and company strategy. In addition, proponents of the finance model overlook the diversity of the board brought by board-level employee representation. This diversity comes in the form of demographic diversity, arising, in particular, from the high level of feminisation among board-level employee representatives, and cognitive diversity illustrated by the extensive knowledge of the company and the different backgrounds of board-level employee representatives compared to other board members.

Explanations of corporate governance from a political perspective view variation in the pattern of corporate governance to arise from economic and, particularly, political conflict. Those that emphasise the impact of political agency argue that corporate governance outcomes result from political alliances or distributional coalitions entered into by representatives of shareholders, management and labour (Aoki 1986; Gourevitch and Shinn 2005; Roe 2003). In contrast to the finance model, labour is thus included as a relevant social actor from the outset by proponents of the political perspective. Although the alliances that the social actors enter into may be tactical or strategic, within the terms of the political perspective a long-term, strategic 'corporatist compromise' characterises continental Western Europe in which an alliance of labour and management has acted to limit the influence of shareholders (Gourevitch and Shinn 2005:205–228).

In all the country clusters examined here, relations between board-level employee representatives and management are more cooperative than are those between board-level employee representatives and shareholder representatives. The basic tenet of the 'corporatist compromise' is thus supported by the findings of this study. In the absence of information on the management–shareholder representative relationship, the findings presented here, however, are by no means conclusive. An additional point concerns the NMS, which were excluded from the initial formulation of the 'corporatist compromise'. The evidence presented in Chapter 6 certainly confirms a greater proximity between board-level employee representatives and managers than between board-level employee representatives and shareholder representatives in the NMS as the presence of a 'corporatist compromise' would suggest. A caveat, however, should be entered regarding the NMS. Board-level employee representatives in the NMS tend to have relatively close, and to desire closer, relationships with shareholder representatives. With the exception of their Germanic counterparts, board-level employee representatives in the NMS are more likely than their counterparts in other country clusters to meet shareholder representatives outside of the board meeting and would prefer to have more frequent contact with shareholder representatives to an extent greater than board-level employee representatives from any other country cluster. These differences between the NMS and continental Western Europe may originate in the transitional and contested nature of the economies in the NMS. In short, it remains to be seen whether the NMS settle on a position more akin to neo-liberal rather than coordinated market economies (Bohle and Grescovits 2007; Meardi 2012). The argument returns to this point later.

The evidence presented here is ambiguous regarding the differentiation between the class, sector and voice models in political perspectives to corporate governance (Gourevitch and Shinn 2005:95–276; Jackson 2005). It is apparent that the distinctions drawn between these three models are not as clear-cut as political approaches to corporate governance would suggest. Whereas the political differentiation between class, sector and voice models anticipates variation in the intensity of relations between board-level employee representatives, management and shareholder representatives, Chapter 6 demonstrated a consistency insofar as in all country clusters relations between board-level employee representatives and shareholder representatives are less cooperative than those between board-level employee representatives and management. Furthermore, in all country clusters articulation between board-level employee representatives and other institutions of labour representation is more intense than that between board-level employee representatives and either management or shareholder representatives. This is not to reject the differentiation between class, sector and voice models *per se*, because there are variations in the intensity of the relationships mentioned earlier that are in the direction anticipated by this differentiation. In the Francophone cluster, for example, relations between board-level employee representatives and managers are the least cooperative, which is as anticipated by the voice model, but are not accompanied by cooperative relations between board-level employee representatives and shareholder representatives, as also anticipated by the voice model.

Putting the firm at the centre of the analysis, advocates of sociological perspectives within the corporate governance literature argue that networks condition, but do not determine, the strategy of the firm towards corporate governance (Hall and Soskice 2001a; Hancké et al. 2007). Networks in this context refer to those arising from cultural and social norms, systems of market regulation, the wide-ranging and varied networks established between firms and other institutions, and internal networks set up to operate the firm. Analysis of relationships between the firm and stakeholders is thus centre stage for advocates of the sociological perspective to corporate governance. Key to the examination of the sociological perspective here is the distinction drawn between CMEs, where market mechanisms are overlaid by a wide range of social and political approaches intended to promote long-term relationships within the firm and between the firm and other institutions, including suppliers of capital; MMEs, where market mechanisms and some forms of coordinated regulation operate in tandem but without the consistent intention of generating long-term relationships as in the CMEs; EMEs, where coordinated regulation, if it is present at all, is immature, not stable and subject to social and political vicissitudes; and the GIIPS, where financial crises and political reform intended to address these crises are promoting wide-ranging social change.[3]

As discussed earlier in the context of the 'corporatist compromise', relations between board-level employee representatives and management are more cooperative than are those between board-level employee representatives and shareholder representatives in all of the country clusters. The intensity of this cooperation confirms that in CMEs, MMEs, EMEs and IGS the basic relationships in the firm differ from those that advocates of sociological perspectives propose for LMEs, namely, relatively close relations between managers and shareholder representatives from which labour is excluded. In addition, the survey results demonstrate that coordination is greater in the CMEs than in the MMEs and IGS. To illustrate several of the instances where this is the case: the power of board-level employee representatives at board meetings is more marked in the CMEs than in the MMEs, the information provision is superior in the CMEs, and board-level employee representatives in CMEs are able to shape the character of restructuring decisions more than their counterparts in the MMEs.

More problematic for sociological perspectives are the survey results obtained for the EMEs. On two counts the expectations of the sociological perspective are realised. First, the influence of board-level employee representatives within CMEs is more pronounced than that of their counterparts within the EMEs. Second, the relationships exhibited between board-level employee representatives and both management and shareholder representatives are consistent with the corporatist compromise, notwithstanding the caveat entered earlier. The relationships within EMEs compared to those within MMEs, however, vary from the expectations of sociological perspectives. In particular, board-level employee representatives in the EMEs think that they are more influential on board decision-making and company restructuring than, are as articulated within the company as, and are more likely to make interventions at the board than, their counterparts in the MMEs. In short, there are indicators of greater maturity in relationships concerned with board-level employee representation in EMEs than in MMEs. While explanation of the pattern of relationships within EMEs, MMEs and IGS is not straightforward within the terms of sociological perspectives three explanations are available. First, a study of board-level employee representation is a study of merely one aspect of coordination, which need not be representative of coordination *per se*. Second, the observed 'maturity' in the relationships concerned with coordination may only be temporary as subsequent social and political change may disturb these relationships. Some evidence of these disturbance effects is presented in the third section of this chapter. Third, the limitations in articulation external to the firm between board-level employee representatives and trade unions in the EMEs support the notion advanced within sociological perspectives that limited trade union support for board-level employee representation impinges on the character of board-level employee representation in the EMEs and may promote some instability (King 2007).

Very much within the confines of sociological perspectives is that the manner of coordination varies between different CMEs. The survey data confirm some differences between CMEs regarding the character of board-level employee representation. Dual- and monistic board systems, the character and intensity of articulation both within and external to the firm, and the manner in which board-level employee representatives exert influence at the board, for example, are far from uniform in the Germanic and Nordic clusters. Furthermore, the survey data support the selection of Germany as the archetypical CMEs insofar as articulation involving Germanic board-level employee representatives is more extensive than elsewhere (Hall and Soskice 2001a). Although commentators highlight the pressures faced by the Germanic system of corporate governance (Höpner 2005; Jackson

2005), the intensity of articulation in such systems suggests that the institutional complementarities arising from the engagement of labour may provide some stability to these systems. One additional note of caution regarding sociological perspectives concerns the relationship *de jure* and *de facto* in board-level employee representation. Sociological perspectives tend to assume that legislation is implemented uniformly once it is enacted. Regarding board-level employee representation this assumption is open to question. In particular, in both the Germanic and Nordic clusters substantial numbers of board-level employee representatives are unable to exert power over strategic company decision-making, because their involvement at board level is restricted to information and consultation.

The Industrial Relations Point of Departure

At the heart of the industrial relations literature on board-level employee representation are debates on industrial democracy and employee participation. In essence, industrial relations scholars regard legislation on industrial democracy enacted in continental Western Europe to result from the increased labour market and political power of labour during the 1970s, which pressured states, particularly when left-of-centre political parties were in power, to introduce legislation on board-level employee representation as a means of re-establishing order in industrial relations (Sassoon 1997:357–382). Similarly, indirect forms of employee participation, including board-level employee representation, are viewed as mechanisms whereby workers can influence decision-making within companies of which they are stakeholders (Pateman 1970; Poole 1975). As Chapter 1 demonstrated, apart from the catch-all 'to democratise work', there is no consensus on the objectives of either industrial democracy or indirect forms of employee participation. Furthermore, there are no detailed comparative analyses of how board-level employee representation might function in practice, although it is recognised that the articulation of representatives operating within the range of institutions of labour representation present within and external to firms is essential if the influence of employee representatives is effectively to be brought to bear (Crouch 1993:54–55; Kjellberg 1983). There is, however, a consensus on the issues raised by these concepts in the context of industrial relations. Three interrelated issues resonate throughout the literature: incorporation, the quality and intensity of participation, and the contestation between the interests of capital and labour.

A strand of the industrial relations literature views board-level employee representation as likely to result in the incorporation of employee representatives to the goals of the firm as they become physically and politically isolated from those that they are supposed to represent. In acknowledging the likelihood of incorporation, Marxist scholars argue that board-level employee representation is associated with the containment of conflict and the mystification of the inherent differences between capital and labour (Clarke 1977; Hyman 1975:141–149).

The argument on incorporation is principally theoretical in that there is no comparative evidence either confirming or denying its existence, or measuring its extent. The survey evidence generated here present several approaches to an examination of incorporation, most of which suggest that incorporation is rarely present among board-level employee representatives. First, it is apparent that most board-level employee representatives intervene during board meetings and that the character of these interventions calls into question the idea of unilateral managerial decision-making at the board. Such interventions do not suggest compliance with a management agenda. Second, a substantial number of board-level employee representatives are intensely articulated with employees and other institutions of labour representation within or external to the firm. Indicators of this articulation include regular contact with employees and representatives from other institutions of labour representation, a reliance on trade unions for training and access to expert advice, the importance attached by board-level employee representatives to information supplied from within other institutions of labour representation, the intensity of reporting back mechanisms, and the holding of multiple representative positions within the company by board-level employee representatives that ensure information transfer through personal engagement. The intensity of this articulation suggests a permanent and continuous exchange between board-level employee representatives and a wide range of labour representatives and employees that would prohibit the isolation of board-level employee representatives, which, in the absence of these conditions, could foster incorporation. Third, board-level employee representatives pursue an agenda that includes issues central to the interests of labour at the board meeting. Although issues such as 'company finance' and 'the structure and organisation of the company' certainly figure large among the concerns of board-level employee representatives, most board-level employee representatives prioritise issues related to human resources.

Additional points specific to two country clusters are pertinent to the examination of incorporation. The majority of the French trade union movement remained sceptical about the establishment of board-level employee representation in the private sector until the early 2000s. This scepticism was, in part, a consequence of the perceived likelihood of incorporation (Sorge 1976). The numerous company crises associated with shareholder value orientations towards corporate governance led to a rethink on board-level employee representation among several French union confederations. The long-running scepticism within the French trade union movement may account for the emphasis placed by Francophone board-level employee representatives on the political leadership provided by trade unions in ensuring articulation between board-level employee representatives and trade unions. In other words, political interventions made by French trade unions through board-level employee representatives constitute a further counter to the possibility of incorporation.

A second cluster-specific point concerning incorporation applies to the NMS. Within the NMS articulation between board-level employee representatives and trade unions does not reach the intensity of, for example, that in the Germanic cluster; and board-level employee representatives in the NMS prioritise the importance of 'company finance' as an agenda item more than their counterparts elsewhere, and to a far greater extent than 'human resources'. These findings suggest that incorporation could, at least, be a possibility within the framework of board-level employee representation within the NMS, particularly as there was no groundswell of support among workers and trade unionists for this form of representation following the collapse of the Soviet-style command economies during the late 1980s. In mitigation of this argument, it is also acknowledged that board-level employee representatives in the NMS intervene at board meetings in a manner comparable to elsewhere and claim to be the most influential on board decision-making. In short, the situation in the NMS regarding incorporation is far from clear-cut.

A second theme that resonates throughout the industrial relations literature concerns the intensity and quality of participation. The intensity of participation is about the range of issues covered by those engaged in the institution of participation and the strategic importance of these issues (Gold and Hall 1990:4; Knudsen 1995:8–10). In practice, the wider the range of issues addressed and the greater their strategic importance, the more intense the level of participation. The intensity of participation may also be influenced by the constitutional arrangements attached to the institution of participation. Constitutional arrangements in this context are often expressed in terms of information, consultation and co-determination rights and the impact of employee representatives within the terms of each right (Knudsen 1995:8–11; Rogers and Streeck 1995).

Debates on the quality of participation focus on distinctions between pseudo-, partial and full participation (Pateman 1970:68–71). Pseudo-participation takes place in circumstances where it is thought by those outside the institution that representatives within the institution are able to influence, if not co-determine, the outcome of a decision-making process, but in practice, neither influence nor co-determine the outcome. Where management practices pseudo-participation, participation becomes a technique of persuasion rather than one of joint decision-making. In circumstances of partial participation board-level employee representatives can influence the outcome of a decision-making process but do not have the same power at their disposal as other board members, whereas in full participation all board members have equal power to determine the outcome of a decision (Pateman 1970:70–71). Constitutional arrangements may influence both the intensity and quality of participation. These arrangements are thus examined after those issues specific to either the intensity or the quality of participation.

On three counts concerning the agenda, board-level employee representation appears to attain an appropriate intensity of participation. First, the breadth of the agenda of board meetings is wide ranging, and relatively few board-level employee representatives report that they are unable to raise an agenda item either as a result of legislation or because of the actions of other board members. Second, most board-level employee representatives have introduced items to the agenda of the board that they feel are appropriate; that is, the agenda is not just a list of items generated by management. Third, agenda items that are strategically important to the firm are raised by board-level employee representatives and are examined by them, if raised by other board members. Furthermore, and affecting all of these three issues, timely information is available in the appropriate form for the majority of board-level employee representatives to enable them to reach considered decisions on the matters raised at the board.

A substantial minority of board-level employee representatives in most country clusters and a majority of Nordic, Francophone and SE board-level employee representatives operate in circumstances of partial participation insofar as they either receive information or are consulted at board level but are unable to exert power over the content of long-term strategic company decision-making. Board-level employee representatives in these circumstances are thus thought to be in positions, at least, to influence decision-making but, in practice, cannot exert power over the outcome of decision-making processes. While partial participation is contrary to the raison d'être of board-level employee representation, it places employee representatives operating within such confines in an invidious position vis-à-vis other representatives of labour, thereby jeopardising any arrangements for articulation that might be in place.

A further theme that resonates throughout the industrial relations literature concerns contestation, usually expressed as that between the interests of capital and labour. Unlike much of the corporate governance literature, industrial relations scholars rarely differentiate between management and shareholder interests in the context of contesting either the principle or the terms of industrial democracy and employee participation. Industrial relations analyses also differ from those of corporate governance in that they emphasise differences within labour towards board-level employee representation. These points apart, however, board-level employee representation is viewed as contested at two levels. At the level of the polity the decision to enact legislation and the content of any legislative proposal is contested by the state, employers and their organisations, and employees and their organisations. Recent developments at this level are examined in the next section of this chapter. At the level of the firm the content and practice of board-level employee representation is contested in a manner similar to that within other institutions of labour representation. In practice, the legislation sets some parameters within which contestation may take place, including, *inter alia*, the breadth of the agenda, where labour generally wishes to extend agendas and the intensity and quality of participation, whereas management may wish to impose limits. Recent evidence suggests that within the firm the strategy of some managers is to shape the content, function and objectives of board-level employee representation in a manner consistent with the shift towards financialisation and deregulation (Pongratz and Voß 2003).

The evidence presented here is cross-sectional rather than longitudinal. It is thus not possible to assess the extent of change over time to 'test' whether the shifts proposed by Pongratz and Voß (2003) are present on a wide-ranging basis. A number of points, however, can usefully be noted. Board-level employee representatives, for example, generally view the provision of information, the breadth of the agenda, relations with other board members, and their ability to intervene at board meetings to be satisfactory. In other words, there is no consistent evidence to suggest that managers have tightened board procedures to the point that large numbers of board-level employee representatives object. The unambiguous exception to this schema is the Francophone cluster within which board-level employee representatives question the quality and timely distribution of information, the application of confidentiality provisions, and relations with other board members. This, of course, is not to argue that these developments are recent and reflect changed economic and political circumstances. To the contrary, it is just as plausible to argue that these circumstances are consistent with adversarial Francophone industrial relations and, as such, are just as likely to have been ever present.

That a substantial minority of board-level employee representatives in most country clusters and a majority in the Nordic, Francophone clusters and in the SEs report that their engagement at the board only constitutes partial participation supports the argument that management restricts the quality of participation at board level, by, for example, shifting decision-making to meetings from which managers exclude board-level employee representatives. Again, it should be acknowledged that this restriction may have been a long-term rather than a recent development in the country clusters. Irrespective of the duration of the phenomenon, the extent of partial participation confirms that legislation does not necessarily set a standard and that in contesting the implementation of the legislation, some managers are able to restrict the power of employee representatives within the board. Similarly, a majority of board-level employee representatives in the Germanic, Nordic, Francophone and NMS clusters think that they are unable to effectively influence the terms of company restructuring. In other words, there is a substantial shortfall in the power of board-level employee representatives today that contrasts with the intentions of the policymakers and legislators at the time that legislation on board-level employee representation was enacted.

THE IMPLICATIONS FOR POLICY AND RECENT DEVELOPMENTS

Impinging on contestation at the level of the polity and within the firm are shifts in political economy and the regulatory environment marked notably by globalisation, financialisation, deregulation and high levels of unemployment relative to those of the 'golden age', all of which have acted to weaken the labour market and political power of labour. At the level of the polity several Western European employers' associations, notably the BDA and BDI in Germany, have argued that shifts in political economy constitute a marked change compared to the period when the legislation on board-level employee representation was enacted and view the extent of this change as sufficient reason to, at least, review the legislation. In 2004, for example, the BDA and BDI published a report calling for the 'modernisation of co-determination' (*Mitbestimmung modernisieren*) in which they plea for the deregulation of the German system by replacing existing statutory rules by flexible arrangements based on company-level negotiations. Although the German government rejected the proposal, the employers' associations have sustained their lobbying activities and have gathered support from influential legal scholars who restated the position of the employers' association in their recommendations for 'the future of EU company law' commissioned by the EC (Antunes et al. 2011:53–54).[4]

The increase in the employment rates of women throughout much of Europe has also prompted the introduction of regulations designed to increase the number and the proportion of women board members (see Chapter 2). The implications of the research findings in terms of the number of women board members are clear. Women are under-represented as directors and the extent of this under-representation would be greater were it not for the relatively large proportion of women that serve as board-level employee representatives. Men, however, constitute the majority of board-level employee representatives in all country clusters and in the SEs. The proportion of women board-level employee representatives is most marked in the Nordic cluster where regulation on gender quotas is the most long-standing, suggesting that such approaches may promote numerical change. There is no evidence from the survey, however, to suggest that women board-level employee representatives pursue different policy agendas, exert more influence or power and express different degrees of satisfaction with board practices than do their male counterparts. The survey results do not allow a detailed examination of how more women board-level employee representatives may promote changes in board processes.

Since the distribution of the survey, the impact of the post-2007 recession has put board-level employee representation under ever-greater pressure in Greece, Ireland and Spain. In these three countries, privatisation plans, elaborated as one of the structural reforms required by the so-called troika, comprising the EC, European Central Bank and the International Monetary Fund, in return for financial support, threaten the existence of board-level employee representation. The coverage of board-level employee representation, which is only to be found in state-owned companies in these countries, is thus gradually being reduced, as privatisation plans are implemented, with the consequence that the number of board-level employee representatives is declining. It is anticipated that none of the existing board-level employee representatives in Greece will 'survive' the dramatic privatisation programme. What looks like a progressive disappearance of board-level employee representation in these three countries, however, to date has been achieved by the transfer of state-owned companies to the private sector rather than by the enactment of legislation eliminating existing rights. In Ireland, recognition of this point led defenders of board-level employee representation to consider changes in the current legal framework so as to preserve the situation, a view shared in a study commissioned by the 'worker director groups' of the Irish Congress of Trade Unions (ICTU), which recommends the extension of board-level employee representation throughout the public sector (TASC 2012).

The recapitalisation and nationalisation of Irish banks in the post-2007 rescue package implemented by the Irish government also prompted arguments that the corporate governance regime in the finance sector should be reformed to include board-level employee representation (ICTU 2008). This position was consolidated at the Congress of 2009 when the Executive Report stated, 'We sought employee representatives on all financial companies' boards, as we can no longer trust the 'shareholder value' appointment and governance system. We are now calling for a more European-style governance structure for private firms in Ireland, based on stakeholder as opposed to shareholder value' (ICTU 2009:15). Subsequently the ICTU extended this position to cover the entire economy, rather than just the finance sector, in calling for consideration of the establishment of 'supervisory boards, as in Germany, with half of the directors nominated by workers and unions' (ICTU 2013:27). Although the response of government to these proposals remains to be seen, the point remains that Irish trade unionism now shows some interest in board-level employee representation in principle.

In contrast, to developments in the rest of Western Europe, legislation enacted in France in June 2013 (*Loi relative à la sécurisation de l'emploi*, Act to Secure Employment) has extended the coverage of board-level employee representation to cover large private-sector companies in addition to the state-owned and privatised companies that were already covered. Although this measure was introduced, as in the past, through the enactment of a law under a Socialist Party–led administration, it originated in a national cross-sectoral agreement signed in January 2013 by the employer associations and three trade union confederations (CFDT, *Confédération française des travailleurs chrétiens* [CFTC] and *Confédération générale des cadres-Confédération française de l'encadrement* [CFE-CGC], but not the CGT and *Force ouvrière* [FO]) that the government transformed into a bill. The compromise that underpins the legislation is part of a broader reform of the labour market with the consequence that the union confederations yielded concessions regarding the coverage of the measure and the number of board-level employee representatives that can serve on the board. The workforce size threshold that triggers compulsory board-level employee representation in private-sector companies is high at 5,000 or more employees in

France or 10,000 employees worldwide, while the proportion of board-level employee representatives is low with only one selected, where the number of board members is twelve or fewer, and two board-level employee representatives, where there are more than twelve board members. The legislation of June 2013 was enacted rather than more wide-ranging legislation, as was initially proposed in the autumn of 2012 by the French government, to reform the regulation of corporate governance. Given that the legislation of June 2013 does not place additional requirements on managements regarding the provision of information and the intensity and quality of participation, both of which the data presented here show to be weak in the Francophone cluster, it is very much open to question whether the extension of the coverage of the legislation will result in additional power within the firm for French board-level employee representatives.

Within the NMS the emphasis is different to that within Western Europe and the impetus for change is the state, albeit supported, if not prompted, by employers' organisations. The centrepiece of arguments in the NMS is that board-level employee representation is inconsistent with the forms of capitalism that are emerging from the post-1990 transition, which have a tendency to resemble LMEs rather than CMEs (Bohle and Grescovits 2007; Meardi 2012). Consistent with this tendency are several attempts to weaken or, in some cases, to eliminate board-level employee representation in NMS. In 2006 the revision of the Companies Acts in Hungary and Slovenia introduced, *inter alia*, the possibility for companies to opt for monistic corporate governance structures in conjunction with a weaker form of employee representation on boards of directors. Contrary to rules that apply in dual systems of corporate governance in Hungary, for example, no minimum standards for employee representation now apply to companies opting for a monistic board of directors. In this case, board-level employee representation is not underpinned by law but is subject to a negotiated agreement between the board of directors and the works council, the latter of which may decide not to introduce employee representation on the board in return for extended rights and duties of the works council (Neumann 2006). In Slovenia, the company law reform resulted in smaller proportions of employee representatives on boards of directors than on supervisory boards (Hojnik 2008). Moreover, the new Companies Act introduced a minimum threshold of 50 employees in both monistic and dual systems whereas none existed previously. Two Slovenian trade unions challenged these changes before the Constitutional Court, which decided that the new regulation was not inconsistent with the national constitution. A more extreme path was followed by the former right/centre-right Czech government. A new act on commercial corporations was enacted in March 2012 and introduced the possibility for companies to opt for a monistic corporate governance structure. As none of the previous legal provisions regarding board-level employee representation were maintained in the revised legislation, there was no longer an obligation for Czech public limited liability companies to have employee representatives on their board after 1 January 2014 when the new law came into force. The proposal of the Polish government was less successful, as its bill of 2010, which had an objective of eliminating board-level employee representation in privatised companies, became stalled after March 2011 because of political disagreements regarding other objectives, including those that deal with the exercise of state intervention in privatised companies, and a shift in political priorities to other sensitive reforms, notably those on pensions. Although the bill of 2010 is no longer on the political agenda, the number of employee representatives in Poland is dramatically decreasing as a consequence of the extensive privatisation process. The database of the Polish Ministry of Treasury, for example, recorded 618 board-level employee representatives at the end of 2009 compared to 197 six years later.[5]

Developments at supranational level are also worth considering insofar as national rights for board-level employee representation are put under pressure by an emerging trend at European level which favours 'regulatory competition': that is, creating the circumstances for companies to shop around among the various national regulatory and legal frameworks to choose the most favourable. According to several rulings of the European Court of Justice, companies are allowed to split the location of their registered seat and real headquarters between two Member States, thus allowing for letterbox companies.[6] This implies that a firm can register in one country and be subject to its national company law, thereby regulating, amongst other things, the composition of corporate governance bodies and board-level employee representation, while conducting all of its business activities in another Member State. By this means companies can circumvent the legal obligation of having employee representatives on the board. In practice, company managements are able to choose whichever national legal framework they prefer and register in a Member State with the least stringent rules on board-level employee representation. To illustrate, 94 large companies now operating in Germany are not required to comply with German co-determination rights, because they are registered in a 'board-level employee representation-free country' and are, according to European case law, perfectly within their rights to arrange their operations in this manner. This number had risen from 43 in 2010 (Sick 2015; Sick and Pütz 2011). By acknowledging that letterbox companies are legal, the European Court of Justice rulings have transformed board-level employee representation 'from an obligatory to a voluntary institution' (Höpner and Schäfer 2015:733).

Concerns about the pressure being put on worker rights is so high that it has prompted the European Parliament to call, in no fewer than five different resolutions, for a regulatory mechanism on the cross-border transfer of seats through a 14th Company Law Directive. At first sight, the fifth call in June 2012 seemed to have had been eventually heard by the EC, which conducted a public consultation on this issue in the first quarter of 2013. The status quo remains, however, as its policy implications have not yet been published two years after the public consultation. The European Parliament is not the sole actor that has reacted to this trend. The ETUC (2014) has also made its position heard by calling for a directive that sets high standards on employee information and consultation, coupled with ambitious minimum standards for board-level employee representation that are applicable to all European company forms.

Turning to the UK where board-level employee representation is absent, reveals some repositioning within the trade union movement, as in the case of Ireland. In the context of political debates on corporate governance, the British TUC, for example, now argues for board-level employee representation (TUC 2014). Originating from criticisms of excessive executive remuneration, the TUC first called for the introduction of regulations to allow employee participation on the remuneration committees of the boards of directors of major companies (TUC 1995), before widening this brief to include board-level employee representation.[7] While the position of several major affiliated trade unions remains ambivalent, the TUC position initially received some support from the Labour Party spokesperson on business (Umunna 2012). A more restricted form of employee representation on remuneration committees was advocated elsewhere (High Pay Commission 2011), although managerial respondents to a survey conducted by the Department of Business, Innovation and Skills were opposed to this more restricted proposal (BIS 2012). The Labour Party adopted the more diluted form of participation in the form of employee representation on remuneration committees in its election manifesto of April 2015 (Labour Party 2015).

These recent developments confirm that board-level employee representation remains contested in principle. The nature and extent of this contestation promote variation in form and practice and ensure that board-level employee representation is dynamic and far from monolithic. We hope that this study contributes to an understanding of the dynamics of board-level representation that is of use to policy-makers and informs academic debates.

NOTES

1. The audit/accounting subcommittee is an exception to this schema as 28.0 per cent of board-level employee representatives participated in such subcommittees whereas 27.1 per cent were not members and had not been invited to join.
2. Works council members with consultative voice are excluded from the average figure for the number of board members.
3. The term *IGS* is used throughout this section to be consistent with the remainder of the publication.
4. The BDA and the BDI argued in their report of 2004 that the German co-determination law was discriminatory, because it does not allow for the representation of workers from foreign subsidiaries. The group of legal experts suggested remedy of this situation was 'introducing the codetermination system provided for by the EU Directive for the SE and the SCE [in which mechanisms of board-level employee representation are an outcome of

negotiations between worker representatives and the employer] also for the domestic forms of company'.

5. Data as of April 2015. Source: Serwis Nadzór Właścicielski, Ministerstwo Skarbu Państwa, http://nadzor.msp.gov.pl/portal/nad/import/6/.
6. The proposal for a European Private Company Statute, put forward by the European Commission in 2008 and which never achieved the necessary political agreement to enable enactment, followed the same pattern (Conchon 2013b). The same is true of the follow-up proposal for a directive on single-member private liability companies issued by the EC in April 2014. Although the possibility of splitting the registered office and administrative seat raised wide-ranging concerns, this contentious point remains within the text of this new initiative.
7. 'Seats for the workforce on company boards would help inject a much-needed dose of reality into boardrooms and put the brakes on the multi-million pay and bonus packages, which are fast becoming the norm in corporate Britain', said TUC General Secretary Frances O'Grady in Autumn 2013; https://www.tuc.org/economic-issues/corporate-governance/workers-company-boards-makes-sound-economic-sense-says-tuc.

Appendix A
Data Compilation and Method

The principal investigative technique was the distribution of a questionnaire to all employee representatives serving at board-level within most European Union Member States and Norway. The questionnaires and reminders were distributed between 2009 and 2012 within seventeen countries: Austria, Czech Republic, Denmark, Finland, France, Germany, Greece, Hungary, Ireland, Luxembourg, the Netherlands, Norway, Poland, Slovakia, Slovenia, Spain and Sweden. In addition, the questionnaire was distributed to board-level employee representatives within companies that had opted for European Company status.

Three countries with board-level employee representation are excluded from the analysis. Croatia was not a Member State of the European Union when the survey was conducted and was not considered for inclusion. Portugal is usually included amongst the countries with legal or conventional provisions on board-level employee representation (Conchon 2013b), but it was excluded from the research. A preliminary census revealed that 49 state-owned Portuguese companies, mainly in the health sector, had one employee representative that sat on one of its corporate bodies. The corporate body on which the employee representatives sit is neither a board of directors (*conselho de administração*) nor a supervisory board (*conselho geral e de supervisão*). In contrast, it is an advisory committee (*conselho consultivo*), with only a consultative remit, rather than decision-making body within which worker representatives have power to influence outcomes and thus was not in the scope of our research. Although a questionnaire was distributed in the Netherlands the country is also excluded from the analysis. Board-level employee representatives in the Netherlands are neither employees of the company nor trade union representatives with interests in the company. Dutch board-level employee representatives also operate under different constitutional expectations than their European counterparts (Goodijk 2010; Rood 1992). They, therefore, have different origins compared to board-level employee representatives elsewhere: for example, many Dutch board-level employee representatives are academics or are employed or have positions in public service; have different relations with trade unions and other organisations that may support board-level employee representatives; and are either articulated with institutions of labour representation within companies in entirely different ways compared to their counterparts elsewhere or are not articulated with such institutions at all. In addition, reference to the returned questionnaires led the authors to suspect that the questionnaires had been distributed incorrectly with the result that people other than board-level employee representatives had completed the questionnaires. For these reasons the Dutch data are not presented in this study, and no further reference to the Dutch data is made in this appendix.

The remainder of this appendix presents detail of the questionnaire design, the methods used to identify board-level employee representatives, the manner of distribution of the questionnaire and the issues linked to the return of the questionnaire.

QUESTIONNAIRE DESIGN

The authors drew up a first draft of the questionnaire. Academics and trade-union experts in the field of workers' participation, including members of the research's advisory board appointed by the Hans-Böckler Foundation, reviewed the draft of the questionnaire and recommended amendments. The reviewers were drawn from countries with wide-ranging rights for board-level employee representation, Austria, Denmark, Germany and Sweden; from countries with weaker provisions but numerous board-level employee representatives, such as France; and from countries with weaker rights and a low number of board-level employee representatives, Luxembourg and Ireland.

The final questionnaire comprised 76 questions grouped around four broad themes: the roles and activities of board-level employee representatives; the priorities and interests of board-level employee representatives; the networks and articulation of board-level employee representatives; and those variables that might influence any of the preceding. To facilitate comparisons the questionnaires distributed within each country included the same questions. Only five questions required adaptation in order to accommodate country specificities. These questions enquired about education, occupation, the legal statutes of companies, and two enquiries concerning the mandates of employee representatives at company-level. As the questions about education, occupation and the legal statutes of companies are not considered in this publication, the adaptations are not described here. The approach adopted for the questions on the mandates of employee representatives at company level is as follows.

Two questions enquire about the current and past representative positions within the company held by respondents and include the following options: staff representative, member of the works council, member of the group/corporate works council, health and safety representative, shop steward, European works council member, other and none. First, depending on the national legal provisions regulating workplace representation and acknowledging that some of these mandates do not exist everywhere, the number of items varied from country to country. Second, trying to interpret these mandates, for example, to establish functional equivalents between national employee representative mandates or bodies, is an issue and a challenge that has long been acknowledged by the scientific community (Gold 2009). The questionnaire relied on adaptation based on linguistic rather than functional equivalents. To implement this approach European and international studies which generate catalogues of existing mandates of employee representative and representative institutions were employed to subsequently establish equivalence (Baker and McKenzie 2009; Blanpain and Engels 2001; Calvo et al. 2008; Carley 1990; Carley et al. 2005; EIRR 2001a; EIRR 2001b; EIRR 2002; ETUC and ETUCO 2003; ETUI 1990; Eversheds and Employment Law Alliance 2005; Fulton 2013a; Gazzane 2006; LRD 2004; Manzella 2015; Schömann et al. 2006).

To ensure a high rate of response, the questionnaire was translated into every national language. This process was handled in three stages. First, a vocational translator completed a basic translation. Second, research team members checked the translation for accuracy, particularly regarding the translation of terms specific to industrial relations and the national usage of such terms. Third, a native speaker with expertise in industrial relations conducted the final check of the questionnaire.

IDENTIFICATION OF THE BOARD-LEVEL EMPLOYEE REPRESENTATIVES

Key to the distribution of the questionnaires was the access to, or the assembly of, databases of employee representatives' name and addresses. Because the characteristics of the overall population were unknown within each participating country, the authors chose to target the entire population of board-level employee representatives rather than specific samples. The identification of board-level employee representatives in each country and European Companies relied on the following delimitation of the scope of the survey:

- Board-level employee representatives who represent the entire workforce and who have an intended decision-making voice, regardless of their means of appointment. Labour directors, representatives of employee-shares schemes and board-level employee representatives in cooperative societies are thus excluded.
- Board-level employee representatives who sit on the supervisory board or board of directors of private, public or state-owned companies, regardless of the size of their workforce and their legal status as long as they have an industrial and commercial character and that they are looking for profit, thus excluding non-profit organisations, foundations, associations or mutual societies.

The identification of named board-level employee representatives that met these criteria comprised two approaches: direct access and indirect access. In addition, a third approach was adopted for those countries where it was not possible to identify named board-level employee representatives. Direct access involved the gathering of existing databases of board-level employee representatives' names and addresses through contacts with national trade union confederations and sectoral/industrial trade unions, trade union–related organisations, training organisations and academic researchers who had conducted a questionnaire survey in their own country. Indirect access included the identification of the companies where some of the board members were employee representatives, usually by reference to legal texts, reports from the state shareholding agency, national business registers and/or stock market indicators. Internet searches of, for example company websites and annual reports, then enabled the assembly of lists of the names and addresses of board-level employee representatives.

For both direct access and indirect access the authors relied on national experts. In the case of direct access the authors were reliant on experts within national trade unions, trade union related organisations and training organisations, as well as academic researchers. Support was drawn from the wide networks set up by the research team, networks convened by the European Trade Union Institute and experts within the European offices of the Friedrich Ebert Stiftung. No fewer than 147 national experts were identified in this way. In the case of indirect access this expertise was supplemented by the collection of each national legal text regulating the representation of employees on the board of companies, in their initial, intermediary and current versions. Some of these legal texts contained a detailed list of companies covered by the regulation. Table A.1 summarises the outcome of both the direct access and indirect access approaches.

In four cases (Czech Republic, Finland, Germany (one-third co-determination) and Slovakia) it was not possible to identify the individual board-level employee representatives to whom the questionnaire should be sent. In these instances lists including the number and the names of companies falling within the scope of the legislation were compiled. Table A.2 provides the detail of the source materials used in these instances. The section on questionnaire distribution that follows explains how board-level employee representatives were reached in these circumstances.

As different approaches were employed for the different systems of German board-level employee representation, Germany is entered on three occasions in Tables A.1 and A.2: for parity representation where employee representatives comprise half of the supervisory board of companies with 2,000 or more employees, Montan representation where employee representatives comprise half of the supervisory board in companies operating in the iron, coal and steel industries with 1,000 or more employees, and systems where employee representatives compose one-third of the supervisory board of companies employing between 500 and 2,000 employees.

Given the inherent limits to such a stocktaking exercise, the total number of individual board-level employee representatives identified for the purposes of this study should be considered as a minimum rather than an exhaustive and complete population. On this basis at the time of the survey there were at least 17,442 board-level employee representatives in thirteen European countries, excluding German representatives within the one-third system, and companies that have opted for European Company status. In addition, there were 5,402 companies within three countries and covered by the German one-third system that came within the scope of national legislation.

QUESTIONNAIRE DISTRIBUTION

Given the scale of the research and the challenges arising from the identification of board-level employee representatives, the initial questionnaire distribution was split into four batches:

- First batch: Austria, Germany [parity], Denmark, Spain, Finland, France, Ireland, Luxembourg, Poland and Sweden (October 2009–June 2010)
- Second batch: SEs, Germany [one-third] and Norway (February 2011–April 2011)
- Third batch: Germany [Montan], Czech Republic, Greece, Slovenia and Slovakia (September 2011–October 2011)
- Fourth batch: Hungary (January 2012)

The manner of distribution of the questionnaires was dependent on the form of access gained to national databases of board-level employee representatives' name and addresses. The authors organised the questionnaire distribution to countries for which they had assembled the database of board-level employee representatives (France, Germany [Montan], Greece, Hungary, Ireland, Luxembourg, SEs and Spain) or of companies hosting board-level employee representatives (Czech Republic, Slovakia and Germany [one-third]), or for which they were provided with databases from national data providers, given the guarantee of fair and specific use of these personal data (Norway, Poland, Slovenia and Sweden). In Austria, Denmark, Finland and Germany [parity], the national data provider handled the questionnaire distribution.

The initial distribution of the questionnaire was by post directly to the board-level employee representative and included a cover letter, a paper copy of the questionnaire and a pre-paid return envelope. In most cases a single reminder was sent either by post or by e-mail. E-mail was used for reasons associated with the research budget, primarily when the cost of a reminder sent by post would have been prohibitive. Reminders were, however, not distributed in four countries (Czech Republic, Hungary, Slovakia

Table A.1 **Outcomes of the Identification of Board-Level Employee Representatives**

		Sources	Limits	Number of identified individuals
Direct Access	**Austria**	Database from trade union–related organisation	May not be exhaustive as includes only board-level employee representatives who attended AK Wien-IfAM training programs	1,382
	Germany (Parity)	Database from trade union related organisation	Excludes non-unionised individuals (about 1,200) and unionised managerial board-level employee representatives	2,743
	Denmark	Trade union's database (from LO-DK—database of the 4 main cartels—and from IDA—the Danish Engineering Union affiliated to the national confederation AC)	Excludes non-unionised individuals Does not cover all the unionised board-level employee representatives as no data was available from FTF (the 2nd-largest confederation of which the Danish financial Services Union—Finansforbundet—is affiliated), from the other AC affiliated organisations, and from Lederne (Danish Association of Managers and Executives) According to a national research conducted in 2003 (Rose 2005), the register of Danish Commerce and Companies Agency counted 3,087 board-level employee representatives	1,180
	Norway	Database from a private business register	None	5,225
	Poland	Database from the Ministry of Treasury	Excludes entirely privatised companies since 1996 Information for some state-owned enterprises is missing	618
	Sweden	Trade union's database	Partially outdated	4,547
	SEs	ETUI database	Excludes 413 SEs for which there is no available information	109

		Sources	Limits	Number of identified individuals
Indirect Access	**Ireland**	1. List of companies: from the legislation on board-level employee representation 2. List of board-level employee representatives held in trade union databases and available on company websites	None	37
	Slovenia	1. List of companies: trade union databases built on data from the national statistical office 2. List of board-level employee representatives: database from a private institution, completed with information from the national business register	Non-exhaustive, missing information for about 50 companies	410
	Germany (Montan)	1. List of companies: database from trade union related organisation 2. List of board-level employee representatives: company websites, national business register	Non-exhaustive	134
	Spain	1. List of companies: government's shareholding agency 2. List of board-level employee representatives: company websites, trade union websites	None	21
	France	1. List of companies: from the legislation on board-level employee representation 2. List of board-level employee representatives: company websites, trade union databases	Information not available for all companies, particularly subsidiaries	542
	Greece	1. List of companies: from the legislation on board-level employee representation (initial and later versions) 2. List of board-level employee representatives: company websites	Lack of information for 14 companies	63

(*Continued*)

Table A.1 (Continued)

	Sources	Limits	Number of identified individuals
Luxembourg	1. List of companies: from the legislation on board-level employee representation, and a list established by the State Treasury 2. List of board-level employee representatives: company websites	List of private companies is not exhaustive	41
Hungary	1. List of companies: from a private business register 2. List of board-level employee representatives: from the official business register	List of companies: partially outdated and limited to 75% of the 2,317 companies due to research time constraints. The official business register is incomplete due to a lack of information on monistic companies and a lack or partial identification of board-level employee representatives	390
		Total	17,442

Table A.2 Outcomes of the Identification of Companies Covered by the Legislation on Board-Level Employee Representation for the Remaining Countries

	Sources	Limits	Number of companies identified
Czech Republic	Database from the national statistical office	None	2,936
Finland	Trade union database	Not based on a systematic census	112
Germany (one-third)	Database produced by a national researcher	None	1,477
Slovakia	Database from the national statistical office	None	877
		Total	5,402

and Slovenia) because the number of questionnaires returned from the initial questionnaire distribution was sufficient for our purposes. Time constraints also influenced this decision.

In those cases where questionnaires were sent to companies rather than individuals (see Table A.2) it was not possible to know how many employee representatives sat on the board. In these instances several copies of the questionnaire were sent to a key representative within the company. In the Czech Republic and Slovakia, the distribution to each company contained two copies of the questionnaire and was addressed to the chair of the supervisory board in Czech companies and to the chair of the management board in Slovak companies who were asked to forward them to board-level employee representative(s) in the company. In Finland, the trade union 'cooperation' working group handled the questionnaire distribution. In Germany (one-third system), the distribution contained three copies of the questionnaire and was addressed to the chair of the works council.

QUESTIONNAIRE RETURNS

Examination of the rate of return comprises two stages: one stage covers the cases where the questionnaires were distributed directly to individual board-level employee representatives, while the second stage reports on cases where the survey was distributed to board or labour representatives within companies rather than named board-level employee representatives. Table A.3 illustrates the outcome of the distribution process to named board-level employee representatives. The French case is an outlier insofar as 530

Table A.3 Rates of Return of Questionnaires Sent to Individuals

Country	Questionnaires distributed	Errors returned	Number of responses	Response rate %[1]
Austria	1,382	0	372	26.9
Denmark	1,180	0	215	18.2
France	530	5	140	26.6
Germany (parity)	2,743	13	885	32.4
Germany (Montan)	134	2	38	28.8
Greece	63	2	13	21.3
Hungary	390	0	91	23.3
Ireland	37	0	10	27.0
Luxembourg	41	0	11	26.8
Norway	5,225	142	1,143	22.5
Poland	618	10	137	22.5
Slovenia	410	0	75	18.3
Spain	21	0	8	38.1
Sweden	4,547	707[2]	948	24.7
European companies (SEs)	109	0	38	34.9
Total	17,430	881	4,124	24.9

1. The response rate was calculated by expressing the number of responses as a proportion of the distribution minus the errors returned.

2. The large number of questionnaires returned in Sweden was attributed to the obsolescence of the database. The distribution took place in November 2009 using a database last updated in early 2008.

questionnaires were distributed yet 542 board-level employee representatives were identified. This discrepancy is the result of the practical difficulties faced in identifying the names of individuals. Although the number of seats held by employee representatives was established, it was not possible to identify the names of twelve individuals; hence, the questionnaire was not distributed to these people. With this point in mind, 17,430 questionnaires were distributed to specific board-level employee representatives, of which 4,124 were returned constituting a response rate of 24.9 per cent.

Two further issues account for the differences between the data mentioned in Table A.3 and the data reported in the analysis. First, 98 out of the 372 Austrian respondents did not complete large sections of the questionnaire and are thus excluded from the analysis. Second, the service provider contracted to transport some questionnaires from Brussels, to where

Table A.4 Numbers of Questionnaires Returned from the Distribution to Companies

Country	Questionnaires distributed	Errors returned	Number of responses
Czech Republic	1,101	2	93
Germany (one-third)	1,477	10	320
Finland	112	0	13
Slovakia	877	2	115
Total	3,898	20	541

the respondents had sent the questionnaires, to Manchester, where the data entry took place, lost 213 Norwegian questionnaires.

Table A.4 presents the outcome of the distributions to companies that had employee representation on the board as determined by national law. In this instance the Czech Republic is the national outlier. The Czech Statistical Office identified 2,936 companies where board-level employee representation was in place. On the grounds of cost, questionnaires were sent to around one-third (1,101) of these companies. Table A.4 shows that questionnaires were sent to 3,898 companies and 541 responses were received. Because the questionnaires are anonymous and respondents were not requested to state the name of their company, there is no possibility of identifying the number of companies from which responses originated. It is thus not possible to calculate a response rate based on the number of companies to which the questionnaires were sent.

Combining the data from Tables A.3 and A.4 in total 4,665 responses were received. Excluding the incomplete Austrian returns (98), the lost Norwegian returns (213) and those returns completed either illegibly or otherwise inadequately completed, 4,155 complete questionnaires were available for analysis.

Appendix B
The Situation *De Jure*

Table B.1 outlines the legislation in force in Europe covering board-level employee representation and focuses exclusively on the rights of employees represented on the supervisory board or board of directors of their company in a deliberative capacity: that is, with the right to vote. Table B.1 excludes provisions concerning employee representation in a consultative capacity, for example, as are found in France. Information reported in Table B.1 relates to the case of public limited companies (Plc), private limited companies (Ltd) and state-owned companies, which are the types of companies that are the subject of this research. The circumstances of cooperatives and savings banks are not addressed.

Table B.1 is structured chronologically by reference to the initial legislation enacted on board-level employee representation. Germany is thus the first listed country as it was there that arrangements for board-level employee representation were first implemented. The year in Table B.1 refers to the initial text: that is, the first legislative measure that regulated board-level employee representation in the country. The explanation of the legal provisions refers to the current situation, thus taking into account amendments to the original legislation or legislation enacted subsequent to the initial measure.

Table B.1 The National Regulation of Board-Level Employee Representation

Country	Year	Legal provisions
Germany	1920	Original Act, repealed (in 1934) *Betriebsrätegesetz vom 4. Februar 1920, §70 / Gesetz über die Entsendung von Betriebsratsmitgliedern in den Aufsichtsrat vom 15. Februar 1922* [Works Council Act of February 4, 1920, Art. 70 / Act on the posting of works council members in the supervisory board of February 15, 1922]
		New Act, revised (in 2004) *Betriebsverfassungsgesetz vom 11. Oktober 1952* [Works Constitution Act of October 11, 1952]
		Act in force *Drittelbeteiligungsgesetz vom 18. Mai 2004* [One-third Participation Act of Mai 18, 2004]
		The workforce directly elects one-third of the supervisory board of companies employing 500 to 2,000 workers. The works council or employees (either 10 per cent of the workforce or 100 employees) nominate candidates. If one or two employee representatives are elected to the board, they must be employees of the company. If more than two employee representatives are elected, at least two of them must be employees of the company.
	1951	Original Act, still in force *Montan-Mitbestimmungsgesetz—Gesetz über die Mitbestimmung der Arbeitnehmer in den Aufsichtsräten und Vorständen der Unternehmen des Bergbaus und der Eisen und Stahl erzeugenden Industrie vom 21. Mai 1951* [Mining Co-determination Act—Act on the participation of employees in the supervisory boards and boards of companies in the mining and iron and steel industry of May 21, 1951]
		Companies employing more than 1,000 employees and operating in the iron, coal and steel industries are obliged to allocate half of the seats on the supervisory board to employee representatives. The works council nominates employee representatives. The works council together with trade unions nominates those who stand for seats reserved for trade union officials. Confirmation of these nominations by the general meeting of shareholders is required. An additional board member, called a 'neutral external person', is appointed to the board by the general meeting of shareholders under the nomination of the supervisory board: this nomination requires a majority on both the employees' side and the side of the shareholder representatives. The neutral external person has a casting vote.

Germany	1976	Original Act, still in force *Mitbestimmungsgesetz vom 4. Mai 1976* [Co-determination Act of May 4, 1976]

In companies with more than 2,000 employees, half the supervisory board are employee representatives who are directly elected by the workforce (or by electoral college delegates in companies with more than 8,000 employees). The pool of board-level employee representatives includes employees of the company and trade union representatives (two, up to three when the total number of board-level employee representatives is ten). The nomination procedure for candidates depends on the category of board-level employee representative. Trade unions organising within the company nominate trade union representatives, who can be external trade union officials. The nomination procedure for board-level employee representatives who are employees of the company depends on their professional status. With regard to the seat reserved for executive managers, 1/20th or 50 executive managers from the company make the nomination. The other employee candidates must be nominated by 1/5th of 100 employees from the same electoral college (executive managers excluded). This system is usually referred to as the 'quasi- or qualified parity codetermination model' given that the chairman of the supervisory board (who is elected by the shareholders representatives on the board) has a casting vote in case of tie.

Situation in state-owned companies

The same rules apply as long as the Plc or Ltd legal statute regulates the state-owned company. On the contrary, there is no board-level employee representation in state-owned companies which are governed by a specific statute ruled by public law (e.g. *Anstalten öffentlichen Rechts*, institutions of public law).

(*Continued*)

Table B.1 (Continued)

Country	Year	Legal provisions
Austria	1947	Original Act *Bundesgesetz vom 28. März 1947 über die Errichtung von Betriebsvertretungen (Betriebsrätegesetz—BRG), §14 (2) 4* [Federal Law of March 28, 1947 on the establishment of works council (Works Council Act), Art. 14 (2), 4] Act in force *Bundesgesetz vom 14. 12. 1973 betreffend die Arbeitsverfassung (Arbeitsverfassungsgesetz, ArbVG), art. 110* [Federal Law of 14 December 1973 concerning Labour Relations (Labour Constitution Act), Art. 110] One-third of the supervisory board of Plc (*AG*) and Ltd (*GmbH*, but with at least 300 employees which is the minimum threshold for the compulsory setting up of a supervisory board) are employee representatives, appointed by the central works council (or works council in companies with only one establishment). Board-level employee representatives must be employees of the company and works councillors with full voting rights at the works council.
	Situation in state-owned companies Most Austrian state-owned companies are also governed by the *Arbeitsverfassungsgesetz* because they have the legal status of Plc (*AG*). There are, however, a few state-owned companies regulated by specific legal provisions. The three most prominent regulations in this regard are • the *ÖIAG Gesetz (Österreichische Industrieholding AG*—Austrian Industry Holding Plc) which follows the one-third representation system with the difference that employee representatives are nominated by the Austrian Chamber of Labour; • The *Arbeitsmarktservicegesetz* (the law that regulates the organisation of the company in charge of the Employment Service) where four out of the total ten board members are employee representatives (three are nominated by trade unions and the Austrian Chamber of Labour and the fourth by the works council); • The *ORF-Gesetz (ORF: Österreichischen Rundfunk*—Austrian Broadcasting Company) whose board (called *Stiftungsrat*—board of trustees) is composed of 35 members of which five are nominated by the central works council.	

Spain	1962	Original Act, repealed (in 1980) *Ley 41/1962, de 21 julio, por la que se establece la participación del personal en la administración de las empresas que adopten la forma jurídica de Sociedades + Decreto 2241/1965, de 15 de julio, por el que se dictan normas de desarrollo y aplicación de la Ley 41/1962 (derogado por Ley 8/1980, de 10 de marzo)* [Act 41/1962 of July 21, establishing the involvement of staff in the administration of firms that adopt the legal form of 'company' + Decree 2241/1965 of July 15, set up rules of application of Act 41/1962 (repealed by Act 8/1980 of March 10)]
	1986	**Situation in state-owned companies** • *Acuerdo sobre participación sindical en la empresa pública con fecha 16 de enero de 1986* [Agreement on trade union participation in the state-owned company of January 16, 1986] In state-owned companies with more than 1,000 employees, employees are represented either on the board of directors or on a joint 'information and supervisory committee' created for this purpose, the choice being subject to company agreement. Where participation is on the board of directors, each representative trade union (which, by definition, organises at least 25 per cent of staff representatives and works council seats, a threshold which is lowered to 10 per cent when it comes to participation on the board of directors of a parent company) nominates one board member. If there is only one majority trade union, it has the right to appoint two members. The board members appointed by trade unions are always in a minority position as legislation stipulates that state representatives on the board of directors cannot be in a minority. • *Acuerdo colectivo para las empresas del sector del Metal del Grupo INI-TENEO con fecha 22 de junio de 1993, art. 10* [Collective agreement for the companies in the metal sector of INI-TENEO group of June 22, 1993, art. 10] NB: This collective agreement corresponds to the development at sectoral level of the 1986 above-mentioned one In INI-TENEO[1] companies operating in the metal sector with more than 500 employees, the rules governing employee representation on the board of directors are exactly the same as those of the 1986 agreement; that is, one board member is nominated for each representative trade union.

(*Continued*)

Table B.1 (Continued)

Country	Year	Legal provisions
Norway	1972	Original Act *Lov om aksjeselskaper av 12. mai 1972* [Act on joint stock companies of May 12, 1972] Acts in force • *Lov om aksjeselskaper nr 044, 1997.06.13, § 6–4, 6–5, 6–35* [Act on private limited companies, No 44, 13 June 1997, Art. 6–4, 6–5, and 6–35] • *Lov om allmennaksjeselskaper nr 045 1997.06.13., § 6–4, 6–5, 6–37* [Act on public limited companies, No 45, 13 June 1997, Art. 6–4, 6–5 and 6–37] Note: legal provisions are further specified within the Royal Decree No 2096 of 13 December 1985 [*FOR 1985–12–13 nr 2096: Forskrift til selskapslovens bestemmelser om de ansattes rett til representasjon I styringsorganene*] The Companies Acts provide employees with the right to elect from among the workforce representatives to serve on boards of directors. This right is not automatic in companies with fewer than 200 employees and has to be triggered by a request from a majority of employees. In companies with 30 to 50 employees, one board-level employee representative may be elected. In companies with more than 50 employees, employees may elect up to one-third of the board, with a minimum of two members. In companies with more than 200 employees that have a corporate assembly,[2] employees may elect from two board members up to a third of the board. In companies with more than 200 employees and not having a corporate assembly, employees have the right to elect one-third of the board plus an additional employee representative.
	1991	**Situation in state-owned companies** Original Act, still in force[3] *Lov om statsforetak av 30. august 1991, nr. 71, §20* [Act on state enterprises of 30 August 1991 No. 71, Art. 20] Rules governing board-level employee representation in companies fully owned by the state are the same as those provided by the act on public limited companies.

<table>
<tr>
<td>Denmark</td>
<td>1973</td>
<td>Original Acts
Lov nr. 370 frá 13. juni 1973 om aktieselskaber
[Act No 370 of June 13, 1973 on public limited companies]
Lov nr. 371 af 13. juni 1973 om anpartsselskaber
[Act No 371 of June 13, 1973 on private limited companies]

Act in force
Lov nr. 470 af 12. juni 2009 om aktie- og anpartsselskaber (selskabsloven) / Lovbekendtgørelse nr. 322 af 11/04/2011, art. 140–143
[Act No 470 of June 12, 2009 on public and private limited companies (Companies Act) / Consolidation Act No 322 of April 11, 2011, Art. 140–143]
Bekendtgørelse om medarbejderrepræsentation i aktie- og anpartsselskaber, BEK nr 344 af 30/03/2012
[Edict on employee representation in public and private limited companies, Edict No. 344 of March 30, 2012]

In companies with more than 35 employees (including employees at overseas sites located in another European Economic Area country), employees may elect, from among their ranks, one-third of the board with a minimum of two employee representatives (three in the parent company of a group). This provision is not compulsory and has to be triggered by a demand from: at least 1/10th of employees, or one or several trade unions at company level which represent at least 1/10th of employees, or a majority of employees in the works council. Once this demand is triggered, a yes/no ballot is organised among employees. If yes votes compose an absolute majority, then board-level employee representatives are elected.</td>
</tr>
<tr>
<td></td>
<td colspan="2">Situation in state-owned companies
The Companies Act also regulates state-owned companies, with the consequence that the same rules on board-level employee representation apply as in the private sector. There are only three exceptions of state-owned companies that are regulated by a specific legal text: DBS (Danske Statsbaner) and Naviair (Navigation Via Air), where the rules on board-level employee representation are similar to those laid out in the Companies Act, and Energinet.dk where the statute stipulates that there are three board-level employee representatives out of eleven board members in total, that is, less than the usual one-third rule.</td>
</tr>
</table>

(*Continued*)

Table B.1 (Continued)

Country	Year	Legal provisions
Luxembourg	1974	Original Act, still in force *Loi du 6 mai 1974 instituant des comités mixtes dans les entreprises du secteur privé et organisant la représentation des salariés dans les sociétés anonymes* [Act of May 6, 1974 establishing joint committees in the private sector and organising the representation of employees in public limited companies] Note: Incorporated into the Labour code (Art. L426–1 to Art. L426–11 of the 2013 version) In the private sector, one-third of the board of a Plc with more than 1,000 employees must be employee representatives elected by staff representatives. Board-level employee representative must be employees of the company. There are exceptions in the iron and steel industry where the most representative national trade unions have the right to directly appoint three board-level employee representatives. In these cases, board-level employee representatives can be nominated from outside the company's workforce.
		Situation in state-owned companies In the public sector, composed here of companies where the state holds at least 25 per cent of the shares, the election process is the same as in the private sector, but the number of board-level employee representatives differs: there is one board-level employee representative per 100 employees, with a minimum of three and a maximum of one-third of the board.

Sweden 1976

Original Act

Lag (1976:351) om styrelserepresentation för de anställda i aktiebolag och ekonomiska föreningar

[Act 1976:351 on employee representation on boards of companies and economic associations]

Note: First enacted in 1973 (*Lag om medbestämmande I Arbetslivet*, Act on Codetermination at the Workplace), the law on board-level employee representation in Sweden became permanent with the enactment of Act 1976:351.

Act in force

Lag (1987:1245) om styrelserepresentation för de privatanställda

[Act 1987:1245 on board representation of private-sector employees]

In companies with more than 25 employees and if local trade unions, defined as those signatory to a collective agreement with the company, so decide, board-level employee representation is set up. Trade unions may appoint two employee representatives (there is no obligation for them to be employees of the company[4]) on the board of directors of companies with more than 25 employees and three board-level employee representatives in companies with more than 1,000 employees *and* operating in several industries. Board-level employee representatives, however, can never form a majority on the board (maximum 50 per cent of the board) because their number cannot exceed the number of other board members. The act provides for an equal number of deputies who also have the right to attend board meeting on a consultative basis.

Situation in state-owned companies

State-owned companies are governed by the same rules on board-level employee representation as private-sector companies, since they usually have the legal status of a Plc or Ltd.

(*Continued*)

Table B.1 (Continued)

Country	Year	Legal provisions
Ireland	1977	**Situation in state-owned companies** Original Act, still in force Worker Participation (State Enterprises) Act No 6/1977, amended by Worker Participation (State Enterprises) Act No 13/1988 In state-owned commercial companies, employees have the right to elect, from among their ranks, one-third of the board of directors (if the number of board member is not divisible by three, the total number of board-level employee representatives is rounded up). Candidates are nominated by trade unions or bodies recognised for collective bargaining. Once elected, the relevant state minister formally appoints the board-level employee representatives.
Poland	1981	**Situation in state-owned companies** Original Act, still in force *Ustawa z dnia 25 września 1981 r. o przedsiębiorstwach państwowych* [Act of September 25, 1981 on state enterprises] In state-owned companies where the privatisation process has not (yet) started, the main governing body—along with senior managers—is the 'workers council', elected by employees. This 'workers council' has the right to adopt business plans, audit accounts and appoint/remove managers.

Poland	1990	Original Act *Ustawa o prywatyzacji przedsiębiorstw państwowych z 13 lipca 1990* [Act on privatisation of state enterprises of July 13, 1990] Act in force *Ustawa z dnia 30 sierpnia 1996 r. o komercjalizaji I prywatyzacji przedsiębiorstw państwowych, art. 11–16* [Act of August 30, 1996 on the commercialisation and privatisation of state enterprises, Art. 11–16] In privatised companies where the state remains the sole shareholder (so-called 'commercialised' companies, which are state-owned companies that have been transformed into a Plc or Ltd), 2/5th of the supervisory board is composed of board-level employee representatives elected by employees. These employee representatives must have passed an exam before the examination commission set up by the Ministry of Treasury. Once the State is no longer the sole shareholder (i.e. in case of 'privatisation', strictly speaking), elected board-level employee representatives hold two to four seats on the supervisory board depending on its size (two in boards up to six members, three in boards between seven and ten members, four in board of eleven or more members).
Greece	1983	**Situation in state-owned companies** Original Act, repealed (in 1996) Νόμος *1365/1983,* Κοινωνικοποίηση των Επιχειρήσεων δημοσίου χαρακτήρα ή κοινής ωφελειας [Act 1365/1983, Socialisation of state-run undertakings and utilities] Repealed by: Νόμος *2414/1996* Εκσυγχρονισμός των Δημοσίων Επιχειρήσεων και Οργανισμών και άλλες διατάξεις, *art.* 6 [Act 2414/1996 on the Modernization of public enterprises and organisations, Art. 6] Act in force Νόμος *3429/2005* Δημόσιες Επιχειρήσεις και Οργανισμοί *(Δ.Ε.Κ.Ο.), 27.12.2005, art. 3, al.* 2 [Act 3429/2005 of 27 December 2005 on Public enterprises and organizations, Art. 3 al. 2] In state-owned companies only (defined as the state holding more than 50 per cent of capital), employees elect one member of the board of directors from among their ranks. The law stipulates that employees must nominate candidates standing for election, but, in practice, they are nominated by trade union branches. Once elected, the appointment of board-level employee representatives requires formal validation by the minister responsible for the company.

(*Continued*)

Table B.1 (Continued)

Country	Year	Legal provisions
France	1983	**Situation in state-owned companies** Original Act, still in force *Loi n°83–675 du 26 juillet 1983 relative à la Démocratisation du secteur public, art. 5- art. 28* [Act No 83–675 of 26 July 1983 on the democratisation of the public sector, Art. 5- art. 28] In state-owned companies, the workforce elects board-level employee representatives. Candidates for election to the board must be employees of the company and nominated either by a trade union or by at least 10 per cent of other employee representatives within the company. In state-owned companies with fewer than 200 employees, between two board members and one-third of the board are elected employee representatives. In state-owned companies with more than 200 employees, the employee side of the board is always one-third. Specific provisions exist for subsidiaries of these state-owned companies: when these subsidiaries have between 200 and 1,000 employees, three members of the board are employee representatives, while they compose one-third of the board in subsidiaries of state-owned companies with more than 1,000 employees.
	1986	Original Act, still in force *Ordonnance n°86–1135 du 21 octobre 1986 modifiant la loi 66–537 sur les sociétés commerciales* [Edict No 86–1135 of 21 October 1986 modifying Act 66–537 on commercial companies] Companies in the private sector may – there is no compulsion – introduce provisions in their articles of association whereby up to four board members (up to five in listed companies with a monistic board structure) and a maximum of one-third of the number of other board members (so, a maximum of a quarter of the total board) are employee representatives elected by the workforce. These employee representatives must be employees of the company and are nominated by either a trade union or 5 per cent of employees (100 employees in companies with more than 2,000 employees).
	1994	Original Act still in force *Loi n° 94–640 relative à l'amélioration de la participation des salariés dans l'entreprise, art. 1* [Act No 94–640 on enhancing employees' participation in the company, Art. 1] The new articles of associations of privatised companies according to the 1993 act on privatisation must state that two to three board members (depending whether the board is larger or smaller than fifteen members) remain employee representatives elected by the workforce from among their ranks.

France	2006	Original Act, still in force *Loi n°2006–1770 du 30 décembre 2006 pour le développement de la participation, art. 33* [Act No 2006–1770 of 30 December 2006 on the development of employee participation, Art. 33] The articles of association of companies privatised under the 1986 act on privatisation and which voluntarily maintained some seats for board-level employee representatives cannot be modified with the view of reducing the number of board-level employee representatives to less than one (in board smaller than fifteen members) or two (in larger boards).
	2013	Original Act, still in force *Loi n°2013–504 du 14 juin 2013 relative à la sécurisation de l'emploi, art. 9* [Act No 2013–504 of 14 June 2013 on employment security, Art. 9] At least one (if the board includes up to 12 members) or at least two (in larger boards) board-level employee representatives have to be appointed on the board of private-sector companies whose consolidated workforce is at least 5,000 employees in France or at least 10,000 employees worldwide. Shareholders decide the appointment mechanism at an extraordinary shareholders' meeting, after the works council has presented its opinion on its favoured option. In the specific case of mandatory board-level employee representation in large private-sector companies, board-level employee representatives can be appointed according to one of the four following options: • Direct workforce election • Appointment by the works council • Appointment by the most representative(s) trade union(s) • If at least two board-level employee representatives are to be appointed: one will be appointed according to one of the three abovementioned options; the second board-level employee representative will be appointed by the European Works Council or the representative body of the European Company if relevant. Board-level employee representatives must be employees of the company per se or one of its France-based subsidiaries (except for board-level employee representatives appointed by the European works council or representative body of the European Company who have to be employees but no restriction as to the location of their company's place of incorporation).

(*Continued*)

Table B.1 (Continued)

Country	Year	Legal provisions
Finland	1987	**Situation in state-owned companies** Original Act, repealed (in 2002) *Laki valtion liikelaitoksista 627/1987, § 14* [Act 627/1987 on State Enterprise, art. 14] Act in force *Laki valtion liikelaitoksista 1062/2010, §7, §10* [Act 1062/2010 on State Enterprise, Art. 7 and art. 10] At least one member of the board of director represents the employees. Board-level employee representatives must be employees of the state-owned company. Government decrees establish the detailed provisions on the composition of the board of directors. Board-level employee representatives have the same rights and duties as the other board members with the following exceptions: they cannot take part in the appointment/dismissal of senior management, in decisions related to the terms and conditions included in the employment contracts of senior management, in decisions related to the terms and conditions of staff employment contracts, or in decisions related to industrial action.
	1990	Original Act still in force *Laki 725/1990 henkilöstön edustuksesta yritysten hallinnossa* [Act 725/1990 on personnel representation in the administration of undertakings] In companies with more than 150 employees, board-level employee representation (number of representatives and choice of the board on which they will sit) can be arranged through an agreement between the employer and at least two personnel groups representing the majority of the workforce. If no agreement is reached and if at least two personnel groups representing the majority of the workforce so demand, board-level employee representation is set up as follows: the management decides on which board (board of directors, supervisory board, management board or similar bodies) board-level employee representatives will sit; the number of board-level employee representatives varies between one and four, representing a quarter of the number of other board members (so a fifth of the total board). Board-level employee representatives are employees of the company appointed by the personnel groups, or the workforce elects them when the personnel groups cannot agree. Where there is only one board-level employee representative, his/her deputy is also entitled to participate in meetings and voice his/her opinion (although he or she has no right to vote).

Hungary	1988	Original Act, repealed (in 2006) *1988. évi VI. törvény a gazdasági társaságokról* [Act VI of 1988 on Business Associations] New Act, revised (in 2013) *2006. évi IV. Törvény a gazdasági társaságokról, 38–39 §* [Act IV of 2006 on Business Association, Art. 38–39] Act in force *2013. évi V. törvény a Polgári Törvénykönyvrõl, 3:124–3:126 §, 3:288 §* [Act V. of 2013 on the Civil Code, art. 3:124 to 3:126 and 3:288] Within companies with more than 200 employees, the works council nominates, after consultation with trade unions, the board-level employee representatives, who are employees of the company. Board-level employee representatives are ultimately appointed by the general meeting of shareholders. In companies operating with a single board structure (only Plc can opt for this monistic structure), the number of board-level employee representatives is arranged according to an agreement reached between the works council and the board of directors. There is no minimum standard applying in this case. In companies with a dual-board structure, board-level employee representatives represent one-third of the supervisory board unless otherwise agreed by the works council and management. The legal provisions also include an opt-out clause, because there could be no board-level employee representation if agreed between the works council and the management.
	Situation in state-owned companies State-owned companies are governed by Plc or Ltd legal status, the rights for board-level employee representation are thus the same as in the private sector.	

(*Continued*)

Table B.1 (Continued)

Country	Year	Legal provisions
Slovak Republic	1990	**Situation in state-owned companies** Original Act, still in force *Zákon č. 111/1990 z 19. apríla 1990 o štátnom podniku, § 20* [Act No 111/1990 of April, 19 1990 on state enterprise, Art. 20] In state-owned companies, half of the supervisory board are employee representatives elected by and from among employees (or elected by delegates if any). An employee representative cannot be the chair of the board. The chair of the board is not an employee of the company. The law does not specify the nomination procedures (it does not state who can propose candidates to the board). If there is a trade union in the company, it then has the right to directly nominate one of the board-level employee representatives who then has to be a member of the trade union.
	1991	Original Act, still in force *Zákon č. 513/1991 Sb., obchodní zákonik, art. 200* [Act No 513/1991 Coll., Commercial Code, art. 200] In Plc (*Akciová Spoločnost*) with a minimum of 50 employees, one-third of the supervisory board are employee representatives elected by employees. The company's articles of association can determine a greater number of employee representatives but this number cannot be higher than the number of other board members elected by the general shareholder meeting. Board-level employee representation may also be set up in smaller companies (with fewer than 50 employees) if such a provision is included in the company's articles of association. Trade unions and/or a minimum of 10 per cent of employees can nominate candidates to the election. There is no restriction with regard to eligibility criteria: that is, there is no obligation for board-level employee representatives to be employees of the company.

Czech Republic[5]	1990	**Situation in state-owned companies** Original Act *Zákon č. 111/1990 z 19. apríla 1990 o štátnom podniku* [Act No 111/1990 of April, 19 1990 on state enterprise] Act in force *Zákon č. 77/1997 Sb., o státním podniku*, art. 13 [Act No 77/1997 Coll., on state enterprises, Art. 13] One-third of the supervisory board are employees of the company, elected by the workforce. Management in agreement with trade unions, if present, establish the electoral regulations.
	1991	Original Act, in force until 31 December 2013 Zákon č. 513/1991 Sb., obchodní zákoník, § 200 [Act No 513/1991 Coll., Commercial Code, Art. 200] In Czech Republic, employee representatives compose one-third of the supervisory board of a Plc with more than 50 employees and are elected by the entire workforce. Board-level employee representatives must be employees of the company or trade union members (external trade union representatives thus can be nominated). The company's articles of association may allow board-level employee representation in companies with fewer than 50 employees. They may also allow employee representatives to compose up to half the supervisory board.

(*Continued*)

Table B.1 (Continued)

Country	Year	Legal provisions
Slovenia	1993	Original Act, still in force *Zakon o sodelovanju delavcev pri upravljanju—ZSDU (Uradni list RS, št. 42/93 z dne 22. 7. 1993) / uradno prečiščeno besedilo (ZSDU-UPB1), členov 78–84a* [Act on Worker Participation in Management—ZSDU (Official Gazette RS, No 42/93 of 22 July 1993) / consolidated version ZSDU-UPB1, art. 78–84a] Board-level employee representation is only compulsory for companies that are not regarded as being 'small'. A small company meets two of the following criteria: fewer than 50 employees, less than €8.8 million of turnover and/or an asset value below €4.4 million. In companies with a dual-board structure, the articles of association determine the proportion of board-level employee representatives to sit on the supervisory board. This proportion cannot be less than one-third or more than a half of the total number of board members. The articles of association also determine the number of board-level employee representatives in companies with a single-board structure (only a Plc can opt for such a monistic structure). In such circumstances there must be at least one employee representative and no less than one employee representative per three board members (so a quarter). In both cases, board-level employee representatives are appointed by the works council from among employees and cannot chair the board (given that the chair of the supervisory board has a casting vote in the event of a tie).
	Situation in state-owned companies State-owned companies regulated by the legal statutes prevailing in the private sector, are subject to the same rules on board-level employee representation.	

Sources: Conchon (2011b), Fulton (2013a), and authors' own research for update thanks to the support of the SEEurope network members.[6]

NOTES

1. INI-TENEO was a state agency acting as the holding company of several state-owned companies and is today known as SEPI (*Sociedad Estatal de Participaciones Industriales*).
2. Unless otherwise agreed by trade unions and management, a 'corporate assembly' (*bedriftsforsamling*) has to be set up in companies with more than 200 employees. The corporate assembly comprises two-thirds of members elected by the general assembly of shareholders and one-third by employees of the company and has far-reaching duties comparable to those of a supervisory board in a dual structure. For instance, the corporate assembly appoints the members of the board of directors and may take decisions on large-scale investments or restructuring.
3. The only regulations mentioned here are those that apply to companies that are entirely owned by the state. Board-level employee representation is also found in other types of public-sector companies in which the same regulations apply. The regulation of board-level employee representation in inter-municipal companies (Lov om interkommunale selskaper nr 06, 1999.01.29 —Act on inter-municipal companies No 06, January 29, 1999, Art. 10) and state-owned companies in the health sector (Lov om helseforetak nr 93 2001.06.15 —Act on health companies No 93, June 15, 2001, Art. 23) is almost identical to that applying to state enterprise, and thus to that applying to Plc and Ltd companies. The same statement applies to state-owned companies governed by specific Acts, such as Posten Norge (postal company) and NSB (national railways company).
4. The law only stipulates that 'employees' representatives *should* be appointed from the employees of the company' (emphasis added).
5. On 1 January 2014, a new Act on commercial corporations (No 90/2012 Coll.) came into force. As none of the previous provisions on board-level employee representation was repeated in the new law, there is no longer any obligation for Czech companies to implement board-level employee representation. According to the interpretation of the law as 'what is not forbidden is allowed', it could be said that Czech companies are still free to decide to keep or introduce board-level employee representation voluntarily.
6. For information about the SEEurope network, see http://www.workerparticipation.eu/European-Company-SE/SEEurope-network.

Bibliography

Ackers, P., Marchington, M., Wilkinson, A. and Goodman, J. 1992. 'The Use of Cycles? Explaining Employee Involvement in the 1990s', *Industrial Relations Journal*, 23 (4):268–283.

Acquisitions Monthly. Various. London: Thomson Reuters.

Adams, R. and Ferreira, D. 2007. 'A Theory of Friendly Boards', *Journal of Finance*, 62 (1):217–250.

Adams, R., Almeida, H. and Ferreira, D. 2005. 'Powerful CEOs and Their Impact on Corporate Performance', *The Review of Financial Studies*, 18 (4):1403–1432.

Adams, R., Hermalin, B. and Weisbach, M. 2010. 'The Role of Boards of Directors in Corporate Governance: A Conceptual Framework and Survey.' *Journal of Economic Literature*, 48 (1):58–107.

Adams, R., Licht, A. and Sagiv, L. 2011. 'Shareholders and Stakeholders: How Do Directors Decide?', *Strategic Management Journal*, 32 (12):1331–1355.

Agnblad, J., Berglöf, E., Högfeldt, P. and Svancar, H. 2001. 'Sweden', pp. 228–258 in Barca, F. and Becht, M. (eds.). *The Control of Corporate Europe*. Oxford: Oxford University Press.

Aguilera, R. and Jackson, G. 2003. 'The Cross-national Diversity of Corporate Governance: Dimensions and Determinants', *Academy of Management Review*, 28 (3):447–465.

Aguilera, R., Filatotchev, I., Gospel, H. and Jackson, G. 2008. 'An Organizational Approach to Comparative Corporate Governance: Costs, Contingencies, and Complementarities', *Organization Science*, 19 (3):475–492.

Ahlering, B. and Deakin, S. 2007. 'Labor Regulation, Corporate Governance, and Legal Origin: A Case of Institutional Complementarity?', *Law and Society Review*, 41 (4):865–908.

AK Wien. 2015. *Frauen Management Report 2015. Frauen in Geschäftsführung und Aufsichtsrat der Top 200 und Börsennotierten Unternehmen*. Vienna: AK Wien.

Antunes, J., Baums, T., Clarke, B., Conac, P., Enriques, L., Hanák, A., Hansen, J., de Kluiver, H., Knapp, V., Lenoir, N., Linnainmaa, L., Soltusinski, S. and Wymeersch, E. 2011. *Report of the Reflection Group on the Future of EU Company Law*. Brussels: European Commission.

Aoki, M. 1986. 'Vertical Information Structure of the Firm', *The American Economic Review*, 76 (5):971–983.

Aoki, M. 1994. 'The Contingent Governance of Teams: Analysis of Institutional Complementarity', *International Economic Review*, 35 (3):657–676.

Aoki, M. 2001. *Towards a Comparative Institutional Analysis*. Cambridge, MA: MIT Press.

Appelbaum, E., Bailey, T., Berg, P. and Kalleberg, A. 2000. *Manufacturing Advantage: Why High Performance Work Systems Pay Off*. Ithaca: Cornell University Press.

Appelbaum, E. and Hunter, L. W. 2004. 'Union Participation in Strategic Decisions of Corporations', pp. 265–291 in Freeman, R., Hersch, J. and Mishel, L. (eds.). *Emerging Labour Market Institutions for the Twenty-First Century*. Chicago: University of Chicago Press.

Armour, J., Deakin, S., Lele, P. and Siems, M. 2009. 'How Legal Rules Evolve? Evidence from a Cross-country Comparison of Shareholder, Creditor, and Worker Protection', *The American Journal of Comparative Law*, 57 (3):579–629.

Bachrach, P. and Baratz, M. 1962. 'Two Faces of Power', *American Political Science Review*, 56 (4):947–952.

Bachrach, R. and Baratz, M. 1963. 'Decisions and Non-decisions: An Analytical Framework', *American Political Science Review*, 57 (3):632–642.

Baker & McKenzie. 2009. *Worldwide Guide to Trade Unions and Works Councils*. Chicago: Baker & McKenzie.

Baldacchino, G. 1997. 'Is-Sistema ta' Management fit-Tarzna: Stharrig, Analizi u Rakkomandazzjonijiet', Report to the Malta Drydocks Task Force. Valletta: Malta Government Press.

Banerjee, S. 2007. *Corporate Social Responsibility: The Good, the Bad and the Ugly*. Cheltenham: Edward Elgar.

Barker, R. 2010. *Corporate Governance, Competition and Political Parties*. Oxford: Oxford University Press.

Barreto, J. 1992. 'Portugal: Industrial Relations under Democracy', pp. 445–481 in Ferner, A. and Hyman, R. (eds.). *Industrial Relations in the New Europe*. Oxford: Blackwell.

Batstone, E., Ferner, A. and Terry, M. 1983. *Unions on the Board. An Experiment in Industrial Democracy*. Oxford: Basil Blackwell.

Bayer, W. 2009. *Drittelbeteiligung in Deutschland*. Düsseldorf: Hans Böckler Foundation.

Beal, E. 1955. 'Origins of Codetermination', *Industrial and Labor Relations Review*, 8 (4):483–498.

Becht, M. and Röell, A. 1999. 'Blockholdings in Europe: An International Comparison', *European Economic Review*, 43 (4–6):1049–1056.

Bedrač, J. 2005. 'The Slovenian System of Worker Board-level Representation', pp. 39–44 in SDA and ETUI. (eds.). *Worker Board-level Representation in the New EU Member States: Country Reports on the National Systems and Practices*. Brussels: Social Development Agency and European Trade Union Institute.

Bendix, R. 1964. *Nation Building and Citizenship: Studies of our Changing Social Order*. London: Wiley.

Bennedsen, M., Kongsted, H. and Nielsen, K. 2008. 'The Causal Effect of Board Size in the Performance of Small and Medium-sized Firms', *Journal of Banking and Finance*, 32 (6):1098–1109.

Ben-Ner, A. 1993. 'Organisational Reforms in Central and Eastern Europe: A Comparative Perspective', *Annals of Public and cooperative Economics*, 3:327–364.

Berggren, C. 1993. *The Volvo Experience: Alternatives to Lean Production in the Swedish Automobile Industry*. Basingstoke: MacMillan.

Berglund, T., Holmen, M. and Rana, R. 2013. 'Causes and Consequences of Employee Representation on Corporate Boards', paper presented at the conference 'Twenty Years after Cadbury, Ten Years after Sarbanes-Oxley: Challenges of Corporate Governance', University of Bath, 24–25 June.

Berle, A. and Means, G. 1932. *The Modern Corporation and Private Property*. New York: MacMillan.

Bermig, A. and Frick, B. 2011. 'Determinanten der 'Übergröße' deutscher Aufsichtsräte', *Schmollers Jahrbuch*, (131):169–194.

Berndt, C. 2000. 'Regulation, Power and Scale: Reworking Capital-labour Relations in German SMEs', Working Paper No. 157, ESRC Centre for Business Research. University of Cambridge.

Bernstein, P. 1976. 'Necessary Elements for Effective Worker Participation in Decision Making', *Journal of Economic Issues*, 10 (2):490–522.

Bettinelli, C. and Chugh, L. 2009. 'Boards of Directors in Europe: A Comparative Analysis', *International Review of Business Research Papers*, 5 (2):62–75.

Bhagat, S. and Black, B. 1999. 'The Uncertain Relationship between Board Composition and Firm Performance', *The Business Lawyer*, 54 (3):921–963.

Bhagat, S. and Black, B. 2002. 'The Non-Correlation between Board Independence and Long-Term Firm Performance', *Journal of Corporation Law*, 27:231–273.

BIS. 2012. 'Executive Remuneration: Summary of Responses', Discussion Paper. London: Department of Business, Innovation and Skills.

Blackburn, R. 2002. 'The Enron Debacle and the Pension Crisis', *New Left Review*, Series 2, No. 14:26–51.

Blair, M. 1995. *Ownership and Control: Rethinking Corporate Governance for the Twenty-first Century*. Washington: Brookings Institution.

Blanpain, R. and Engels, C. 2001. (eds.). *Comparative Labour Law and Industrial Relations in Industrialized Market Economies. VIIth revised edition*. The Hague: Kluwer Law International.

Blasi, J. and Kruse, D. 1991. *The New Owners: The Mass Emergence of Employee Ownership in Public Companies and What It Means for American Business*. New York: Harper Business.

Block, F. 2007. 'Understanding the Diverging Trajectories of the United States and Western Europe: A Neo-Polanyian Analysis', *Politics and Society*, 35 (1):3–33.

Blumberg, P. 1968. *Industrial Democracy: The Sociology of Participation*. London: Constable.

Blyth, M. 2003. 'Same as It Never Was: Temporality and Typology in the Varieties of Capitalism', *Comparative European Politics*, 1 (2):215–225.

Bohle, D. and Greskovits, B. 2007. 'Neo-liberalism, Embedded Neo-liberalism, and Neo-corporatism: Towards Transnational Capitalism in Central-Eastern Europe', *West European Politics*, 30 (3):443–466.

Bøhren, Ø. and Strøm, R. 2005. 'The Value Creating Board: Theory and Evidence', Research Report No. 8, Oslo: BI.

Boneberg, F. 2010. 'The Economic Consequences of One-third Co-determination in German Supervisory Boards: First Evidence for the Service Sector from a New Source of Enterprise Data', Working Paper No. 177, University of Lüneberg.

Boone, A., Field, L., Karpoff, J. and Raheja, C. 2007. 'The Determinants of Corporate Board Size and Composition: An Empirical Analysis', *Journal of Financial Economics*, 85 (1):66–101.

Borbély, S. 'Hungary: EU Enlargement and the Trade Unions', *South East Europe Review*, 1 (1):97–107.

Boselie, J. 2013. 'Human Resource Management and Performance', pp. 18–36 in Bach, S. and Edwards, M. (eds.). *Managing Human Resources: Human Resource Management in Transition*. Chichester: John Wiley.

Botero, J., Djankov, S., La Porta, R., Lopez-de-Silanes, F. and Shleifer, A. 2004. 'The Regulation of Labor', *Quarterly Journal of Economics*, 119 (4):1339–1382.

Boxall, P. and Purcell, J. 2011. *Strategy and Human Resource Management*. 3rd Edition. Basingstoke: Palgrave MacMillan.

Boyer, R. 2000. 'Is a Finance-led Growth Regime a Viable Alternative to Fordism? A Preliminary Analysis?', *Economy and Society*, 29 (1):111–145.

Boyer, R. 2005. 'How and Why Capitalisms Differ', *Economy and Society*, 34 (4):509–557.

Brachinger, R. 2004. *Berichte aus der Aufsichtsratspraxis. Ergebnisse der Aufsichtsrätebefragung 2003/2004*. Vienna: AK-Consult.

Brannen, P. 1983. *Authority and Participation in Industry*. London: Batsford.

Brickley, J., Coles, J. and Jarrell, G. 1997. 'The Leadership Structure: Separating the CEO and Chairman of the Board', *Journal of Corporate Finance*, 3 (3):189–220.

Briefs, U. 1989. 'Co-determination in the Federal Republic of Germany: An Appraisal of a Secular Experience', pp. 63–74 in Szell, G., Blyton, P. and Cornforth, C. (eds.). *The State, Trade Unions and Self-management*. Berlin: de Gruyter.

Brulin, G. 1995. 'Sweden: Joint Councils under Strong Unionism', pp. 189–216 in Rogers, J. and Streeck, W. (eds.). *Works Councils: Consultation, Representation and Cooperation in Industrial Relations*. Chicago: University of Chicago Press.

Brust, L. 2002. 'Making Markets and Eastern Enlargement: Diverging Convergence?', *West European Politics*, 26 (2):121–140.

Büggel, A. 2010. 'Gesellschafts- und Mitbestimmungsrecht in den Ländern der Europäischen Gemeinschaft', *Arbeitshilfen für Aufsichsräte*, No. 11, Düsseldorf: Hans-Böckler-Stiftung.

Buiges, P. 1993. 'Evaluation des Concentrations: Entreprises et Pouvoirs Publics Face-à-Face', *Economie Internationale*, 55:91–108.

Buiges, P., Ilkowitz, F. and Lebrun, J.-F. 1990. 'The Impact of the Internal Market by Industrial Sector: The Challenge for Member States', *Social Europe*, Special Issue. Luxembourg: Office for Official Publications of the European Communities.

Bullock, Lord, A. 1977. *Report of the Committee of Inquiry on Industrial Democracy*. Cmnd 6706. London: Her Majesty's Stationary Office.

Butler, H. and Ribstein, L. 1995. *The Corporation and the Constitution*. Washington, DC: American Enterprise Institute.

Cable, J. and Fitzroy, F. 1980. 'Cooperation and Productivity: Some Evidence from West German Experience', *Economic Analysis and Workers' Management*, 14 (2):163–180.

Calvo, J., Vigneau, C., Belopavlovič, N., Rodríguez Contreras, R., and Fulton, L. (eds.). 2008. *Employee Representatives in an Enlarged Europe. Vol. 1 and 2*. Luxembourg: Office for official publications of the European Communities.

Carley, M. 1990. 'Employee Participation in Europe. Works Councils, Worker Directors and Other Forms of Participation in 15 European Countries', *European Industrial Relations Review*, Report No. 4. London: European Industrial Relations Review.

Carley, M. 1996. *Worker Directors: A Comparative Study of Five Countries. Part One: Background and Regulation*. Dublin: European Foundation for the Improvement of Living and Working Conditions.

Carley, M. 1997. *Worker Directors: A Comparative Study of Five Countries*. Dublin: European foundation for the Improvement of Living and Working Conditions.

Carley, M. 2005. 'Board-level Employee Representatives in Nine countries: A Snapshot', *Transfer: European Review of Labour and Research*, 11 (2):231–243.

Carley, M., Baradel, A. and Welz, C. 2005. *Works Councils: Workplace Representation and Participation Structures*, Dublin: European Foundation for the Improvement of Living and Working Conditions.

CCOO. 1989. *Propuesta Sindical Prioritaria*. Madrid: Comisiones Obreras.

Chandler, A. 1977. *The Visible Hand: Managerial Revolution in American Business*. Cambridge, Mass.: Harvard University Press.

Chandler, A. 1990. *Scale and Scope: The Dynamics of Industrial Capitalism*. Cambridge, Mass.: Harvard University Press.

Charkham, J. 2005. *Keeping Better Company: Corporate Governance Ten Years On*, 2nd Edition. Oxford: Oxford University Press.

Clarke, T. 1977. 'Industrial Democracy: The Institutionalized Suppression of Industrial Conflict?', pp. 351–382 in Clarke, T. and Clements, L. (eds.). *Trade Unions under Capitalism*. London: Fontana.

Clegg, H. 1951. *Industrial Democracy and Nationalization*. Oxford: Blackwell.

Clegg, H. 1960. *A New Approach to Industrial Democracy*. Oxford: Basil Blackwell.

Clegg, H. 1976. *Trade Unionism under Collective Bargaining: A Theory Based on Comparisons of Six Countries*. Oxford: Basil Blackwell.

Coates, K. and Topham, T. 1977. *The Shop Stewards Guide to the Bullock Report.* Nottingham: Spokesman.

Coffee, J. 2005. 'A Theory of Corporate Scandals: Why the USA and Europe Differ', *Oxford Review of Economic Policy*, 21 (2):198–211.

Coffee, J. 2006. *Gatekeepers: The Professions and Corporate Governance.* Oxford: Oxford University Press.

Collier, J. and Esteban, R. 2007. 'Corporate Social Responsibility and Employee Commitment', *Business Ethics: A European Review*, 16 (1):19–33.

Conchon, A. 2009. 'Les administrateurs salariés dans les entreprises françaises: une approche quantitative', pp. 103–112 in Auberger- Barré, M.-N. and Conchon, A. (eds). *Les administrateurs salariés et la gouvernance d'entreprise.* Paris: La documentation française.

Conchon, A. 2011a. 'Employee Representation in Corporate Governance: Part of the Economic of the Social Sphere', ETUI Working Paper, No. 2011.08. Brussels: European Trade Union Institute.

Conchon, A. 2011b. 'Board-level Employee Representation Rights in Europe: Facts and Trends', ETUI Report No. 121. Brussels: European Trade Union Institute.

Conchon, A. 2012. 'Are Employee Participation Rights Under Pressure ? Trends at National and EU Level', ETUI Policy Brief No. 7. Brussels: European Trade Union Institute.

Conchon, A. 2013a. 'La Participation aux Décisions Stratégiques de l'Entreprise: Influence ou Pouvoir des Administrateurs Salariés', *Participations* (5): 127–149.

Conchon, A. 2013b. *Workers' Voice in Corporate Governance: A European Perspective.* Economic Report Series. London: Trades Union Congress.

Conchon, A. 2013c. 'National Participation Rights in an EU Perspective: The SE Rules as a Key Safeguard', pp. 291–309 in Cremers, J., Stollt, M. and Vitols, S. (eds.) *A Decade of Experience with the European Company.* Brussels: European Trade Union Institute.

Conchon, A. and Waddington, J. 2011. 'Board-level Employee Representation in Europe: Challenging Commonplace Prejudices', pp. 91–111 in Vitols, S. and Kluge, N. (eds.). *The Sustainable Company: A New Approach to Corporate Governance.* Brussels: European Trade Union Institute.

Conyon, M., Gregg, P. and Machin, S. 1995. 'Taking Care of Business: Executive Compensation in the UK', *Economic Journal*, 105 (430):704–714.

Cordova, E. 1982. 'Workers' Participation in Decisions within Enterprises: Recent Trends and Problems', *International Labour Review*, 121 (2):125–140.

Coriat, B. 'Labor and Capital in Crisis: France, 1966–82', pp. 17–38 in Kesselman, M. (ed.). *The French Workers' Movement.* London: George Allen & Unwin.

Cox, T. and Mason, B. 2000. 'Interest Groups and the Development of Tripartism in East Central Europe', *European Journal of Industrial Relations*, 6 (3):325–347.

Cremers, J. and Carlson, A. 2013. 'SEs in the Czech Republic', pp. 107–122 in Cremers, J., Stollt, M. and Vitols, S. (eds.). *A Decade of Experience with the European Company.* Brussels: ETUI.

Cremers, J. and Wolters, E. 2011. 'EU and National Company Law: Fixation on Attractiveness', Report 120. Brussels: European Trade Union Institute.

Cressey, P. 1992. 'Trade Unions and New Technology: European Experience and Strategic Questions', pp. 236–265 in Beirne, M. and Ramsay, H. (eds.). *Information Technology and Workplace Democracy.* London: Routledge.

Crouch, C. 1993. *Industrial Relations and European State Traditions.* Oxford: Clarendon.

Crouch, C. 2004. *Post Democracy.* Cambridge: Polity Press.

Crouch, C. 2005. *Capitalist Diversity and Change: Recombinant Governance and Institutional Entrepreneurs.* Oxford: Oxford University Press.

Crouch, C. 2011. *The Strange Non-Death of Neo-liberalism*. Cambridge: Polity Press.

Culpepper, P. 1999. 'Introduction: Still a Model for the Industrialised Countries?', pp. 1–34 in Culpepper, P. and Finegold, D. (eds.). *The German Skills Machine: Sustaining Comparative Advantage in a Global Economy*. New York: Berghahn Books.

Cziria, L. 1995. 'The Czech and Slovak Republics', pp. 61–80 in Thirkell, J., Scase, R. and Vickerstaff, S. (eds.). *Labour Relations in Eastern Europe: A Comparative Perspective*, London: University College, London Press.

Dachler, P. and Wilpert, B. 1978. 'Conceptual Dimensions and Boundaries of Participation in Organizations: A Critical Evaluation', *Administrative Science Quarterly*, 23 (1):1–39.

Dahl, R. 1961. *Who Governs? Democracy and Power in an American City*. New Haven and London: Yale University Press.

Davies, P. 2003. 'Workers on the Board of the European Company?', *Industrial Law Journal*, 32 (2):75–96.

Davies, P. and Hopt, K. 2013. 'Corporate Boards in Europe. Accountability and Convergence', *American Journal of Comparative Law*, 61 (2):301–376.

Davies, P., Hopt, K., Nowak, R. and van Solinge, G. 2013. 'Boards in Law and Practice: A Cross-country Analysis in Europe', pp. 3–15 in Davies, P., Hopt, K., Nowak, R. and van Solinge, G. (eds.). *Corporate Boards in Law and Practice: A Comparative Analysis in Europe*. Oxford: Oxford University Press.

Deeg, R. 1999. *Finance Capitalism Unveiled: Banks and the German Political Economy*. Ann Arbor: The University of Michigan Press.

Deeg, R. 2005. 'Change from Within: German and Italian Finance in the 1990s', pp. 169–202 in Streeck, W. and Thelen, K. (eds.). *Beyond Continuity: Institutional Change in Advanced Political Economies*. Oxford: Oxford University Press.

Deeg, R. 2009. 'The Rise of Internal Capitalist Diversity? Changing Patterns of Finance and Corporate Governance in Europe', *Economy and Society*, 38 (4):552–579.

Deeg, R. and Jackson, G. 2007. 'Towards a more Dynamic Theory of Capitalist Variety', *Socio-Economic Review*, 5 (1):149–179.

Delery, J. and Doty, D. 1996. 'Modes of Theorizing in Strategic Human Resource Management: Tests of Universalistic, Contingency and Configurational Performance Predictions', *Academy of Management Review*, 4 (39): 802–835.

Demb, A. and Neubauer, F. 1992. *The Corporate Board: Confronting the Paradoxes*. Oxford: Oxford University Press.

Dølvik, J.E. and Waddington, J. 2005. 'Can Trade Unions Meet the Challenge? Unionisation in the Marketised Services', pp. 316–341 in Bosch, G. and Lehndorff, S. (eds.). *Working in the Service Sector: A Tale from Different Worlds*. London: Routledge.

Doucouliagos, C. 1995. 'Worker Participation and Productivity in Labour-managed and Participatory Capitalist Firms: A Meta-Analysis', *Industrial and Labor Relations Review*, 49 (1):58–77.

Dufour, C. and Hege, A. 2002. *L'europe syndicale au quotidien*. Brussels: PIE-Peter Lang.

Dukes, R. 2005. 'The Origins of the German System of Worker Representation', *Historical Studies in Industrial Relations*, (19):31–62.

Duménil, G. and Lévy, D. 2004. *Capital Resurgent: Roots of the Neoliberal Revolution*. Cambridge, MA: Harvard University Press.

Duran, M. and Pull, K. 2014. 'Der beitrag der Arbeitnehmervertreter zur fachlichen und geschlechtlichen Diversität von Aufsichtsräten: Erkenntnisse aus eine qualitativ-explorativen Analyse', *Industrielle Beziehungen*, 21 (4):329–351.

Duriez, B., Ion, J. and Pincon, M. 1991. 'Institutions statistiques et nomenclatures socioprofessionnelles. Essai comparatif : Royaume-Uni, Espagne, France', *Revue française de sociologie*, 32 (1):29–59.

Easterbrook, F. and Fischel, D. 1983. 'Voting in Corporate Law', *Journal of Law and Economics*, 26 (2):395–427.

Edwards, T. 2004. 'Corporate Governance, Industrial Relations and Trends in Company-level Restructuring in Europe: Convergence towards the Anglo-American Model?', *Industrial Relations Journal*, 35 (6):518–535.

Ehrenstein, I. 2014. '651 Unternehmen sind mitbestimmt', *Mitbestimmung Magazin*, No. 5:58–59.

Eidenmüller, H., Engert, A. and Hornuf, L. 2009. 'Incorporating under European Law: The Societas Europaea as a Vehicle for Legal Arbitrage', *European Business Organization Law Review*, 10 (1):1–33.

EIRR. 2001a. 'Information and Consultation of Workers across Europe: Part One', *European Industrial Relations Review*, No. 334, November:13–21.

EIRR. 2001b. 'Information and Consultation of Workers across Europe: Part Two', *European Industrial Relations Review*, No. 335, December:13–18.

EIRR. 2002. 'Information and Consultation of Workers across Europe: Part Three', *European Industrial Relations Review*, No. 336, January:30–36.

EMF. 2003. *The European Company—SE. EMF Guidelines*. Brussels: European Metalworkers' Federation.

EMF. 2004. *European Multi-stakeholder Forum on Corporate Social Responsibility: Final Results and Recommendations*. Brussels: European Multinational Forum.

Engelen, E. and Konings, M. 2010. 'Financial Capitalism Resurgent: Comparative Institutionalism and the Challenges of Financialisation', pp. 601–624 in Morgan, G., Campbell, J., Crouch, C., Pedersen, O. and Whitley, R. (eds.). *The Oxford Handbook of Comparative Institutional Analysis*. Oxford: Oxford University Press.

Engelen, P.-J., van den Berg, A. and van der Laan, G. 2012. 'Board Diversity as a Shield During the Financial Crisis', pp. 259–285 in Boubaker, S., Gand Nguyen, B. and Khuong Nguyen, D. (eds.). *Corporate Governance. Recent Developments and New Trends*. Berlin: Springer-Verlag.

Enriques, L. and Volpin, P. 2007. 'Corporate Governance Reforms in Continental Europe', *Journal of Economic Perspectives*, 21 (1):117–140.

Ernst & Young. 2009. *Study on the Operation and the Impacts of the Statute for a European Company (SE). Final report*. Brussels: Ernst & Young.

Escobar, M. 1995. 'Spain: Works Councils or Unions?', pp. 153–188 in Rogers, J. and Streeck, W. (eds.). *Works Councils: Consultation, Representation and Cooperation in Industrial Relations*. Chicago: University of Chicago Press.

Esping-Andersen, G. 1990. *The Three Worlds of Welfare Capitalism*. Princeton, NJ: Princeton University Press.

ETUC. 2003. *Make Europe Work for the People*. Action Programme Adopted at the ETUC 10th Statutory Congress, 26–29 May 2003. Brussels: European Trade Union Confederation.

ETUC. 2011. *ETUC Strategy and Action Plan*. Brussels: European Trade Union Confederation.

ETUC. 2012. *5th Annual ETUC 8 March Survey 2012*. Brussels: European Trade Union Confederation.

ETUC. 2014. *Towards a New Framework for More Democracy at Work*. Resolution adopted by the Executive Committee, 21–22 October. Brussels: European Trade Union Confederation.

ETUC and ETUCO. 2003. *Worker Representation Systems in the European Union and the Accession Countries*. Brussels: European Trade Union Confederation and European Trade Union College.

ETUC and ETUI. 2014. *Benchmarking Working Europe 2014*. Brussels: European Trade Union Institute.
ETUI. 1990. *Workers' Representation and Rights in the Workplace in Western Europe*. Brussels: European Trade Union Institute.
Eurofound. 2015. *Third European Company Survey—Overview report: Workplace Practices—Patterns, Performance and Well-being*. Luxembourg: Publications Office of the European Union.
European Commission. 2008. *Employee Representatives in an Enlarged Europe: Volumes 1 and 2*. Directorate-General for Employment, Social Affairs and Equal Opportunities. Luxembourg: Office for Official Publications of the European Communities.
European Commission. 2010. *Green Paper. Corporate Governance in Financial Institutions and Remuneration Policies*. COM(2010) 284 final, Brussels.
European Commission. 2011. *Green Paper. The EU Corporate Governance Framework*. COM(2011) 164 final, Brussels.
European Commission. 2012a. *Action Plan: European Company Law and Corporate Governance: A Modern Legal Framework for More Engaged Shareholders and Sustainable Companies*. COM(2012) 740 final, Strasbourg.
European Commission. 2012b. *Women in Economic Decision-making in the EU: Progress Report*. Luxembourg: Publications Office of the European Union.
European Commission. 2013. *Proposal for a Directive of the European Parliament and of the Council amending Council Directives 78/660/EEC and 83/349/EEC as regards disclosure of non-financial and diversity information by certain large companies and groups*. COM (2013) 207 final, Strasbourg.
Eversheds & Employment Law Alliance. 2005. *Information and Consultation Survey*. London: Eversheds & Employment Law Alliance.
Fagan, C., González Meneèdez, M. and Gómez Ansón, S. 2012. (eds.). *Women on Corporate Boards and in Top Management: European Trends and Policy*. Basingstoke: Palgrave Macmillan.
Fairbrother, P. and Griffin, G. 2002. (eds.). *Changing Prospects for Trade Unionism*. London: Continuum.
Faleye, O., Mehrotra, V. and Morck, R. 2006. 'When Labor has a Voice in Corporate Governance', *Journal of Financial and Quantitative Analysis*, 41 (3):489–510.
Fama, E. 1980. 'Agency Problems and the Theory of the Firm', *Journal of Political Economy*, 88 (2):288–307.
Fama, E. and Jensen, M. 1983. 'Separation of Ownership and Control', *Journal of Law and Economics*, 26 (2):301–325.
Fama, E. and Jensen, M. 1985. 'Organizational Forms and Investment Decision', *Journal of Financial Economics*, 14 (1):101–119.
Fanto, J., Solan, L. and Darley, J. 2011. 'Justifying Board Diversity', *North Carolina Law Review*, 89 (3):901–935.
Farrell, K. and Hersch, P. 2005. 'Additions to Corporate Boards: The Effect of Gender', *Journal of Corporate Finance*, 11 (1):85–106.
Fauver, L. and Fuerst, M. 2006. 'Does Good Corporate Governance Include Employee Representation? Evidence from German Corporate Boards', *Journal of Financial Economics*, 82 (4):673–710.
Fishman, R. 1990. *Working-class Organization and the Return to Democracy in Spain*. Ithaca: Cornell University Press.
Fligstein, N. 1990. *The Transformation of Corporate Control*. Cambridge, MA: Harvard University Press.
Fonow, M. and Franzway, S. 2009. 'Sites for Renewal: Women's Activism in Male-dominated Unions in Australia, Canada and the United States', pp. 177–191 in Foley, J. and Baker, P. (eds.). *Unions, Equity and the Path to Renewal*. Vancouver: University of British Columbia Press.

Frege, C. 2007. *Employment Research and State Traditions: A Comparative History of Britain, Germany and the United States*. Oxford: Oxford University Press.

French, J., Israel, J. and Ås, D. 1960. 'An Experiment in Participation in a Norwegian Factory', *Human Relations*, 13 (1):3–19.

Frick, B. and Lehmann, E. 2005. 'Corporate Governance in Germany: Ownership, Codetermination and Firm Performance in a Stakeholder Economy', pp. 122–147 in Gospel, H. and Pendleton, A. (eds.). *Corporate Governance and Labour Management: An International Comparison*. Oxford: Oxford University Press.

Fulton, L. 2006. *The Forgotten Resource: Corporate Governance and Employee Board-level Representation: The Situation in France, the Netherlands, Sweden and the UK*. London: Labour Research Department.

Fulton, L. 2009. *Worker Representation in Europe*. Labour Research Department and European Trade Union Institute. Available at www.worker-participation.eu/National-Industrial-Relations.

Fulton L. 2013a. 'From a European Blueprint to National Law', pp. 67–89 in Cremers, J., Stollt, M. and Vitols, S. (eds.). *A Decade of Experience with the European Company*. Brussels: European Trade Union Institute.

Fulton, L. 2013b. *Worker Representation in Europe*. Labour Research Department and European Trade Union Institute, available at www.worker-participation.eu/National-Industrial-Relations.

Gahleitner, H. 2013. *Mitwirkung im Aufsichtsrat. Grundzüge des Gesellschaftsrechts für Arbeitnehmervertreterinnen II*. Vienna: Verlag des ÖGB.

Gahleitner, S. and Preiss, J. 2003. *Economics, Law, Co-decision. The Essentials of Corporate Law for Workers' Representatives II: Supervisory Board Participation*. Vienna: VOGB and AK Österreich.

Ganz, M. 2000. 'Resources and Resourcefulness', *American Journal of Sociology*, 105 (4):1003–1062.

Gazzane, S. 2006. *Health and Safety Representation of Employees in EU Countries*. Brussels: European Trade Union Institute.

Gerner-Beuerle, C., Paech, P. and Schuster, E.-P. 2013. *Study on Directors' Duties and Liability*. London: LSE Enterprise.

Gerum, E. 2007. *Das deutsche Corporate Governance-System. Eine empirische Untersuchung*. Stuttgart: Schäffer-Poeschel Verlag.

Gerum, E. and Debus, M. 2006. *Die Größe des Aufsichtsrats als rechtspolitisches Probelm. Einige empirische Befunde*. Düsseldorf: Hans-Böckler-Stiftung.

Gill, C. and Krieger, H. 1999. 'Direct and Representative Participation in Europe: Recent Survey Evidence', *The International Journal of Human Resource Management*, 10 (4):572–591.

Glass, E. 2009. *Mitbestimmung in Societas Europaea. Ein Blick auf die Umsetzung des Rechtsstatuts und dessen Wirkung, unter Berücksichtigung der Vereinbarungen zur Mitarbeiterbeteiligung*. Master thesis, University of Hamburg.

Globerson, A. 1970. 'Spheres and Levels of Employee Participation in Organisations: Elements of a Conceptual Model', *British Journal of Industrial Relations*, 8 (2):252–262

Goergen, M., Manjon, M. and Renneboog, L. 2008. 'Is the German System of Corporate Governance Converging towards the Anglo-American Model?', *Journal of Management and Governance*, 12 (1):37–71.

Gold, M. 2005. 'Worker Directors in the UK and the Limits of Policy Transfer from Europe since the 1970s', *Historical Studies in Industrial Relations*, 20:29–65.

Gold, M. 2009. 'Employee Participation at European Union Level: Was it Worth the Wait? The Concept of "Functional Equivalence" Revisited', paper presented at the 15th International Industrial Relations Association World Congress, 24–27 August, Sydney.

Gold, M. 2011. 'Taken on Board: An Evaluation of the Influence of Employee Board-level Representatives on Company Decision-making across Europe', *European Journal of Industrial Relations*, 17 (1):41–56.

Gold, M. and Hall, M. 1990. *Legal Regulation and the Practice of Employee Participation in the European Community*. Dublin: European Foundation for the Improvement of Living and Working Conditions.

Gold, M., Kluge, N. and Conchon, A. 2010. *'In the Union and on the Board': Experiences of Board-level Employee Representatives across Europe*. Brussels: European Trade Union Institute.

Gold, M. and Rees, C. 2013. 'What Makes an Effective European Works Council? Considerations Based on Three Case Studies', *Transfer*, 19 (4):539–551.

Goodijk, R. 2000. 'Corporate Governance and Workers' Participation', *Corporate Governance: An International Review*, 8 (4):303–310.

Goodijk, R. 2006. 'Supervisory Board and Works Council in the Netherlands', Research Paper, January, University of Groningen.

Goodijk, R. 2010. *Corporate Governance and Works Councils: A Dutch Perspective*. Presented at the IIRA European Congress, 28 June–1 July, Amsterdam.

Gorton, G. and Schmid, F. 2004. 'Capital, Labor and the Firm: A Study of German Codetermination', *Journal of the European Economic Association*, 2 (5):863–905.

Gospel, H. 1992. *Markets, Firms and the Management of Labour in Modern Britain*. Cambridge: Cambridge University Press.

Gospel, H. and Pendleton, A. 2005. (eds.). *Corporate Governance and Labour Management: An International Comparison*. Oxford: Oxford University Press.

Gostiša, M. 2001. *Struktura, način kadrovanja in usposobljenost delavskih predstavnikov v nadzornih svetih*. Ljubljana: Študijski Center za Industrijsko Demokracijo.

Gourevitch, P. 2003. 'The Politics of Corporate Governance Regulation', *Yale Law Journal*, 112 (7):1829–1880.

Gourevitch, P. and Shinn, J. 2005. *Political Power and Corporate Control: The New Global Politics of Corporate Governance*. Princeton: Princeton University Press.

Government Commission. 2013. *German Corporate Governance Code*. Frankfurt am Main: Government Commission German Corporate Governance Code.

Goyer, M. 2006. 'Capital Mobility, Varieties of Institutional Investors, and the Transforming Stability of Corporate Governance in France', pp. 195–219 in Hancké, B., Rhodes, M. and Thatcher, M. (eds.). *Beyond Varieties of Capitalism: Conflict, Contradictions and Complementarities in the European Economy*. Oxford: Oxford University Press.

Goyer, M. 2010. 'Corporate Governance', pp. 423–451 in Morgan, G., Campbell, J., Crouch, C., Pedersen, O. and Whitley, R. (eds.). *The Oxford Handbook of Comparative Institutional Analysis*. Oxford: Oxford University Press.

Goyer, M. and Hancké, B. 2005. 'Labour in French Corporate Governance: The Missing Link', pp. 173–196 in Gospel, H. and Pendleton, A. (eds.). *Corporate Governance and Labour Management: An International Comparison*. Oxford: Oxford University Press.

Grabbe, H. 2003. 'European Integration and Corporate Governance in Central Europe: Trajectories of Institutional Change', pp. 247–266 in Federowicz, M. and Aguilera, R. (eds.). *Corporate Governance in a Changing Economic and Political Environment: Trajectories of Institutional Change*. Houndmills: Palgrave MacMillan.

Greenfield, K. 1998. 'The Place of Workers in Corporate Law', *Boston College Law Review*, 39 (2):283–327.

Gregg, P., Machin, S. and Syzmanski, S. 1993. 'The Disappearing Relationship between Directors' Pay and Corporate Performance', *British Journal of Industrial Relations*, 31 (1):1–10.

Greifenstein, R. and Kißler, L. 2010. *Mitbestimmung im Spiegel der Forschung*. Berlin: Sigma Edition.

Guglielmi, G. 2005. 'Les juristes, le service public et les entreprises publiques aux XIXe-XXe siècles', *Revue d'histoire moderne et contemporaine*, 3 (52–3) :98–118.

Guillebaud, C. 1928. *The Works Council: A German Experiment in Industrial Democracy*. Cambridge: Cambridge University Press.

Gumbrell-McCormick, R. and Hyman, R. 2013. *Trade Unions in Western Europe: Hard Times, Hard Choices*. Oxford: Oxford University Press.

Hagen, I. M. 2007. 'Employee Representatives at Board Level: Ensuring Productivity or Democracy at Work?', Paper presented to the 8th European Regional congress of the IIRA, 3–6 September, University of Manchester.

Hagen, I. M. 2008. *Ansatte i styret. Statusrapport 2007*. Oslo: Fafo Rapport No. 09.

Hagen, I. M. 2010. *Det mektige mindretallet. Ansattereresentasjon i styret mellom Corporate Governance of Industrial Relations*. Oslo: Fafo Rapport 2010:02.

Hagen, I. M. 2011. 'Employee-elected Directors on Company Boards: Stakeholder Representatives or the Voice of Labour?', pp. 121–140 in Blanpain, R., Bromwich, W., Rymkevich, O. and Senatori, I. (eds.). *Rethinking Corporate Governance: From ShareholderValue to Stakeholder Value*. Alphen aan den Rijn: Kluwer Law International.

Hagen, I. M. 2014. 'Board-level Employee Representatives in Norway, Sweden and Denmark: Differently Powerless or Equally Important?', pp. 139–161 in Hauptmeier, M. and Vidal, M. (eds.). *Comparative Political Economy of Work*. Basingstoke: Palgrave Macmillan.

Hall, P. 2005. 'Institutional Complementarity: Causes and Effects', *Socio-Economic Review*, 3 (2):373–377.

Hall, P. 2007. 'The Evolution of Varieties of Capitalism in Europe', pp. 39–85 in Hancké, B., Rhodes, M. and Thatcher, M. (eds.). *Beyond Varieties of Capitalism: Conflict, Contradictions, and Complementarities in the European Economy*. Oxford: Oxford University Press.

Hall, P. and Gingerich, D. 2009. 'Varieties of Capitalism and Institutional Complementarities in the Political Economy: An Empirical Analysis', *British Journal of Political Science*, 39 (3):449–482.

Hall, P. and Soskice, D. 2001a. 'An Introduction to Varieties of Capitalism', pp. 1–70 in Hall, P. and Soskice, D. (eds.). *Varieties of Capitalism: The Institutional Foundations of Comparative Advantage*. Oxford: Oxford University Press.

Hall, P. and Soskice, D. 2001b. (eds.). *Varieties of Capitalism: The Institutional Foundations of Comparative Advantage*. Oxford: Oxford University Press.

Hamskär, I. 2012. 'The Importance of Worker Representatives on Company Boards and Their Right to Consult with Their Trade Union Organisation and Its Management', pp. 197–210 in Vitols, S. and Heuschmid, J. (eds.). *European Company Law and the Sustainable Company: A Stakeholder Approach: Volume II*. Brussels: European Trade Union Institute.

Hancké, B. and Goyer, M. 2005. 'Degrees of Freedom: Rethinking the Institutional Analysis of Economic Change', pp. 53–77 in Morgan, G., Whitley, R. and Moen, E. (eds.). *Changing Capitalisms? Internationalization, Institutional Change and Systems of Economic Organization*. Oxford: Oxford University Press.

Hancké, B., Rhodes, M. and Thatcher, M. 2007. (eds.). *Beyond Varieties of Capitalism: Conflict, Contradictions, and Complementarities in the European Economy*. Oxford: Oxford University Press.

Harrison, J. and Freeman, R. 1999. 'Stakeholders, Social Responsibility and Performance: Empirical Evidence and Theoretical Perspectives', *The Academy of Management Journal*, 42 (5):479–485.

Hart, O. 1995. 'Corporate Governance: Some Theory and Implications', *The Economic Journal*, 105 (430):678–689.

Hassel, A. 1999. 'The Erosion of the German System of Industrial Relations', *British Journal of Industrial Relations*, 37 (3):483–505.
Hassel, A. and Rehder, B. 2001. 'Institutional Change in the German Wage Bargaining System. The Role of Big Companies', MPIfG Working Paper No. 01/9, Köln.
Havel, B. 2005. 'An Outline of Czech Company Law', *European Business Organization Law Review*, 6 (4):581–623.
Hazama, H. 1997. *The History of Labour Management in Japan*. London: MacMillan.
HBS and ETUI. 2004. (eds.). *Workers' Participation at Board Level in the EU-15 Countries: Reports on National systems and Practices*. Brussels: Hans-Böckler-Stiftung and European Trade Union Institute.
Heathfield, D. 1977. (ed.). *The Economics of Co-Determination*. London: MacMillan
Heidrick & Struggles. 2011. *European Corporate Governance Report 2011. Challenging Board Performance*. Chicago: Heidrick & Struggles International Inc.
Heller, F. 1971. *Managerial Decision-making: A Study of Leadership Styles and Power-sharing among Senior Managers*. London: Tavistock.
Heller, F. 1998. *Organizational Participation: Myth and Reality*. Oxford: Oxford University Press.
Heller, F., Drenth, P., Koopman, P. and Rus, V. 1988. *Decisions in Organisations: A Longitudinal Study of Routine, Tactical and Strategic Decisions*. London: Sage.
Heppnerová, D. 2005. 'The Czech System of Worker Board-level Representation', pp. 3–5 in SDA and ETUI (eds.). *Worker Board-level Representation in the New EU Member States: Country Reports on the National Systems and Practices*. Brussels: Social Development Agency and European Trade Union Institute.
Herrigel, G. 1996. *Industrial Constructions: The Sources of German Industrial Power*. Cambridge: Cambridge University Press.
High Pay Commission. 2011. *Cheques with Balances: Why Tackling High Pay is in the National Interest. Final Report*. London: High Pay Commission.
Hitchens, K. 1990. 'Hungary', pp. 347–366 in van der Linden, M. and Rojahn, J. (eds.). *The Formation of Labour Movements 1870–1914*. Leiden: E.J. Brill.
Hojnik, J. 2008. 'Corporate Governance Reform in Slovenia and the Current Place of Workers' Voice—State of the Art in Slovenia under the EU Presidency', *Transfer: European Review of Labour and Research*, 14 (1):137–141.
Hojnik, J. 2009. 'Indirect Management and Implications for Industrial Relations of the European Company Statute: The Case of Slovenia', pp. 201–226 in Gold, M., Nikolopoulos, A. and Kluge, N. (eds.). *The European Company Statute. A New Approach to Corporate Governance*. Bern: Peter Lang.
Hollandts, X. 2010. 'Les déterminants du choix de la structure du conseil : une étude empirique sur les sociétés cotées françaises', Centre d'études et de recherches du groupe ESC Clermont, Cahiers de Recherche No. 3.
Hollingsworth, J. 1997. 'Continuities and Changes in Social Systems of Production: The Cases of Japan, Germany and the United States', pp. 265–310 in Hollingsworth, J. and Boyer, R. (eds.). *Contemporary Capitalism: The Embeddedness of Institutions*. Cambridge: Cambridge University Press.
Höpner, M. 2001. 'Corporate Governance in Transition: Ten Empirical Findings on Shareholder Value and Industrial Relations in Germany', Discussion Paper 01/5, Köln: Max-Planck-Institut für Gesellschaftsforschung.
Höpner, M. 2003. 'European Corporate Governance Reform and the German Party Paradox', Discussion Paper 03/4, Köln: Max-Planck-Institut für Gesellschaftsforschung.
Höpner, M. 2005. 'What Connects Industrial Relations and Corporate Governance? Explaining Institutional Complementarity', *Socio-Economic Review*, 3 (2):331–358.

Höpner, M. and Schäfer, A. 2015. 'Integration among Unequals. How the Heterogeneity of European Varieties of Capitalism Shapes the Social and Democratic Potential of the EU', pp. 725–745 in Magone, J. (ed.). *Routledge Handbook of European Politics*. London: Routledge.

Howell, C. 1992. *Regulating Labor: The State and Industrial Relations Reform in Postwar France*. Princeton, New Jersey: Princeton University Press.

Howell, C. 2003. 'Varieties of Capitalism: And Then There Was One?', *Comparative Politics*, 36 (1):103–124.

Hughes, S. 1992. 'Living with the Past: Trade Unionism in Hungary since Political Pluralism', *Industrial Relations Journal*, 23 (4):293–303.

Huiban, J.-P. 1984. 'The Industrial Counterproposal as an Element of Trade Union Strategy', pp. 224–237 in Kesselman, M. (ed.). *The French Workers' Movement: Economic Crisis and Political Change*. London: George Allen and Unwin.

Hume-Rothery, R. 2004. 'Implementing the Directive: A View from UK business', pp. 80–92 in Fitzgerald, I. and Stirling, J. (eds.). *European Works Councils: Pessimism of the Intellect, Optimism of the Will?*. London: Routledge.

Hutton, W. 1995. *The State We're In*. London: Jonathan Cape.

Hyman, R. 1975. *Industrial Relations: A Marxist Introduction*. London: MacMillan.

Hyman, R. 1997. 'The Future of Employee Representation', *British Journal of Industrial Relations*, 35 (3):309–336.

Ichniowski, C., Shaw, K. and Prennushi, G. 1997. 'The Effect of Human Resource Management Practices on Productivity: A Study of Steel Finishing Lines', *American Economic Review*, 87 (3):291–313.

ICTU. 2008. *Nationalise the Banks*. Dublin: Irish Congress of Trade Unions.

ICTU. 2009. *Report of the Executive Council to Conference*. Biennial Delegate Conference, Tralee, 7th–10th July.

ICTU. 2013. *Report of the Executive Council: Biennial Delegate Conference*. Belfast, 2–4 July. Dublin: Irish Congress of Trade Unions.

Iversen, T. 2007. 'Economic Shocks and Varieties of Government Responses', pp. 278–304 in Hancké, B., Rhodes, M. and Thatcher, M. (eds.). *Beyond Varieties of Capitalism: Conflict, Contradictions and Complementarities in the European Economy*. Oxford: Oxford University Press.

Jackson, G. 2005. 'Towards a Comparative Perspective on Corporate Governance and Labour Management: Enterprise Coalitions and National Trajectories', pp. 284–309 in Gospel, H. and Pendleton, A. (eds.). *Corporate Governance and Labour Management: An International Comparison*. Oxford: Oxford University Press.

Jackson, G., Höpner, M. and Kurdelbusch, A. 2005. 'Corporate Governance and Employees in Germany: Changing Linkages, Complementarities and Tensions', pp. 84–121 in Gospel, H. and Pendleton, A. (eds.). *Corporate Governance and Labour Management: An International Comparison*. Oxford: Oxford University Press.

Jackson, S., May, K. and Whitney, K. 1995. 'Understanding the Dynamics of Diversity in Decision-making Teams', pp. 204–261 in Guzzo, R. and Salas, E. (eds.). *Team Effectiveness and Decision Making in Organizations*. San Francisco: Jossey-Bass.

Jacobi, O. and Hassel, A. 1995. 'Germany: Does Direct Participation Threaten the German Model?', Working Paper No. WP/95/67/EN. Dublin: European Foundation for the Improvement of Living and Working Conditions.

Janis, I. 1972. *Victims of Groupthink. A Psychological Study of Foreign Policy Decisions and Fiascos*. Boston: Houghton Mifflin Company.

Jansen, T. 2013. *Mitbestimmung in Aufsichtsräten*. Wiesbaden: Springer VS.

Jensen, M. 1986. 'Agency Costs of Free Cash Flow, Corporate Finance and Takeovers', *American Economic Review*, 76 (2):323–329.

Jensen, M. 1993. 'The Modern Industrial Revolution: Exit and the Failure of Internal Control Systems', *Journal of Finance*, 48 (3):831–880.
Jensen, M. and Meckling, W. 1976. 'Theory of the Firm: Managerial Behaviour, Agency Costs and Ownership Structure', *Journal of Financial Economics*, 3 (4):305–360.
Jensen, M. and Meckling, W. 1979. 'Rights and Production Functions: An Application to Labor-managed Firms and Codetermination', *The Journal of Business*, 52 (4):469–506.
Jirjahn, U. 2011. 'Ökonomische Wirkungen der Mitbestimmung in Deutschland: ein Update', *Schmollers Jahrbuch*, 131 (1): 3–57.
Johnson, S., La Porta, R., Lopez-de-Silanes, F. and Shleifer, A.R. 2000. 'Tunneling', *American Economic Review*, 90 (2):22–27.
Jones, D. and Kato, T. 1995. 'The Productivity Effects of Employee Stock-ownership Plans and Bonuses', *The American Economic Review*, 85 (3):91–414.
Junkes, J. and Sadowski, D. 1999. 'Mitbestimmung im Aufsichsrat: Steigerung der Effizienz oder Ausdünnung von Verfügungsrechten?, pp. 53–88 in Frick, B., Kluge, N. and Streeck, W. (eds.). *Die wirtschaftlichen Folgen der Mitbestimmung*, Frankfurt/Main: Campus.
Jürgens, U., Lippert, I. and Gaeth, F. 2008. *Information, Kommunikation und Wissen im Mitbestimmungssystem*. Baden-Baden: Nomos verlag.
Kaufman, A. and Englander, E. 2005. 'A Team Production Model of Corporate Governance', *The Academy of Management Executive*, 19 (3):9–22.
Kaufman, B. 2004. *The Global Evolution of Industrial Relations: Events, Ideas and the IIRA*. Geneva: International Labour Office.
Kay, J. and Silberston, A. 1995. 'Corporate Governance', *National Institute Economic Review*, 153:84–97.
Kelemen, M., Stollt, M. and Carlson, A. 2013. *News on European Companies (SE)*. July 2013. Brussels: European Trade Union Institute.
Keller, B. and Werner, F. 2008. 'Negotiated Forms of Worker Involvement in the European Company (SE): First Empirical Evidence and Conclusions', *Management Revue*, 19 (4):291–306.
Keller, B. and Werner, F. 2010. 'Industrial Democracy from a European Perspective: The Example of SEs', *Economic and Industrial Democracy*, 20 (5):1–15.
Keller, B. and Werner, F. 2012. 'New Forms of Employee Involvement at European Level: The Case of the European Company (SE)', *British Journal of Industrial Relations*, 50 (4):620–643.
Kessler, I., Undy, R. and Heron, P. 2004. 'Employee Perspectives on Communication and Consultation: Findings from a Cross-national Survey', *The International Journal of Human Resource Management*, 15 (3):512–532.
Kester, G. 1980. 'Transition to Workers' Self-management: Its Dynamics in the Decolonizing Economy of Malta', Working Paper, Institute of Social Studies, The Hague.
Kinderman, D. 2005. 'Pressure from Without, Subversion from Within: The Two-Pronged German Employer Offensive', *Comparative European Politics*, 3 (4):432–463.
King, C. and van de Vall, M. 1978. *Models of Industrial Democracy: Consultation, Co-determination and Workers' Management*. The Hague: Mouton Publishers.
King, L. 2007. 'Central European Capitalism in Comparative Perspective', pp. 307–327 in Hancké, B., Rhodes, M. and Thatcher, M. 2007. (eds.). *Beyond Varieties of Capitalism: Conflict, Contradictions, and Complementarities in the European Economy*. Oxford: Oxford University Press.
Kjellberg, A. 1983. *Facklig organisering i tolv länder*. Lund: Arkiv.
Kjellberg, A. 1992. 'Sweden: Can the Model Survive?', pp. 88–142 in Ferner, A. and Hyman, R. (eds.). *Industrial Relations in the New Europe*. Oxford: Blackwell.
Klambauer, M. 2008. *Case Study Report on Strabag SE*. Brussels: European Trade Union Institute and Hans Böckler Stiftung.

Kluge, N. 2008. 'Workers' Participation in BASF SE and the European Debate on Corporate Governance', *Transfer*, 14 (1):127–132.

Kluge, N. and Stollt, M. (eds.). 2006. *The European Company: Prospects for Worker Board-level Participation in the Enlarged EU*. Brussels: Social Development Agency and European Trade Union Institute.

Kluge, N. and Stollt, M. 2009. 'Administrateurs salariés et gouvernement d'entreprise: un élément clef du modèle social européen', pp. 81–91 in Conchon, A. and Auberger, M.-N. (eds.). *Les administrateurs salariés et la gouvernance d'entreprise*. Paris: La Documentation Française.

Knudsen, H. 1995. *Employee Participation in Europe*. London: Sage.

Knudsen, H., Müller, T. and Rehfeldt, U. 2008. *Converting MAN B&W Diesel AG into MAN Diesel SE. Negotiations and the agreement on employee involvement*. Brussels: ETUI and HBS.

Knyazeva, A., Knyazeva, D. and Raheja, C. 2013. 'The Benefits of Focus vs. Heterogeneity: Dissimilar Directors and Coordination within Corporate Boards', SSRN paper, available online at http://ssrn.com/abstract=2083287.

Kommission zur Moderniserung der deutschen Unternehmensmitbestimmung. 2006. *Bericht der wissenschaftlichen Mitglieder der Kommission*. Berlin: Bundesregierung.

Kořalka, J. 1990. 'The Czech Workers' Movement in the Hapsburg Empire', pp. 321–346 in van der Linden, M. and Rojahn, J. (eds.). *The Formation of Labour Movements 1870–1914*. Leiden: E.J. Brill.

Köstler, R. 2011. 'Die Europäische Aktiengesellschaft. Eine Einführung in die Europäische Aktiengesellschaft mit Anmerkungen zur grenzüberschreitenden Verschmelzung', *Arbeitshilfe für Aufsichtsräte*, No. 6, 5th edition, Hans-Böckler Stiftung.

Köstler, R. 2013. 'SEs in Germany', pp. 123–131 in Cremers, J., Stollt, M. and Vitols, S. (eds.). *A Decade of Experience with the European Company*. Brussels: European Trade Union Institute.

Köstler, R. and Büggel, A. 2003. 'The European Company and Company Law and Existing Legislative Provision for Employee Participation in the EU Member States', Report No. 79. Brussels: European Trade Union Institute.

Köstler, R., Müller, M. and Sick, S. 2013. *Aufsichtsratspraxis. Handbuch für die Arbeitnehmervertreter im Aufsichtsrat*. Frankfurt am Main: Bund-Verlag.

Köstler, R. and Pütz, L. 2013. 'Neueste Fakten zur SE und zur grenzüberschreitenden Verschmelzung—Mitbestimmte Unternehmen sind zufrieden', *Die Aktiengesellschaft*, No. 12:180–181.

Köstler, R. and Rose, E. 2011. *Mitbestimmung in der Europäischen Aktiengesellschaft (SE). Betriebs- und Dienstvereinbarungen. Analyse und Handlungsempfehlungen*. Frankfurt am Main: Bund-Verlag.

Koukiadaki, A. 2009. 'Reflexive Regulation of Employee Involvement at EU-level: Implementation and the Example of the United Kingdom', pp. 109–141 in Gold, M., Nikolopoulos, A. and Kluge, N. (eds.). *The European Company Statute. A New Approach to Corporate Governance*. Bern: PeterLang.

Koutroukis, T. 2009. 'Employee Participation in the European Company: Implications for the Greek Industrial Relations System', pp. 143–163 in Gold, M., Nikolopoulos, A. and Kluge, N. (eds.). *The European Company Statute. A New Approach to Corporate Governance*. Bern: Peter Lang.

Kozek, W., Federowicz, M. and Morawski, W. 1995. 'Poland', pp. 109–135 in Thirkell, J., Scase, R. and Vickerstaff, S. (eds.). *Labour Relations in Eastern Europe: A Comparative Perspective*, London: University College, London Press.

Kraft, K. and Ugarkovis, M. 2006. 'Gesetzliche Mitbestimmung und Kapitalrendite', *Jahrbücher fur Nationalökonomie und Statistik*, 226:588–604.

Krajcir, P. 2005. 'Practitioner Report: Slovak Republic', pp. 37–38 in SDA and ETUI. (eds.). *Worker Board-level Representation in the New EU Member States: Country Reports on the National Systems and Practices*. Brussels: Social Development Agency and European Trade Union Institute.

Kravaritou, Y. 1994. *European Employment and Industrial Relations Glossary: Greece*. Luxembourg, Office for Official Publications of the European Communities: Sweet and Maxwell.

Kritsantonis, N. 1992. 'Greece: From State Authoritarianism to Modernization', pp. 601–628 in Ferner, A. and Hyman, R. (eds.). *Industrial Relations in the New Europe*. Oxford: Blackwell.

Labour Party. 2015. *Britain Only Succeeds When Working People Succeed. This Is a Plan to Reward Hard Work, Share Prosperity and Build a Better Britain*. Labour Party Manifesto. London: Labour Party.

La Porta, R., Lopez-de-Silanes, F., Shleifer, A. and Vishny, R. 1997. 'Legal Determinants of External Finance', *The Journal of Finance*, 52 (3):1131–1150.

La Porta, R., Lopez-de-Silanes, F., Shleifer, A. and Vishny, R. 2000. 'Investor Protection and Corporate Governance', *The Journal of Financial Economics*, 58 (1–2):3–27.

Lavesen, M. and Kragh-Stetting, J. 2011. *Håndbog for medarbejderrepræsentanter 2011*. Odense: Erhvervsskolernes Forlag.

Lazonick, W. 2010. 'Innovative Business Models and Varieties of Capitalism: Financialization of U.S. Corporations', *Business History Review*, 84 (2):675–702.

Lazonick, W. 2013. 'The Financialization of the U.S. Corporation: What Has Been Lost and How It Can Be Regained', *Seattle University Law Review*, 36 (4):857–909.

Lazonick, W. and O'Sullivan, M. 2000. 'Maximizing Shareholder Value: A New Ideology for Corporate Governance', *Economy and Society*, 29 (1):13–35.

Ledwith, S. 2012. 'Gender Politics in Trade Unions. The Representation of Women between Exclusion and Inclusion', *Transfer: European Review of Labour and Research*, 18 (2):185–199.

Levinson, K. 2000. 'Codetermination in Sweden: Myth and Reality', *Economic and Industrial Democracy*, 21 (4):457–473.

Levinson, K. 2001. 'Employee Representatives on Company Boards in Sweden', *Industrial Relations Journal*, 32 (3):264–274.

Likert, R. 1961. *New Patterns of Management*. New York: McGraw-Hill.

Lippert, I., Huzzard, T., Jürgens, U. and Lazonick, W. 2014. *Corporate Governance, Employee Voice and Work Organization*. Oxford: Oxford University Press.

Lipton, M. and Lorsh, J. 1992. 'A Modest Proposal for Improved Corporate Governance', *Business Lawyer*, 48 (1):59–77.

LRD. 2004. *Worker Representation in Europe*. London: Labour Research Department.

Lukes, S. 1974. *Power: A Radical View*. London: MacMillan.

Lund, R. 1980. 'Indirect Participation, Influence and Power: Some Danish Experiences', *Organization Studies*, 1 (2):147–160.

MacDuffie, J. 1995. 'Human Resource Bundles and Manufacturing Performance: Organizational Logic and Flexible Production Systems in the World Auto Industry', *Industrial and Labor Relations Review*, 48 (2):197–221.

Mahoney, J. and Thelen, K. 2010. 'A Theory of Gradual Institutional Change', pp. 1–37 in Mahoney, J. and Thelen, K. (eds.). *Explaining Institutional Change: Ambiguity, Agency and Power*. Cambridge: Cambridge University Press.

Mahoney, P. 2001. 'The Common Law and Economic Growth: Hayek Might Be Right', *The Journal of Legal Studies*, 30 (2):503–525.

Manne, H. 1965. 'Mergers and the Market for Corporate Control', *Journal of Political Economy*, 73 (2):110–120.

Manzella, P. 2015. 'Lost in Translation: Language and Cross-national Comparisons in Industrial Relations', *E-journal of International and Comparative Labour Studies*, 4 (1):1–20.

Marchington, M., Goodman, J., Wilkinson, A. and Ackers, P. 1992. *New Developments in Employee Involvement*. Research Series No. 2. Manchester: Manchester School of Management.

Marchington, M. and Wilkinson, A. 2005. 'Direct Participation and Involvement', pp. 398–423 in Bach, S. (ed.). *Managing Human Resources: Personnel Management in Transition*. Oxford: Blackwell.

Marchington, M., Wilkinson, A., Ackers, P. and Goodman, J. 1993. 'The Influence of Managerial Relations on Waves of Employee Involvement', *British Journal of Industrial Relations*, 31 (4):553–576.

Marginson, P. 2000. 'The Eurocompany and Euro Industrial Relations', *European Journal of Industrial Relations*, 6 (1):9–34.

Markovits, A. 1986. *The Politics of West German Trade Unions*. Cambridge: Cambridge University Press.

Martinez Lucio, M. 1992. 'Spain: Constructing Institutions and Actors in a Context of Change', pp. 482–523 in Ferner, A. and Hyman, R. (eds.). *Industrial Relations in the New Europe*. Oxford: Blackwell.

Martinez Lucio, M. 2010. 'Labour Process and Marxist Perspectives on Employee Participation', pp. 105–130 in Wilkinson, A., Gollan, P., Marchington, M. and Lewin, D. (eds.). *The Oxford Handbook of Participation in Organizations*. Oxford: Oxford University Press.

Massa-Wirth, H. and Seifert, H. 2005. 'German Pacts for Employment and Competitiveness: Concessionary Bargaining as a Reaction to Globalization and European Integration?', *Transfer: European Review of Labour and Research*, 11 (1):26–44.

Mayer, C. and Alexander, I. 1990. 'Banks and Securities Markets: Corporate Financing in Germany and the United Kingdom', *Journal of the Japanese and International Economies*, 4 (4):450–475.

McBride, A. 2001. *Gender Democracy in Trade Unions*. Aldershot: Ashgate.

McKersie, R. 2001. 'Labor's Voice at the Strategic Level of the Firm', *Transfer*, 7 (3):480–493.

Meardi, G. 2002. 'The Trojan Horse for the Americanization of Europe? Polish Industrial Relations Towards the EU', *European Journal of Industrial Relations*, 8 (1):77–99.

Meardi, G. 2012. *Social Failures of EU Enlargement: A Case of Workers Voting with their Feet*. London: Routledge.

Mertens, H.-J. and Schanze, W. 1979. 'The German Codetermination Act of 1976', *Journal of Comparative Law and Securities Regulation*, 2 (1):75–88.

Miller, D. and Stirling, J. 1998. 'European Works Council Training: An Opportunity Missed?', *European Journal of Industrial Relations*, 4 (1):35–56.

Milliken, F. and Martins, L. 1996. 'Searching for Common Threads: Understanding the Multiple Effects of Diversity on Organizational Groups', *The Academy of Management Review*, 21 (2):402–433.

Molina, O. and Rhodes, M. 2007. 'The Political Economy of Adjustment in Mixed Market Economies: A Study of Spain and Italy', pp. 223–252 in Hancké, B., Rhodes, M. and Thatcher, M. 2007. (eds.). *Beyond Varieties of Capitalism: Conflict, Contradictions, and Complementarities in the European Economy*. Oxford: Oxford University Press.

Mommsen, H. 1989. *The Rise and Fall of Weimar Democracy*. London: The University of North Carolina Press.

Morck, R., Shleifer, A. and Vishny, R. 1988. 'Management Ownership and Market Valuation: An Empirical analysis', *Journal of Financial Economics*, 20 (1):293–315.

Morin, F. 2000. 'A Transformation in the French Model of Shareholding and Management', *Economy and Society*, 29 (1):36–53.

Mouriaux, R. 1984. 'The CFDT: From the Union of Popular Forces to the Success of Social Change', pp. 75–92 in Kesselman, M. (ed.). *The French Workers' Movement*. London: George Allen & Unwin.

Movitz, F. and Levinson, K. 2013. 'Employee Board Representation in the Swedish Private Sector', pp. 471–484 in Sandberg, Å. (ed.). *Nordic Lights: Work, Management and Welfare in Scandinavia*. Stockholm: SNS Förlag.

Mückenberger, U. 2011. 'Chances and Obstacles for International Trade Union Strategies in the CSR Field', pp. 145–166 in Vitols, S. and Kluge, N. (eds.). *The Sustainable Company: A New Approach to Corporate Governance*. Brussels: European Trade Union Institute.

Mulder, M. 1971. 'Power Equalization through Participation?', *Administrative Science Quarterly*, 16 (1):31–38.

Müller, G. 1987. *Mitbestimmung in der Nachkriegszeit*. Düsseldorf: Schwann-Bagel.

Müller, G. 1991. *Strukturwandel und Arbeitnehmerrechte*. Essen: Klartext Verlag.

Müller-Jentsch, W. 1986. *Soziologie der industriellen Beziehungen*. Frankfurt am Main: Campus Verlag.

Müller-Jentsch, W. 2003. 'Re-assessing Co-determination', pp. 39–56 in Weitbrecht, H. and Müller-Jentsch, W. (eds.). *The Changing Contours of German Industrial Relations*. München und Mering: Rainer Hampp Verlag.

Müller-Jentsch, W. 2008. 'Industrial Democracy: Historical Development and Current Challenges', *Management Revue*, 19 (4):260–273.

Munck, R. 2000. 'Labour and Globalisation', *Work, Employment and Society*, 14 (2):385–393.

Mykhnenko, V. 2007. 'Strengths and Weaknesses of Weak Coordination: Economic Institutions, Revealed comparative Advantages, and Socio-Economic Performance of Mixed Market Economies in Poland and Ukraine', pp. 351–378 in Hancké, B., Rhodes, M. and Thatcher, M. (eds.). *Beyond Varieties of Capitalism: Conflict, Contradictions, and Complementarities in the European Economy*. Oxford: Oxford University Press.

Nagel, B. 2007. *Die Beteiligungsrechte der Arbeitnehmer bei der formwechselnden Umwandlung einer deutschen AG in eine Europäische Gesellschaft (SE)*. Düsseldorf: Hans-Böckler Stiftung.

Naumann, R. 2004. 'Portugal', pp. 88–101, in HBS and ETUI (eds.). *Workers Participation at Board Level in the EU-15 Countries*. Brussels: Hans Böckler Stiftung and European Trade Union Institute.

Neumann, L. 1997. 'Circumventing Trade Unions in Hungary: Old and New Channels of Wage Bargaining', *European Journal of Industrial Relations*, 3 (2):183–202.

Neumann, L. 2006. 'New Company Act Reduces Role of Board-level Employee Representatives', EIROnline, Available at http://www.eurofound.europa.eu/eiro/2006/11/articles/hu0611039i.htm

Nygaard Thorkildsen, S. and Haugland Gaure, A. 2013. *Board Size in Private Firms*, Master thesis under the supervision of Øyvind Bøhren, Oslo: BI Norwegian Business School.

O'Connor, M. 1993. 'The Human Capital Era: Reconceptualising Corporate Law to Facilitate Labor-Management Cooperation', *Cornell Law Review*, 78 (5):899–965.

OECD. 1999. *OECD Principles of Corporate Governance*. Paris: Organisation for Economic Co-operation and Development.

OECD. 2004. *OECD Principles of Corporate Governance*. Paris: Organisation for Economic Co-operation and Development.

O'Kelly, K. 2000. 'Shifting from Voluntarism to National Agreements', pp. 339–365 in Waddington, J. and Hoffmann, R. (eds.). *Trade Unions in Europe: Facing Challenges and Searching for Solutions*. Brussels: European Trade Union Institute.

O'Kelly, K. 2004. 'Ireland: Shall We Dance?', pp. 163–178 in Huzzard, T., Gregory, D. and Scott, R. (eds.). *Strategic Unionism and Partnership: Boxing or Dancing?* Houndmills: Palgrave MacMillan.

O'Kelly, K. 2006. *Employee Board-Level Representation Project: First Results of a Survey*. Presented at the 5th Transnational Seminar of the European Commission funded 'Project for Employee Board-level Representatives', Budapest, 19–21 January.

Ost, D. and Weinstein, M. 1999. 'Unionists against Unions: Towards Hierarchical Management in Post-communist Poland', *East European Politics and Societies*, 13 (1):1–33.

Osterloh, M. and Frey, B. 2006. 'Shareholders Should Welcome Knowledge Workers as Directors', *Journal of Management and Governance*, 10 (3):325–345.

Pagano, M. and Volpin, P. 2005. 'The Political Economy of Corporate Governance', *The American Economic Review*, 95 (4):1005–1030.

Papoulias, D. and Lioukas, S. 1995. 'Participation in the Management of Public Enterprises: Experience from Greek Utilities', *Annals of Public and Cooperative Economics*, 66 (3):275–298.

Paris, J.-J., Rode, N. and Van Deijk, A. 2012. 'National Training Practices for Employee Representatives on Board Level', Consultingeuropa Research Report. Brussels: Consultingeuropa.

Parker, D. 1993. 'Unravelling the Planned Economy: Privatisation in Czecho-Slovakia', *Communist Economies and Economic Transformation*, 5 (3):391–404.

Paster, T. 2012. 'Do German employers Support Board-level Codetermination? The Paradox of Individual Support and Collective Opposition', *Socio-Economic Review*, 10 (3):471–495.

Pateman, C. 1970. *Participation and Democratic Theory*. Cambridge: Cambridge University Press.

Patra, E. 2009. 'The Regulation of Industrial Relations in the European Company: Challenges Facing Managers and Employee Representatives', pp. 165–190 in Gold, M., Nikolopoulos, A. and Kluge, N. (eds.). *The European Company Statute. A New Approach to Corporate Governance*. Bern: Peter Lang.

Pettigrew, A. 1992. 'On Studying Managerial Elites', *Strategic Management Journal*, 13 (2):163–182.

Pfeffer, J. and Salancik, G. 1978. *The External Control of Organizations: A Resource Dependence Perspective*. New York: Harper & Row.

Phelan, C. 2007. (ed.). *Trade Union Revitalisation Trends and Prospects in 34 Countries*. Bern: Peter Lang.

Pinto, M., Martins, P. and Nunes de Carvalho, A. 1996. *European Employment and Industrial Relations Glossary: Portugal*. Luxembourg, Office for Official Publications of the European Communities: Sweet and Maxwell.

Piore, M. 2003. 'Discussion of 'Towards a New Socio-Economic Paradigm'. Society as a Precondition for Individuality: Critical Comments', *Socio-Economic Review* 1 (1):119–122.

Pistor, K. 1999. 'Codetermination: A Sociopolitical Model with Governance Externalities', pp. 163–193 in Blair, M. and Roe, M. (eds.). *Employees and Corporate Governance*. Washington, DC: Brookings Institution Press.

Pongratz, H. and Voß, G. 2003. 'From Employee to Entreployee: Towards a Self-entrepreneurial Work Force', *Concepts and Transformations*, 8 (3):239–254.

Pontusson, J. 2005. 'Varieties and Commonalities of Capitalism', pp. 163–188 in Coates, D. (ed.). *Varieties of Capitalism: Varieties of Approaches*. Basingstoke: Palgrave MacMillan.

Poole, M. 1975. *Workers' Participation in Industry*. London: Routledge and Kegan Paul.

Poole, M. 1982. 'Theories of Industrial Democracy: The Emerging Synthesis', *The Sociological Review*, 30 (2):181–207.

Porter, M. 1990. *The Competitive Advantage of Nations*. London: MacMillan.

Poutsma, E. 2001. *Recent Trends in Employee Financial Participation in the European Union*. Dublin: European Foundation for the Improvement of Living and Working Conditions.

Poutsma, E. and Braam, G. 2005. 'Corporate Governance and Labour Management in the Netherlands: Getting the Best from Both Worlds?', pp. 148–172 in Gospel, H. and Pendleton, A. (eds.). *Corporate Governance and Labour Management: An International Comparison*. Oxford: Oxford University Press.

Prašnikar, J. and Gregorič, A. 2002. 'The Influence of Workers' Participation on the Power of Management in Transitional Countries: The Case of Slovenia', *Annals of Public and Cooperative Economics*, 73 (2):269–297.

Prowse, S. 1994. 'Corporate Governance in an International Perspective: A Survey of Corporate Control Mechanisms among Large Firms in the United States, the United Kingdom, Japan and Germany', BIS Economic Papers No. 41. Basle: Bank for International Settlements.

Privatisation Barometer. 2011. *The PB Report 2010. Here Comes another Privatization Wave*. Milan: Fondazione Eni Enrico Mattei.

PTK. 2011. *Bolagsstyrelseledamot. En handbook för arbetstagarrepresentanter i bolagsstyrelser*. Stockholm: Privattjänstemannakartellen.

Pulignano, V. 2006. 'The Diffusion of Employment Practices of US-based Multinational in Europe: A Case Study Comparison of British- and Italian-based Subsidiaries', *British Journal of Industrial Relations*, 44 (3):497–518.

Pütz, L. 2014. *Statistik: SEs in Europa. Stand: 01.10.2014*. Düsseldorf: Hans-Böckler Stiftung.

Raabe, N. 2005. 'Aus dem Aufsichtsratsalltag', *Magazin Die Mitbestimmung*, 52 (7):38–42.

Ramsay, H. 1977. 'Cycles of Control: Worker Participation in Sociological and Historical Perspective', *Sociology*, 11 (3):481–506.

Ramsay, H. 1980. 'Phantom Participation: Pattern of Power and Conflict', *Industrial Relations Journal*, 11 (3):46–59.

Regini, M. 2003. 'Tripartite Concertation and Varieties of Capitalism', *European Journal of Industrial Relations*, 9 (3):251–263.

Rehfeldt, U., Voss, E., Pulignano, V., Kelemen, M., Telljohann, V., Fulton, L., Neumann, L., Mester, D., Schütze, K. and Wilke, P. 2011. *Employee Involvement in Companies under the European Company Statute*. Dublin: European foundation for the improvement of living and working conditions.

Renaud, S. 2007. 'Dynamic Efficiency of Supervisory Board Codetermination in Germany', *Labour*, 21 (4–5):689–712.

Ribarova, E., Mihailova, T., Slavcheva, S., O'Kelly, K., Vaughn, F., Leonardi, S., Seperic, D. and Bouquin, S. 2010. *Informia. Information and Consultation in Europe. Analysis of the Legislative Framework and Practice*. Sofia: CITUB.

Rizzo, S. 2006. 'Is Employee Board Level Representation on the Way Out?', www.timesofmalta.com.

Roe, M. 1994. *Strong Managers, Weak Owners: The Political Roots of American Corporate Finance*. Princeton, NJ: Princeton University Press.

Roe, M. 2003. *Political Determinants of Corporate Governance: Political Context, Corporate Impact*. Oxford: Oxford University Press.

Roe, M. and Gordon, J. 2004. *Convergence and Persistence in Corporate Governance*. Cambridge: Cambridge University Press.

Rojahn, J. 1990. 'Poland', pp. 487–521 in Van der Linden, M. and Rojahn, J. (eds.). *The Formation of Labour Movements 1870–1914: An International Perspective*. Leiden: E.J. Brill.

Rogers, J. and Streeck, W. 1995. *Works Councils: Consultation, Representation and Cooperation in Industrial Relations*. Chicago: University of Chicago Press.

Rokkan, S. 1970. *Citizens, Elections, Parties: Approaches to the Comparative Study of the Processes of Political Development*. Oslo: Universitetsforlaget.

Rood, M. 1992. 'The Netherlands', *Bulletin of Comparative Labour Relations*, 23:199–214.

Rose, C. 2005. 'Medarbejdervalgte bestyrelsesmedlemmer i danske virksomheder', *Tidsskrift for Arbejdsliv*, 7 (3):34–50.

Rose, C. 2008. 'The Challenges of Employee-Appointed Board Members for Corporate Governance: The Danish Experience', *European Business Organization Law Review*, 9 (2):215–235.

Rose, C. and Kvist, H.-K. 2004. *Employee Directors: What is their Say?* Copenhagen: Co-Industri.

Rose, E. 2013. 'The Workers' Voice in SE Agreements', pp. 207–225 in Cremers, J., Stollt, M. and Vitols, S. (eds.). *A Decade of Experience with the European Company*. Brussels: ETUI.

Rose, E. and Köstler, R. 2014. *Mitbestimmung in der Europäischen Aktiengesellschaft (SE). Betriebs- und Dienstvereinbarungen. Analyse und Handlungsempfehlungen*, 2nd edition. Frankfurt am Main: Bund-Verlag.

Rosenbohm, S. 2013a. 'The SE's Impact on Transnational Information and Consultation: Trends and Developments from a Company Perspective', pp. 189–205 in Cremers, J., Stollt, M. and Vitols, S. (eds.). *A Decade of Experience with the European Company*. Brussels: ETUI.

Rosenbohm, S. 2013b. 'Verhandelte Arbeitnehmerbeteiligung. Ein empirischer Vergleich der Formen vor und nach der Gründung einer Europäischen Aktiengesellschaft', *Industrielle Beziehungen*, 20 (1):8–35.

Roth, M. 2010. 'Employee Participation, Corporate Governance and the Firm: A Transatlantic View Focused on Occupational Pensions and Co-Determination', *European Business Organization Law Review*, 11 (1):51–85.

Roth, M. 2013. 'Corporate Boards in Germany', pp. 253–365 in Davies, P., Hopt, K., Nowak, R., and van Solinge, G. (eds.). *Corporate Boards in Law and Practice. A Comparative Analysis in Europe*. Oxford: Oxford University Press.

Rothstein, B. 2001. 'Social Capital in the Social Democratic Welfare State', *Politics and Society*, 29 (2):207–241.

Rueda, D. 2005. 'Insider-Outsider Politics in Industrialized Democracies: The Challenge to Social Democratic Parties', *American Political Science Review*, 99 (1):61–74.

Rueda, D. 2006. 'Social Democracy and Active Labour-Markey Policies: Insiders, Outsiders and the Politics of Employment Promotion', *British Journal of Political Science*, 36 (3):385–406.

Rueda, D. 2007. *Social Democracy Inside Out: Partisanship and Labor Market Policy in Industrialized Democracies*. Oxford: Oxford University Press.

Ryan, H. and Wiggins, R. 2004. 'Who Is in Whose Pocket? Director Compensation, Bargaining Power and Board Independence', *Journal of Financial Economics*, 73 (3):497–524.

Sairo, K. 2001. *Henkilöstön Hallintoedustus Metalli-ja Elekroniikkateollisuuden Yrityksissä*. Helsinki: Metallityöväen Liiton Tutkimustoiminnan Julkaisuja.

Sandberg, Å. 1995. *Enriching Production: Perspectives on Volvo's Uddevalla Plant as an Alternative to Lean Production*. Aldershot: Avebury.

Santoro, G. 2012. 'L'apport des accords instituant la représentation collective des travailleurs dans les sociétés européennes', pp. 141–160 in Moreau, M.-A. (ed.).

La représentation collective des travailleurs. Ses transformations à la lumière du droit comparé. Paris: Dalloz.
Saracibar, A. 1986. 'El Reto Sindical de la Participación obrera en España', *Claridad*, 13:5–25.
Sasso, L. 2009. 'The European Company: Does It Create Rules for the Market or a Market for the Rules?', pp. 279–307 in Gold, M., Nikolopoulos, A. and Kluge, N. (eds.). *The European Company Statute. A New Approach to Corporate Governance*. Frankfurt am Main: Peter Lang.
Sassoon, D. 1997. *One Hundred Years of Socialism*. London: Fontana.
Schmidt, V. 2002. *The Futures of European Capitalism*. Oxford: Oxford University Press.
Schmitter, P. 1995. 'Organised Interests and Democratic Consolidation in Southern Europe', pp. 284–314 in Gunther, R., Diamandouros, P. and Puhle, H.-J. (eds.). *The Politics of Democratic Consolidation: Southern Europe in Comparative Perspective*. Baltimore: The Johns Hopkins University Press.
Schömann, I., Clauwaert, S. and Warneck, W. 2006. 'Information and Consultation in the European Community: Implementation Report of Directive 2002/14/CE', Report No. 97. Brussels: European Trade Union Institute.
Schömann, I., Sobczak, A., Voss, E. and Wilke, P. 2008. *Codes of Conduct and International Framework Agreements: New Forms of Governance at Company Level*. Dublin: European Foundation for the Improvement of Living and Working Conditions.
Schulten, T., Zagelmeyer, S. and Carley, M. 1998. *Board-level Employee Representation in Europe*. EIRonline Study.
Schütze, K. 2011. *Employee Involvement in Companies under the European Company Statute (ECS). Case study: Fresenius SE*. Dublin: European Foundation for the Improvement of Living and Working Conditions.
Schweiger, C. 2014. *The EU and the Global Financial Crisis. New Varieties of Capitalism*. Cheltenham and Northampton: Edward Elgar Publishing.
Schwimbersky, S. and Gold, M. 2013. 'The European Company Statute: A Tangled History', pp. 49–66 in Cremers, J., Stollt, M. and Vitols, S. (eds.). *A Decade of Experience with the European Company*. Brussels: European Trade Union Institute.
Schwimbersky, S. and Rehfeldt, U. 2006. *Case Study Report on Plansee SE*. Brussels: European Trade Union Institute and Hans-Böckler-Stiftung.
SDA and ETUI. 2005. (eds.). *Worker Board-level Representation in the New EU Member States: Country Reports on the National Systems and Practices*. Brussels: Social Development Agency and European Trade Union Institute.
Senčur Peček, D. 2011. 'The Participation of Employees in Company Bodies as Regulated in Law of the Republic of Slovenia', pp. 161–189 in Löschnigg, G. (ed.). *Arbeitnehmerbeteiligung in Unternehmensorganen im internationalen Vergleich*, Wien: ÖGB Verlag.
Shleifer, A. and Vishny, R. 1997. 'A Survey of Corporate Governance', *Journal of Finance*, 52 (2):737–783.
Shleifer, A. and Wolfenzon, D. 2002. 'Investor Protection and Equity Markets', *Journal of Financial Economics*, 66 (1):3–27.
Sick, S. 2013. 'Worker Participation in SEs: A Workable, Albeit Imperfect Compromise', pp. 93–106 in Cremers, J., Stollt, M. and Vitols, S. (eds.). *A Decade of Experience with the European Company*. Brussels: ETUI.
Sick, S. 2015. 'Der deutschen Mitbestimmung entzogen: Unternehmen mit ausländer Rechtsform nehmen zu', Report der Mitbestimmungsförderung, No. 8. Düsseldorf: Hans Böckler Stiftung.
Sick, S. and Pütz, L. 2011. 'Der deutschen Unternehmensmitbestimmung entzogen: Die Zahl der Unternehmen mit ausländischer Rechtsform wächst', *WSI Mitteilungen*, 64 (1):34–40.

Skupień, D. 2010. 'Developments in Board-room Representation in Poland', SE-Europe internal paper, Brussels: European Trade Union Institute.

Skupień, D. 2011. 'Board-level Employee Participation in Polish Limited-liability Companies', pp. 139–159 in Löschnigg, G. (ed.). *Arbeitnehmerbeteiligung in Unternehmensorganen im internationalen Vergleich*. Wien: ÖGB Verlag.

Sorge, A. 1976. 'The Evolution of Industrial Democracy in the Countries of the European Community', *British Journal of Industrial Relations*, 14 (3):274–294.

Speth, R. 2004. *Die Politischen Stategien der Initiative Neue Soziale Marktwirtschaft*. Düsseldorf: Hans-Böckler-Stiftung.

Steinko, A. 2004. 'Spain', pp. 102–110 in HBS and ETUI (eds.). *Workers Participation at Board Level in the EU-15 Countries*. Brussels: Hans Böckler Stiftung and European Trade Union Institute.

Stelina, J. 2005. 'The Polish System of Worker Board-level Representation', pp. 26–30 in SDA and ETUI. (eds.). *Worker Board-level Representation in the New EU Member States: Country Reports on the National Systems and Practices*. Brussels: Social Development Agency and European Trade Union Institute.

Stenstrand, T., Bruun, N. and Neumann, L. 2007. *Elcoteq SNB negotiations. Experiences and procedures*. Brussels: ETUI and HBS.

Stirling, J. 2004. 'Connecting and Communicating: European Works Council Training for Global Networks', pp. 183–197 in Fitzgerald, I. and Stirling, J. (eds.). *European Works Council: Pessimism of the Intellect, Optimism of the Will?*. London: Routledge.

Stoleroff, A. 2000. 'Portugal: Union Development within the Changing Contexts of Political Economy and Industrial Relations', pp. 451–498 in Waddington, J. and Hoffmann, R. (eds.). *Trade Unions in Europe: Facing Challenges and Searching for Solutions*. Brussels: European Trade Union Institute.

Stollt, M. and Kelemen, M. 2013. 'A Big Hit or a Flop? A Decade of Facts and Figures on the European Company (SE)', pp. 25–47 in Cremers, J., Stollt, M. and Vitols, S. (eds.). *A decade of experience with the European Company*. Brussels: ETUI.

Stollt, M. and Wolters, E. 2011. *Worker Involvement in the European Company (SE): A Handbook for Practitioners*. Brussels: European Trade Union Institute.

Strauss, G. 1998. 'An Overview', pp. 8–39 in Heller, F., Pusić, E., Strauss, G. and Wilpert, B. (eds.). *Organizational Participation. Myth and Reality*, Oxford: Oxford University Press.

Streeck, W. 1992. 'Codetermination: After Four Decades', pp. 137–168 in Streeck, W. (ed.). *Social Institutions and Economic Performance: Studies of Industrial Relations in Advanced Capitalist Countries*. London: Sage.

Streeck, W. 1995. 'Works Councils in Western Europe: From Consultation to Participation', pp. 313–348 in Rogers, J. and Streeck, W. (eds.). *Works Councils: Consultation, Representation and Cooperation in Industrial Relations*. Chicago: University of Chicago Press.

Streeck, W. 1997. 'Neither European nor Works Council: A Reply to Paul Knutsen', *Economic and Industrial Democracy*, 18 (2):325–337.

Streeck, W. 2009. *Re-Forming Capitalism: Institutional Change in the German Political Economy*. Oxford: Oxford University Press.

Sudreau, P. 1975. *La réforme de l'entreprise*. Paris: Union générale d'éditions, collection 10/18.

Summers, J. and Hyman, J. *Employee Participation and Company Performance. A Review of the Literature*. York: Joseph Rowntree Foundation.

Svensson, T. and Öberg, P. 2005. 'How Are Coordinated Market Economies Coordinated? Evidence from Sweden', *West European Politics*, 28 (5):1075–1100.

Swenson, P. 2002. *Capitalists against Markets: The Making of Labor Markets and Welfare States in the United States and Sweden*. Oxford: Oxford University Press.

Swenson, P. and Pontusson, J. 2000. 'The Swedish Employer Offensive against Centralized Wage Bargaining', pp. 77–106 in Iversen, T., Pontusson, J. and Soskice,

D. (eds.). *Unions, Employers and Central Banks: Macroeconomic Coordination and Institutional Change in Social Market Economies*. Cambridge: Cambridge University Press.
TASC. 2012. *Good for Business? Worker Participation on Boards*. Dublin: Think Tank for Action on Social Change.
Taylor, R. 2000. 'Workers' Rights and Responsibilities in the Modern Company', pp. 101–112 in Parkinson, J., Gamble, A. and Kelly, G. (eds.). *The Political Economy of the Company*. Oxford: Portland Press.
Tchobanian, R. 1995. 'France: From Conflict to Social Dialogue?', pp. 115–152 in Rogers, J. and Streeck, W. (eds.). *Works Councils: Consultation, Representation and Cooperation in Industrial Relations*. Chicago: University of Chicago Press.
Thelen, K. 2000. 'Why German Employers Cannot Bring Themselves to Dismantle the German Model', pp. 138–169 in Iversen, T., Pontusson, J. and Soskice, D. (eds.). *Unions, Employers and Central Banks*. Cambridge: Cambridge University Press.
Thelen, K. and van Wijnbergen, C. 2003. 'The Paradox of Globalization: Labor Relations in Germany and Beyond', *Comparative Political Studies*, 36 (8):859–880.
Thill, P. 2013. 'The Dynamics of Worker Participation in SEs in Luxembourg: Towards Reinforced Rights?', pp. 133–145 in Cremers, J., Stollt, M. and Vitols, S. (eds.). *A Decade of Experience with the European Company*. Brussels: European Trade Union Institute.
Timming, A. 2006. 'The Problem of Identity and Trust in European Works Councils', *Employee Relations*, 28 (1):9–25.
Toth, A. 2000. 'Hungary: Attempts to Reform a Workers' Movement without Mass Participation', pp. 305–338 in Waddington, J. and Hoffmann, R. (eds.). *Trade Unions in Europe: Facing Challenges and Searching for Solutions*. Brussels: European Trade Union Institute.
TUC. 1995. *Pay and Perks, Narrowing the Gap: The TUC's Evidence to the Greenbury Committee*. London: Trades Union Congress.
TUC. 2012. *Worker Representation on Remuneration Committees: Why Do We Need It and How Would It Work in Practice?* London: Trades Union Congress.
TUC. 2014. *Final Agenda. Motions and Nominations for the 146th Annual Trades Union Congress*. London: Trade Union Congress.
Turner, L. 1996. 'The Europeanization of Labour: Structure before Action', *European Journal of Industrial Relations*, 2 (3):325–344.
Umunna, C. 2012. 'I Don't Deny I'm Ambitious Says the Rising Star of Labour, Chuka Umunna', *Independent*, 2nd October.
Urban, H.-J. 2012. 'Crisis, Corporatism and Trade Union Revitalisation in Europe', pp. 219–241 in Lehndorff, S. (ed.). *A Triumph of Failed Ideas*. Brussels: European Trade Union Institute.
Van Apeldoorn, B. and Horn, L. 2007. 'The Marketisation of European Corporate Control: A Critical Political Economy Perspective', *New Political Economy*, 12 (2):211–235.
van de Vall, M. 1970. *Labor Organizations*. Cambridge: Cambridge University Press.
Van der Velden, S., Dribbusch, H., Lyddon, D. and Vandaele, K. (eds.). 2007. *Strikes around the World, 1968–2005*. Amsterdam: Aksant.
van het Kaar, R. 2013. 'SEs in the Netherlands', pp. 147–162 in Cremers, J., Stollt, M. and Vitols, S. (eds.). *A Decade of Experience with the European Company*. Brussels: ETUI.
Vickerstaff, S. and Thirkell, J. 2000. 'Instrumental Rationality and European Integration: Transfer or Avoidance of Industrial Relations Institutions in Central and Eastern Europe', *European Journal of Industrial Relations*, 6 (2):237–251.
Villiers, C. 2006. 'The Directive on Employee Involvement in the European Company: Its Role in European Corporate Governance and Industrial Relations',

International Journal of Comparative Labour Law and Industrial Relations, 22 (2):183–211.

Visser, J. and Hemeriijck, A. 1997. *A Dutch Miracle: Job Growth, Welfare Reform and Corporatism in the Netherlands*. Amsterdam: Amsterdam University Press.

Vitols, S. 2004. 'Negotiated Shareholder Value: The German Version of an Anglo-American Practice', *Competition & Change*, 8 (4):357–374.

Vitols, S. 2010. 'The European Participation Index (EPI): A Tool for Cross-National Quantitative Comparison', ETUI Background Paper, available online at www.worker-participation.eu/About-WP/European-Participation-Index-EPI.

Vliegenthart, A. 2007. 'Regulating Employee Representation in Post-socialist Supervisory Boards', *South-East Europe Review*, 10 (4):67–82.

Vliegenthart, A. 2009. 'Who Is Undermining Employee Involvement in Post-socialist Supervisory Boards? National, European and International Forces in the Revision of Hungarian Company Law', *Journal of East European Management Studies*, 14 (3):265–285.

Vliegenthart, A. and Horn, L. 2007. 'The Role of the EU in the (Trans)formation of Corporate Governance Regulation in Central Eastern Europe-The Case of the Czech Republic', *Competition & Change*, 11 (2):137–154.

Volonté, C. 2015. 'Boards: Independent and Committed Directors?', *International Review of Law and Economics*, 41:25–37.

Vranicki, P. 1965. 'On the Problem of Practice', *Praxis*, No. 1:41–48.

Waddington, J. 2011. *European Works Councils: A Transnational Industrial Relations Institution in the Making*. London: Routledge.

Watanabe, S. 1991. 'The Japanese Quality Circle: Why It Works', *International Labour Review*, 130 (1):57–81.

Webb, S. and Webb, B. 1913 (originally published 1897). *Industrial Democracy*. London: Longmans.

Weckes, M. 2015. 'Geschlechterverteilung in Vorständen und Aufsichtsräten', Hans-Böckler Report, No. 10. Hans-Böckler Stiftung: Düsseldorf.

Western, B. 1997. *Between Class and Market: Postwar Unionization in the Capitalist Democracies*. Princeton, NJ: Princeton University Press.

Weston, S. and Martinez Lucio, M. 1998. 'European Works Councils: More than a Busman's Holiday', *Employee Relations*, 20 (6):551–564.

Wheeler, J. 2002. 'Employee Involvement in Action: Reviewing Swedish Codetermination', *Labor Studies Journal*, 26 (4):71–97.

Whitley, R. (ed.). 1992. *European Business Systems: Firms and Markets in Their National contexts*. London: Sage.

Whitley, R. 1999. *Divergent Capitalisms: The Social Structuring and Change of Business Systems*. Oxford: Oxford University Press.

Whittall, M. 2000. 'The BMW European Works Council: A Cause for European Industrial Relations Optimism?', *European Journal of Industrial Relations*, 6 (1):61–83.

Williams, K. 2000. 'From Shareholder Value to Present-Day Capitalism', *Economy and Society*, 29 (1):1–12.

Wilson, R. 1990. 'The Changing Occupational Structure of Employment, 1971–95', *International Journal of Manpower*, 3 (1):44–53.

Wright, M., Filatotchev, I. and Buck, T. 1997. 'Corporate Governance in Central and Eastern Europe', pp. 212–232 in Keasey, K., Thompson, S. and Wright, M. (eds.). *Corporate Governance: Economic, Management and Financial Issues*. Oxford: Oxford University Press.

Würz, S. 2003. (ed.). *European Stock-taking on Models of Employee Financial Participation: Results of Ten European Case Studies*. Wiesbaden: Nomus.

Yermack, D. 1996. 'Higher Valuation of Companies with a Small Board of Directors', *Journal of Financial Economics*, 40 (2):185–212.

Index